New Beginnings in Literary Studies

New Beginnings in Literary Studies

Edited by

Jan Auracher and Willie van Peer

Cambridge Scholars Publishing

New Beginnings in Literary Studies, Edited by Jan Auracher and Willie van Peer

This book first published 2008 by

Cambridge Scholars Publishing

15 Angerton Gardens, Newcastle, NE5 2JA, UK

British Library Cataloguing in Publication Data
A catalogue record for this book is available from the British Library

Copyright © 2008 by Jan Auracher and Willie van Peer and contributors

All rights for this book reserved. No part of this book may be reproduced, stored in a retrieval system, or transmitted, in any form or by any means, electronic, mechanical, photocopying, recording or otherwise, without the prior permission of the copyright owner.

ISBN (10): 1-84718-594-0, ISBN (13): 9781847185945

TABLE OF CONTENTS

Preface ix

Introduction:

The Inhumanity of the Humanities 1
by Willie van Peer

Part I:
Structures and Their Processing

Analyzing Words to Understand Literature 24
by James W. Pennebaker and Molly Ireland

Sweet Fragrances from Indonesia: A Universal Principle Governing Directionality in Synaesthetic Metaphors 49
by Yeshayahu Shen and David Gil

Automatic Analyses of Language, Discourse, and Situation Models .. 72
by Art Graesser, Moongee Jeon, Zhiqiang Cai, and Danielle McNamara

Discovering Frantext 89
by Véronique Montémont

Unigrams, Bigrams and LSA: Corpus Linguistics Explorations of Genres in Shakespeare's Plays 108
by Max Louwerse, Gwyneth Lewis, Jie Wu

This Way to the War 130
by Robert Hogenraad

Reading Different Types of Narrative Texts: A Study of Cognitive and Emotional Responses 145
by Aldo Nemesio, M. Chiara Levorato, and Lucia Ronconi

Image Schemas in Narrative Macrostructure: Combining Cognitive Linguistic with Psycholinguistic Approaches 158
by Michael Kimmel

Fiction and Belief Change: Exploring Boundaries 185
by Melanie C. Green and Jennifer Garst

Part II:
Influences of Readers' Background on Media Perception

Compassion and Disgust as Markers of Cultural Differences in Reading Violence in Literary Texts 198
by Paul Sopčák

Culture and Reading: The Influence of Western and Eastern Thought Systems on the Understanding of Fairy Tales 218
by Yehong Zhang

Translating Foregrounding: A Comparative Study of Chinese and Canadian Readers 238
by Gao Wei, David S. Miall, and Don Kuiken

Is This Typical Japanese? Influences of Stereotypes on Text Reception 251
by Jan Auracher and Akiko Hirose

From Sacred to Profane: The Effects of Reading Violent Religious Literature on Subsequent Human Aggression 267
by Robert D. Ridge and Colin W. Key

Narrative Comprehension and Enjoyment of Feature Films: An Experimental Study 286
by Bradford Owen

Of Men Who Read Romance and Women Who Read Adventure Stories... An Empirical Reception Study on the Emotional Engagement of Men and Women while Reading Narrative Texts 308
by Özen Odağ

Part III:
The Personal in Literary Response

The more you see, the more you get: How Spectators' Use
Their Limited Capacity for Attention in Responses to Formal
Aspects of Film 332
by Jèmeljan Hakemulder

Remindings, Understanding and Involvement: A Close Reading
of the Content and Context of Remindings 352
by Cecilia Therman

Media Reception, Language Acquisition and Cultural Identity
as Seen by Migrant Minority Children and their Parents 372
by Petra Wieler and Janina Petzold

Virtual Communities – Real Readers: New Data in Empirical
Studies of Literature 390
by Maciej Maryl

Literariness and the Process of Evaluation 407
by Marisa Bortolussi, Peter Dixon, and Blaine Mullins

What Is, Empirically, a Great Book? Or: Literary Dialogues
and Canon Formation 423
by David Fishelov

Contributors 446

PREFACE

In August 2006 the 10th biennial conference of the International Society for the Empirical Study of Literature and the Media (IGEL, a German acronym[1] dating from the time the Society was founded at the Unversity of Siegen in Germany) was held on Lady's Isle in Lake Chiem near Munich, at the occasion of the Society's 20th birthday.

The book that is in front of you contains a selection of the papers presented at this conference.

We have chosen to give the volume the title NEW BEGINNINGS IN LITERARY STUDIES, since we are convinced that such new beginnings are needed, as often in life, but also that the contributions contained in this volume indeed deliver such new perspectives. They are innovative in terms of themes that are opened up, approaches that are applied, methods

---

[1] Internationale Gesellschaft für Empirische Literaturwissenschaft; IGEL also means hedgehog in German, which is why this little animal turns up on the website: http://www.igel.lmu.de/platform/index.php

of analysis employed, and above all, by the combination of different disciplines. All contributions combine methods from different fields. In this sense the volume is a *truly* interdisciplinary one. The emphasis is also on empirical approaches, which still present a novelty to most scholars in literary studies.

The volume opens with a critical appraisal of the humanities by Willie van Peer (Munich), which was the presidential address at the conference. The chapter shows how the humanities are no longer the guardians of human values, but instead have fallen into an abyss of mostly poorly-related technicalities; the chapter advocates to give humanity back to the humanities by concentrating on functional issues, and probing these through empirical research, providing examples at every turn of the argument. Chapter two, by James Pennebaker (Texas) forms a clear illustration of the richness of insights that can be generated when social psychology, linguistics and literary studies are interwoven. Their combination brings us one step closer to understanding the mysteries of literary communication.

In a similar way, Yeshayahu Shen (Tel Aviv) brings together methods from cognitive studies, linguistics, and anthropology to throw light on the structure and understanding of synaesthetic metaphors in daily language and in literature.

Apart from Pennebaker, several other authors employ computer software to cast light on the nature and structure of (literary) texts. Graesser, Jeon, Cai, and McNamara (Memphis) illustrate its use in an analysis of *Einstein's Dreams*. Véronique Montémont (Nancy) introduces the French database and software 'Frantext' and provides ample examples how it can be used in stylistic analysis. Louwerse, Lewis and Wu (Memphis) apply techniques from corpus linguistics in order to categorize Shakespeare's plays, showing how, purely based on an analysis of the texts, the computer comes to almost identical categorizations as literary historians. The contribution by Hogenraad (Louvain-la-Neuve) is not, strictly speaking, about literature. We have included it nevertheless, because it reveals so manifestly the power of computer analysis of language: Hogenraad was successful before in predicting the outbreak of the Iraq war, solely on the basis of a computer analysis of the language of decision makers. In this chapter he predicts that there will be no war with Iran – at least not for the time being.

Structural analysis of literary texts is one thing. The other is how such structures are processed by readers. Cognitive psychology nowadays provides reliable methods to examine such comprehension processes. Nemesio, Levorato and Ronconi had readers read an original story by

Borges and one from which the initial paragraph had been removed. Both groups responded to a number of questions, which – after a statistical analysis – revealed three major factors influencing the story's processing: their emotional participation in the story, the violation of their expectations and their cognitive appraisal of the textual features that form the foundation to comprehend the story. Kimmel (Vienna) develops a new way of looking at story comprehension: instead of looking at the way readers process language propositions, he proposes that processing a story (his example is Joseph Conrad's *Heart of Darkness*) makes use of image schemas that are cognitive, but not linguistic. The research by Green and Garst (University of North Carolina) is interesting and innovative in that it probes the persuasive force of different kinds of stories. It turns out that realistically presented fictional stories influence readers' real-world beliefs, but that individual readers may have different standards for 'realism' in stories.

Texts do not have *a* meaning, but are perceived differently by individuals. Contrary, however, to the 'everything-goes' view of post-structuralist approaches the contributions in this volume try to detect observable relations between readers' attributes and their reading strategies. This new direction is based on the assumption that readers do not exist in a social vacuum and are therefore not completely isolated in their cognitive development. Moreover, an 'ideal reader', who is representative for all readers, does not exist. Rather, specific characteristics of readers influence their understanding, such as cultural and social background, personality traits, educational level, language spoken, gender, etc.

Several contributions take a closer look at the interdependence between cultural socialisation, cultural values, cognition and reading. Paul Sopčák (Alberta) assessed emotional and judgmental reactions of readers from Germany, Brazil and the USA to texts containing graphic descriptions of physical violence. His results show a clear connection between the general attitude towards violence in each culture and the reaction to the virtual violence in texts, suggesting a culturally biased evaluation of fiction. Similarly, Zhang (Göttingen) registers the epistemic distinction between Western and East-Asian cultures as *analytic* and *holistic* respectively to capture differences in the perception of fairy tales, comparing young readers from Germany and China in their perception and appraisal of narrative categories when reading traditional German and Chinese fairy tales. While Sopčák and Zhang analysed the influence of cultural background on the processing of content, Gao, Miall, and Kuiken (Alberta) investigate the appreciation of stylistic features in literary texts by readers from different cultures. In particular they survey effects of translations on its reception. By assessing reading times and ratings for strikingness per segment of poems in the original Chinese version as well as in an English translation, Gao Wei et al. found a close correspondence of these measures between Chinese and Canadian participants, suggesting that the stylistic variations in Chinese were largely recreated in the English translation. A slightly different approach is taken by Auracher and Hirose (Munich), who focus on the bias exerted by stereotypes about a culture when reading traditional texts. They confronted German readers with a Grimm's fairy tale, claiming it to be of either Japanese or Italian origin. Their analysis reveals that readers tend to find stereotypical meanings based rather on pre-information and the concomitant expectations than on actual content.

Apart from cultural backgrounds, several contributions analyse the influence of readers' personality, gender or values on their media perception. Ridge and Key (Brigham Young) scrutinise the influence of religiously sanctified violence on consequent aggression. Their research does not only demonstrate a significant relation between the sanction of violence by a deity and the willingness for aggressive behaviour of readers, but also a positive correlation of consequent aggression with readers' religiousness.

The particular value of quantitative approaches, however, reveals itself not only in the confirmation of general theories, but in equal measure in the failure to corroborate theories – that is, to falsify them. Owen (Southern California), for example, applied Graesser's constructionist theory to motion pictures and tested the impact of individual differences in *cognitive ability, need for cognition* and *experience with challenging films* on the enjoyment of story comprehension. Three re-edited versions of a film with varying levels of cognitive challenge were presented to different groups. Surprisingly, his results suggest that feelings for the characters may outweigh narrative comprehension in generating viewer enjoyment, whereas other parameters such as film version, and the assessed personality traits did not significantly interact with enjoyment. Also Odag's (Bremen) research thoroughly questions firmly believed theoretical claims about gender differences. In her research she compares emotional involvement in literary texts of male and female readers in relation to the category of the work and its thematic focus. Contrary to predictions of feminist theory and in opposition to former survey results, male participants scored higher than females on questionnaire scales assessing emotional involvement.

Finally, a number of contributions throw new light on the functions that literature fulfills. Hakemulder (Urecht), for instance, looks at the foundations of such functions: since many of the stories we read (or, in this case, watch as movies) are known to us prior to reading or viewing, the question becomes why we wish to be exposed to them again (and again). The answers that Hakemulder provides on the basis of four experimental studies point to the importance of form, and especially the deviation from 'usual' ways of presentation, thus opening up a whole new theoretical framework. Therman (Helsinki) examines the way literary stories may call forward biographical remindings. Contrary to previous research, she finds that imagination may play a more important role in understanding and responding to a text than the mere fact the text evokes personal memories. In all this, however, we are always looking at adults. What Wieler and Petzold (Berlin) do in their chapter is drawing attention to the fact that these skills in treating narrative are predicated on prior socialization. In their qualitative research, they look at how indigenous and migrant children and families make use of different strategies to use narratives and different media in developing and maintaining a cultural identity. These media are rapidly changing the literary landscape, as Maryl (Warsaw) shows in his contribution. His argument is that we can use these new developments for our research purposes: internet book-clubs or book recommendation systems provide a plethora of information on what people read, for what purposes, what they recommend and for what reasons, how elements of content, plot or structure influence evaluations. In a well-balanced approach, Maryl describes – on the basis of concrete examples of such internet discussions – the advantages but also the limitations of using such internet materials for research on literature. Evaluation is also the topic of Bortolussi, Dixon and Mullins (Alberta), one that is highly controversial in literary studies. The authors develop a typology of different kinds of evaluation sources and processes, and subsequently ask readers to evaluate different kind of stories. Their analysis reveals different factors that play a role in such judgments. Over lengthy periods of time, such evaluations lead to canon formation: which texts to retain and recommend. Fishelov's (Jerusalem) approach is refreshing in that it turns away from the often ideologically laden discussions over the canon by empirically investigating which literary works (in the West) have generated most references in the internet. The results of this search form a much more reliable basis to discuss issues of literary value and the canon than has hitherto been the case.

The authors in this volume come from different cultures and academic fields, all building bridges between various approaches, methods and theories. They all aim for a deservedly new beginning in literary studies.

Acknowledgements

Financial support of the German Research Foundation (DFG, Deutsche Forschungsgemeinschaft) for the 2006 IGEL Conference in Munich is hereby gratefully acknowledged.

Permission has kindly been granted by John Benjamins Publishing Company, Amsterdam/Philadelphia to reprint the table on page 175-176 of Mona Baker's "A corpus-based view of similarity and difference in translation" in *International Journal of Corpus Linguistics* 9:2 in the chapter by David Miall. The permission is gratefully acknowledged here.

Permission to reproduce Titian's *Venus of Urbino* here has been kindly granted by the Uffizi Museum in Florence.

Permission to reproduce a detail from Bernini's *The Ecstacyof St Theresa* has been kindly granted by the photographer Maurizio di Puolo.

INTRODUCTION

THE INHUMANITY OF THE HUMANITIES

WILLIE VAN PEER

Abstract

In this chapter[1] I argue that traditional methods of treating literature and the arts have evolved into technical ways of dealing with them, without much alignment to why these texts and works are there in the first place. I will give some clear (and, I believe, convincing) examples, which I claim are prototypical for the way the humanities deal with the functional side of their objects of study. The conclusion from here must be that, in spite of all appearances, and certainly in spite of what most humanists believe and propagate, the humanities are characterized more by the lack of humanity with which they treat art and literature. Notwithstanding individual exceptions and local tendencies to counter such poverty, this tendency is widespread and internalized at deep levels by professionals in university institutions, and mirrors itself in the personality of students of the humanities, as one study clearly articulates.

I will then assert that in empirical research we can and do make this link to the vital functions that literature fulfils, precisely by studying what literature (or art) does to the lives of individuals and groups. I will give a typical example of such research, and show how it may bring us back to the roots of what literature is and does.

---

[1] The following is the text of a plenary presidential address given at the 2006 IGEL conference near Munich. In order to largely preserve the oral character of the presentation I have renounced the use of notes as much as possible and kept references to a minimum. I hope the argument will thus speak for itself. I wish to express sincere thanks to Jan Auracher, Jemeljan Hakemulder, Max Louwerse, David Miall and Sonia Zyngier for incisive criticism on an earlier version of this chapter, from which my argument has significantly profited. All remaining shortcomings are mine, of course.

1. The Value of Writing and Reading Literature

Toward the end of *On Writing* Stephen King talks about the function of literature:

> Writing isn't about making money, getting famous, getting dates, getting laid, or making friends. In the end, it's about *enriching the lives* of those who will read your work, and enriching your own life, as well. (2000, 275; my italics)

Enriching the lives of readers! Such a view of literature has consequences. Could it mean that students in the humanities, and especially students of literature, could therefore have richer lives than those in other subjects? The cumulative effect of being continuously exposed to and confronted with the bounty (of feeling, of ideas, of values, of imagination, and so forth) contained in literary texts should presumably result in a richer personality. One could even argue that herein lies the value of the humanities, that they provide individuals and society with a wider array and a wider panorama of human values, what Charles Murray has called the 'transcendental goods'. In his monumental work *Human Accomplishment* he argues that...

> "[A]n artist's conception of the purpose of a human life and the measure of excellence in a human life provides a frame within which the varieties of the human experience are translated into art. Good art often explores the edges of the frame, revealing to us the depths to which human beings can fall as well as the heights to which they can climb." (2003, 421)

If art and literature involve us emotionally in such depths and heights of human existence, then one may reasonably expect that regular immersion in such emotions will turn readers into emotionally richer persons.

These processes could result then, in different personality traits, depending on the amount of exposure to literature and art. Now as a theoretical claim this is a tall order, and one that certainly needs finer specification. I believe that the previous argument may hold in general, but I know also that it certainly does *not* hold for students. At least one extensive and systematic investigation of personality differences between students of the humanities and the sciences, revealed no such differences at all – in some cases even the opposite of what is claimed above holds! Eirini Tsiknaki, a former Ph.D. student of mine, compared 78 students of both areas of study on a number of parameters (Tsiknaki 2005). It is indeed the case that students of the humanities indicate that they read more than students of the sciences (t = 2.62, df =76, p < .0005)[2], also read (on top of their literary reading assignments for their courses) significantly more literature in their leisure time (t = 1.67, df = 75, p < .05), also enjoy reading literature more (t = 2.76, df = 76, p < .003), so that the conditions for a reasonable comparison are fulfilled. Out of the many hypotheses investigated by Tsiknaki, I will concentrate here on one, namely the one relating to 'emotional intelligence' of both groups of participants. Emotional intelligence is a concept first proposed by Payne (1985), further developed by Salovey and Mayer (1990) and popularized by Goleman (1995). It refers to the ability to recognize and 'understand', as well as the skill to 'manage' emotions of oneself and of others. Tsiknaki had participants of both disciplines fill out an extensive questionnaire that had been developed and calibrated by professional psychologists to measure a person's emotional intelligence. The outcome of the questionnaire is a so-called EQ, an 'emotional intelligence quotient': as with IQ, the higher a person's EQ, the more this person is emotionally 'intelligent'. If the function of reading literature as outlined by Stephen King and Charles Murray would hold, then one would expect students of the humanities to score higher for emotional intelligence than science studies. Is this the case?

Below is a scatterplot of the responses of all Tsiknaki's participants: the horizontal axis represents the EQ-value as measured through the questionnaire (each dot being a participant or group of participants), the vertical axis the amount of literature read. The line is the average tendency of the relationship between horizontal and vertical axis, i.e. the relationship between literary reading frequency on the one hand and emotional intelligence on the other.

The reader may be in for a shock at this point: as can be seen, the line tilts slightly to the right hand side. This means that there is an *inverse* relation between the two variables: *high* frequency of literary reading is associated with *lower* level of emotional intelligence! And vice versa: higher levels of emotional intelligence are to be found predominantly among participants who read less, i.e. the scientists. This is exactly the opposite of what we had predicted. Moreover, this association between weak emotional intelligence and high reading frequency approaches

---

[2] These p-values indicate the error probability, i.e. the chances that the observed differences between the groups are caused by error or chance. They are also an indication of the probability that the observed group difference is a contingent characteristic of these groups. In other words, low p-values mean that the data may be generalized beyond the sample of participants.

significance in statistical terms ($r = -0.169$, $p < .07$, $N = 78$). A t-test for independent samples, comparing average responses for humanities vs. science students even shows a highly significant difference in this respect ($t = 2.65$, $df = 76$, $p < .01$). This means that there is only a 1 % chance that this difference is due to error; or: repeating the study a hundred times would result in only one test deviating from the current outcome.

Figure 1: Relationship reading frequency (vertical) / emotional intelligence (horizontal)

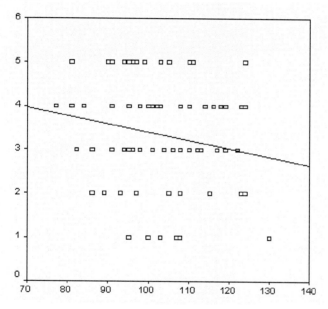

This is a first sense in which one observes the inhumanity[3] of the humanities: in spite of the plausibility of the hypothesis, and against the cherished self-image of the humanities as bearers of human values, literary departments at universities are no better at instilling these values in their students, certainly not as far as emotional intelligence is concerned. Stronger even, the results of this study reveal the opposite: it is students of the natural sciences, who read much less than humanities students, who

---

[3] I am using the word here as meaning: lacking humanity or emotional warmth, or: not suited for human beings. There is in English also a meaning of the word inhumanity as referring to cruelty or brutality. This sense is explicitly *not* meant here, of course.

score highest on this scale of emotional richness. An inference may be drawn here: although classroom methods in lectures and seminars were not studied as part of this research, the poor showing of the humanities students may be due to the "inhuman" nature of their experience in the literature classroom, which conduces to lower emotional intelligence. This suggested inhumanity is a supposition only, but a reasonable one, based on knowledge of what happens in classrooms.

2. The Object of Humanities' Studies

So we do have a problem in the humanities. After Dilthey (1883 / 1989) introduced his distinction between understanding (*verstehen*) and explaining (*erklären*) the humanities have prided themselves on being different from the sciences. Understanding...

> "[W]as seen by Dilthey as the typical way in which the humanities try to understand the world through an operation that centres, not on causality, as in the natural sciences, but on trying to unravel the personal meaning of the phenomena involved." (van Peer, Hakemulder, and Zyngier 2007, 2)

And this attitude extended itself beyond the realm of methodology. The humanities are not just different in terms of the way in which they go about their business (when compared to the natural sciences), they also adhere to different values. The prototypical associations made with the study of the humanities are: quality, subjectivity, individuality, humaneness. The sciences, by contrast, are believed to deal with quantities, objectivity, impersonal data, and with cold calculation. The list can be extended a*d libitum*. It is a list that is made up and maintained mainly by humanists. What interests us here is less such individual characterizations than a general world view that most people in the humanities have of themselves and others. It seems to boil down to the view that the humanities deal in what is deep down, really humane, benign, mild, open-minded and understanding, the quintessence of what is taken to be human, while the sciences would fail such a perspective. They would even lack the insights to articulate such concerns. Let us look in closer detail, however, what the object of study in the humanities entails, and how scholars go about it.

In a fundamental paper, Uri Margolin (2003) brings us closer to the above-mentioned aim of analysing what the study object of the humanities is and entails. The total literary system, he argues, consists of two equally indispensible and irreducible components:

(1) a set of objects and codes (text types, genres, styles);
(2) a correlated set of historically occurring individual and collective situations, activities and practices bearing on these objects.
(Margolin 2003, 2)

Indeed, what we call 'literature' in general consists first and foremost as a corpus of texts: oral and written, popular and canonical, historical and contemporary. This is the first component of the system as defined by Margolin: symbolic objects with their particular content, structure and particular features. But there is more than just an arbitrary set of texts. We can also study the origins of such texts, the autographs or manuscripts and their genealogy, their forms and their styles, in what categories one can classify them, how certain categories show specific characteristics of language and style not contained in other types. All this belongs to the study of the first component.

But we can also study how, where and why these texts emerged and how they were disseminated, how people reacted to them initially, what form these reactions took, how they influenced other reactions, what individual effects were produced by their reading, in what way the texts influenced mentalities or institutional practices of a group or a society. It is clear in this case that we are not just studying the objects referred to in category (1), but instead what people *do* with these objects, forming the study field number (2). In this case we are basically investigating the functions these objects fulfill in the lives of individuals and/or social groups. Another way of saying this is that category (1) is concerned with some specific *products*, while category (2) relates to *processes* that contextually embrace these products.

One may want to question whether the distinction between (1) and (2) is tenable in all cases, whether there are no fuzzy areas, or whether it is always profitable to maintain the distinction. Others might want to dispute whether the distinction by Margolin is sufficient – maybe some scholars want to add further dimensions, but Margolin's proposal has at least the advantage of being conceptually clear *and* parsimonious. For this reason, I will follow Margolin's distinction and the way he reasons about it.

Also, Margolin's argument is not so much that these two components exist, but that to study literature in its totality emplies studying both, or better even, the relation between the two components, and that this entails some kind of empirical work. To study the functional aspect means to write literature's social or institutional history as well as investigate individual processes of comprehension, cognitive, emotional, attitudinal and behavioural effects, and these aims require empirical research methods: critical study of sources, reception studies, reader reactions, and so forth. Only to study such functional aspects, however, neglects the characteristics of the objects and codes, and hence is a form of unacceptable reductionism, leading to a form of social and individual 'book keeping'. Hence one must also study the products themselves that fulfill these functions. But only to study these objects eliminates the humane that relates to literary texts, namely what human people do with these objects, why, and how they do so – and is therefore a form of unacceptable reductionism as well, leading to a poetics in an individual and social 'vacuum' and a fetishism of texts and codes (as we witness in Post-Structuralism and Deconstruction in their various guises). Whence we must also study their functional side.

My claim now is that the humanities by and large hide behind a technical elaboration of Margolin's first field (the objects and codes) in order to duck the more fundamental issues of the second field (the functions these objects fulfil), thereby reducing the study of literature to the technical description of inanimate objects (be they symbolic), thus rendering inhuman what is ultimately and intimately human. It is this concentration on technicalities and the concomitant neglect of the human side that may explain the low emotional intelligence of humanities students compared to the scientists. Of course I would not want to claim that it is always and everywhere the case that the humanities slight their human side. Of course there are colleagues who do take the human side of the arts and literature seriously – if one only thinks of the work of Martha Nussbaum (2001), for instance. But my personal impression is that its neglect is widespread if not endemic in the humanities. For many people in the humanities their work is a job like any other job, in which you have to excel in certain details, but in which no requirements are made or upheld concerning the teaching of values beyond the by now ritual repetition of the race/class/gender issues in the English speaking parts of academia.

But here opponents could counter that precisely by concentrating on such issues the humanities deliver a 'humanising' of topics for study. Also, much postmodern criticism is concerned with such ‚human' issues, e.g., new historicist accounts of social conditions reflected in a particular text. Since, however, this is often used as a basis for attacking a writer for not having the same values as the critic, this seems to be a major source of the inhuman. Consider the ills flowing from postmodern approaches, the "posthuman": this usually involves the hegemony of "race/class/gender" in which literary texts are treated with suspicion. Here is a major source of that loss of emotional connection between student and literature. How can one expect a certain ‚humanity' to grow in students if they are continuously instructed to distrust authors and texts? How to conceive of the humanity of literary studies when the author has been declared dead[4], where a prominent journal (*Philosophy and Literature*) awards prizes of the annual "Bad Writing Contest" to some of the most visible and prominent professors[5], and where the Sokal affair[6] showing the discpline's inability to guard academic standards of research and publication has taken the credibility out of the discipline's. As Denis Dutton (1995, 38) has so eloquently expressed it: "no sense of joy or love for the arts is ever allowed to emerge."

Lest my intention be mistaken: this is not a plea for 'softness' – quite the contrary, my point is (and will be further elaborated later) that this disregard for the 'human' side goes hand in hand with a neglect of a rigorous methodology. It is precisely this lack of rigorous methods when inspecting claims in the humanistic disciplines that is at the basis of much inhumanity. What I am claiming is not that we should be 'soft' in the humanities. If we want to further increase our understanding of ourselves as human beings, we will have to bow to the rigours of rational analysis and to the inexorable tests to which we submit our theoretical views. To draw a parallel with medicine: it is nice when a physician sympathizes with the suffering of a patient, but that is not what we ultimately expect from the physician, but rather a deeper understanding of the causes of the disease we are suffering from, so that decisive therapy may ensue.

But that is not the way the humanities in general and literary studies in particular proceed. Functional questions are rare in those disciplines: functional topics are even shunned systematically. Why is there something like literature in the first place? And what exactly is literature? Why is its presence universal in human cultures? Why are so many structural characteristics of literary texts so similar in so many, often unrelated, cultures? What emotions are generated during reading and how do these influence readers' further emotional life? What are the effects of reading literature on individuals and on social groups, or on society as a whole - effects on cognition, on attitudes, on behaviour, on subjective well-being, on health? Since we use the word *belles-lettres* to refer to literature, what exactly is it that we find beautiful? And what *is* beauty? The reader will be hard-pressed to find much research on these crucial questions, which is odd in a sense, when theoretical reflection on literature in the West took

---

[4] See Burke (1998).
[5] See http://denisdutton.com/bad_writing.htm (inspected 22.09.07).
[6] See http://www.physics.nyu.edu/faculty/sokal/index.html. See also Sokal and Bricmont (1998).

off with such fundamental questions in the works of Plato and Aristotle. It looks as if literary studies systematically avoid these questions. True, they are not easy questions; fundamental questions never are. But in every discipline there is at least a determined effort to come to terms with them. Not so in the study of literature, and not so in other related areas in the humanities. As Mario Bunge, not completely tongue-in-cheek, once remarked:

> "... [A] comment on Cicero's discussion of Clitomachus' account of Carneades' views is likely to be regarded as the summit of serious scholarship." (2001, 208)

3. Fear of Humanity

Apparently, literary scholars seem to have found refuge in technical questions concerning literary works – or that, at least, is my personal impression. In order to become more concrete, let me give you an example of what I mean. I admit that it is only an example, although it can be augmented with many more, and certainly does not exclude that other, non-technical approaches are applied to the study of literature. Yet, also these other approaches typically avoid functional questions of the type highlighted above. The example comes from *A Tramp Abroad*, the non-fictional account of Mark Twain's travels through central and southern Europe, which appeared in 1880. In it, Twain recounts an experience he had in the Uffizi museum in Florence, which he describes as follows:

> "You enter [the Uffizi] and proceed to that most-visited little gallery that exists in the world – the Tribune – and there, against the wall, without obstructing rap or leaf, you may look your fill upon the foulest, the vilest, the obscenest picture the world possesses – Titian's Venus. It isn't that she is naked and stretched out on a bed – no, it is the attitude of one of her arms and hand. If I ventured to describe that attitude there would be a fine howl – but there the Venus lies for anybody to gloat over that wants to – and there she has a right to lie, for she is a work of art, and art has its privileges. I saw a young girl stealing furtive glances at her; I saw young men gazing long and absorbedly at her, I saw aged infirm men hang upon her charms with a pathetic interest. How I should like to describe her – just to see what a holy indignation I could stir up in the world ... yet the world is willing to let its sons and its daughters and itself look at Titian's beast, but won't stand a description of it in words....There are pictures of nude women which suggest no impure thought – I am well aware of that. I am not railing at such. What I am trying to emphasize is the fact that Titian's Venus is very far from being one of that sort. Without any question it was

painted for a bagnio and it was probably refused because it was a trifle too strong. In truth, it is a trifle too strong for any place but a public art gallery." (Mark Twain 1880)[7]

The work in question is Titian's *Venus of Urbino*, painted in 1538, which is reproduced overleaf. It is one of the earliest paintings of a female nude[8] in the history of Western art after Classical Antiquity. Its content speaks for itself: we see a woman, stretched out on a bed. She is stark naked with the exception of a ring on her left hand and a bracelet on her right wrist, her left hand resting on her pubic area (is she touching her sex?), looking the spectator straight in the eyes. With his typical frankness, Twain claims that the picture is sexually charged. Maybe many of us will agree, but the astonishing fact is that over the past 450 years this fact has attracted no attention whatsoever from art historians! This astonishing fact is in stark contrast to reactions of some Christian fundamentalists, for instance the 'Christian Front for Virtue, Decency and Morals' in Germany, who demand the immediate removal of all 'indecent' works of art from museums; Titian's picture decorates their website (www.rasputin.de/CF/kunst.html). At least these people have understood something basic about the painting that the art historians seem to have missed.

---

[7] Available online at Project Gutenberg:
http://www.gutenberg.org/files/119/119-h/p7.htm
[8] With one exception: Giorgione's *Sleeping Venus*, painted around 1510. Giorgione (1477 – 1510) had, in contrast to Titian, who lived up to the age of 80 years, a very brief life, hence not even having the opportunity to further develop the genre; only six of his paintings are known.

Figure 2: Titian's *Venus of Urbino*

So one wonders what has been said and written about Titian's Venus? The answer to that question provides an interesting catalogue of what I mean when I speak of the inhumanity of the humanities. Of course the exquisite quality and masterly control of all the techniques of oil painting, as well as its artful composition, have been endlessly extolled. Then there are detailed iconographic studies of the woman's hair and its place in contemporary fashion. But not only that: there are discussions about the delicate texture of the skin, as well as the folds in the sheet. (Folds in the sheet? How did they get there in the first place?) Note also the rich textiles and how they are rendered in paint. And what about the flowers in the women's right hand? Which flower is it? Why has one of them dropped on to the bed? And what is the lapdog doing on the bed? Is it really sleeping or only pretending? Does its presence tell us of some hidden meaning in the painting? What kind of tiles do we see? What is the women with the textiles draped over her shoulder doing? What does her different hairdo tell us? Why does she have these textiles over her shoulder and why is she rolling up her sleeves? And what is the little girl looking for in the trunk? What do the patterns on the trunk mean? What symbols are there on the tapestry on the outside wall? Do they carry a specific meaning? What landscape do we see through the window outside? As the reader can gauge from this brief catalogue, there are so many urgent questions to be resolved, that art historians have been kept quite busy for four and a half centuries. Only: the one and only thing they have resolutely avoided discussing is the emotional impact of the woman on the bed: her vulnerability in relation to ours. It seems as if *fear of humanity* reigns in the humanities. And note one technical aspect that is little discussed: the 'Venus' is represented here without any of the usual attributes of a Goddess of Love and Fertility from Antiquity, a further sign of her role in the picture.

Of course there are interesting and also partly important iconographic aspects of the painting that should be investigated and dealt with. But one expects some kind of balance between the study of technical details and the reasons why we should study them. In Margolin's terms: we sacrifice everything in the functional component to technicalities about the objects. And that is the crucial point: these dozens of technical studies largely ignore the fact that the picture is ultimately an erotic one. For the first time in European visual history a sexual desire is represented: the woman shows herself openly, her nipples are erect, her attitude is inviting, without shame – she even looks a little dominant at what we may perhaps presume are male spectators. The image was created by a man, for the enjoyment of (at the time) other men. But only few people (except Mark Twain) are prepared to admit that it expresses a male gaze of sexual desire. And art historians least of all! For further information on the neglected erotic aspects of Titian's painting, see Freedberg (1989), Goffen (1997) and at ART at SUNY[9]. I hasten to add here that nowadays a good deal of attention is spent on erotic and sexual aspects in art and literature, for instance in feminist and cultural studies, but the bulk of such publications are found in the last twenty years, and a hundred years after Mark Twain published his view on Titian. And one could also criticise the methodological basis of such studies, usually involving a high degree of subjectivity and speculativeness. I hope to demonstrate later that these limitations can be overcome through a more rigorous methodology.

Now I am not suggesting that we should see Titian's *Venus* as some kind of soft porn, even when it is undeniably erotic. But there is also another side to it: the cautious approach to the enigma of female sexuality, the celebration of female beauty, the spiritual power of sensuality, and a profound reflection on the power of the human gaze. And all this in a

---

[9] http://employees.oneonta.edu/farberas/arth/arth213/Titian_Venus_urbino.html

breathtaking demonstration of the artist's powers to probe (and partly reveal) the deepest currents of human existence.

If this were the sole case to which one could point the argument would be poor, of course. But it is not. Look at the picture below. It is a detail from a sculpture by Bernini, created some hundred years after Titian's *Venus*. Simon Schama, in his *Power of Art* asks the rhetorical question: "Who can look at Bernini's *Extasy of St. Theresa*, 1644-7, with an innocent eye?" (2006, 78)

Figure 3: Bernini's *St Theresa*

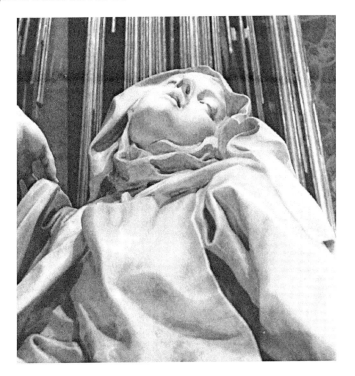

As in Titian's case, it is female sexuality that is at the heart of the matter. Although the face of St. Theresa shows unmistakable signs of corporal surrender, art critics do not allow any erotic associations with it. To quote Schama in full:

"Typical is the authority who writes that to see the work as being in any way erotic 'limits it severely' – although, equally typically of this kind of comment, he doesn't bother to say why. We are left with the wagged finger and imputation that, if we are to understand Bernini's intentions, we had better banish any such modern vulgarity from our heads. It is utterly unhistorical, these interpreters insist, to imagine that the Pope's architect, the supreme sculptor of Rome, a man who practiced Jesuitical discipline, every day, could conceive of representing the mystical levitation of a saint as a moment of orgasmic convulsion. But as a matter of fact, the modern anachronism is not the union of body and soul that so many 17-century poets and writers obsessed about, but its demure separation into sensual and spiritual experience. Ecstacy in Bernini's time was understood, and experienced, as sensuously indivisible." (2006, 78)

Schama is exceptional as (art) historian that he puts aside the technical details and concentrates on the sculpture's central function. As with Titian's painting, there are dozens of technical questions one can (and in some cases should) investigate, but Bernini surely did not create his work for us to ponder over such details without a firm look at what is there at the centre of it. And that is: a woman all but fainting under the unbearable duress of corporal and spiritual ecstasy - as the title of the work announces clearly enough. Just how powerful is art, Schama asks. His answer, in all its simplicity and candour, amounts to the simple definition: "The power of art is *the power of unsettling surprise*." (2006, 7; my italics) I will add later that this is also part of the answer to an earlier question: what is beauty? Beauty is what the power of art is about, and beauty is the power of unsettling surprise.

It is the inhumanity of the humanities that they do not wish to become too deeply involved with this power of beauty, with this unsettling surprise. It is so much safer to stay with some technical details. Could it be that the students of the humanities in Tsiknaki's study did not score higher on the test of emotional intelligence because they had been dealing almost exclusively with such technical details of literary works during their training at university? And that science students, not being in the least familiar with such technical issues, view human emotions and relations in a much more authentic way?

4. An Alternative

Obviously the humanities are in serious problems – granted that one may generalise beyond the two examples provided in the previous section. And I do believe that, counterexamples notwithstanding, the large majority of work in literary studies are *not* dealing with such functional questions as I have just reviewed and illustrated. So what is to be done?

In this section I will give an example of a piece of research I have carried out with colleagues[10] that may illustrate a different tack, one which will confront such basic questions head on and at the same time throw us back on to the functions of art and literature in the hearts and minds of human beings.

The purpose of this research was to investigate Schama's claim about the power of *unsettling surprise*[11] embedded in Margolin's categorization. To test the link of such surprise to *beauty* a simple reading experiment was carried out. A 'poem' was composed, consisting of the line 'I love you not' repeated identically eight times, thus building up a strong pattern of expectation in the reader, which is broken in the final, ninth, line which ran 'I love you notwithstanding'. Given the pattern of expectation previously built up, the final line may present some degree of surprise in the reader. But it is not the surprise in itself that we were interested in, but its relationship to perceived beauty! The lines were projected on a screen one by one; after each line readers were requested to judge the beauty of the poem so far on a 10-point scale. We did not define the term 'beauty' but left this to each reader's interpretation. Note that any such interpretative variation will work *against* any hypothesis concerning the relationship between surprise and beauty, as it will create semantic noise. If, in spite of such looseness of definition, we found strong agreement among participants, this could be taken as strong evidence for such a link. Because we were interested whether such a link would be universal or more likely to be culture-bound we ran the experiment in seven different countries: Brazil, Egypt, Finland, Germany, Netherlands, Tunisia, and Ukraine. All in all some 420 students took part in these reading experiments. The general result can be seen in Figure 4 below:

---

[10] Jemeljan Hakmulder, of Utrecht University and Sonia Zyngier, of the Federal University of Rio de Janeiro. For a description of the framework of this research, see van Peer, Zyngier and Hakemulder (2007).

[11] The idea is not new. As a matter of fact, in literary studies the theory of foregrounding is a systematic elaboration of the idea; see, for an overview the thematic issue on foregrounding in *Language and Literature* 16 (2), 2007.

Figure 4: Perceived beauty through surprise

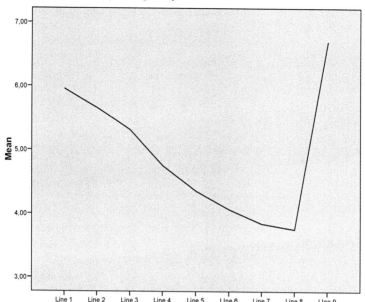

The horizontal axis represents the 9 lines of the 'poem', the vertical axis has the average ratings of each line in terms of perceived beauty. Two things are immediately clear in this graph. First, ratings start somewhere in the middle of the scale for the first line, then gradually drop to a low point: this is what one would expect, given the fact that readers were confronted with the identical formulation line after line. Secondly, one sees a dramatic jump at the final line (9), meaning that on average readers perceived the poem as considerably more beautiful after having processed the last, and surprising, line. The differences in rated beauty after having read line 9 and all other lines is statistically significant (as measured with a Mann Whitney test) at p-levels lower than one in thousand, perhaps one in ten thousand ($p < .001$). This result corroborates Schama's claim: the surprise of the alternative perspective and wording in the final line made for a powerful impression of beauty on our readers. It remains open to what extent this surprise was also 'unsettling' as Schama named it, but even if this were not the case (which is likely, given the artificial nature of the 'poem' and the lack of literary qualities in its author) the result is nevertheless remarkable. How much more powerful indeed would a really unsettling surprise be!

But this is only the average response to the poem, across the seven nations. Are there marked differences between cultures in this respect? There are, as can be readily seen in Figure 5, which contains average beauty ratings for the penultimate line (8) and the final line (9), separated out for different cultural groups.

Figure 5: Cultural differences in response to lines 8 and 9

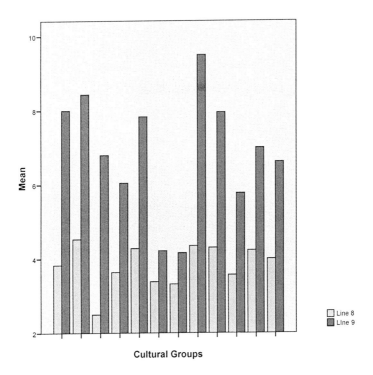

There is considerable variation in the height of the bars in this figure, both for line 8 and for line 9, a clear indication that cultures differ with respect to the rated beauty of both lines. An ANOVA[12] reveals that for all

---

[12] This is an analysis of variance: basically it compares the distribution of the responses *between* the different nationalities with the distribution *within* each of the respective groups. When the former is considerably larger than the latter, this

nine lines the cultural differences were highly significant. In other words, though Figure 4 showed us a general picture in which surprise 'created beauty', Figure 5 mitigates this impression, in that it reveals significant differences in the reactions of readers belonging to different cultures – which is something anyone with trans-cultural experience will immediately appreciate.

However, this is not the whole story. Have another look at Figure 5: one also notices that in spite of the cultural variation one thing is stable across the board: the perceived beauty of the 'surprise line' is always higher than that of the penultimate line! This means, then, that two forces are at work simultaneous: variation at the cultural level and constancy across cultures. In other words: our research demonstrates how both relativistic *and* universalistic forces are at work side by side. Although cultures do differ in the beauty rankings allocated they also abide by a general, law-like mechanism of associating surprise with beauty. Thus, local traditions are yoked to global rules, which, in turn, are realized differently locally. We hereby get rid of endless bickering over relativism and universalism: clearly *both* forces are at work simultaneously!

5. Conclusion

In this chapter I have first shown that the usual supposition upon which the study of art and literature is predicated is not fulfilled when one looks at the personality structure of students in these fields. I have then outlined a perspective (taken from Margolin) on the object of study typical of the humanities. In the course of the argument it became clear how literary studies concentrates one-sidedly on one of the two major object areas, neglecting the study of the functional aspects of literary texts in human life. I have illustrated this basic inhumanity of the humanities with some examples, and have proposed an alternative, empirical way out of this embarrassment: to return to the basic questions that literature and the arts raise: its function in the lives of human beings. The experiment presented made clear in what way perception of beauty is embedded in cognitive and emotional structures that go beyond cultural conventions, though being influenced by them.

This is rather counter-intuitive. Most scholars in the humanities view empirical studies, with the emphasis they often place on objectivity, on

---

results in statistically significant differences between groups. In this case, all intercultural differences had p-values lower than .001 but two, who have p-values below .05, the conventional level of statistical significance.

operationalization, and on quantitative measurement, as anathema to literary studies – and definitely against what they perceive as the human enterprise of their discipline. Yet as the example may have shown, it is exactly the empirical approach illustrated above that has an eye for the human aspect of literature. To get the gist of this inimicality against empirical studies as part of the humanities, let me draw attention to the position of Jonathan Culler, who writes: "The question is not what actual readers happen to do but what an ideal reader must know implicitly in order to read and interpret works in ways which we consider acceptable, in accordance with the institution of literature" (1975, 123-4). Can anyone believe this? Note that Jonathan Culler is not some obscure figure in literary studies: he is one of the most respected and most visible scholars in the field. His books have been uninterruptedly on reading lists worldwide for more than thirty years. But studying literature under real conditions is not something he envisages as a worthwhile enterprise – instead the proposal is to study what a fictional reader (for an ideal reader is a fiction) does! (Note also that Culler claims in effect that his own idea of the conventions of reading are what should be studied!) In any case it is yet another symptom of the dearth of humanity in the humanities: It means a total lack of interest in what actually happens with literature in reality. In other words: reality is unimportant to the literary scholar, and the real experiences of real people with real literary texts is at most peripheral. Suppose a world-wide authority in medicine proclaims: the question is not what would heal actual patients. Or the chemist proclaims that what these substances actually do is of no relevance. Or the historian declares that the question is not what actually happened. But in literary studies, this seems to be the ultimate wisdom, *not* to look at what really happens. Thus the reproach of more traditionally oriented scholars against empirical studies has to be turned on its head: it is the former, rather than the latter, who approach literature and the arts in a way that is devoid of real human concerns.

Of course a certain detachment from one's object of research is often required and necessary. Yet to cut the umbilical cord with the real world of phenomena one studies would sound suicidal to most natural scientists nowadays, or would resemble being catapulted back into the Middle Ages, where followers of Aristotle (as many are now following Culler in literary studies) fanatically believed that men have 34 teeth, women only 32. Aristotle, who had been married several times, apparently never asked one of his wives to open her mouth to check.

But detachment is one thing, the other is the link to why we are studying the things we are studying: are these issues relevant to human life? My claim is that we need to give back humanity to the humanities If we carry out such research as exemplified here[13], in which human issues are *not* trivialised but taken seriously, in which results can be openly inspected and replicated, and in which the rich diversity of human life is investigated with the best methods that we have, we may be successful in re-introducing humanity in the humanities.

Works Cited

Bortolussi, Marissa and Peter Dixon. 2003. *Psychonarratology. Foundations for the empirical study of literary response.* Cambridge: Cambridge University Press.
Bunge, Mario. 2001. *Philosophy in Crisis. The need for reconstruction.* Amherst: Prometheus Books.
Burke, Séan. 1998. *The Death and Return of the Author: Criticism and Subjectivity in Barthes, Foucault, and Derrida.* Edinburgh: Edinburgh University Press.
Culler, Jonathan. 1975. *Structuralist Poetics: Structuralism, linguistics, and the study of literature.* London: Routledge & Kegan Paul.
Dilthey, Wilhelm 1989. *Introduction to the Human Sciences.* Princeton, NJ: Princeton University Press. [Orig. ed. 1883].
Dutton, Denis. 1995. Mythologies of Tribal Art. In *African Arts* 28, no. 3, pp. 32-43.
Freedberg, David. 1989. *The Power of Images: Studies in the History and Theory of Response.* Chicago: University of Chicago Press.
Gerrig, Richard. 1993. *Experiencing Narrative Worlds. On the psychological activities of reading.* New Haven, CT: Yale University Press.
Goffen, Rona. 1997. *Titian's Women.* New Haven, CT: Yale University Press.
Goleman, D. 1995. *Emotional Intelligence.* New York: Bantam Books.
Hakemuder, Jemeljan. 2000. *The Moral Laboratory. Experiments examining the effects of reading literature on social perception and self-concept.* Amsterdam / Philadelphia: John Benjamins.

---

[13] I have given only one example here, and a very simple one at that. For readers interested in more empirical work on literature, I would like to refer to the following book publications: Bortolussi and Dixon (2003), Gerrig (1993), Hakemulder (2000), Kreuz and MacNeally (1996), Louwerse and van Peer (2002), Martindale (1990), Miall (2006), Schram and Steen (2001), Steen (1994), van Peer (1986), van Peer and Chatman (2001), van Peer, Hakemulder and Zyngier (2007), Zwaan (1993).

King, Stephen. 2000. *On Writing. A memoir of the craft.* New York: Pocket Books.
Kreuz, Roger and Susan MacNeally (eds). 1996. *Empirical Approaches to Literature and Aesthetics.* Norwood, NJ: Ablex Publ. Comp.
Louwerse, Max and Willie van Peer (eds). 2002. *Thematics. Interdisciplinary Studies.* Amsterdam / Philadelphia: John Benjamins.
Margolin, Uri. 2003. *Studying literature and being empirical: A multifaceted conjunction.* http://www.redes.lmu.de/portal/modules.php?name=Downloads& cid=2.
Martindale, Colin. 1990. *The Clockwork Muse: The predictability of artistic change.* New York: Basic Books.
Miall, David. 2006. *Literary Reading. Empirical and theoretical studies.* New York / Bern: Peter Lang.
Murray, Charles. 2003. *Human Accomplishment. The pursuit of excellence in the arts and sciences, 800 B.C. to 1950.* New York: HarperCollins.
Nussbaum, Martha. 2001. *Upheavals of Thought. The intelligence of emotions.* Cambridge: Cambridge University Press.
Payne, W.L. 1985. A Study of Emotion: developing emotional intelligence; self integration; relating to fear, pain and desire. *Dissertation Abstracts International*, 47, No. 1(a), p. 203A.
Salovey, P. and J.D. Mayer. 1990. Emotional intelligence. *Imagination, Cognition, and Personality* 9: 185-211.
Schama, Simon. 2006. *Power of Art.* London: BBC Books.
Schram, Dick and Gerard Steen (eds). 2001. *The Psychology and Sociology of Literature.* Amsterdam / Philadelphia: John Benjamins.
Sokal, Alan D. and Bricmont, Jean. 1998. *Fashionable Nonsense: Postmodern Intellectuals' Abuse of Science.* New York: Picador: New York.
Steen, Gerard 1994. *Understanding Metaphor in Literature. An empirical approach.* London: Longman.
Tsiknaki, Eirini. 2005. *Literatur und Persönlichkeitsentwicklung. Eine empirische Untersuchung zur Erfassung des Zusammenhangs zwischen literarischem Lesen und Emotionaler Intelligenz* (Literature and Personality Development. An empirical investigation of the relationship between literary reading and emotional intelligence). Munich: Meidenbauer.
Twain, Mark. 1880. *A Tramp Abroad.* Hartford, CT: American Publishing Company.
van Peer, Willie. 1986. *Stylistics and Psychology. Investigations of foregrounding.* London: Croom Helm.

van Peer, Willie and Seymour Chatman (Eds). 2001. *New Perspectives on Narrative Perspective*. Albany, NY: SUNY Press.

van Peer, Willie and Jemeljan Hakemulder and Sonia Zyngier. 2007. *Muses and Measures. Empirical research methods for the humanities*. Newcastle-upon-Tyne: Cambridge Scholars Publications.

van Peer, Willie, Sonia Zyngier, and Jemeljan Hakemulder. 2007. Foregrounding: Past, Present, Future. In *Stylistics: Prospect and Retrospect*, eds. David Hoover and Sharon Lattig, 1-22. Amsterdam / Atlanta: Rodopi.

Zwaan, Rolf. 1993. *Aspects of Literary Comprehension*. Amsterdam / Philadelphia: John Benjamins.

PART I

STRUCTURES AND THEIR PROCESSING

Chapter One

Analyzing Words to Understand Literature

James W. Pennebaker and Molly E. Ireland

Abstract

The words people use in everyday language can reveal a great deal about their personalities, motivations, and social situations. Some of the most important psychological clues can be found in function words – such as pronouns, prepositions, and articles. Recent findings based on computer analyses suggest that function words can help to understand the psychological states of authors as well as their characters and themes in literature. Implications for applying new methods from computational linguistics and psychology to books, plays, and other literary forms are discussed.

Analyzing Words to Understand Literature

The magic of literature is that powerful memories, feelings, and images can be aroused in the reader through written words on a page. Most scholars, in an attempt to understand this process, focus on the underlying themes or broad writing style in the works they study. Rarely is this analysis boiled down to the authors' uses of the words themselves. It borders on the absurd to wax poetic about Shakespeare's use of pronouns or Browning's mastery of prepositions. It would be akin to critiquing the architecture of the Musée d'Orsay by discussing the types of nails or mortar used in its building.

This is a paper on the nails and mortar of great literature. By analyzing the words people use in their writing or even in their natural speech, we can come to a better understanding of the authors and their audience. This endeavour is not as absurd as it may sound. We all tend to speak in different ways depending on our moods, our audiences, and our intentions. Many of these variations may be subtle and not directly detectable by the average reader or listener. Nevertheless, they imperceptibly shape the evaluations and actions of the audience.

This way of thinking is possible because we are standing at the threshold of a new age in the empirical study of literature. Recent breakthroughs in computer sciences, statistics, computational linguistics, and psychology are ushering in powerful new analytic approaches to the study of words and their use. In this chapter, we briefly describe some recent findings about word level analyses and point to the promise of these tools in better understanding authors, their work, and their impact on their audience.

Words and Ways to Study Them

The average English language modern novel is generally composed of at least 100,000 words; the typical Shakespeare play has around 23,000 words; Wordsworth had a penchant for poems that were about 105 words long even though he occasionally published much longer ones. How can we understand a novel, play, or poem by simply counting the words the author used? Which kinds of words should we be counting?

Most word counting approaches distinguish between two broad classes of words – those that reflect content and those that reflect linguistic style. Depending on your training, you might refer to them as closed-class versus open-class words, nouns and regular verbs versus function words, or content-heavy versus junk words. Most early content analyses focused on content-heavy words that suggested specific themes. By analysing a chapter or entire book, one could detect theme-related words that specifically talked about objects or events such as family, nature, illness, and money. Generally, nouns and regular verbs define the primary categories and actions dictated by the author. It makes sense. If you are going to write a book, it is a good idea to say something. Indeed, our research would encourage all aspiring authors to try to include a good number of nouns and regular verbs to help construct a compelling story.

There is much more to writing than content, however. As readers, we are highly attentive to the ways writers convey a message. Even controlling for the content of a narrative, an author's writing style can be dense, informal, playful, convoluted, or mysterious. Just as there is linguistic content, there is also linguistic style – how people put their words together to create a message.

What accounts for "style"? As an example, James Joyce, Gertrude Stein, and Adrienne Rich each wrote about the nature of poetry. Each of these authors has a unique style in their writing that is detectable across genres. Which author is responsible for which quotation?

Author A: Poetry is doing nothing but using losing refusing and pleasing and betraying and caressing nouns. That is what poetry does, that is what poetry has to do no matter what kind of poetry it is.

Author B: Poetry is above all a concentration of the power of language, which is the power of our ultimate relationship to everything in the universe.

Author C: Poetry, even when apparently most fantastic, is always a revolt against artifice, a revolt, in a sense, against actuality.

All three authors are saying equivalent things. Nevertheless, their ways of expressing themselves suggest other issues. Author A is playful; author B is more formal and stiff; author C tends to be more complex and perhaps lyrical than the others. We can define these different styles by looking at the authors' use of articles (and therefore concrete nouns), large versus small words, punctuation, and dozens of other dimensions. Their linguistic styles can be discerned by paying attention to "junk words" – those words that do not convey much in the way of content. These junk words, usually referred to as function words or particles, serve as the cement that holds the content words together. It is also instructive to note that the ways people use these function words in one context is highly correlated with the ways they use them in other settings. As proof, you could probably guess which authors go with which quotation: A = Gertrude Stein, B = Adrienne Rich, and C = James Joyce.

Function words include pronouns, prepositions, articles, conjunctions, and auxiliary verbs. Whereas the average native English speaker has an impressive vocabulary of well over 100,000 words, fewer than 400 are function words. This deceptively trivial percentage (less than 0.04%) of our vocabulary accounts for over half of the words we use in daily speech (see Chung and Pennebaker 2007, for discussion of these statistics). Despite the frequency of their use, they are the hardest to master when learning a new language (Weber-Fox and Neville 2001). They are also almost invisible to both the speaker and listener. For example, can you estimate how frequently you have seen articles (a, an, the) in this chapter so far? Has this paper used more or fewer articles than you would expect in normal speech? [Hint: the answer is much more: 8.1% in this chapter compared to 4.0% in normal speech]. Despite rarely paying them any conscious attention, function words have a powerful impact on the listener/reader and, at the same time, reflect a great deal about the speaker/writer. Returning to the three authors describing poetry, their different uses of function words mark them in predictable ways. The ways people use function words, then, reflect their linguistic style.

Humans, of course, are highly social animals. If we examine the human brain and compare it with every other mammal, the frontal lobe of the cerebral cortex is disproportionately large. In recent years, researchers have begun to emphasize the frontal lobe in guiding our social behaviours (e.g., Gazzaniga 2005, Damasio 1995). Most social emotions, the skill of reading others' emotions and intentions, and the ability to connect with others are highly dependent on an intact frontal lobe.

Language, too, has an important link to frontal lobe function. In general, the majority of language functions are housed in the temporal and frontal lobes. Within the left temporal lobe (at least for most people) is Wernicke's area. Wernicke's area is critical for both understanding and generating most advanced speech – including nouns, regular verbs, and most adjectives. Broca's area, on the other hand, is situated in the left frontal lobe. Damage to Broca's area – while Wernicke's area is intact – results in people speaking in a painfully slow, hesitating way, often devoid of function words. People with functioning Broca's area - but with damage to Wernicke's area – exhibit a completely different social style. These people often speak warmly and fluidly while maintaining eye contact with the target person. The only problem is that they primarily use function words with no content at all (e.g., Miller 1995). Even at the brain level, then, function words are linked to social skills.

A closer analysis of function words points to their social roles more clearly. Pronouns, for example, are words that demand a shared understanding of their referent between the speaker and listener. Consider the completely normal sentence, "I can't believe that he gave it to her." It is easy to imagine someone saying this to us and knowing exactly what is meant. This sentence makes absolutely no sense, however, unless you know who the "I", "he", "her", and "it" refer to. In a normal conversation, we would know who the various players and objects were based on shared knowledge between the speaker and listener. Some social skills are required here. The speaker assumes that the listener knows who everyone is. The listener must be paying attention and know the speaker to follow the conversation. So the mere ability to understand a simple conversation replete with function words demands social knowledge.

For the last few years, we have begun to track the usage of function words across multiple settings. Most of these studies have focused on pronouns and, occasionally, on articles and prepositions. Given that function words are so difficult to control in everyday speech and writing, examining the use of these words in natural language samples has provided a non-reactive way to explore social and personality processes.

It is beyond the scope of this chapter to summarize the many computerised strategies available to researchers interested in the analysis of function and content words (see Pennebaker, Mehl, and Niederhoffer 2003, for a general review). Some methods, for example, simply count words related to particular themes (e.g., the DICTION program, Hart et al. 2005), others look for words or phrases that reveal psychoanalytic concerns or themes related to drives or motives (e.g., the General Inquirer, Stone et al. 1966). Other strategies take a more inductive approach and seek to find broad similarities in word patterns over time or across genres (e.g., Graesser and Petschonek 2005, Martindale 1990, Mergenthaler 1996, Weintraub 1989). Various inductive methods have been evolving from the world of artificial intelligence. One such program, called Latent Semantic Analysis (LSA, Foltz 1996), compares the similarity of any two texts in terms of their content.

In our lab, we have been relying on a text analysis program that we developed called Linguistic Inquiry and Word Count, or LIWC (Pennebaker, Francis, and Booth 2001; Pennebaker, Booth, and Francis 2007). LIWC searches for and counts both content and style words within any given text file. LIWC was developed by having groups of judges evaluate the degree to which about 2,000 words or word stems were related to each of several dozen categories. The categories include negative emotion words (sad, angry), positive emotion words (happy, laugh), standard function word categories (1st, 2nd, and 3rd person pronouns, articles, prepositions), and various content categories (e.g., religion, death, occupation). For each text sample (e.g., poem, essay, book), LIWC computes the percentage of total words that these and other linguistic categories represent.

It should be noted that LIWC, like all other computer programs, does a poor job of appreciating context. Computerized approaches are unable to gauge irony, sarcasm, and the use of metaphors. In most languages, including English, words often have different meanings in different settings. The LIWC program, for example, counts the word "mad" as an anger and negative emotion word. Phrases such as "I'm mad about my lover" and "he's mad as a hatter" are simply miscoded. Word count programs are ultimately probabilistic. In short, one must appreciate the significant shortcomings of computerised text analysis strategies. What they gain in speed and reliability, they often lose in coding errors. In general, the best way to optimise the value of computerised methods is to analyse large samples representing tens of thousands of words.

Using Words to Understand Authors' Psychological States

As suggested above, the analysis of function words has the potential to reveal a great deal about people's social and psychological states. In this section, we briefly describe some of our research, linking function word use to characteristics of writers.

Demographics: sex and age

There are *sex* differences in the use of virtually all function words: pronouns, prepositions, articles, and auxiliary verbs. In a study of over 10,000 text files, we have found that females tend to use 1st person singular pronouns at a consistently higher rate than do males (e.g., Newman et al. 2007). Possible reasons for this difference could be that females are generally more self-focused than men, are more prone to depression than men, or that women are more socially complex and use pronouns to acknowledge other perspectives. Another reliable sex difference is that males' natural speech contains higher rates of article and noun use, which suggests categorisation, or concrete thinking.

Age differences in function words are also robust. In analyses of personal writings collected during experiments or surveys from several thousand people, we found that people use fewer personal pronouns – especially first person singular words – with age (Pennebaker and Stone 2003). This, along with the greater use of exclusive words, suggests that as people age, they make more distinctions and psychologically distance themselves from their topics. In other words, older people speak with greater cognitive complexity. Interestingly, analysis of the use of emotion-laden words indicates that as people age, the more they use positive emotion words and the less they use negative emotion words. The aging project was interesting because all participants did their writing in the late 1990s or early 2000s. A potential problem might be that the effects were attributable to a cohort effect. That is, people born in a particular decade may all write in somewhat similar ways since they all had similar life experiences. Apparent differences in age, then, could simply reflect differences in the decades in which people were born and grew up.

An alternative strategy was to analyse individuals' writings over the course of their lives. We accomplished this by studying the collected works of a number of well-established poets, playwrights, and novelists (for summary of results, see Pennebaker and Stone 2003).

Table 1. Simple correlations with word categories and the authors' age.

		Austen	Shakespeare	Yeats
Function words				
Articles	A, the	0.14	0.21	0.16
Conjunctions	But, since	-0.18	-0.46	-0.39
Personal Pronouns	I, you, them	-0.69	0.10	-0.50
1st pers singular	I, me, my	-0.49	-0.22	-0.13
Auxiliary verbs	Is, have	0.64	0.40	0.05
Prepositions	With, over	0.03	-0.18	-0.45
Negations	No, never	0.56	0.25	0.15
Quantifiers	Few, much	0.54	0.63	0.15
Emotion processes				
Positive emotions	Love, good	0.03	0.00	0.11
Negative emotions	Angry, ugly	-0.23	-0.10	-0.24
Cognitive processes				
Insight words	Understand, know	0.35	0.44	0.46
Discrepancy	Would, could	0.54	0.51	0.10
Tentative	Maybe, perhaps	0.79	0.38	0.53
Certainty	Absolute, certain	0.49	0.50	0.00
Inclusives	And, with	-0.38	-0.45	-0.62
Exclusives	But, without	0.77	0.12	0.59
N		13	37	33

Note: Within-author correlations are based on Jane Austen's 13 books, Shakespeare's 37 plays, and W.B. Yeats' 33 collections of poems. For a within-author Pearson correlation to be statistically significant (p < .05 2-tailed test), it must be |.55| for Austen, |.32| for Shakespeare, and |.34| for Yeats. That is, a significant correlation for Austen must be greater than .55 or less then -.55.

To appreciate the links between aging and word use, Table 1 includes the analyses of the collected works of Jane Austen, William Shakespeare, and William Butler Yeats. The numbers in the table are the simple correlations between each person's use of various types of words and the authors' age during the course of their writing career. So, for example, the older Jane Austen was, the more she tended to use articles (r = .14), as did Shakespeare (.21) and Yeats (.16). Considering the general pattern of these correlations, one can see that aging is generally associated with works of literature subtly changing to reflect the authors' own psychological state. The later plays, poems, and books by these authors tended to use fewer personal pronouns, more quantifiers, and markers of greater cognitive complexity.

Depression

Across multiple studies, we have found that use of 1st person singular pronouns – especially the word "I" – is associated with negative affective states (see also Weintraub 1989). When asked to write about coming to college, currently depressed students use more 1st person singular pronouns than either formerly depressed or never depressed students. In addition, formerly depressed students use more 1st person singular pronouns than never-depressed students (Rude, Gortner, and Pennebaker 2004). In natural speech captured over several days of tape recordings, use of "I" is more frequent among those with high depression scores than those with low depression scores (Mehl 2004). In both studies, pronouns are a better marker of depression than use of negative emotion words.

In the analysis of the poetry of suicidal versus nonsuicidal poets, poets who eventually committed suicide used 1st person singular pronouns at higher rates than those who did not commit suicide (Stirman and Pennebaker 2001). Ironically, suicidal poets do not use more negative emotion words than other poets. Overall, suicidal poets' language use showed that they were focused more on the self, and less socially integrated than non-suicidal poets. Consider, for example, the lines of two American poets born about the same time – Sylvia Plath and Denise Levertov – both writing about the misery of relationships:

Sylvia Plath

"I shut my eyes and all the world drops dead;
I lift my lids and all is born again.
(I think I made you up inside my head.)

The stars go waltzing out in blue and red,
And arbitrary blackness gallops in:
I shut my eyes and all the world drops dead.

I dreamed that you bewitched me into bed
And sung me moon-struck, kissed me quite insane.
(I think I made you up inside my head.)

God topples from the sky, hell's fires fade:
Exit seraphim and Satan's men:
I shut my eyes and all the world drops dead.

I fancied you'd return the way you said,
But I grow old and I forget your name.
(I think I made you up inside my head.)

I should have loved a thunderbird instead;
At least when spring comes they roar back again.
I shut my eyes and all the world drops dead.
(I think I made you up inside my head.)"

—Mad Girl's Lovesong (1953)

Denise Levertov

The ache of marriage:
thigh and tongue, beloved,
are heavy with it,
it throbs in the teeth

We look for communion
and are turned away, beloved,
each and each

It is leviathan and we
in its belly looking for joy, some joy
not to be known outside it

two by two in the ark of
the ache of it.

—The Ache of Marriage (1962)

What makes the use of 1st person singular pronouns in these two poems interesting is that you can see how Plath's use of "I" suggests that she is embracing her loss and sadness. Levertov, on the other hand, seems to be holding her aching away at arms' length – almost as if she is looking at it from a more distant (and safer) third person perspective. Indeed, as one reads the collected works of these two impressive authors, it is apparent how the two differ in owning or embracing their feelings of loss, alienation, and depression. Plath may be the better poet for this reason. With the tool of 1st person singular pronouns, she takes us closer to the edge so that we can get a feeling of her personal despair.

The Language of Arrogance, Insecurity, and Loss

Closely linked to depression are the feelings of loss that come from failure or rejection. Over the last few years, we have been tracking individual case studies of people who face significant life changes. Following a front page article in the *New York Times* in 2000, we became intrigued with the apparent personality changes that members of the press were witnessing in Rudolph Giuliani, who had been mayor of New York City since 1993. Soon after his election, Giuliani surprised many of his close friends by adopting a somewhat cold, even arrogant style in dealing with the media and other political leaders. In late Spring 2000, Giuliani's life turned upside down within a 2-week period: he announced the breakup of his marriage, his affair with another woman was made public, he was diagnosed with prostate cancer, and he withdrew from the senate race against Hillary Clinton. Within a couple of months, members of the press reported that his personality had changed and he was now warm, honest, even charming.

Text analyses comparing his responses to questions in press conferences during his early years as mayor to those surrounding his personal upheavals revealed that his use of language had indeed changed dramatically. Compared to his first years as mayor, Giuliani demonstrated a dramatic increase in his use of 1st person singular pronouns, a drop in big words, and an increase in his use of both positive and negative emotion words (Pennebaker and Lay 2002). Equally intriguing was his shift in 1st person plural pronouns. The cultural stereotype is that words such as "we" and "us" reflect the speaker's close emotional ties to others. Sometimes this is true; just as often, it is not. Males especially use "we" in a distancing or royal form: "we need to analyse that data" or "we aren't going to put up with higher taxes." In Giuliani's case, his language shifts suggested an interesting personality switch from cold and distanced to someone who was more warm and immediate.

A parallel transformation was that of Shakespeare's *King Lear*. In Shakespeare's play of the same name, King Lear starts off as an arrogant ruler who demands that his daughters publicly declare their love and admiration for him. His favourite daughter, Cordelia, refuses and ultimately leaves England and marries the King of France. Wars, fights, recriminations, and misery follow. (Note: this is the *Cliff's Notes* version of the play). In the final act, the mortally wounded King Lear confronts the corpse of his beloved daughter. His warmth and humanity are apparent to all. Read Shakespeare's first and last speeches by Lear:

Act 1, Scene 1. King Lear speaks:

Know we have divided in three our kingdom; and it is our fast intent to shake all cares and business from our age, conferring them on younger strengths while we unburdened crawl toward death. Our son of Cornwall, and you, our no less loving son of Albany, we have this hour a constant will to publish our daughters' several dowers, that future strife may be prevented now. ... Tell me, my daughters (since now we will divest us both of rule, interest of territory, cares of state), which of you shall we say does love us most? That we our largest bounty may extend where nature does with merit challenge.

Act 5, Scene 3. King Lear's final lines:

Oh, you are men of stone. Had I your tongues and eyes, I'd use them so that heaven's vault should crack. She's gone forever! I know when one is dead, and when one lives. She is dead as earth. ... A plague upon you, murderers, traitors all! I might have saved her; now she's gone for ever! Cordelia! Stay a little. What is it that you say? Her voice was ever soft, gentle, and low ... I have seen the day, with my good biting falchion. I would have made them skip. I am old now, and these same crosses spoil me. Who are you? My eyes are not of the best. I'll tell you straight. ... Pray you undo this button. Thank you, sir. Do you see this? Look on her!

The analyses of these two speeches make for a fascinating parallel with the changes we witnessed with Mayor Giuliani. As depicted in Table 2, during the arrogant periods, both Lear and Giuliani used low rates of 1st person singular and emotion words and, at the same time, high rates of 1st person plural and big words. These patterns were reversed for both when faced with life-changing (and, in Lear's case, life-ending) personal upheavals. Life imitates art and science is here to record it.

Table 2. Language use by Shakespeare's King Lear and Mayor Rudolph Giuliani

	Lear Act 1	Giuliani 1st years	Lear Last act	Giuliani Crisis
I, me, my	2.0	2.1	7.4	7.0
We, us, our	12.0	2.5	0	1.0
Positive emotion	4.7	1.8	3.1	2.2
Negative emotion	0.7	1.5	0.7	0.6
Big words	18.9	17.0	7.4	12.5

The Shakespeare analyses are the first and last speeches by King Lear; the Giuliani data are based on press conferences during the first 4 years of Giuliani's administration and during the two months immediately following his announcement of his prostate cancer. Numbers are percentage of Giuliani's total words within any given press conference.

Status

Of all the function words, the relative use of 1st person singular pronouns is a particularly robust marker of the status of two people in an interaction. Within dyads, we have found that the person whose use of I-words is lower tends to be the higher status participant. In the analysis of the incoming and outgoing emails of 11 undergraduates, graduate students, and faculty, the rated status of the interactant was correlated -.40 with the relative use of 1st person singular pronouns (Chung and Pennebaker 2007). These effects are easily replicated in the laboratory as well. For example, we have asked pairs of students to simply talk informally with one another for 15 minutes in order to get to know one another. At the end of the conversation, both members of the pair were asked to rate who was more dominant. Overall, the one rated most dominant used fewer 1st person singular pronouns (Kacewicz, Pennebaker, Burris, and Davis 2008).

Playwrights and other authors intuitively detect these language shifts in portraying the roles of their characters. Pronoun shifts associated with dominance are seen in some of the earliest recorded literature. For example, one of the last works of Euripides, *The Bacchae*, was discovered soon after his death in 404 BC. Having spent most of his life in Athens, Euripides was concerned with the corruption and instability of the political world around him. The two main characters in his play are Dionysus and Pentheus. At the beginning, the god Dionysus moves to the city of Thebes to try to establish a new cult. Pentheus, the arrogant young king of Thebes, seeks to destroy the cult and soon has Dionysus imprisoned. Earthquakes, lightning, and mayhem follow. Through the cleverness of Dionysus, Pentheus ultimately relinquishes his power, is humiliated, and beheaded (with the help of his own mother). Dionysus becomes king; suffering, grief, and grim acceptance follow.

As can be seen in Table 3, use of 1st person singular pronouns nicely tracks the power shifts. At the beginning of the play, the arrogant Pentheus uses relatively few I-words whereas the subservient god Dionysus uses them at very high rates. Compare the first lines of both their initial speeches.

> **PENTHEUS:** It so happens **I've** been away from Thebes, but **I** hear about disgusting things going on, here in the city—women leaving home to go to silly Bacchic rituals, cavorting there in mountain shadows, with dances honouring some upstart god, this Dionysus, whoever he may be. Mixing bowls in the middle of their meetings are filled with wine. They creep off one by one to lonely spots to have sex with men, claiming they're Maenads busy worshipping. But they rank Aphrodite, goddess of sexual desire, ahead of Bacchus.

> **DIONYSUS:** **I've** arrived here in the land of Thebes, **I**, Dionysus, son of Zeus, born to him from Semele, Cadmus' daughter, delivered by a fiery midwife—Zeus' lightning flash. Yes, **I've** changed **my** form from god to human, appearing here at these streams of Dirce, the waters of Ismarus. **I** see **my** mother's tomb—for she was wiped out by that lightning bolt. It's there, by the palace, with that rubble, the remnants of her house, still smouldering from Zeus' living fire—Hera's undying outrage against **my** mother.

Table 3. Use of 1st person singular pronouns from Euripides's *The Bacchae*

	Pre-conflict	Early conflict	Post-conflict
Pentheus	3.17	3.62	6.68
Dionysus	7.26	5.87	2.83

Numbers are based on LIWC analyses and represent percentage of total words that are first person singular pronouns within the first (pre-conflict) and last (post-conflict) speeches by Pentheus and Dionysus. The early conflict data are based on the first interactions between the two characters.

During their initial tense interchanges, their relative use of 1st person singular begins to moderate. In their final scenes after Dionysus has clearly taken control, their use of I-words have completely switched. Pentheus, who is now in a delusional and flirtatious state, uses 1st person singular in almost every sentence in his last lines of the play. Dionysus, however, is now behaving in a king-like way – focusing his attention on others and not himself.

> **PENTHEUS:** Are we going to take some levers with us? Or shall **I** rip the forests up by hand, putting arm and shoulder under mountain peaks? ... You mention a good point. **I'll** use no force to get the better of these women. **I'll** conceal myself there in the pine trees. ... That's good. **I** can picture them right now, in the woods, going at it like rutting birds, clutching each other as they make sweet love. ... Lead on— through the centre of our land of Thebes. **I'm** the only man in all the city who dares to undertake this enterprise. That will be **my** mother.... That's why **I'm** going.... You're pampering **me**! ... You've really made up your mind to spoil **me**. ... Then **I'll** be off to get what **I** deserve.
>
> **DIONYSUS**: Now you must leave— abandon your city for barbarian lands. Agave, too, that polluted creature, must go into perpetual banishment. And Cadmus, you too must endure your lot. Your form will change, so you become a dragon. Your wife, Harmonia, Ares' daughter, whom you, though mortal, took in marriage, will be transformed, changing to a snake. As Zeus' oracle declares, you and she will drive a chariot drawn by heifers. You'll rule barbarians. With your armies, too large to count, you'll raze many cities. Once they despoil Apollo's oracle, they'll have a painful journey back again. But Ares will guard you and Harmonia. In lands of the blessed he'll transform your lives. That's what **I** proclaim— **I**, Dionysus, born from no mortal father, but from Zeus. If you had understood how to behave as you should have when you were unwilling, you'd now be fortunate, with Zeus' child among your allies.

Admittedly, these are analyses of texts originally written in Ancient Greek. Through various translations, it is possible that the wording gradually shifted to match current versions of high versus low dominance. This is ultimately an empirical question that we should soon be able to answer with our next generation of the LIWC computerized text program that can theoretically analyse language in multiple languages – including Ancient and Modern Greek.

Deception

Pronouns and other function words also provide hints about the truthfulness of statements. Conjunctions, negations, and certain prepositions are used to make important distinctions about categories. A particularly interesting class of words is exclusive words. These include words like "but", "except", "without", and "exclude". Factor analytically, these words typically load with negations (no, not, never), and are associated with greater cognitive complexity (Pennebaker and King 1999). Across multiple experiments where people have been induced to describe or explain something honestly or deceptively, the combined use of 1st person singular pronouns and exclusive words predicts honesty (Newman et al. 2003). In other words, when people are telling the truth (as opposed to lying), they are more likely to "own" it by making it more personal and, at the same time, are more likely to describe their story in a more cognitively complex way.

Applying these finding to literature might seem daunting at first. While the linguistic markers of lies are straightforward, deception and our perception of it are not. Pure lies are rare. Through cognitive contortionism, liars sometimes believe their lies or interweave truth with fiction. "[I]t's not a lie . . . if *you* believe it," George Costanza philosophized on the American sitcom *Seinfeld* (Leifer 1995). Along these lines, in 2005 Stephen Colbert gave us "truthiness," a satirical reification of truth in the context of American politics: according to Colbert, facts and empirical evidence don't stand a chance against willfully-ignorant intuition and blind certitude (Eichler and Purcell 2005). Truthiness and other more slippery varieties of deception are not limited to political pundits. They are common and are often found in literature. The challenge for future research is to determine the degree to which perceived truths – that are, in fact, lies – are revealed by their own linguistic fingerprints. That is, can we detect believed truths from believed lies whether in reality or in fiction.

Despite all these impediments, LIWC can supplement our understanding of deception in literature. As an example, we analysed selections from John Kennedy Toole's (1980) *A Confederacy of Dunces*. The hero of this novel, Ignatius J. Reilly, is a quixotic fool. Everything he says is a fantastic reinterpretation of reality. He honestly believes that cities outside his New Orleans are filled with subliterate villains and that Boethius, the medieval philosopher wrongly executed for treason, is his brother in both brilliance and injustice. Given these delusions, separating his honest beliefs about the world from his outright lies seems challenging. Despite this, LIWC analyses reveal clear differences: Ignatius uses 1st person singular pronouns much less often when deliberately telling lies than when he feels that he is being honest: 4.9%, compared with 7.3% in his honest communications. For example, in the first of the following two excerpts he is lying to his employer about missing merchandise. In the second he is attempting to truthfully tell the reader about his new job.

Deception: Perhaps he was very hungry. Perhaps some vitamin deficiency in his growing body was screaming for appeasement. The human desire for food and sex is relatively equal. If there are armed rapes, why should there not be armed hot dog thefts?

Honesty: As I told you before, I have succeeded in laying a patina, as it were, over the turbulence and mania of our office. All non-essential activities in the office are slowly being curtailed. At the moment I am busily decorating our throbbing hive of white-collared bees (three).

In the deceptive example, Ignatius is attempting to distance himself from his lies by going on a pseudo-psychological tangent. In the second, the frequent "I" usage suggests that he is eager to own his good deeds which, although exaggerated, he truly believes.

Other psychological states

In this section, we have provided a small number of findings of function words and their links to psychological states. In the last few years, we have also discovered that function words provide a novel perspective on how individuals and entire societies cope with emotional upheavals such as the September 11, 2001 attacks (Cohn, Mehl, and Pennebaker 2004) or the death of Princess Diana (Stone and Pennebaker 2002). Other analyses have helped us in identifying healthy versus unhealthy close relationships (Slatcher and Pennebaker 2006). Analyses of function words have also been found to differ as a function of people's sexual orientation (Groom and Pennebaker 2005), testosterone levels (Pennebaker, Groom, Loew, and Dabbs 2004), or adjustment to eating disorders (Lyons, Mehl, and Pennebaker 2006). Indeed, many of these findings are holding up across languages and cultures (Ramirez-Esparza and Pennebaker 2006).

What is less clear is why we are finding so many links between word use and psychological states. Ultimately, function words reflect attentional processes as well as cognitive processes. The use of 1st person singular, for example, is a marker of where the individual is paying attention. Individuals who use almost exclusively I-words appear to pay less attention to relationships with others, and so seem to be less socially integrated than those who refer to others more often. Words that refer to cause and effect indicate that the author thinks about the world like an empiricist, searching for catalysts and linked series of events. In many ways, we are just beginning to understand the theoretical explanations for function word use. That such strong and reliable patterns are emerging is a testament to our analytic approach. We suspect that the general methodological approach we are developing has great potential for psychological researchers as well as computational linguists. For literary scholars who might spend decades attempting to peer into an author's head via personal letters and journals, the modest headway we have made so far is not insignificant.

Using Words to Assess the Authors' Impact on Readers

Whereas the first part of this chapter focuses on the ways words – especially function words – reflect the psychological state of the authors, the remainder of the chapter explores how the authors' words influence the readers or listeners. That is, how and when does an author's linguistic style influence his or her audience?

It is a sensation familiar to most: we read something, and suddenly, for a minute or much longer, the author is pulling our strings. Our normal speech patterns are temporarily replaced by the author's. Suddenly the schizoid speech patterns of one of Dostoevsky's neurotic antiheroes flow out of our mouths or into e-mails more naturally than our own. It can be disturbing not only because we may not identify—or may not *want* to identify—with the author we are suddenly mimicking. The eeriness arises from the fact that this appears to be entirely unintentional. Yet this sensation of linguistic style matching is both intuitively familiar and empirically observable, and it does not appear to be limited to a specific literary style or tradition.

The experience of accidental imitation is not limited to literature, of course. Humans are social animals; we imitate each other all the time. Nonverbal research indicates that coordination is crucial to human interaction. Most components of human communication, including facial expression, nonverbal vocal behaviour, kinesics, visual behaviour, and proxemics, are coordinated (Harper, Wiens, and Matarazzo 1978). Children tend to synchronise their actions with their parents' even before they are capable of speech. Condon and Sander (1974) found that newborns' body movements are synchronised with adult speech. Later work in linguistic-kinesic interactions suggested that speech and social interactions of children with autism, dyslexia, stuttering, and learning disabilities generally show a lack of synchrony in both verbal behaviour and body movements (e.g., Wylie 1985). In other words, synchrony is apparently fundamental to functional social interaction.

Linguistic synchrony is also common in the context of conversations. By analysing the conversations of pairs of college students in experimental settings as well as with politicians in their natural environment, Niederhoffer and Pennebaker (2002) found that individuals tend to mimic each other's linguistic style during both online and face-to-face dyadic interactions. This tendency towards dyadic synchrony is referred to as linguistic style matching, or LSM. LSM is operationalized by calculating the synchrony between each interactant's use of pronouns, prepositions, articles, and other function words. Content words are not given a specific role in the LSM algorithm: of course if two individuals are discussing a specific topic, e.g., horse racing, then they will both use words like "horse" and "jockey" a number of times. Content word synchrony is often evidence of nothing but the tendency to stay on-topic.

Across multiple studies where we have measured LSM, the most striking finding is that style matching is almost always present. It is unrelated to the degree to which the interactants like each other, have a formal or informal relationship, or have a shared history. It can be detected at a turn-by-turn level in an interaction or even at the broader conversation level. Indeed, we have evidence that strangers who are asked to interact with one another begin style-matching within the first 10-20 seconds of the interaction. It appears, then, to be a basic rule underlying human verbal communication.

If LSM is a basic feature of spoken and written interactions, it would follow that it could implicitly occur between author and reader, between speaker and listener. It is also likely that some readers and listeners would be more prone to this process than others. Indeed, pilot investigations in our lab are beginning to yield exciting results. Recently approximately 840 students in two Introductory Psychology sections were given four essay questions as part of class writing assignments. Each question was written using a very different linguistic style. For example, the following two sentences introduced social facilitation and cognitive dissonance questions, respectively:

> As described in the book, social facilitation results when a group of people (e.g., friends, strangers, maybe even enemies[?]) observe a person's behaviour. If the behaviour is well-learned (i.e., well-practiced), the behaviour is usually (but not always) performed more quickly; if it is complex or not well-learned, the performance of the behaviour can be made slower or more inaccurate (this depends, of course, on the behaviour)...

> [I]t's super easy to see how cognitive dissonance can make you do crazy things .... hmmm, like, make you enjoy something that you normally

wouldn't. So, the idea is that if you have two ideas that are inconsistent with one another you, well, feel kinda anxious. And this nervous feeling is dissonance—which you hate…

The first is overly complex and a bit convoluted. The parenthetical asides distract from the main idea, and a semicolon makes the sentence unnecessarily complex. The second example, which we call Valley-Girl-eze, is extremely informal and personal. Both are comprehensible, but not particularly well-written. Despite these divergent styles, students tended to come up with examples of social facilitation and cognitive dissonance using linguistic styles that matched the question. For the social facilitation question, students used bigger words, longer sentences, fewer pronouns, and fewer present tense verbs compared to the cognitive dissonance question.

More intriguing, however, are some of the psychometrics of LSM across the four writing assignment questions. First, the more that people exhibit LSM on one question, the more they do so on others (cross-question correlations average around $r = .25$). Second, the more that people tend to exhibit LSM, the better they do on class exams and the higher they score on measures of absorption, which has been found to be linked to hypnotisability (Glisky and Kihlstrom 1993). Although weak, there are significant correlations between LSM and agreeableness (r's average around .12) but no other Big Five measures such as extraversion. No differences emerge for sex or most other individual differences.

When we ask ourselves why we are suddenly imitating the speech patterns of some recently-read author, a few hypotheses come to most people's minds. The absorption findings are particularly promising since they tend to tap the degree to which people become immersed in their visual, auditory, or fantasy worlds. It is possible that those high in absorption in the current project were more immersed in the assignment in general.

There is psychological evidence for the idea that absorption, enjoyment, and reading comprehension are linked with LSM. Green and Brock (2000) studied the psychological role of transportation, or the degree to which individuals become cognitively, emotionally, and perceptually involved in written narratives. They found that individuals who reported a high degree of transportation after reading a story reported greater agreement with beliefs implicit in that story. Highly-transported individuals also perceived these stories to be more realistic. The narratives that reliably induced significant levels of transportation in all participants tended to be either very popular or generally accepted as belonging to the canon of classic literature (e.g., anthologised short fiction in Green and

Brock 2000). In other words, individuals who were transported by a narrative also expressed beliefs that were in sync with those found in the author's writing, and this synchrony was most often found in literature that is, according to most objective standards, enjoyable.

LSM and highly-transported individuals' expression of narrative-consistent beliefs both may be manifestations of a common social-cognitive mechanism. Both are linked to the facilitation of social interaction through synchrony and both seem to occur unintentionally. However, it is unclear whether LSM is the process by which readers are able to enjoy, be persuaded by, or be transported by literature or only the byproduct of these things. It is also difficult to tell, at this time, whether LSM is a corollary of real or only perceived transportation and enjoyment. If LSM actually is a reliable predictor of a reader's comprehension of or agreement with an author's work, then it might be reasonable to assume that LSM serves a function.

LSM's original linguistic function may have been to persuade, or synchronise attitudes. If this is true, it makes sense that it would do this by facilitating perspective-taking. It is after all easier to see things from another's perspective if you suddenly find yourself speaking like them. Perspective-taking is the cornerstone of good social interaction. It develops at as early as 24-months, and for good reasons: deception, empathy, and virtually any social cognition would be impossible without the ability to understand what another person might be feeling or thinking (Moll and Tomasello 2006).

Recent neuropsychological inquiries into the mirror neuron system provide further evidence for the importance of basic processes of imitation. Mirror neurons are a class of visuomotor neurons that show identical activity when a person or a monkey sees an action performed and when they themselves perform that action (Rizzolatti and Craighero 2004). For example, the same neurons that would be activated if you were to actually clench your fist are activated when you imagine clenching your fist, when you see a person making a fist, and when you hear the sentence, "Jane is making a fist." Perhaps LSM is a byproduct of the related processes of neural imitation and perspective-taking, and perhaps it would be impossible to be entertained, transported, or persuaded by literature without these socially driven, reflex-like behaviours. (For a more complete review of the mirror neuron system, see Rizzolatti and Craighero 2004.)

These are all empirical questions which will have to be answered in future experiments. This research has the potential to be very exciting for champions of literature. Literature-lovers often feel that the novels, poems, and plays they have experienced over the course of their life have fundamentally shaped their present-day identity. LSM research may provide empirical evidence that literature does indeed change us at an elemental level. Our research with LIWC has shown that the words we use are important indicators of physical and mental health, personality, and mental states. If literature changes the way we use language, perhaps it also changes our selves in essential, empirically observable ways.

Summary and Conclusions

A text-analytic approach to the study of literature is not new. However, recent breakthroughs in computational linguistics and new software technology have the potential to change the ways we do business. These new methods are capable of processing billions of words in mere minutes, leaving hand-coding methods of text analysis far behind in terms of reliability, economy, and speed. Function words especially allow us to get a clear and concise picture of a large corpus of text very quickly. The ubiquity and timelessness of function words allows us to analyse the antiquated language of Shakespeare or Euripides as easily as any 21st century author. Our findings have also been consistent across different cultures and languages. In addition to the original English language LIWC, Polish, Spanish, Turkish, and Korean LIWCs are in varying stages of development and validation.

Our research with LIWC has given us unprecedented insight into the minds of both authors and literary characters. Simply by looking at personal pronouns, we are capable of predicting people's current and future health, depression, deception, social status, and relationship stability, among other things. Currently we are researching the effects of literature on readers' own natural language use, specifically by looking at how readers often unintentionally mimic an author's writing style. We call this linguistic style matching, or LSM. It is a universal experience and a part of what makes literature a unique joy, but at this point its causes and effects are unknown. Preliminary research is promising, however, and soon we hope to know exactly how, to what degree, and why literature changes our selves and the way we speak.

Literature is an extraordinarily valuable art form for researchers across multiple disciplines. It does not only entertain. By recording thousands of years of authors' philosophical, sociological, and psychological insights into the human experience, it educates us and records history. However, because literature is an art, its specific meaning is often unclear. Scholars sometimes spend their lives defending their interpretation of an author's work. While computerized text analysis is not a skeleton key that will immediately solve all literary riddles, it can give us priceless information about authors, their work, and the effects of their work on its readers.

Acknowldegments

Preparation of this chapter was aided by funding from the Army Research Institute.

Works Cited

Chung, Cindy K. and James W. Pennebaker. 2007. The psychological function of function words. In *Social Communication: Frontiers of Social Psychology*, edited by K. Fiedler, 343-359. New York: Psychology Press.

Cohn, Michael A., Matthias R. Mehl, and James W. Pennebaker. 2004. Linguistic markers of psychological change surrounding September 11, 2001. *Psychological Science* 15(10): 687-693.

Condon, William S. and Louis W. Sander. 1974. Synchrony demonstrated between movements of the neonate and adult speech. *Child Development* 45(2): 456-462.

Damasio, Antonio R. 1995. *Descartes' Error: Emotion, Reason, and the Human Brain*. New York, NY: Harper Collins.

Eichler, Glenn and Tom Purcell. 2005. Episode 1. *The Colbert Report*. © Comedy Central.

Foltz, Peter W. (1996). Latent semantic analysis for text-based research. *Behavior Research Methods, Instruments & Computers* 28: 197-202.

Gazzaniga, Michael S. 2005. *The Ethical Brain*. New York, NY: Dana Press.

Glisky, Martha L. and Jennifer F. Kihlstrom. 1993. Hypnotizability and facets of openness. *International Journal of Clinical & Experimental Hypnosis* 41: 112-123.

Graesser, Arthur C. and Sarah L. Petschonek. 2005. Automated systems that analyse text and discourse: QUAID, Coh-Metrix, and AutoTutor. In W. R. Lenderking and D. Revicki, eds., *Advancing Health Outcomes Research Methods and Clinical Applications* (McLean, VA, US: Degnon Associates).

Green, Melanie C. and Timothy C. Brock. 2000. The role of transportation in the persuasiveness of public narratives. *Journal of Personality and Social Psychology* 79(5): 701-721

Groom, Carla and James W. Pennebaker. 2005. The language of love: Sex, sexual orientation, and language use in online personal advertisements. *Sex Roles* 2(7/8): 447-461.

Harper, Robert Gale, Arthur N. Wiens, and Joseph D. Matarazzo. 1978. *Non-verbal Communication: The State of the Art*. New York, NY: Wiley & Sons.

Hart, Roderick P., S.E. Jarvis, W.P. Jennings, and D. Smith-Howell. 2005. *Political Keywords: Using Language that Uses Us*. New York: Oxford University Press.

Joyce, James. 1959. Lecture at University College, Dublin, 1902. In Ellsworth Mason and Richard Ellmann, eds., *The Critical Writings of James Joyce* (New York, NY: Viking).

Kacewicz, Ewa, James W. Pennebaker, Ethan Burris, and Matthew Davis. 2008. *Language Correlates of Status and Dominance*. Paper submitted for publication. Austin, TX: The University of Texas at Austin.

Leifer, Carol. 9 February 1995. The Beard. *Seinfeld*, season 6, ep. 102. Andy Ackerman, dir. © Sony Pictures.

Levertov, Denise. 1962. "The Ache of Marriage." In Denise Levertov, *Poems, 1960-1967* (New York, NY: New Directions).

Lyons, Elizabeth J., Matthias R., Mehl, and James W. Pennebaker. 2006. Linguistic self-presentation in anorexia: Differences between pro-anorexia and recovering anorexia internet language use. *Journal of Psychosomatic Research* 60: 253-256.

Martindale, Colin. 1990. *A Clockwork Muse: The Predictability of Artistic Change*. New York, NY: Basic Books.

Mehl, Matthias R. 2004. The sounds of social life: Exploring students' daily social environments and natural conversations. Unpublished Doctoral Dissertation.

Mergenthaler, Erhard. 1996. Emotion-abstraction patterns in verbatim protocols: A new way of describing psychotherapeutic processes. *Journal of Consulting and Clinical Psychology* 64(6): 130-1315.

Miller, George A. 1995. *The Science of Words*. New York, NY: Scientific American Library.

Moll, Henrike and Michael Tomasello. 2006. Level 1 perspective-taking at 24 months of age. *British Journal of Developmental Psychology* 24(3): 603-613.

Newman, Matthew L., Carla J. Groom, Lori D. Handleman, and James W. Pennebaker. 2007 in press. Gender differences in language use: An analysis of 14,000 text samples. *Discourse Processes*.

Newman, Matthew L., James W. Pennebaker, Diane S. and Jane M. Richards 2003. Lying words: Predicting deception from linguistic style. *Personality and Social Psychology Bulletin* 29: 665-675.

Niederhoffer, Kate G. And James W. Pennebaker. 2002. Linguistic style matching in social interaction. *Journal of Language and Social Psychology* 21: 337-360.

Pennebaker, James W., Roger J. Booth, and Martha E. Francis. 2007. *Linguistic Inquiry and Word Count (LIWC): LIWC2007*. Austin, TX: www.LIWC.net.

Pennebaker, James W., Martha E. Francis, and Roger J. Booth. 2001. *Linguistic Inquiry and Word Count (LIWC): LIWC2001*. Mahwah, NJ: Lawrence Erlbaum Associates.

Pennebaker, James W., Carla J. Groom, and Daniel Loew, and James Dabbs. 2004. Testosterone as a social inhibitor: Two case studies of the effect of testosterone treatment on language. *Journal of Abnormal Psychology* 113(1): 172-175.

Pennebaker, J. W., and Laura A. King. 1999. Linguistic styles: Language use as an individual difference. *Journal of Personality & Social Psychology* 77: 1296-1312.

Pennebaker, James W. and Thomas C. Lay. 2002. Language use and personality during crises: Analyses of Mayor Rudolph Giuliani's press conferences. *Journal of Research in Personality* 36(3): 271-283.

Pennebaker, James W., Matthias R. Mehl, and Kate Niederhoffer. 2003. Psychological aspects of natural language use: Our words, our selves. *Annual Review of Psychology* 54: 547-577.

Pennebaker, James W. and Lori D. Stone. 2003. Words of wisdom: Language use over the lifespan. *Journal of Personality and Social Psychology* 85: 291-301.

Plath, Sylvia. 1953. "Mad Girl's Lovesong." In Estate of Sylvia Plath, *The Collected Poems of Sylvia Plath*. 1981. New York, NY: Harper & Row.

Ramirez-Esparza, Nairan, and James W. Pennebaker. 2006. Do good stories produce good health? Exploring words, language, and culture. *Narrative Inquiry* 16: 211-219.

Rich, Adrienne. 1978. Introduction. In *The Work of a Common Woman* by Judy Grahn. New York, NY: The Crossing Press.

Rizzolatti, Giacomo and Laila Craighero. 2004. The mirror-neuron system. *Annual Review of Neuroscience* 27: 169-192.

Rude, Stephanie, Eva-Maria Gortner, James W. Pennebaker. 2004. Language use of depressed and depression-vulnerable college students. *Cognition & Emotion* 18(8): 1121-1133.

Slatcher, Richard B. and James W Pennebaker. 2006. How do I love thee? Let me count the words: The social effects of expressive writing. *Psychological Science* 17(8): 660-664.

Stein, Gertrude. 1935. Poetry and Grammar. *Lectures in America.* New York: Random House.

Stirman, Shannon Wiltsey and James W. Pennebaker. 2001. Word use in the poetry of suicidal and nonsuicidal poets. *Psychosomatic Medicine* 63(4): 517-522.

Stone, Lori D. and James W. Pennebaker. 2002. Trauma in real time: Talking and avoiding online conversations about the death of Princess Diana. *Basic and Applied Social Psychology* 24: 172-182.

Stone, Philip J., Dexter C. Dunphy, Marshall S. Smith, and Daniel M. Ogilvie. 1966. *The General Inquirer: A Computer Approach to Content Analysis.* Cambridge, MA: MIT Press.

Toole, John Kennedy. 1980/1987. *A Confederacy of Dunces.* New York, NY: Grove Press.

Weber-Fox, Christine and Helen J. Neville. 2001. Sensitive periods differentiate processing of open- and closed-class words: An ERP study of bilinguals. *Journal of Speech, Language and Hearing Research* 44(6): 1338-1354.

Weintraub, Walter. 1989. *Verbal Behavior in Everyday Life.* New York, NY: Springer Publishing.

Wylie, Laurence. 1985. Language learning and communication. *The French Review* 58(6): 777-785.

CHAPTER TWO

SWEET FRAGRANCES FROM INDONESIA:
A UNIVERSAL PRINCIPLE GOVERNING
DIRECTIONALITY IN SYNAESTHETIC
METAPHORS

YESHAYAHU SHEN AND DAVID GIL

Abstract

Synaesthetic metaphors are metaphorical expressions that consist of a mapping between two sensory modalities (e.g., *sweet silence, cold light*). Previously, it was suggested by Ullmann that there is a tendency in various poetic corpora to use synaesthetic metaphors in which the metaphor Target (tenor) is from a higher sensory modality (e.g., SIGHT or SOUND) than the Source, as in *sweet melodies*, or *cold light*. Subsequently the Directionality Principle was confirmed by further investigations, which span a variety of languages (European, Middle Eastern and East Asian), periods and genres (for a brief review, see Shen and Aisenman, forthcoming). In this paper we present a preliminary exploration of synaesthetic metaphors in Indonesian, a language that is far removed from Hebrew and other European languages in terms of geographical space, genealogical affiliation, grammatical structure, and cultural influences. If Indonesian turns out to be similar to Hebrew and other European languages then the case for universality is substantially boosted. While the corpus study shows that Indonesian synaesthetic metaphors look very much like those previously described in other languages, the experimental study—the first to be done outside of Hebrew—suggests that the structure of synaesthetic metaphors observed in texts reflects underlying principles of cognitive simplicity, as encapsulated in the Directionality Principle. Both studies suggest that the principles governing the structure of synaesthetic metaphors proposed on the basis of Hebrew and other Eurasian languages may indeed be universal.

1. Introduction

Figure 1: The Sweet Fragrance supermarket in Indonesia

In Indonesia, on the island of Borneo, in the town of Pontianak, there is a supermarket called *Harum Manis* (shown in Figure 1 above). *Harum* means 'fragrant' or 'fragrance', while *Manis* means 'sweet' or "sweetness'. The name of the shop may thus be translated into English as 'Sweet Fragrance'.

Is it a mere accident that the store was called *Harum Manis* and not *Manis Harum*, or 'Fragrant Sweetness'? After all, the two words have similar meanings, denoting pleasant sensations, and also similar grammatical behaviour, presumably belonging to the same part of speech. This suggests that either order should have been equally appropriate. However, this is not the case; in actual fact, there are good reasons why *Harum Manis* was chosen and *Manis Harum* rejected. These reasons are what this paper is all about. Of course, not just names of supermarkets follow the principle illustrated here; poets, too, as a rule make similar choices. In doing so they make use of a universal rule govering the structure of metaphors, one that literary scholars must start exploring if they wish to understand what makes literature tick.

2. Metaphors and Synaesthesia

Harum manis, and its English counterpart, *sweet fragrance*, are examples of metaphors based on a relationship of synaesthesia, or *synaesthetic metaphors*.

A *metaphor* is a linguistic structure that involves a mapping between two distinct domains, referred to as *target* and *source* (or, alternatively, *tenor* and *vehicle*), such as the following English examples:

(1) (a) smooth character
    (b) green idea.

In the above examples, the nouns, *character* and *idea*, represent the target domains, while the adjectives, *smooth* and *green*, represent the corresponding source domains. Typically, as in the above examples, the target domain involves an abstract concept, while the source domain has to do with a concept that is more concrete.

Synaesthesia is a systematic relationship between elements from two distinct sensory modalities. For example, hearing a particular note on the piano, such as C#, might cause a person to see a certain colour, such as an orangey brown; such a person would be undergoing a synaesthetic experience based on a relationship between the sensory modalities of sound and sight.

A synaesthetic metaphor is a metaphor in which target and source domains are associated with different sensory modalities. In our Indonesian supermarket example above, the target domain, *harum* 'fragrant', belongs to the sensory modality of smell, while the source domain, *manis* 'sweet', belongs to the sensory modality of taste. Two other examples of synaesthetic metaphors in English are the following:

(2) (a) soft light
    (b) sweet melodies.

In (2a), *light*, the target domain, is associated with the sense of sight, while *soft*, the source domain, is associated with the sense of touch. And in (2b), *melodies*, the target domain, is associated with the sense of sound, whereas *sweet*, the source domain, is associated with the sense of taste.

But it is not just in everyday speech, where a *sour smell*, *sweet silence*, a *cold voice* and a *smooth movement* are features of language.

Consider the famous poem *Voyelles* (Vowels) by the French poet Arthur Rimbaud, which starts with

> A noir, E blanc, I rouge, U vert, O bleu
> (A black, E white, I red, U green, O blue).

A clear (albeit extreme) case of the blending of different senses: hearing (the five vowels listed) and seeing (the five colours associated with the vowels). Other well known literary examples relate the modalities of taste and sound, as in: "Heard melodies are sweet, but those unheard are sweeter;" (Keats's "Ode on a Grecian Urn"); the modalities of sight and sound as in: "the lily-voices of the cicadas" (Iliad III, 152); those of smell and voice: "a loud perfume…" (Donne in Elegy *Perfume*); and, the joining of touch and sound that is introduced by Crawshaw (*Musick's Duel:* "There might you heare her kindle her soft voice").

It is clear from these very few examples that poets exploit the linguistic resources available in their culture to express meanings that they apparently would not be able to communicate without the use of such devices. What do these everyday and literary examples tell us?

3. The Directionality Principle

Synaesthetic metaphors pose a variety of challenging research questions that have attracted the interest of scholars in linguistics, literary studies and cognitive psychology alike: What is the basis for the identification of similarities between concepts associated with different sensory modalities? Are there differences between poetic and non-poetic usages of synaesthetic metaphors? How and when does the ability to use synaesthetic metaphors develop? To what extent are synaesthetic metaphors universal?

The major question addressed in this paper is the following one: Are there constraints on the directionality of synaesthetic metaphors? Or in other words: Are concepts from certain sensory domains more likely to function as target domains while concepts from other sensory domains are more commonly found in the role of source domains, or is it the case that concepts from any sensory modality can be mapped onto concepts from any other sensory modality with equal likelihood?

For metaphors in general, not necessarily synaesthetic ones, the directionality question has been investigated by Ortony, Vondruska, Foss and Jones (1985), Shen (1997), and many others. For specifically synaesthetic metaphors, the directionality question has been studied by Ullman (1957), Tsur (1992), Shen (1997), Shen and Cohen (1998), Yu (2003), Shen and Aisenman (forthcoming), and others.

The first study of the directionality of synaesthetic metaphors is Ullman's (1957) pioneering research of poetic synaesthesia. Ullman's point of departure is that the various sensory modalities form a hierarchy with respect to their degree of differentiation:

(3)　　*Hierarchy of Sensory Modalities*
　　　　sight > sound > smell > taste > touch

In accordance with the above hierarchy, sight is the highest, or most differentiated sense, followed, in that order, by sound, smell and taste, with touch as the lowest, or least differentiated sense.

One may wonder what the motivation may be for the above hierarchy, and, indeed, a number of scholars have offered various explanations for it; see, for example Ullman (1957), Tsur (1992), Shen (1997), Shen and Cohen (1998) and Popova (2005). One possible explanation is discussed briefly in the next section of this paper. However, for the purposes of this paper, we accept the hierarchy as a given fact; our main focus is on using it as an analytical tool facilitating an insightful description of the patterns of usage displayed by synaesthetic metaphors.

Given the Hierarchy of Sensory Modalities, synaesthetic metaphors are presented with two structural possibilities, which can be exemplified with reference to our Indonesian supermarket:

(4)　(a)　　sweet fragrance
　　　(b)　　fragrant sweetness

In (4a), *fragrance,* the target domain, is associated with the sense of smell, while *sweet*, the source domain, is associated with the sense of taste; accordingly, the mapping is upwards on the hierarchy, from a lower sensory domain to a higher one. Conversely, in (4b), *sweetness,* the target domain, is associated with the sense of taste, while *fragrant*, the source domain, is associated with the sense of smell; accordingly, the mapping is downwards on the hierarchy, from a higher sensory domain to a lower one.

Ullman (1957) looked at over 2000 synaesthetic metaphors from 8 poets representing 19th century poetry in three languages, English, French and Hungarian. His main finding can be summarized as follows:

(5) *Directionality Principle*
With greater than chance frequency, synaesthetic metaphors involve mappings upwards on the Hierarchy of Sensory Modalities (with the exception of sight and sound, which behave in similar fashion).

In other words, in synaesthetic metaphors, the target domain tends to be associated with a sensory modality lower down on the hierarchy, and the source domain with a sensory modality higher up on the hierarchy.

For example, in (2), both metaphors conform to the Directionality Principle in (5): in (2a) *soft light*, the mapping is from touch to sight, while in (2b) *sweet melodies*, the mapping is from taste to sound. But what about the two examples in (4): In (4a) *sweet fragrance*, the structure, once again, is in conformity with the Directionality Principle, with the mapping from taste to smell. However, in (4b) *fragrant sweetness*, the mapping violates the Directionality Principle, since in this case it is downwards, from smell to taste. Thus, the Directionality Principle accounts for the structure of the Indonesian supermarket name, and the choice of *Harum Manis* 'Sweet Fragrance' over the alternative *Manis Harum* 'Fragrant Sweetness'. But does the Directionality Principle really apply also to names for supermarkets in distant Indonesia, or is *Harum Manis* just a fortuitous coincidence?

4. Universality and Cognitive Simplicity

More generally, Ullman's study raises the question to what extent the Directionality Principle is universal, that is to say, to what extent it applies to synaesthetic metaphors in other languages and in other genres.

A variety of further investigations suggest that indeed, the Directionality Principle is applicable well beyond the specific languages and genres examined in Ullman's original study: among such studies are Dombi (1974) for Hungarian poetry, Williams (1976) for Japanese prose, Day (1996) for German and American English prose, Manor (1996) for Hebrew prose, Shen and Cohen (1998) for Modern Hebrew poetry, Yu (2003) for Chinese literary and non-literary prose, Arsenic (2005) for Serbo-Croatian poetry, and Shen and Gadir (forthcoming) for Biblical Hebrew. The above studies span a variety of languages, periods and genres. Linguistically, they are representative of Europe, the Middle-East and also East Asia. Historically, although focusing on the 20th century, they examine also works from the 19th century (as did Ullman's original study), and go back to antiquity with Biblical Hebrew. In terms of genres, they include both poetry and prose, the latter of both literary and non-literary varieties. In particular, some of the studies, such as those by Shen and Gadir and by Shen and Cohen, span several decades, and thus include different sub-periods of modern poetry, as defined by conventional literary studies. It is a generally accepted view in literary studies that consecutive literary generations rebel against their predecessors with respect to conventions of linguistic usage as well as various other aspects of poetic texts; see Shen (1997) for details. Accordingly, the fact that the Directionality Principle for synaesthetic metaphors remains valid across successive literary generations suggests that this principle reflects basic and invariant properties of human cognition.

Further evidence for the Directionality Principle derives from examination of the ways in which words change their meanings over time. One very common pattern of meaning change involves a metaphorical expression which in the distant past might have been used in a novel and creative fashion, but which over the course of many years becomes conventionalized, and is used with greater and greater frequency, so much so that the metaphorical nature of the expression becomes weakened and ultimately lost: the result is an expansion of the literal meaning of the source expression to include also its erstwhile metaphorical function. For example, in Indonesian, the original meaning of the word *keras* was 'hard', and this remains its basic meaning today. However, at some point in the past, the word *keras* was applied to expressions denoting sounds, resulting in synaesthetic metaphors in which *keras* was understood to mean 'loud', as, for example in the expression *suara keras* 'loud voice'. In such metaphors, *keras*, the source domain, is associated with the sense of touch, while the various target domains are associated with the sense of sound; thus, these metaphors are in accordance with the Directionality Principle. Over the course of time, these metaphors became conventionalized and increasingly common, to the extent that contemporary dictionaries of Indonesian now list 'loud' as a secondary meaning of *keras*. While it is probably still the case that speakers of Indonesian consider the basic meaning of *keras* to be 'hard', usages of *keras* to mean 'loud' are well on the way to losing their metaphorical nature, at which time the meaning change will have reached completion. In the case of *keras*, the meaning change is thus from the sensory modality of touch to that of sound, which is upwards on the Hierarchy of Sensory Modalities.

In general, the Directionality Principle predicts that when words denoting sensory perceptions change their meanings to ones associated with different sensory modalities as a result of the conventionalization of a synaesthetic metaphor, then the direction of the change will be upwards on the Hierarchy of Sensory Modalities. And indeed, a variety of studies of diachronic meaning change in different languages have shown that it proceeds in accordance with the Directionality Principle; see, for example, Williams (1976) for English and Japanese, Yu (1992) for Chinese, and Shen and Gadir (forthcoming) for Hebrew.

Thus, there is already considerable evidence suggesting that the Directionality Principle may be universal. But why should this be the case? In general, universals of language may be due to any or all of the following factors: chance, language contact and subsequent borrowing, inheritance from a hypothetical common proto-language, and universal properties of human cognition. In the case at hand, the widespread distribution of synaesthetic metaphors patterning in accordance with the Directionality Principle clearly rules out chance, and also renders a borrowing explanation extremely unlikely. Moreover, the patterns of diachronic meaning change discussed above suggest that the Directionality Principle is not just an accidental property inherited from some proto-language but rather an active force governing the formation of metaphors in contemporary languages. Thus, we are led towards an explanation for the Directionality Principle couched in terms of universal properties of human cognition.

One possible explanation for the Directionality Principle stems from the observation that, in the Hierarchy of Sensory Modalities, lower sensory modalities are more concrete or "accessible" than higher sensory modalities. To the extent that this is the case, the Directionality Principle for synaesthetic metaphors can be viewed as a particular instantiation of the more general directionality principle mentioned in Section 2 above, to the effect that source domains tend to be more concrete, target domains more abstract. This explanation is developed in Shen and Cohen (1998), Shen and Aisenman (forthcoming), and Shen and Gadir (forthcoming).

If in fact the Directionality Principle is part of human cognition, then this ought to be observable experimentally. In particular, if synaesthetic metaphors conforming to the Directionality Principle are cognitively simpler or more basic, then we would expect subjects to judge such metaphors as more natural, to assign them interpretations with greater ease, and to be able to recall them more successfully. In a series of experiments conducted on speakers of Hebrew, Shen and Cohen (1998) and Shen and Aisenman (forthcoming) show that these predictions are borne out. Thus, the experimental evidence suggests that metaphors conforming to the Directionality Principle are indeed cognitively simpler. However, to the best of our knowledge, no similar experiments have so far been conducted with speakers of any languages other than Hebrew. Once again, the question arises whether similar facts obtain in other languages, that is to say, whether synaesthetic metaphors conforming to the Directionality Principle are cognitively simpler across the languages of the world.

5. Synaesthetic Metaphors in Indonesian

In this chapter, we present some preliminary studies of synaesthetic metaphors in Indonesian. Indonesian is chosen as a language that is far removed from Hebrew and other European languages in terms of geographical space, genealogical affiliation, grammatical structure, and cultural influences. If Indonesian turns out to be similar to Hebrew and other European languages then the case for universality is substantially boosted. The studies presented herein are part of a large-scale ongoing investigation of metaphors and related tropes in Indonesian and other languages of Indonesia, seeking out patterns of universality and diversity in the realm of figurative language.

Indonesian, sometimes also referred to as Bahasa Indonesia, is the national language of Indonesia, spoken by around two hundred million people, albeit not all natively. As is generally the case for large languages, there is a great amount of variation along several independent dimensions. *Standard Indonesian* is the formal variety of the language, and that most commonly described in the linguistic literature. However, nobody speaks Standard Indonesian as their first native language; children acquiring Indonesian start out with one or more varieties of colloquial Indonesian, and only later acquire the standard language. Colloquial Indonesian exhibits a substantial amount of regional variation, with varying degrees of mutual intelligibility between dialects; in addition, colloquial Indonesian varieties are all very different from the standard language. Since the present studies were carried out in the capital city, Jakarta, the variety of colloquial Indonesian that we shall be concerned with here is that generally referred to as *Jakarta Indonesian*. (Somewhat confusingly, Jakarta Indonesian is occasionally referred to simply as "Colloquial Indonesian"; however, this usage fails to take into account the existence of other regional varieties of colloquial Indonesian.) Some grammatical studies of Jakarta Indonesian can be found in Wouk (1989, 1999), Cole, Gil, Hermon and Tadmor (2001), Tjung (2006), Sneddon (2006) and Gil (2006, forthcoming). Jakarta Indonesian and Standard Indonesian are not autonomous entities; rather, they represent the two idealized endpoints on a continuum of language varieties, or lects; see Sneddon (2003). In reality, speakers are constantly moving up and down the lectal cline, from basilect to acrolect and back again. What this means is that any given naturalistic text may combine features of Jakarta and Standard Indonesian. Moreover, when subjects are presented with experimental tasks, it is not always possible to tell whether they are performing them in Jakarta or Standard Indonesian (even when the experiments involve linguistic stimuli that are unambivalently in one or another variety). Accordingly, in this paper, we shall use the term "Indonesian" to refer to the entire range from Jakarta to Standard Indonesian.

What we are interested in is whether synaesthetic metaphors in Indonesian behave the same way as in other languages. Already we have encountered examples suggesting that this might be the case: the supermarket called *Harum Manis* 'Sweet Fragrance', and the meaning change of *keras* from 'hard' to 'loud'—both conforming to the Directionality Principle. But one swallow does not make a spring. In what follows, we shall present results from two studies of synaesthetic metaphors, one corpus-based, the other experimental, showing that the Directionality Principle does indeed govern the structure of synaesthetic metaphors in Indonesian.

5.1. The Corpus Study

As noted above, corpus studies demonstrating the validity of the Directionality Principle have been conducted for several European languages, ancient and modern Hebrew, and also two East Asian languages, Chinese and Japanese. Still, in many respects, the Eurasian landmass constitutes a single linguistic area with many shared features setting it apart from other geographical regions; see, for example, many of the chapters of the *World Atlas of Language Structures* (Haspelmath, Dryer, Gil and Comrie eds. 2005). Therefore, it is of interest to conduct similar studies on languages from other parts of the world, such as, for example, Indonesian, spoken in insular Southeast Asia.

The present study is based on a corpus of written Indonesian, culled, for the most part, from the internet, consisting of texts of a variety of genres, including poetry, short stories, and journalistic articles. The corpus is coded for various sorts of figurative language, including metaphors of various kinds, among which are the synaesthetic metaphors of concern in the present paper. The compilation and coding of the corpus is an ongoing project; accordingly, the results presented in this paper are of an interim nature.

So far, the corpus has yielded a total of 125 synaesthetic metaphors. Of these, 121 are in accordance with the Directionality Principle, while just 4 are in violation of it. Thus, the Indonesian corpus study joins forces with the previous studies mentioned above, providing strong additional support for the universality of the Directionality Principle.

A few examples of Indonesian synaesthetic metaphors from the corpus are given in (6) - (10) below. In each example, the sensory modalities of the target and source domains are indicated, followed by the text itself, with the synaesthetic metaphor in boldface. (In (8) and (10) there are two different synaesthetic metaphors within each example.)[1]

(6) *sight > touch*
['The newest colours in the Chic Colour series from the Majirel Spring Summer Colour Collection consist of three captivating colours that can be suited to skin colour, namely Agua Chic with choice of aquatic colour with hints of green and blue,']
Pure   Chic   untuk   **warna**   yang   lebih   **lembut**
Pure   Chic   for   **colour** REL   more   **soft**
dan   feminin
and   feminine
'Pure Chic for a **softer** and more feminine **colour**'
['and salmon pink and Exo Chic in exotic mahogany purple suitable for chocolate coloured skin.']

(7) *sound > taste*
Kedai kopi   itu   sekarang melantunkan
shop coffee DEM-DEM:DIST now   AG-reflect-EP
lagu-lagu   enak   kesukaan   Yoshio
DISTR-song   delicious ABSTR-like-ABSTR   Yoshio
'The coffee shop now plays lots of **delicious songs** that are Yoshio's favourites'"

---

[1] Each example is presented in three lines: text, interlinear gloss, and free translation into English. In examples (6) and (8), some of the surrounding text is shown in square brackets, in free translation into English, in order to provide further information concerning the context in which the synaesthetic metaphor occurs. The interlinear glosses make use of the following abbreviations: ABSTR abstract; AG agent-oriented voice; ASSOC associative; AUG augmentive; DEAG deagentive; DEM demonstrative; DEPAT depatientive; DIST distal; DISTR distributive; EP end-point-oriented voice; NEG negative; PFCT perfect; REL relative; SG singular; VOC vocative; 1 first person.

(8) *sound > touch / sound > touch*
Suaranya   lembut mengalun   "Paaaak   Bagyo"
voice-ASSOC **soft**   AG-swell   VOC-father Bagyo
'Her soft voice swelled "Mister Bagyo"'
['The first two "aa" low, the last two "aa" heightening.']
Bunyi "k" tidak tajam melainkan tersentak
sound k   NEG   sharp AG-other-EP DEAG-pull
medok
heavy.accent
'**The sound "k" not sharp**, but startling with its heavy accent'

(9) *smell > taste*
Setelah   tiga   bulan   berada   dalam   tanah
one-PFCT three month DEPAT-exist inside earth
aku   menggali kembali kotoran   yang telah
1SG   AG-dig   return dirty-AUG REL   PFCT
berbau   asam itu
DEPAT-smell sour DEM-DEM:DIST
'After it was in the earth for three months, I dug up the muck that was already **smelling sour**'

(10) *smell > touch / smell > taste*
Udara balai   desa   lama-lama   jadi
air   public.building village DISTR-old   become
tajam oleh **aroma** keringat. **Asam, asin, asem.**
sharp by   **odour** sweat   **sour salty sour**
'The air in the old village halls became **sharp** with the odour of **sweat. Sour, salty, sour.**'

In (6), *warna*, the target domain, is associated with the sense of sight, while *lembut*, the source domain, is associated with the sense of touch. In (7), *lagu-lagu*, the target domain, is associated with sound, whereas *enak*, the source domain, is associated with taste. In (8), in the first case, *suaranya*, the target domain, is associated with sound, while *lembut*, the source domain, is associated with touch; similarly, in the second case, *bunyi "k"*, the target domain, is associated with sound, whereas *tidak tajam*, the source domain, is associated with touch. In (9), *berbau*, the target domain, is associated with smell, while *asam*, the source domain, is associated with taste; this metaphor accordingly exhibits the same pattern of sensory modalities as the *Harum Manis* "Sweet Fragrance" supermarket name. Finally, in (10), in the first case, *aroma*, the target domain, is associated with smell, while *tajam*, the source domain, is associated with touch; the same *aroma* also functions as the target domain of a second metaphor, in which *asam, asin, asem*, the source domain, is associated with taste. These examples, and many others like them in the corpus, show that synaesthetic metaphors in Indonesian texts typically involve mappings upwards on the Hierarchy of Sensory Modalities, in accordance with the Directionality Principle.

5.2. The Experimental Study

The Indonesian corpus study suggests that for Indonesian speakers, too, synaesthetic metaphors conforming to the Directionality Principle may be cognitively simpler than others violating it. But is this really the case? As noted above, the cognitive reality of the Directionality Principle has previously been tested only for Hebrew. Our plan is to replicate all the Hebrew experiments inIndonesian; however, so far, we have had occasion to conduct just a single experiment, testing subjects' 'naturalness' judgments of synaesthetic metaphors in conformity with and in violation of the Directionality Principle. (The structure of the experiment and its results are presented in Table 1.)

The experiment was presented to subjects in the form of a sheet of paper containing 20 stimuli. Each stimulus consists of a synaesthetic metaphor in two forms: one conforming to the Directionality Principle, the other violating it. Subjects were asked to circle the form that they judged to be the more natural of the two. The 20 stimuli test all 10 possible combinations of the 5 sensory modalities, with 2 stimuli per combination. In Table 1, the first two columns present the sensory domains, the next two columns the Indonesian words chosen, and the two columns after that their English glosses. Note that one of the 20 combinations, number 15, happens to involve the words forming the name of the Indonesian supermarket.

Sweet Fragrances from Indonesia

No	sense 1	item 1	sense 2	item 2	gloss 1	gloss 2	var 1 (%)	var 2 (%)
1	sight	merah	sound	nyaring	red	high-pitched	82	80
2	sight	cerah	sound	dengung	bright	buzzing	25	27
3	sight	kuning	smell	anyir	yellow	rancid	77	82
4	sight	putih	smell	sengat	white	putrid	40	32
5	sight	hijau	taste	rasa	green	taste	27	27
6	sight	gelap	taste	pahit	dark	bitter	45	32
7	sight	kilat	touch	tajam	shiny	sharp	85	75
8	sight	hitam	touch	dingin	black	cold	72	57
9	sound	denyut	smell	pesing	throbbing	urine-smell	85	77
10	sound	desah	smell	wangi	wheezing	fragrant	72	67
11	sound	gedebuk	taste	tawar	thudding	bland	52	67
12	sound	dengkur	taste	asam	grunting	sour	57	82
13	sound	bunyi	touch	keras	sound	hard	90	97
14	sound	debar	touch	lembek	throbbing	soft	65	92
15	smell	harum	taste	manis	fragrant	sweet	97	75
16	smell	gosong	taste	pedas	burnt-smell	peppery	52	52
17	smell	amis	touch	licin	fish-smell	smooth	65	57
18	smell	apek	touch	panas	musty	hot	20	15
19	taste	gurih	touch	kasar	savoury	rough	70	77
20	taste	asin	touch	lembut	salty	soft	62	80

Table 1: The Naturalness Judgment Experiment for Synaesthetic Metaphors in Indonesian

The experiment is constructed in two alternative variants differing with respect to the grammatical construction of the synaesthetic metaphor. These two alternative variants may be exemplified with reference to stimulus 15:

(11)   Variant A: harum manis   manis harum
       Variant B: harumnya manis   manisnya harum

Variant A of the experiment involves the *bare juxtaposition* construction, in which the two words occur alongside each other without any additional grammatical marking. Variant B of the experiment involves the *-nya* construction, in which the first word is marked with the associative enclitic *-nya*, whose meaning ranges between that of a definite article such as 'the' and that of a possessive pronoun such as 'its'. Thus, subjects given Variant A of the experiment had to choose between forms such as *harum manis* and *manis harum*, while subjects given Variant B had to choose between forms such as *harumnya manis* and *manisnya harum*.

The motivation for testing two different constructions is to make sure that we know which of the two words in each expression is the target domain and which the source domain. Indonesian, especially in its colloquial varieties, allows for a much greater degree of grammatical flexibility than most European languages; see Gil (2005a,b) for the Riau dialect of Indonesian, similar facts obtain also for Jakarta Indonesian. For example, a bare juxtaposition construction such as *harum manis* allows for at least the following two potential interpretations: (a) an *attributive* interpretation, in which the second word modifies the first, 'sweet fragrance', and (b) a *conjunctive* interpretation, in which both words are equally ranked, 'fragrant and sweet'. Whereas the attributive interpretation gives rise to a metaphor in which the first element, the head of the expression, is the target domain, and the second element, the attribute, is the source domain, the conjunctive interpretation does not result in a metaphorical expression—its interpretation is more closely akin to that of a zeugma. In order to ensure that subjects obtain a metaphorical reading, the *-nya* construction is introduced, as its effect is to narrow down the range of possible interpretations. Thus, in a construction such as *harumnya manis*, the most readily available interpretation is a predicative one, in which the first word is understood as the subject, and the second word as its predicate, 'the/its fragrance is sweet'. This interpretation is clearly metaphorical, with the first element as target domain and the second element as source domain.

Each variant of the experiment has two different versions in which the stimuli are randomized in different orders, and the relative order of the two forms within each stimulus is also different. In each version, there are some stimuli in which the form conforming to the Directionality Principle occurs on the left (as in (11) above) and others in which it occurs on the right.

A total of 80 subjects, native speakers of Indonesian resident in Jakarta, took part in the experiment: 40 for each variant, and 20 for each version within each variant. The results of the experiment are given in the last two columns of Table 1, for variants 1 and 2 respectively. The figures show the percentage of subjects that chose the form of the synaesthetic metaphor conforming to the Directionality Principle.

The results of the experiment show that subjects tended to prefer synaesthetic metaphors conforming to the Directionality Principle over their alternatives that violate it. Of the 20 stimuli, 15 scored over 50% for both variants, while just 5 scored under 50% for both variants. (The latter group are shaded grey.) In general, then, the results of the bare juxtaposition and -*nya* variants are quite similar, suggesting that subjects interpreted both variants in accordance with the same principles. A chi-squared test shows that the overall preference for synaesthetic metaphors conforming to the Directionality Principle is significant at $p < 0.01$.

Nevertheless, the results of the experiment show considerable variation from one stimulus to another, for which we do not expect to be able to come up with a single unified explanation. Each word and each pair of words has its own story, its own idiosyncratic features, which affect the way in which it is judged by the experimental subjects. All we can do is to speculate briefly on a few of the other factors that may underlie some of the observed variation.

To begin with, it may be noted that of the 5 stimuli that scored under 50%, one, namely stimulus 2, involves the two highest sensory domains, sight and sound. As noted in the formulation of the Directionality Principle in (5) above, sight and sound constitute an exception to the generalization concerning directionality; hence stimulus 2 need not be considered as a counterexample to the Directionality Principle.

Like other figures of speech, synaesthetic metaphors may be ranked on a scale ranging from highly innovative and hence extremely rare to highly conventionalized and accordingly very common. With respect to the exerimental task, one might expect subjects to be more consistent in their judgments of metaphors that are more highly conventionalized and to which they have already presumably been exposed. Thus, if the experiment had been targeted specifically at conventionalized metaphors, the results would have been "better", that is to say, conforming more closely to the Directionality Principle. However, such results would have been little more than a recapitulation of the findings from the corpus study, telling us what we already know. Instead, an attempt was made to test synaesthetic metaphors of a more innovative nature, in the hope that subjects faced with such stimuli would be forced to exercise their relevant cognitive faculties creatively and in real time, rather than simply calling upon a memorized list of familiar conventionalized collocations. However, in actual fact, it proved to be very difficult to come up with 20 different stimuli satisfying the experimental design and also exhibiting an equal degree of innovativeness.

In an attempt to evaluate the degree of innovativeness of the experimental stimuli, a post hoc analysis was conducted making use of the MPI Jakarta Child Language Corpus. The MPI Jakarta Child Language Corpus consists of over 2,300,000 words of naturalistic conversation in Jakarta Indonesian, of which roughly half is spoken by young children, and the remaining half by adults, largely, though not entirely, directed towards children. Although the MPI Jakarta Child Language Corpus may appear, on the face of it, to provide a less than optimal hunting ground for synaesthetic metaphorical expressions, arguably such a corpus of naturalistic speech actually provides a more faithful reflection of the range of linguistic phenomena to which ordinary speakers of Indonesian are exposed in the course of their everyday lives, and which might, accordingly, impinge on their performance as experimental subjects. This is because most people, most of the time, make use of language in its primary oral mode, rather than its derivative written medium.

Table 2 below presents the frequency of occurrence in the MPI Jakarta Child Language Corpus of the 40 individual words in the experimental stimuli, arranged according to the five sensory modalities. The frequencies are defined in terms of number n of tokens per million words, on a roughly logarithmic scale, as follows: very high ($1000 < n$), high ($100 < n \leq 1000$), mid ($10 < n \leq 100$), low ($0 < n \leq 10$), very low ($n = 0$). For each word, the frequency measure takes into account occurrences of the word both in bare form and with additional prefixes and/or suffixes.

As evident from Table 2, the distribution of word frequencies varies across the different sensory modalities. Sight has the most frequent words, due largely to the common use of colour terms. In contrast, sound has the least frequent words, so much so that when constructing the experiment, we had to go a dictionary to find appropriate words. The remaining three sensory modalities fall in between sight and sound. What Table 2 shows, then, is that in constructing the experimental stimuli, there was simply no practical way to ensure that all of the words chosen would be of comparable frequency.

	sight	sound	smell	taste	Touch
very high	merah				
high	gelap hijau hitam kuning putih	bunyi	wangi	manis pedas rasa	dingin keras panas tajam
mid			amis gosong	asam asin pahit tawar	kasar lembek licin
low	cerah kilat	dengkur denyut nyaring	apek harum pesing sengat	gurih	lembut
very low		debar degung desah gedebuk	anyir		

Table 2: Frequency of Words in the MPI Jakarta Child Language Corpus

Of course, what has a potential effect on subjects' judgments is not the frequencies of individual words but rather the frequencies of their collocations as synaesthetic metaphors. Accordingly, the MPI Jakarta Child Language Corpus was searched for synaesthetic metaphors corresponding to each of the 20 experimental stimuli. The search included expressions instantiating any grammatical construction whatsoever (bare juxtaposition, -*nya*, or other) provided the two words are present and constitute a synaesthetic metaphor. For 18 out of the 20 stimuli, no such combinations were found in the corpus. What this suggests, then, is that by and large, the experiment achieved its goal of testing subjects' creative, real-time cognitive abilities: when choosing one order over another, they were doing so primarily because it sounded better on the fly, not because they remembered having heard a similar collocation in the past. Thus, to the extent that subjects' judgments were consistent with the Directionality Principle, this suggests that synaesthetic metaphors conforming to the Directionality Principle are not just more frequent in texts, but also cognitively simpler or more basic.

But what of the remaining two stimuli, those that did show up as synaesthetic metaphors in the corpus? One of them, stimulus 13, involves the conventionalized meaning extension of *keras* 'hard' to mean 'loud' as discussed in Section 4 above; the combination of *keras* with *bunyi* 'sound', as in stimulus 13, occurs exactly once in the corpus:

(12) *sound > touch*
Keras nggak, **bunyinya?**
hard   NEG   sound-ASSOC
'Is the **sound loud**?'

In the above example, *bunyinya*, the target domain, is associated with sound, while *keras*, the source domain, is associated with touch. Example (12) thus corresponds to Variant B of stimulus 13, albeit with an inverted word order. The high frequency of this particular metaphor, as reflected by its presence the corpus, is undoubtedly the reason why, of all the 20 stimuli, stimulus 13 is the one in which subjects most consistently chose the order conforming to the Directionality Principle, at 90% and 97% respectively for the two variants.

However, the second of the two stimuli which showed up as synaesthetic metaphors in the corpus, stimulus 5, is more problematic. In the corpus there are four instances of synaesthetic metaphors combining *hijau* 'green' and *rasa* 'taste', and all four violate the Directionality Principle. These four tokens occur in a single stretch of discourse, involving a young boy aged 3 years and 3 months, playing with a collection of coloured blocks which he picks up, one after another, pretends to eat, and then comments on their taste by means of a sequence of synaesthetic metaphors involving the word *rasa* 'taste' in construction with the appropriate colour terms, including, as per stimulus 5, the word *hijau* 'green'. Following is one example of the child's speech, instantiating the combination in stimulus 5 plus a similar one involving the colour blue:[1]

---

[1] In example (13), *hijau* 'green' is spelled *ijo*, as is customary in colloquial Jakarta Indonesian. The form *nyam* is an onomatopoeic word representing the sound of eating.

(13) *taste > sight / taste > sight*
        Itu   bukan **rasa** **ijo**,   r(asa)... ra(sa)...
        DEM-DEM:DIST NEG   taste   green   taste   taste
        biru, nyam   nyam   nyam   nyam   nyam
        blue *nyam* *nyam* *nyam*   *nyam* *nyam*
        'That doesn't taste green, that tastes blue, *nyam nyam nyam nyam nyam*'

In (13), *rasa*, the target domain, is associated with taste, while *ijo* and *biru*, the source domains, are associated with sight. Thus, the synaesthetic metaphors in (13) and other similar examples in the same discourse involve mappings downwards on the Hierarchy of Sensory Modalities, in violation of the Directionality Principle. As was the case for example (12), the occurrence of the synaesthetic metaphor in the corpus is consonant with the judgments offered by the experimental subjects, though, in the present case, in mirror-image form. Thus, for stimulus 5, only 27% of subjects chose the predicted form; the remaining 73% preferred the form exemplified in example (13), in violation of the Directionality Principle.

As suggested by both of the above examples, frequency in naturalistic speech may be an additional factor governing subjects' judgments of naturalness in the experimental task. However, this leaves unanswered the question why, in both the MPI Jakarta Child Language Corpus and the experimental study, combinations of *rasa* and a colour term, as in stimulus 5, form synaesthetic metaphors in violation of the Directionality Principle. A possible answer to this question is provided by Viberg (1984), who shows that the principles governing synaesthetic metaphors are different for verbs than they are for other parts of speech. Although parts-of-speech distinctions are difficult to draw in Indonesian, the word *rasa* does stand out in relationship to the other words in the experiment drawn from the modality of taste. Whereas the other words refer primarily to specific taste qualities, such as 'sour', 'bitter' and so forth, *rasa* refers to the abstract notion of taste or to the activity of tasting, in which latter case it has the semantic attributes characteristic in most languages of verbs. Thus, the different behaviour of synaesthetic metaphors involving the word *rasa* may be part and parcel of a more general tendency involving verbs or verb-like words, as proposed by Viberg.

Having come this far, we may now return to our supermarket name *Harum Manis* 'Sweet Fragrance'. In the experiment, for stimulus 15, subjects exhibited a very strong preference for *harum manis*, 97%, over its alternative form, *manis harum*, just 3%. Although this particular synaesthetic metaphor did not occur in the MPI Jakarta Child Language

Corpus, its observed usage as a supermarket name, albeit in a far-away city on another island, suggests that subjects just might have encountered it sometime somewhere in the past, which may account, in part, for their overwhelming preference for the attested form *harum manis*. But this does not explain why the supermarket was called *Harum Manis* and not *Manis Harum* in the first place. However, as argued in this paper, the choice of the supermarket name was no fortuitous coincidence—cognitively simpler synaesthetic metaphors make for better commercial brand names.

6. Conclusion

Synaesthetic metaphor is a frequent device in literary and religious texts, occurring "in the earliest literature of the West (*e.g.*, in *Iliad* 3.152, where the voices of the old Trojans are likened to the *lily-like* voices of cicalas; in *Iliad* 3.222, where Odysseus' words fall like winter snowflakes; and in the *Odyssea* 12.187 in the *honey-voice* of the Sirens...). Hebrews 6.5 and Revelations 1.12 refer to *tasting* the word of God and *seeing* a voice." (Preminger 1974, 840)

In this paper we presented a preliminary exploration of synaesthetic metaphors in Indonesian. While the corpus study shows that Indonesian synaesthetic metaphors look very much like those previously described in other languages, the experimental study – the first to be done outside of Hebrew – suggests that the structure of synaesthetic metaphors observed in texts reflects underlying principles of cognitive simplicity, as encapsulated in the Directionality Principle. Both studies suggest that the principles governing the structure of synaesthetic metaphors proposed on the basis of Hebrew and other Eurasian languages may indeed be universal.

Acknowledgements

The work reported on in this paper would not have been possible without the infrastructure provided by the Max Planck Institute Jakarta Field Station and its coordinator Uri Tadmor. In particular, we are grateful to Tessa Yuditha for assistance in running the experiment, to Dini Andarini and Dian Mayasari for compiling and coding the figurative-language corpus, to Brad Taylor for designing the FileMaker Pro database in which the corpus is housed, and to all the other members of the Jakarta Field Station for encouragement, support, and ongoing discussions of metaphors and other kinds of figurative language in Indonesian. We also thank Will van Peer for invaluable comments and suggestions.

The first author's research was supported by grant number 969/07 from the Israel Science Foundation, administered by the Israel Academy of Sciences and Humanities.

Works Cited

Arsenic, Vladimir (2005) "Synaesthetic Metaphors in Serbo-Croatian Modern Poetry", unpublished manuscript, Department of Poetics and Comparative Literature, Tel Aviv University, Tel Aviv.

Cole, Peter, David Gil, Gabriella Hermon and Uri Tadmor (2001) "The Acquisition of In-Situ WH-Questions and WH-Indefinites in Jakarta Indonesian", in A. H.-J. Do, L. Domínguez and A. Johansen eds., *Proceedings of the the 25th Annual Boston University Conference on Language Development, Volume 1*, Cascadilla Press, Somerville, 169-179.

Day, Sean (1996) "Synaesthesia and Synaesthetic Metaphors", *PSYCHE* 2: 32.

Dombi, Erzsebet (1974) "Synaesthesia and Poetry", *Poetics* 11: 23-44.

Gil, David (2005a) "Isolating-Monocategorial-Associational Language", in H. Cohen and C. Lefebvre eds., *Categorization in Cognitive Science*, Elsevier, Oxford, 347-379.

—. (2005b) "Word Order Without Syntactic Categories: How Riau Indonesian Does It", in A. Carnie, H. Harley and S.A. Dooley eds., *Verb First: On the Syntax of Verb-Initial Languages*, John Benjamins, Amsterdam, 243-263.

—. (2006) "The Acquisition of Voice Morphology in Jakarta Indonesian", in N. Gagarina and I Gülzow eds., *The Acquisition of Verbs and Their Grammar: The Effect of Particular Languages*, Springer, Dordrecht, 201-227.

—. (forthcoming) "The Acquisition of Syntactic Categories in Jakarta Indonesian", *Studies in Language*.

Haspelmath, Martin, Matthew Dryer, David Gil and Bernard Comrie eds. (2005) *The World Atlas of Language Structures*, Oxford University Press, Oxford.

Manor, Yifat (1996) "Synaesthetic Metaphors in Prose", unpublished manuscript, Department of Poetics and Comparative Literature, Tel Aviv University, Tel Aviv.

Ortony, Andrew, Ruth Vondruska, Mark Foss and Lawrence Jones (1985) "Salience, Similes, and the Asymmetry of Similarity", *Journal of Memory and Language* 24: 569-594.

Popova, Yanna (2005) "Image Schemas and Verbal Synaesthesia", in B. Hampe ed. *From Perception to Meaning: Image Schemas in Cognitive Linguistics*, Mouton de Gruyter, Berlin, 395-419.
Preminger, Alex ed. 1979. *Princeton Encylopedia of Poetry and Poetics*. London: The Macmillan Press.
Shen, Yeshayahu (1997) "Cognitive Constraints on Poetic Figures", *Cognitive Linguistics* 8.1: 33-71.
Shen, Yeshayahu and Michal Cohen (1998) "How Come Silence Is Sweet But Sweetness Is Not Silent: A Cognitive Account of Directionality in Poetic Synaesthesia", *Language and Literature* 7.2: 123-140.
Shen, Yeshayahu and Ravid Aisenman (forthcoming). "Heard Melodies Are Sweet, But Those Unheard Are Sweeter". Journal of Pragmatics.
Shen, Yeshayahu and Osnat Gadir (forthcoming) "Synaesthesia, Cognition and Diachronic Meaning Extension", *Leshonenu* (in Hebrew).
Sneddon, James Neil (2003) "Diglossia in Indonesian", *Bijdragen tot de Taal-, Land- en Volkenkunde* 159: 519-549.
—. (2006) *Colloquial Jakartan Indonesian*, Pacific Linguistics, Canberra.
Tjung, Yassir Nasanius (2006) *The Formation of Relative Clauses in Jakarta Indonesian, A Subject-Object Asymmetry*, PhD Dissertation, University of Delaware, Newark, DE, USA.
Tsur, Reuven (1992) *Toward a Theory of Cognitive Poetics*, Elsevier, Amsterdam.
Ullman, Shimon (1957) "Panchronistic Tendencies in Synaesthesia", in S. Ullman ed. *The Principles of Semantics*, Blackwell, Oxford, 266-289.
Viberg, Åke (1984) "The Verbs of Perception: A Typological Study", in B. Butterworth, B. Comrie and Ö. Dahl eds. *Explanations for Language Universals*, Mouton, Berlin, 123-162.
Williams, Joseph M. (1976) "Synaesthetic Adjectives: A Possible Law of Semantic Change", *Language* 52.2: 461-478.
Wouk, Fay (1989) *The Impact of Discourse on Grammar: Verb Morphology in Spoken Jakarta Indonesia*,. PhD Dissertation, UCLA, Los Angeles.
—. (1999) "Dialect Contact and Koineization in Jakarta, Indonesia", *Language Sciences* 21: 61-86.
Yu, Ning (1992) "A Possible Semantic Law in Synaesthetic Transfer", *The SECOL Review* 16: 20-39.
—. (2003) "Synaesthetic Metaphor: A Cognitive Perspective", *Journal of Literary Semantics* 32: 19-34.

CHAPTER THREE

AUTOMATIC ANALYSES OF LANGUAGE, DISCOURSE, AND SITUATION MODELS

ART GRAESSER, MOONGEE JEON, ZHIQIANG CAI, AND DANIELLE MCNAMARA

Abstract

Coh-Metrix is a new system on the web that is capable of measuring texts on hundreds of metrics of discourse cohesion and language complexity at the same time. In contrast to more traditional ways of analysing texts in literary studies, Coh-Metrix has a number of automated measures that cover all levels of text analysis, including characteristics of words, syntax, referential cohesion, semantic cohesion, and dimensions of the situation model. In order to illustrate the capabilities of Coh-Metrix in this chapter, we report an analysis of *Einstein's Dreams*, a best selling novel written by a physicist, Alan Lightman. The book is a series of short chapters about villages in Switzerland in which the citizens have radically different assumptions about time and such assumptions have a salient impact on their lives. We used Coh-Metrix to analyse these chapters on different measures of language, discourse, and cohesion; the characteristics of these chapters were compared to a normative sample of science and narrative texts. Our central guiding question is whether the chapters in *Einstein's Dreams* are more similar to narrative or to scientific text, given it is a novel written by a scientist. We discovered that most measures were most similar to narrative text, but many were similar to science, so there is no simple answer to the question. Colleagues are encouraged to use Coh-Metrix for multi-leveled analyses of text corpora.

Automatic Analyses of Language, Discourse, and Situation Models

There has been a dramatic increase in computer analyses of large text corpora during the last decade. This can be partly explained by revolutionary advances in computational linguistics,[1] discourse processes,[2] the representation of world knowledge,[3][4] and corpus analyses.[5] Thousands, or even millions, of texts can be quickly accessed and analysed on hundreds of measures in a short amount of time. Data mining is emerging as a standard methodology in a broad spectrum of fields that range from cyber security to Shakespeare.

We believe that members of IGEL and literary studies in general would benefit from advances in corpus linguistics and computational linguistics. It will always be important to analyse the contents of texts at deep conceptual levels of analysis that can only be achieved by humans who are trained in literary studies. However, it is frequently useful to accompany such annotated analyses of human experts with computer analyses in order to provide a more objective and defensible foundation to scholarly claims. Sometimes the computer analyses produce counterintuitive results that invite further reflection by scientists and nonscientific scholars.

During the last 5 years we have developed a system called Coh-Metrix (http://cohmetrix.memphis.edu),[6][7] a computational tool that produces indices of the linguistic and discourse characteristics of a text. The values on these indices can be used in many different ways to investigate the cohesion of the explicit text and the coherence of the mental representation of the text. Our definition of *cohesion* consists of characteristics of the explicit text that play some role in helping the reader mentally connect ideas in the text.[8] The definition of *coherence* is the subject of much debate. Theoretically, the coherence of a text is defined by the interaction between linguistic representations and knowledge representations. When we put the spotlight on the text, however, coherence can be defined as

---

[1] In order to make for easier readability of this chapter, references to the various aspects of Coh-Metrix are listed in footnotes. With regard to computational linguistics, see Jurafsky and Martin (2000).
[2] Graesser, Gernsbacher, and Goldman (2003).
[3] Lenat (1995).
[4] Landauer et al. (2007).
[5] Biber, Conrad, and Reppen (1998).
[6] Graesser et al. (2004).
[7] McNamara, Louwerse, and Graesser (2002).
[8] Graesser, McNamara, and Louwerse (2003).

characteristics of the text (i.e., aspects of cohesion) that are likely to contribute to the coherence of the mental representation. Coh-Metrix provides indices of such cohesion characteristics.

Coh-Metrix

There are 60 indices in Coh-Metrix version 2.0 that is available to the public. The user of Coh-Metrix enters a text into the web site and it prints out measures of the text on metrics that span different levels of discourse and language. Coh-Metrix was designed to move beyond standard readability formulae, such as Flesch-Kincaid Grade Level.[9] Traditionally, readability formulae rely exclusively on word length, sentence length, and sometimes word frequency to scale texts on readability. For example, the Flesch-Kincaid Grade Level is computed as shown in formula #1, where *Words* equals mean words per sentence and *Syllables* equals mean syllables per word.

$$\text{Grade Level} = .39 * Words + 11.8 * Syllables - 15.59$$

Sentence length and word length are only a start in analyzing texts, but surprisingly these two variables robustly predict reading time. The 60 Coh-Metrix measures include some simple measures to compute, such as number of words in the text, number of sentences, number of paragraphs, syllables per word, words per sentence, and sentences per paragraph.

Coh-Metrix analyses texts on many levels of language and discourse that go well beyond these simple measures, however. Some indices refer to characteristics of individual words, as has been achieved in many other computer facilities.[10] Most of the Coh-Metrix indices include deeper or more processing-intensive algorithms that analyse syntax, referential cohesion, semantic cohesion, and dimensions of the situation model. A snapshot of the landscape of indices is provided below. It should be noted that the researchers at the University of Memphis have over 600 measures in their research web site, but approximately 60 of these are available in the public website. In what follows, we will first list some typical measures of text structure provided by Coh-metrix, before using the program in an example of concrete text-analysis. This list will inevitably contain some technical explanations that are needed in order to understand

---

[9] Klare (1974-75).
[10] Pennebaker and Francis (1999).

the later textual investigation; we invite the reader to exert some patience in this.

1. **Word measures**. Coh-Metrix measures words on a large number of characteristics, most of which will not be defined in this chapter (see the help system on the web site http://cohmetrix.memphis.edu). There are measures of word frequency in the English language, the distinction between content words (e.g., noun, main verb, adjective) versus function words (e.g., prepositions, articles, conjunctions), concreteness of words, and the level of the words in a semantic abstraction hierarchy (called hypernym count). Mean values of words on these indices are computed for the relevant words in the text. Coh-Metrix incorporates several lexicons, including CELEX,[11] WordNet,[12] the MRC Psycholinguistic Database,[13] and the Brill (1995)[14] part-of-speech classifier.

Word measures are sometimes directly relevant to cohesion. In particular, some word classes have the function of connecting clauses and other constituents in the text. There are different categories of connectives, such as additive (*also, moreover*), temporal (*and then, after, during*), causal *(because, so)*, and logical (*therefore, nevertheless*) connectives.[15][16][17] There are negations (*not, n't*) that span different levels of constituent structure. The *incidence* of these word classes is measured as the number of occurrences per 1000 words. A text with higher cohesion would have a higher incidence of word classes that connect constituents. Another important word class consists of pronouns (*it, he, hers*), which present problems of cohesion when the comprehender does not know the referent of these pronouns. Pronouns often require a conversational or social context to resolve, as opposed to their referring to other text constituents.

2. **Syntax**. Coh-Metrix measures sentence syntax with the assistance of syntactic parsers[18] that assign parts-of-speech and syntactic tree structures to sentences. There are a number of indices of syntactic complexity. A noun-phrase incidence score computes the number of noun-phrases per 1000 words. The mean number of modifiers per noun-phrase is

---

[11] Baayen, Piepenbrock, and van Rijn (1993).
[12] Fellbaum (1998).
[13] Coltheart (1981).
[14] Brill (1995).
[15] Halliday and Hasan (1976).
[16] Louwerse (2002).
[17] Sanders, Spooren, and Noordman (1992).
[18] Charniak (2000).

an index of the complexity of referencing expressions. For example, *the very arrogant frustrated man* is a complex noun-phrase with 4 modifiers of the head noun *man*. The number of words before the main verb of the main clause is an index of working memory load; the reader needs to keep a large number of words in working memory before getting to the main idea of the sentence.[19] Sentences with a high number of higher-level constituents per word are more structurally embedded and therefore more complex. The structural similarity of pairs of sentences is also measured. Texts have higher syntactic cohesion when pairs have similar syntax.

3. Referential and semantic cohesion. Referential cohesion occurs when a noun, pronoun, or noun-phrase refers to another constituent in the text. For example, in the sentence *When people are happy, they have the impression that time moves quickly,* the word *they* refers to the word *people*. A referring expression (E) is the noun, pronoun, or noun-phrase that refers to another constituent (C). C is designated as the referent of E. In the example sentence, the word *they* is the referring expression E, whereas the referent C is the word *people*. One form of co-reference that has been extensively studied is argument overlap.[20] This occurs when a noun, pronoun, or noun-phrase in one sentence is a co-referent of a noun, pronoun, or noun-phrase in another sentence. The word "argument" is used in a special sense in this context, namely it is a contrast with predicates in propositional representations.[21] Another form of co-reference is stem overlap, where a noun in one sentence has a similar morphological root as a content word in another sentence. For example, *When people are happy, they have the impression that time moves quickly. When happiness ends, the obstacles slow down everything. Happiness* and *happy* have common stems, so there is stem overlap. Yet another form of co-reference is anaphoric pronominal co-reference; a pronoun in one sentence refers to a referent in another sentence. Coh-Metrix computes the referents of pronouns on the basis of syntactic rules, semantic fit, and discourse pragmatics by some existing algorithms proposed by Mitkov (1998)[22] and Lappin and Lease (1994)[23]. Coh-Metrix 2.0 has indices for pronominal co-reference, but these will not be discussed further in the present chapter.

In addition to referential cohesion indices, Coh-Metrix has indices that assess the extent to which the content of sentences or paragraphs is similar

---

[19] Graesser et al. (2006).
[20] Kintsch and Van Dijk (1978).
[21] Ibid.
[22] Mitkov (1998).
[23] Lappin and Leass (1994).

semantically or conceptually. Cohesion and coherence are predicted to increase as a function of similarity. One index of semantic similarity is content word overlap, which is the proportion of content words in two excerpts that share common content words. Latent Semantic Analysis (LSA) is a second method of computing similarity that considers implicit knowledge. LSA is a statistical technique for representing world knowledge, based on a large corpus of texts. LSA uses singular value decomposition, a general form of principle component analysis, to condense a very large corpus of texts to 100-500 dimensions.[24][25] The conceptual similarity between any two text excerpts (e.g., word, clause, sentence, text) is evaluated by these 100-500 functional dimensions.

There are two ways to measure each of the co-reference and semantic similarity metrics. The first consists of adjacent sentence cohesion; the indices are computed only on the contiguous pairs of sentences. Global cohesion is based on all pairs of sentences in a paragraph. It is also possible to compute LSA metrics between paragraphs, but these are not reported in this chapter.

Lexical diversity provides a simple, but less computationally expensive, approach to computing semantic cohesion of a text. The lexical diversity metric in Coh-Metrix is the type-token ratio score.[26] This is the number of unique words in a text (i.e. types) divided by the overall number of words (i.e. tokens) in the text. Semantic, conceptual, and co-referential cohesion has a high negative correlation with type-token ratio.

4. Situation model dimensions. Many aspects of a text can contribute to the *situation model* (or mental model), the referential content or microworld of what a text is about.[27][28] Text comprehension researchers have investigated at least five situational dimensions: causation, intentionality, time, space and protagonists.[29][30] All of these situational dimensions can be indicated in a text by connectives, particles, nouns, and verbs. In Coh-Metrix 2.0, the protagonist dimension is not analysed. For some measures, we assess the ratio of cohesion particles (connectives and other words that help connect constituents) to the density of relevant referential content. For example, the content of intentional information

---

[24] Landauer, Foltz, and Laham (1998).
[25] Landauer et al. (2007).
[26] Templin (1957).
[27] Graesser, Singer, and Trabasso (1994).
[28] Kintsch (1998).
[29] Zwaan, Langston, and Graesser (1995).
[30] Zwaan, and Radvansky, (1998).

includes intentional actions performed by agents (as in stories, scripts, and common procedures), whereas the cohesion particles include infinitives and intentional connectives (*in order to, so that, by means of*). In the case of temporal cohesion, we assess the uniformity of the sequence of main verbs with respect to tense and aspect. It is beyond the scope of this chapter to define these situation model dimensions in more detail. The Coh-Metrix help facility is available at the web site for more details.

Einstein's Dreams

Alan Lightman's book *Einstein's Dreams*[31] has a series of chapters about fictional villages in Switzerland in which the citizens' assumptions about time deviate from the normal TIME schema in Western cultures. Anomalies on the temporality dimension have illuminating repercussions on causality, agent goals, spatiality, properties of characters, and agent emotions. For example, the citizens in one village know about their entire future, whereas the future is uncertain in our normal reality. The fact that the future is known lowers the anxiety in the citizens and forces the losers in life to cope with their unfortunate lot. In another village, the citizens have no memory for the past, which forces them to rediscover and reinvent themselves each day. Time flows backward instead of forward in one of the villages, whereas time stands still in another. As one might expect, some readers are challenged in the attempt to comprehend the stories that are many transformations away from our everyday TIME schemas.[32]

The author of this unusual novel is a physicist who had studied the evolution of Albert Einstein's ideas before Einstein discovered his theory of relativity. Lightman's academic background had an interesting combination of physics and history. However, *Einstein's Dreams* is also narrative fiction, so Alan Lightman would presumably need to incorporate the language and voice that is closely aligned to the narrative genre. This raises an interesting question: Is the language in *Einstein's Dreams* most akin to science or to narrative? Stated differently, does Alan Lightman write more like a scientist or a novelist? We conducted a study with Coh-Metrix to answer these questions.

Our methodological approach to exploring this question was very straightforward. We used Coh-Metrix 2.0 to analyse a corpus of 10 chapters that were randomly sampled from *Einstein's Dreams*. These were the same 10 chapters that had been investigated in the empirical study

---

[31] Lightman (1993).
[32] Graesser et al. (1998).

conducted on how college students comprehend these texts.[33] We compared the Coh-Metrix values in this Einstein's Dreams corpus with a normative corpus of science and narrative texts that are representative of what high school students typically read. The normative corpus was a sample of texts prepared by Touchstone Applied Science Associates (TASA). TASA classifies the texts into the science versus narrative categories, as well as other genres/registers. The TASA categorization provides an independent, objective, operational definition for classifying the texts into these two categories. We randomly selected 100 science texts and 100 narrative texts from the TASA corpus. The sampled texts were at approximately the 7th grade level according to the Flesch-Kincaid Grade Level because the mean grade level of the Einstein's Dream's (ED) texts was 6.90. The mean numbers of words per text were 667, 276, and 290, respectively, for ED, science, and narrative texts; the corresponding mean numbers of sentences were 44.1, 21.8, and 16.1. Therefore, the ED texts were over twice as long as the science and narrative texts in the TASA sample. In summary, the main empirical question is whether the Einstein's Dreams corpus has a profile of language and discourse features that look more like the TASA science texts or the TASA narrative texts.

A skeptical colleague might wonder why one needs a computer to analyse the extent to which these texts from *Einstein's Dreams* are more similar to the narrative versus the science genres. Why would it not be sufficient to ask literary experts to make such judgments? We would have three replies to the skeptic. One reply is that experts often disagree in their judgments, whereas a computer analysis would provide some objective foundation for resolving such disagreements. A second reply is that many texts are hybrid genres, a mixture of more than one genre. When texts with such mixed genres occur, it is reasonable to consider a large number of metrics or criteria so the scholar can explore the different ways that a text is in one genre or the other. A third reply is that the automated analyses allow the researchers to consider large corpora of texts in their assessments. An assessment of hundreds of texts would take too long and test the patience of most scholars.

---

[33] Ibid.

Results

Are the Einstein's Dreams Chapters More Like Science or Narrative?

One of the foundational research questions in discourse processes is how the language and discourse characteristics differ among texts in different genres, conversational registers, or other theoretical schemes for text classification.[34][35] Researchers from different fields do not agree on what the ideal categories or dimensions should be, but example contrasts are made between narrative and informational texts, oral versus print, socially interactive versus decontextualized texts, and so on. From the standpoint of the present study, we make the contrast between narrative texts and science texts.

Table 1 presents the results of the Coh-Metrix analyses that were performed on the ED texts, science texts, and narrative texts. The Coh-Metrix indices are segregated into the word-level measures, syntax, referential and semantic cohesion, and situation model dimensions. The Einstein column lists mean values of the indices, averaging over the 10 chapters sampled from the book. The TASA science and narrative texts have columns for means and standard deviations, based on the sample of 100 texts from each genre. Given the sample size of 100 for the TASA texts, one can derive the 95% confidence intervals for assessing whether a particular score is outside of the range of the mean, given an alpha level of .05. The general formula would be Mean ± [1.96 * SD / SQRT(100)]. For example, the mean number of negations for narrative is 9.6 and the standard deviation (SD) is 7.2. The 95% confidence interval would be 9.6 ± 1.4. That is, scores between 8.2 and 11.0 are not significantly different than the mean of 9.6. The mean negation score for science texts is only 6.3, which is clearly outside of the range for narrative texts. Therefore we would conclude that science texts have a lower incidence of negations (per 1000 words) than do narrative texts. Moreover, the fact that the mean number of negations for the Einstein's Dreams texts is 14.1 would indicate that (a) the samples from this text are more like narrative texts than science texts and (b) there is an unusually high number of negations in the ED text. Negations are comparatively difficult for humans to process, which perhaps partly explains why ED is challenging for even college students.

---

[34] Biber (1988).
[35] Louwerse et al. (2004).

There is a column in Table 1 filled with the letters *N, S, n,* and *s.* The capital N signifies that the ED texts are more like narrative than science texts, whereas S signifies the ED are more like science texts. The small letters indicate that the ED texts are in between the narrative to science continuum, but the ED scores lean toward one of the two. This cell was left blank for logical connectives and NP incidence because these scores were nearly the same for science and narrative texts. As can be seen, the number of measures in the narrative direction outscores that of science 20 to 9. However, the results are hardly uniform across measures. At this point we will turn to interpreting the results presented in Table 1.

Table 1: Coh-Metrix Analysis of Einstein's Dreams

	Einstein		Science 7th-M	7th-SD	Narrative 7th-M	7th-SD
WORD LEVEL						
Logarithm of frequency of content words	2.278	N	2.239	0.154	2.272	0.145
Concreteness content words	410.0	S	414.8	32.4	397.6	32.6
Noun concreteness in hierarchy (hypernym)	4.980	S	4.862	0.502	5.279	0.514
Verb concreteness in hierarchy (hypernym)	1.480	N	1.424	0.189	1.492	0.194
All connectives	66.8	S	69.7	19.4	79.0	19.4
Additive connectives	37.3	S	36.4		46.1	
Temporal connectives	11.6	N	9.1		12.6	
Causal connectives	10.1	N	25.1		22.5	
Logical connectives	29.8		30.8		31.0	
Negations	14.1	N	6.3	6.4	9.5	7.2
Personal pronouns	67.8	s	43.4	26.9	95.2	33.9
Pronoun ratio per noun-phrase	0.236	s	0.154	0.097	0.339	0.118
SYNTAX						
NP incidence	288.0		283.6	23.2	280.8	17.8
Modifiers per NP	0.814	N	0.909	0.180	0.795	0.139

82   Automatic Analyses of Language, Discourse, and Situation Models

Higher level constituents per word	0.732	n	0.719	0.041	0.744	0.035
Words before main verb of main clause	4.199	N	3.820	1.119	3.931	1.518
Syntactic structure similarity adjacent	0.147	S	0.152	0.041	0.093	0.030
REFERENTIAL AND SEMANTIC COHESION						
Adjacent argument overlap	0.423	N	0.632	0.167	0.492	0.206
Global Argument overlap	0.260	n	0.442	0.159	0.422	0.180
Adjacent stem overlap	0.263	N	0.616	0.179	0.244	0.184
Global stem overlap	0.171	N	0.427	0.169	0.213	0.126
Content word overlap	0.093	N	0.154	0.058	0.085	0.043
LSA sentence adjacent	0.116	N	0.425	0.112	0.283	0.093
LSA sentence all	0.090	N	0.324	0.110	0.248	0.087
Type-token ratio	0.723	S	0.657	0.091	0.822	0.063
SITUATION MODEL DIMENSIONS						
Causal content	34.4	N	52.0	18.4	30.5	12.1
Causal cohesion	2.140	N	1.208	1.153	3.048	2.422
Intentional content	19.6	N	13.3	10.3	18.5	9.0
Intentional cohesion	1.110	N	2.372	2.299	1.314	1.212
Temporal cohesion	0.860	N	0.837	0.090	0.847	0.089
Spatial cohesion	0.445	S	0.466	0.094	0.485	0.073

1. Word-level indices. The content words in narrative have significantly higher word frequencies than those in science texts, whereas the ED texts are similar to narrative. The measures of concreteness are a bit inconsistent. The concreteness values of content words (second row in Table 1) are based on human ratings from the MRC corpus that has only a few thousand words.[36] In contrast, noun and verb concreteness (third and

---

[36] Coltheart (1981).

fourth row) was based on over 100,000 words in Wordnet[37]; more concrete words have higher *hypernym* counts, which consist of superordinate levels in a semantic hierarchy. The latter indices of concreteness showed an expected trend of narrative texts being more concrete than science. That being said, ED texts are more like narrative with respect to verbs and more like science with respect to nouns. Word frequency and concreteness are interesting characteristics of individual words, but they have little or no relevance to cohesion or coherence.

A mixed picture emerges when considering connectives that link constituents in the texts. The incidence of connectives is higher for narrative than science texts. When the categories of connectives are segregated according to classifications introduced by Halliday and Hasan (1976)[38], there are more additive and temporal connectives in narrative, but causal connectives are a bit higher in science and logical connectives are about the same in the two genres. The ED texts are similar to narrative texts with respect to temporal and causal connectives, but to science texts with respect to additive connectives.

As expected, pronouns are approximately twice as prevalent in narrative text than in science text. The pronoun incidence in ED texts is more similar to science than narrative texts. Alan Lightman apparently was more specific in grounding the entities in his microworlds with nouns rather than using pronouns. Pronouns are, of course, a threat to cohesion and coherence to the extent that readers have trouble inferring the referents of the pronouns. This is one sense that Lightman wrote more like a scientist than a novelist.

2. Syntax. The syntactic composition of sentences systematically differs for science and narrative texts. Science texts have more dense noun-phrases (i.e. more modifiers per noun-phrase) whereas narrative texts have more words before the main verb of the main clause (i.e. a greater load on working memory) and have more higher-level constituents per word. The complexity of the syntactic constructions in ED texts was uniformly more similar to narrative texts than expository texts. In contrast, the syntactic similarity between adjacent sentences was higher for science than narrative texts. Apparently, there is more diversity in syntactic composition among sentences in narrative than science and the ED texts were closer to the science texts.

---

[37] Fellbaum (1998).
[38] Halliday and Hasan (1976).

3. **Referential and semantic cohesion.** The type-token index of lexical diversity shows higher scores for narrative than science texts. Therefore, there is more redundancy and cohesion among the content words in the latter. Indeed, all measures of referential and semantic cohesion were higher, and typically substantially higher, for science texts than narrative texts: adjacent and global argument overlap, stem overlap, content word overlap, and LSA sentence similarity. Whereas the ED texts were most similar to science texts on type-token ration, they were most similar to narrative texts on all other measures of referential and semantic cohesion. Clearly, there is no simple generalization to be gleaned from these results.

4. **Situation model dimensions.** The four dimensions of the situation model are causality, intentionality, temporality, and spatiality.[39] [40] Narrative texts have more intentional content with animate beings performing actions in pursuit of goals. In contrast, material causality is affiliated with science texts more than narrative texts. With regard to cohesion (which is different than the amount of content), the pattern of causal cohesion shows higher cohesion (i.e. a ratio of causal particles to events) in narrative texts than science texts, whereas science texts had higher intentional cohesion scores. Thus, the measures of amount of content are clearly different, in this case the opposite, of the amount of cohesion. For all of these scores, as well as the temporal cohesion scores, the ED texts were more similar to narrative than expository texts. The one exception is for spatial cohesion: on this ED shows the lowest score of all. It appears that the situation model content, cohesion, and coherence in ED texts is more akin to narrative than science texts, except for the spatial dimension. There is no obvious reason why the spatial dimension would differ from the other dimensions of the situation model.

Discussion

One might ask how the above analyses present new beginnings for the study of literature? Perhaps the best answer to this question is that it is unlikely that a traditional stylistic analysis of Alan Lightman's novel would have revealed, in so much detail, what was revealed in the Coh-Metrix analyses. We discovered that Alan Lightman tended to write more like a novelist than a scientist in terms of the concreteness of verbs,

---

[39] Zwaan et al. (1995).
[40] Zwaan and Radvansky (1998).

syntax, referential cohesion, semantic cohesion, temporal and causal connectives, and with respect to most dimensions of the situation model. In contrast, the language of science is more prominent in the novel when examining spatial cohesion, type-token ratio, syntactic similarity between adjacent sentences, additive connectives, pronouns, and the concreteness of nouns. Therefore, there is no simple answer to the question of whether *Einstein's Dreams* is more similar to science than narrative texts. The genre appears to be a hybrid between narrative and science. The results are hardly elegant, which is refreshing for the scholars who are inspired by complexity but somewhat bewildering for those who desire simple conclusions.

We are currently developing a number of other measures of cohesion, but have not yet analysed these sufficiently to release them to the public. For example, we are in the process of developing indices on genre uniformity, the ease of identifying topic sentences in paragraphs, and on given-new information contrasts. One of the most influential analyses of genre has been that of Biber (1988), who used a factor analysis to classify a large corpus of texts on the basis of 67 features of language and discourse. We have automated nearly all of these features so that Coh-Metrix can compute the extent to which a text fits different genres (such as narrative, science, versus history texts). However, Coh-Metrix incorporates many other characteristics of text and other algorithms that Biber never considered when he performed his analysis of genre nearly 20 years ago. Each genre has an associated diagnostic set of connectives, discourse markers, and other signalling devices. Statistical analyses identify the features that diagnostically predict whether text T is in genre/class G. Texts can subsequently be scaled on global genre cohesion in two ways. First, a text has higher genre cohesion when it cleanly fits into one prototypical genre/class G. Second, there is higher global cohesion when there is a higher density of diagnostic features associated with the dominant genre/class G.

Another analysis contrasts *new* from *given* information by segregating constituents that are introduced for the first time in the text from references to previous text constituents.[41] Previous analytical treatments of the given-new distinction have been compositional and symbolic, whereas we have explored LSA-based algorithms[42] to segregate *new* versus *given* information automatically as sentences are comprehended, one by one.

---

[41] Prince (1981).
[42] Hempelmann et al. (2005).

This chapter provides only a glimpse of the analyses that can be conducted on texts with Coh-Metrix. There is an open frontier of questions to explore now that Coh-Metrix and other computer systems can automatically and quickly analyse large corpora. We encourage our colleagues to google Coh-Metrix and use this tool in their research. However, we also warn the reader that the results may not be as simple and clear-cut as our theories and intuitions.

Acknowledgements

The research on this chapter was supported by the Institute of Education Sciences (IES R305G020018-02). Any opinions, findings, and conclusions or recommendations expressed in this material are those of the authors and do not necessarily reflect the views of IES. Requests for reprints should be sent to Art Graesser, Department of Psychology, 202 Psychology Building, University of Memphis, Memphis, TN 38152-3230.

Works Cited

Baayen, R. H., R. Piepenbrock, and H. van Rijn, eds. 1993. *The CELEX Lexical Database* (CD-ROM). University of Pennsylvania, Philadelphia (PA): Linguistic Data Consortium.

Biber, D. *Variations across speech and writing.* 1988. Cambridge, MA: Cambridge University Press.

Biber, D., S. Conrad, and R. Reppen. 1998. *Corpus linguistics: Investigating language structure and use.* Cambridge: Cambridge University Press.

Brill, E. 1995. Transformation-based error-driven learning and natural language processing: A case study in part-of-speech tagging. *Computational Linguistics* 21: 543-66.

Charniak, E. 2000. A maximum-entropy-inspired parser. In *Proceedings of the First Conference on North American Chapter of the Association For Computational Linguistics.* San Francisco. CA: Morgan Kaufmann Publishers: 132-139.

Coltheart, M. 1981. The MRC psycholinguistic database quarterly. *Journal of Experimental Psychology* 33A: 497-505.

Fellbaum, C, ed. 1998. *WordNet: An electronic lexical database.* Cambridge, MA: MIT Press.

Graesser, A. C., Z. Cai, M. M. Louwerse, and F. Daniel. 2006. Question Understanding Aid (QUAID): A web facility that helps survey methodologists improve the comprehensibility of questions. *Public Opinion Quarterly* 70: 3-22.

Graesser, A.C., M. A. Gernsbacher, and S. Goldman, eds. 2003. *Handbook of discourse processes*. Mahwah, NJ: Erlbaum.

Graesser, A. C., M. A. Kassler, R. J. Kreuz, and B. McLain-Allen. 1998. Verification of statements about story worlds that deviate from normal conceptions of time: What is true about Einstein's Dreams? *Cognitive Psychology* 35: 246-301.

Graesser, A. C., D. S. McNamara, and M. M. Louwerse. 2003. What do readers need to learn in order to process coherence relations in narrative and expository text? In *Rethinking reading comprehension*, edited by A. P. Sweet and C. E. Snow, 82-98. New York: Guilford Publications.

Graesser, A. C., D. S. McNamara, M. M. Louwerse, and Z. Cai. 2004. Coh-Metrix: Analysis of text on cohesion and language. *Behavior Research Methods, Instruments, and Computers* 36: 193-202.

Graesser, A. C., M. Singer, and T. Trabasso. 1994. Constructing inferences during narrative text comprehension. *Psychological Review* 101: 371-95.

Halliday, M. A. K., and Hasan, R. 1976. *Cohesion in English*. London : Longman.

Hempelmann, C. F., D. Dufty, P. McCarthy, A. C. Graesser, Z. Cai, and D. S. McNamara. 2005. Using LSA to automatically identify givenness and newness of noun-phrases in written discourse. In *Proceedings of the 27th Annual Meetings of the Cognitive Science Society*, edited by B. G. Bara, L. Barsalou, and M. Bucciarelli, 941-946. Mahwah, NJ: Erlbaum.

Jurafsky, D., and Martin, J.H. 2000. *Speech and language processing: An introduction to natural language processing, computational linguistics, and speech recognition*. Upper Saddle River, NJ: Prentice-Hall.

Kintsch, W. 1998. *Comprehension: A paradigm for cognition*. Cambridge: Cambridge University Press.

Kintsch, W., and T. A.Van Dijk. 1978. Toward a model of text comprehension and production. *Psychological Review* 85: 363-94.

Klare, G. R. 1974-75. Assessing readability. *Reading Research Quarterly* 10: 62-102.

Landauer, T. K., P. W. Foltz, and D. Laham. 1998. An introduction to latent semantic analysis. *Discourse Processes* 25: 259-84.

Landauer, T., D. McNamara, S. Dennis, and W. Kintsch, eds. 2007. *Handbook of Latent Semantic Analysis.* Mahwah, NJ: Erlbaum.

Lappin, S., and H. J. Leass. 1994. An algorithm for pronominal coreference resolution. *Computational Linguistics* 20: 535-61.

Lenat, D. B. 1995. CYC: A large-scale investment in knowledge infrastructure. *Communications of the ACM* 38: 33-8.

Lightman, A. P. 1993. *Einstein's Dreams.* New York, NY: Random House, Inc.

Louwerse, M. M. 2002. An analytic and cognitive parameterization of coherence relations. *Computational Linguistics*: 291–315.

Louwerse, M. M., P. M. McCarthy, D. S. McNamara, and A. C. Graesser. 2004. Variation in language and cohesion across written and spoken registers. In *Proceedings of the 26th Annual Conference of the Cognitive Science Society*, edited by K.D. Forbus, D. Gentner, and T. Regier, 843-848. Mahwah, NJ: Erlbaum.

McNamara, D. S., M. M. Louwerse, and A. C. Graesser. 2002. *Coh-Metrix: Automated cohesion and coherence scores to predict text readability and facilitate comprehension.* Institute for Intelligent Systems, University of Memphis, Memphis, TN.

Mitkov, R. 1998. Robust pronoun resolution with limited knowledge." In *Proceedings of the 18th International Conference on Computational Linguistics*. EDITOR, 869-875. Montreal, Canada: PUBLISHER.

Pennebaker, J.W., and M. E. Francis. 1999. *Linguistic inquiry and word count (LIWC).* Mahwah, NJ: Erlbaum.

Prince, E. 1981. Towards a taxonomy of given-new information. In *Radical Pragmatics*, edited by P. Cole. New York: Academic Press: 223-256.

Sanders, T. J. M., W. P. M. Spooren, and L. G. M. Noordman. 1992. Toward a taxonomy of coherence relations. *Discourse Processes* 15: 1-35.

Templin, M. C. 1957. *Certain language skills in children, their development and interrelationships.* Minneapolis, MN: University of Minnesota Press.

Zwaan, R. A., and G. A. Radvansky. 1998. Situation models in language comprehension and memory. *Psychological Bulletin* 123: 162-85.

Zwaan, R. A., M. C. Langston, and A. C. Graesser. 1995. The construction of situation models in narrative comprehension: An event-indexing model. *Psychological Science* 6: 292-97.

CHAPTER FOUR

DISCOVERING FRANTEXT

VÉRONIQUE MONTÉMONT

Abstract

Developed by the ATILF-CNRS research unit in Nancy (France), Frantext is emphatically the most important literary data-base in the francophone world (the word "literary" being here understood in its widest sense so as to include, for instance, a number of philosophical works).

This paper shall trace the history of the data-base, address its contents, and discuss some of the difficulties pertaining to the assessment of results. Indeed, once the data has been collected, it must be ascribed a meaning and placed within a referential framework. For these tasks to be conducted optimally, relevance thresholds require to be formulated and the results compared to those reached on account of searches through other bodies of texts.

Frantext's highly sophisticated research tool offers a unique capability in that it features "grammars", or combinations of search functions. These can be used to identify complex semantic units, such as numbers, or to delineate with ease a precise network of words within a sizeable body of texts. From a narrative standpoint, the results make it possible to underline the aesthetic or symbolic value of given recurrences or, contrariwise, of certain omissions.

Given the fascinating heuristic perspectives uncovered by Frantext, its development is operating apace. The aim of Frantext is to continue to expand the body of texts on offer and to provide ever-more ergonomic and high-performance research tools for the academic community. In this way, Frantext can contribute significantly to the valorization of the empirical approach that statistical studies makes possible in the literary field.

0. Digital databases

Nowadays, thanks to the development of digital networks and easy access to internet, the use of digital corpora has become commonplace. Several national libraries have already acquired digital collections or plan to adopt them soon. In France, for example, the Gallica database managed by the French National Library includes more than 90,000 references. In England, the British Library offers online access to a site called "Treasures in full"[1], where one can read manuscripts of famous English works, including Shakespeare's dramas.

Forty years ago, such gigantic projects of mass digitization were still in the realm of utopia. The Gutenberg Project, launched by Michael Hart in 1971, is a pioneer in the field of digital databases; it contains now more than 19,000 books in several languages. But it still relies on the scanning of texts by volunteers, and it sometimes encounters copyright conflicts, owing to quite restrictive clauses in American and European law. Furthermore, its possible growth has been restricted for a long time by technical limits which mean it took almost 40 years to gather the base which exists today.

The democratization of the internet radically changed the situation: technical progress, including ADSL lines and high-performing OCR tools allow us now to digitize many books and even to download a complete work in a few seconds. New possibilities appeared when Google announced on December 14, 2004 its "Google Print Libraries Project," which aims to digitize 15 million books from the libraries of major American universities. During the months following this announcement, search engines such as Yahoo! and online booksellers such as Amazon.com announced that they planned to offer free access as well to entire book chapters. This hegemonic attempt, considered by publishers and authors as a copyright violation and therefore a direct economic threat, also triggered an immediate counter-attack through the impetus of Jean-Noël Jeanneney, the director of the French National Library (Jeanneney 2005, 7 ff). Several major European libraries decided to work together to launch the TEL project, which is now under debate by the European Parliament.

Nevertheless, whether public or private, these projects suffer from the same defect. Most of the time texts have been digitized as images; in the Gallica database, less than 1% of the works are readable as plain text. This protects the source texts against massive copying, but it also prevents

---

[1] http://www.bl.uk/treasures/treasuresinfull.html

queries and textual searches. In other cases, for example in the Gutenberg Project, plain text downloading is actually possible. But since works are under copyright for 75 to 95 years (if published after 1923) in the U.S.A. and for 70 years in Europe, all recent books are excluded from free public databases. From a technical point of view, texts remain easily readable, but most of the time, systematic queries are reduced to the "search" function of a word processor or they require the downloading and installing of specific software. The files provide few indications about the edition used, and this can also hamper scientific research. Developing alternative systems with a scientific purpose while both respecting copyright laws and enabling complex queries remains, therefore, an essential objective.

The Frantext database created and developed in Nancy in 1984 (Bernet and Pierrel, forthcoming) may seem very limited in scope if we compare it with the huge systems mentioned above: it consists of "only" 3,800 French texts, but it includes several unique functions that set it apart. Although its corpus is varied and interesting[2], and its search engine is quite sophisticated, many literary researchers are reluctant to base their analyses on statistical data. Based on lists and scores, lexical statistics are, however, a reliable empirical way to study texts, since they provide at a glance information that an ordinary reading cannot: how many times words are used, which are the most frequently used, which grammatical categories (verbs, nouns, articles) or punctuation marks are the most frequent. The first prominent French research projects on lexical statistics, also called textual statistics, began in the eighties. Charles Muller (1964), who analysed Corneille's dramas from this new perspective, was the pioneer of this method. He was followed by Charles Bernet, whose essay on Racine's vocabulary was published in 1967, and by Etienne Brunet (1985, 1987), who carried out an analysis of Zola's and Proust's vocabulary. More recently, the "Hubert de Phalèse" collective made up of Henri Béhar's research group, has been publishing a yearly commented lexical index of the works studied each year for *agrégation* — the most famous French education competitive recruitment examination.

Those data can then be included in various interpretation charts, depending on the perspective chosen by the researcher: a result can validate a psychoanalytic reading as well as a stylistic one (Gicquel 1999).

---

[2] It is also the richest equipped with a search engine as far as French literature is concerned, and it remains far away from the Gutenberg Project French corpus. "The most important textual database [as French literature is concerned] is French. Its name is Frantext." [La plus grande base de données textuelles [pour les ressources françaises] du monde est française. Il s'agit de Frantext.] (Bernard 1999, 21)

Statistics obviously does not attempt to replace a deep knowledge of texts, but instead offers precise criteria to analyse their content and structure. The method allows comparisons based on lexical facts, and thus gives us the opportunity to substitute concrete observation to what can be sometimes perceived as former impressionistic intuitions, based more on individual sensivity than on a close examination of lexical data. Henri Béhar stresses the fact that in some thematic reading cases, "authors do not share the same vision of what thematics is and have no stable linguistic ground on which to rest their argument" (Béhar 1996, 186)[3]. Even though it is but one method among others, and demands to be used in a larger theoretical interpretative system[4], let us consider how useful a statistical approach might be in an academic field, i.e. literature, even if these methods have been and occasionally still are considered suspiciously by researchers as far as their scientific adequacy with respect to the literary object they claim to analyse?[5]

In order to demonstrate this, I will first summarize the history of the Frantext database before explaining how to use it for research. I will then examine conditions that must be met to make sense of the results, followed by some of the methodological perspectives.

1. Frantext: a Short History

Frantext is a database which has its own search engine, Stella (Bernet and Pierrel, to be published). Today it includes 3,773 texts, comprising about 210 million words and a thousand authors. 80% of its digitized

---

[3] The fact can be observed in Jean-Pierre Richard's or, more recently, Jean-Michel Maulpoix's works, whose are highly receptive to texts aesthetics features and whose style, almost empathic, prominently involves reader's sensivity.

[4] We would like to emphasize that we do not consider statistics a «pure» way of access to meaning. On the contrary, it always involves references to history, sociology, psychoanalysis, stylistic or biographical observations in order to provide a relevant reading.

[5] Some works of lexical or textual statistics, even recent, often begin by recalling the historical strong opposition, sometimes still vivid, between a sensitive reading and another based on quantified datas. Christian Baudelot (1994) stresses the prejudice according to which statistical reading might be "sacrilegious". Michel Bernard (1999, 8) depicts a statistic method considered as an "alien invader in the field of literature". Bernard Gicquel (1999) also insists on the opposition often raised between stylistics and statistics, described as two "discrepant approaches". Last, Henri Béhar (1996) uses the *golem*'s metaphor to describe computer and insists on "formidable misunderstandings" that computer specialists and literary criticits had to overcome.

works are literary texts, 20% are either scientific or technical. A great number of these texts belong to 19th and 20th century literature (which make about 67% of the corpus). From an historical point of view, this collection, before being officially a *database*, was at first proposed to provide examples for a huge dictionary, the *Trésor de la langue française*. This series of 17 volumes defines about 100,000 words chosen in such a way as to present a nearly exhaustive view of the French language in the 20th century. To meet these objectives, literary and technical texts have been digitized in order to constitute a database from which quotations were excerpted and used to enrich definition.

When the project was launched at the beginning of the sixties, using computers to write a dictionary was seen as a genuinely original approach: epistemologically, a connection can be made with cybernetics and structuralism, which both were in vogue at the time (Dosse 1992). Once the dictionary was successfully completed, a decision had to be made about the data. Since the collection formed one of the richest resources of digitized French literature, it would have been wasteful to give it up. That is why in 1984 Jacques Dendien, the computer engineer who conceived the system, wrote a performing search engine called Stella (Dendien 1986). Thanks to this tool, a researcher can immediately find an element in a work or in a corpus; it takes a few seconds to get a result even if 3,000 thousands works are queried at the same time.

The database was given the name "Frantext"; however, it was not available online and could not be used outside the laboratory. In 1992, the Internet gave a new life to Frantext by enabling researchers to access it through web subscription. Many subscribers are foreign libraries; others are strictly obliged to vouch that they are students or researchers. Though everyone agrees on the usefulness of a widely opened database, we have to be aware that several hundred of the offered texts are still under copyright, which explains that none of them is readable online; however, after discussions with publishers, consulting short extracts online is possible in order to see one or several words in their original context. 500 copy free texts are downloadable on the CNRTL (Centre National de Ressources Textuelles et Lexicales) site[6], also developed by the ATILF team since spring 2006.

---

[6] www.cnrtl.fr.

2. Database Contents

Before talking about the specific issues of research done with Frantext, let us first see how it works and what exactly it enables us to do. Since the database is managed by the CNRS (National Center for Scientific Research), the selection of texts depends on scientific criteria as well as on linguistic or literary points of view. The nucleus comes from a thousand texts considered as the most representative of French literature and chosen among various genres and different periods: poetry, novels, drama, memoirs. More than half of them have been published in the 20th century. The base has been progressively enriched with non-literary texts, including, for example, cookbooks or sportscasters' memories, and new corpora, sometimes linked to contemporary or current events, are regularly added: Goncourt prize winners, the annual series of works to be studied for the *agrégation*, or complete works celebrating anniversaries such as Victor Hugo's complete works entered in the 2002 Frantext to celebrate the bicentennial of his birth.

When the decision is made to enter a new work in Frantext, the best edition of a text, i.e., the most reliable from a academic point a view, is selected and then digitized by two OCR programs running concurrently. Remaining errors after comparison of both versions are so rare that the outcome is nearly perfect: the error rate is lower than in the French Gallimard's collection "La Pléiade", considered as the ultimate reference for French literary texts.

Texts, as far as the most recently entered are concerned, are then marked up in XML, which permits the keeping of typographic characteristics such as bold text, italics, or underlining, while identifying proper nouns and foreign language words, in Latin, for instance. Most texts follow the TEI (Text Encoding Initiative) in order to be able to exchange eventual files in partnership with other online libraries that are readable on any system.

The text is then installed in the database. Several pieces of information are entered at this time, including the author's name, the title, the first date of publication, the publisher, the name of the editor if known, and the literary genre. This issue is one the most debatable ones and calls for periodic redefinition, in so far as literary genres, their standards and designations may vary. That will lead us to introduce new describers in Frantext such as "autofiction" (Schaeffer 2001, 11) and to open a new interface equipped with Boolean operators. Thanks to these various adaptations, the text is now ready to be queried with the search engine Stella.

3. How to Choose a Corpus and Sort the Vocabulary

When users access Frantext, the first step consists in choosing a corpus.[7] One may select only one author or only one book, but can also submit queries by genre, date, or period. For instance, to compare stylistic features, it is possible to create a corpus of eighteenth century dramas or to conduct a search on French novels written between 1950 and 1970. Grammatical categorization, which consists in sorting vocabulary items according to grammatical type (nouns, verbs, adjectives) also permits to observe relevant syntactic features or to see which class predominates. This kind of grouping is especially useful when the objective is a thematic study. The possibility of selecting a cohesive corpus makes both diachronic and synchronic inquiries possible, and allows for a historical or sociological perspective. For instance, by seeking the occurrences of the word "photography", we may see how this new medium progressively took its place in XXth century culture; or, by gathering occurrences of "écrire son journal" ("writing one's diary"), we may observe when this social practice appeared in literature and how it was considered by authors throughout the centuries (Montémont 2008, Brunet 1993).

Another interesting function is the ability to analyse vocabulary. A single operation can extract and sort the entire vocabulary used in a book or in a corpus, as well as count how many times each form has been used. The list can be classified according to its increasing or decreasing rate or by alphabetical order. This function can be useful for quantifying a corpus by locating the terms most often used (with high frequency) as well as those rarely used, or even genuinely rare (hapax).

In 2006 an ATILF team started a Georges Perec[8] dictionary project: the first step of our work consisted in listing the vocabulary of a corpus of eight books, in order to identify which words are most or least frequently used. Since in French polysemic words are quite frequent, we also use the base to display the word in its context (up to 350 characters) in order to

---

[7] "The first thing to be made before conducting a research is to constitute a corpus." ["La sélection d'un corpus de travail est l'étape préalable à toute recherche"], (Bernet and Kahn 2007) The *Centre d'ingénierie documentaire* of ENS-LSH (Lyon, France) offers 7 comprehensive tutorials online, explaining how to use Frantext and its various functions.

[8] Georges Perec: French writer, born in 1936, died in 1982. Perec was an Oulipian writer and used strong constraints to compose his books: *La Disparition* (1969) is written without using *e*, the most frequently used letter in French. He also wrote *Les Choses* (1965) and *La Vie Mode d'emploi* (1978), a huge novel built according to a building's plan, which tells the story of each flat and of each of its tenants.

distinguish its ambiguous meanings. Let us take the example of the word *canapé*: in French, it refers to a kind of *sofa*, but it also means a piece of bread garnished with various foods. This distinction can be crucial in an article dedicated by Perec to *seats*; it led us to discover that *canapé* (= seat), with its 21 occurrences, is clearly less frequently employed than *couch* (46 occurrences) and *sofa* (7 occurrences), although these words are nearly synonymous. This can be explained by Perec's deep interest in psychoanalysis: the "vastes divans, capitonnés de cuir marron" (Perec 1995, 134) sounds like a very Freudian description...Without this quantified comparison, the peculiar focus on this word would have remained hidden, and the results corroborate the theory of encrypted themes developed by Bernard Magné (Magné 1999, 23). The dictionary definition will take this dimension into account, pointing out the specific distribution of synonymy, and in this case emphasizing the way in which the biographical pattern enriches a word's semantic content. Considering that we are about to treat 2,500 words, many of which present similar problems, it is easy to understand how useful these quick displays of excerpts can be, especially since they refer to a precise edition and even to a precise page, which allows a researcher to go back to the printed text and its larger context if needed.

4. How to Evaluate a Score?

From a general point of view, any query always returns a result. But the result is only a digit, and despite its scientific aspect, we must be aware that it is the researcher's task to bring out its meaning. Various scholars, grounding their research on lexical statistics, agree on this point: data must always be interpreted in their context. What is more, each result requires a critical examination of the basis used to extract it, and requires the selection of a parallel corpus to offer points of comparison. A great range of approaches and methods now exists: frequency range (Lebart et Salem), Zipf's law, binomial law, Brunet's "W index" (Cossette 1994). Each of them has its own qualities and limitations, the main point being, as far as methodology is concerned, the ability to elaborate a protocol, to explain it, and to strictly maintain it as the research proceeds.

To achieve this purpose, a result always requires comparison with other scores in the list of vocabulary. Our way to determine its level of relevance is to examine the list sorted by decreasing order starting from the beginning. It is easy to notice that the most frequently used words are auxiliary words: determiners, auxiliary verbs, as well as coordination and subordination conjunctions. In a semantic approach of vocabulary though, they are less useful than adjetives, nouns or verbs. This is the reason why we look for the first adjective, verb, noun or adverb of the list conveying a semantic stronger content: this leads us to exclude prepositions, conjunctions, and, depending on cases, some verbs as "dire" when a novel contains many dialogues. One word is chosen to mark the threshold between the relevant / irrelevant zone. Then, we add scores of each word located in the irrelevant zone, and deduce the sum from the total numbers of lemmas. The rest is divided by tens, and constitutes lexical areas numbered from 10 (the highest score) to 1 (the lowest score). If a word is located in area 10 or 9, it can be assumed it is *often* employed by the author and it particularly deserves our attention. For example, a novel by Marguerite Duras entitled *Un Barrage contre le Pacifique* (Duras 2003*)* is made of 4,788 discrete lexical units. Area 10 registers many words such as *voir* (*to see*, 305 occurrences)*, regarder* (*to look at*, 201), *yeux* (*eyes*, 91), that demonstrate how important the visual dimension is for Duras, who is also a film-maker. In area 10 the important lexical field of money is also shown to be an essential topic in a novel where characters live in great poverty: *argent* (money), *diamant* (*diamond*), *francs*. Duras' book is a violent pamphlet against the colonial upper-class and she depicts her family as being as poor as the Indochinese people they live with. The vocabulary list shows how obsessive this dimension becomes and thus provides elements for a political reading of the book.

5. Lists and proximity searches

A reader can also carry out an investigation on an entire isotopy, or group of words relating to the same topic, thanks to the "list" function. For example, in the work of Marguerite Duras quoted above, the theme of alcohol is also crucial. It appears in the text through an especially rich vocabulary: *alcohol, drunken, wine, bottle, whisky, cognac*, etc. It is possible to make a query for each of these words, but Frantext offers a more efficient procedure. First, various words are entered in a list called "alcohol". Then, with a single query, written **&+l+alcohol**[9], all the elements are found and ordered in a file. The query nevertheless does not include lemmatised forms and the user should enter each form (for example singular and plural) of a word before saving the list, or separate the queries word by word and use **&m / &c** to obtain a lemmatised score. This explains that the "list" function is easier to apply to substantives and adjectives than to verbs; if needed, a complex sequence gathering various

---

[9] & = query function, l = list.

forms of substantives and verbs can be elaborated with a "grammar" (see below). One can also make a proximity search, which aims to show how some words are systematically associated with others. A word called the "pivot" and a threshold of proximity are defined by a digit between 1 and 300. By using the list function and the **&m / &c key**, a pivot considered as a lemmatized element can be searched under its various forms. The lower the threshold, the more significant the search results. Let us again consider the example of the verb *to drink* in Duras' novel: as *drink* can take a direct object, we will define a proximity threshold of 3 (article / + adjective / + noun), to find out which beverages characters drink. Few occurrences of *tea, water* and *milk* can be observed. Instead, most of the vocabulary concerns other beverages: *wine, wormwood, alcohol, champagne, demi* (beer glass), *cognac, rum,* and *whisky*. Thus we can deduce a clear prevalence of the lexical network of alcohol and focus on the psychological and social dimension attached to these substances: for example, cognac and champagne are drunk by the protagonists, who are extremely poor, only when they are the guests of the colonial upper-class.

6. Writing a "Grammar"

The most attractive function offered by Frantext is without doubt its grammars. The word "grammar" here is given a specific meaning: it is the name chosen to describe a sequence of research functions running together. They enable the user to precisely locate some complex sequences or several elements at the same time in a text. For example, this researcher had to carry out a study about the role played by numbers in the work of Jacques Roubaud, a French writer who is also a mathematician. The first thing to know was how many times the author mentioned numbers. But the corpus under consideration consisted of five works, a total of 2,000 pages, that prevented listing occurrences manually. This kind of result is difficult to get, since there are several ways of writing a number: either in Arabic or in Roman numerals, either in digits or in words. On a lower level, the number can be broken up into a series of digits or words, with or without hyphens: *trente-trois, cent vingt-sept*. The most efficient way to solve the problem and to get a result while adding various expressions of number consists in combining them. First, various elements have to be put in identifiable groups to get a "rule", which describes each element searched. For example, the rule "Arabic_numerals" gathers all digits from 0 to 9 ("|" means *or*)

Véronique Montémont 99

Arabic_numerals:
0|1|2|3|4|5|6|7|8|9

Other rules describe textual ways to write a number:

single_cardinal_numbers:
deux|trois|quatre|cinq|six|sept|huit|neuf|dix|onze|douze|treize|quatorze|quinze|
seize|vingt|vingts|trente|quarante|cinquante|soixante|cent|cents|mille|million|millions|milliard|milliards

Then we need to specify which combinations may be relevant: by adding others rules, we can seek not only single digits but also two-, three-, or four-digit numbers. In Roubaud's cycle entitled *Le Grand Incendie de Londres*[10], the query returned 6,744 results, which represent approximately 3 occurrences per page. Compared to seven other authors, two of them, Perec and Queneau, belonging to "Oulipo", the same literary group as Roubaud, one can see that numbers represent 1.2% of the total vocabulary. This score is inferior to that of Perec, who had incorporated numbers as a constraint in his famous novel *La vie mode d'emploi* (2.6%), but it is really close the score obtained by the mathematician Henri Poincaré (1.4%)! On the one hand, this strongly suggests that numbers and their properties are indeed close to an obsession in Roubaud's work. One the other hand, thanks to frequencies indexes, it highlights the most frequently used words so that it is then possible to focus on some of them, since they appear to play a major symbolic role, and have some mathematical properties.

Let's see in which context those numbers appear: 6 and 12, for instance, are respectively a "perfect" and an "abundant" number following arithmetic tradition, and they are the basis of the alexandrine structure, precisely because of these combinatorial properties. So they are given by Roubaud as keys for the occidental poetic tradition. Given that each of them appears more than 130 times, Frantext may help us to sort the cases where numbers play their ordinary role, measuring time or counting things ("six months", "six hours", "six levels") and those where numbers become a metatextual and metapoetic topic. For this purpose it is relevant to seek, among the 6,744 extracts, those including an article, indicating that the number is the object of a commentary:"le 6", "le 12" : "le 6 a sa place

---

[10] Roubaud, J. *Le grand incendie de Londres* (Paris: Le Seuil, 1989), *La Boucle* (Paris: Le Seuil, 1993), *Mathématique:* (Paris: Le Seuil, 1997), *Poésie:* (Paris: Le Seuil, 2000), *La Bibliothèque de Warburg* (Paris: Le Seuil, 2002)

parce que c'est le nombre de la sextine"[11] ("six has its place because it's the sestina's figure"); "le 12 a un sens dans mon grand registre de nombres, qui lui vient de l'alexandrin" ("twelve has a meaning in my own major number list that comes from the alexandrine")[12]. These results allows us to deduce that numbers are not considered as tools but seen as giving access to the harmony of a secret world which poetry tries to mirror.

Thematic research concerning the body in the work of the French author Raymond Queneau's provided the opportunity to write another complex grammar. The lexical field concerning the body is a very rich one: body parts and organs present a large lexical repertoire. Moreover, is it enriched in Queneau's novels by the frequent use of slang or familiar language: *bavoter, merdouille, gambille, crachouiller*, words which the reader might not even find in the usual dictionaries at hand. The author pays much attention to forms used only within determined social groups, like *loucherbem* (Parisian butchers' slang). He often uses funny metaphors: "ne pas laisser rouiller ses dents"[13] ("not to let one's teeth rust" = to eat a lot). Moreover, Queneau developed his own style by using a 'phonetic' way of writing words: *douas* for *doigts* (fingers), *pouatrine* for *poitrine* (breast), *danlgosier* for *dans le gosier* (in the throat). His writing therefore includes many phonetic neologisms, which require a carefully written grammar. Several words, queried under their lemmatized forms, were not included in Frantext nomenclature and should be written exactly as they appear in the text: *pulmoneux*[14] (a neologism derived from *poumon*), *ronflotant* (*snoozing a little*).

At the same time this grammar permits one to seek more than 450 pre-determined lemmata in a corpus made up of 840,357 words: Frantext here provides a concrete track and gives a global overview of this lexical field. It represented more than 8,900 forms, which seems to be a major score. Since the result was so large, the grammar "body" was divided into six rules to increase its efficiency: organs, actions, excretions, eating and drinking, disease, asthma. Some rules, such as "excretions" or "eating and drinking", aimed to analyse more precisely how characters, often aggravated by poverty or hunger, fell prey to violent impulses. As far as excretion is concerned, words to describe organic matters are surprisingly varied. Queneau was indeed inspired by an ancient philosophical theory elaborated by Pierre Roux, who defines excretion as a kind of global

---

[11] Roubaud, J. *Le grand incendie de Londres*, 302.
[12] Roubaud, J. *Le grand incendie de Londres*, 189.
[13] Queneau, R., *Pierrot mon ami* (Paris; Gallimard, 1942), 93.
[14] Queneau, R., *Loin de Rueil* (Paris; Gallimard, [1944] "Folio", 2003), 20.

phenomena extended to earth and even to inanimate objects. (Queneau 2002) What is more, Queneau was deeply influenced by Freudian theory (Queneau 1996, Freud 1987, esp. chapter 21) – he himself underwent psychoanalysis – and he knew the prominent role of the anal-sadistic phase, which became a haunting theme in his writing. The same analysis could be carried out with respect to the lexical field of food and drink, which is also abundant; it could be related to Freud's oral phase, allowing a better understanding of why some characters act like ogres.

In such complex cases, Frantext allows us to write as many rules as needed in order to combine and even to factorize them, and even to seek through one single request form made from various elements (figures or words). By gathering so many lemmas and organizing them in thematic rules, grammars make ambitious research aims possible. But one of the major issues is the ability to propose an interpretive framework so as to assign meaning to the data collected.

7. Comparison corpora

The search engine enables the collection of untreated data such as words, lemmata, and digits. But in the case of literature, these data, which can be quantified and considered as discrete elements, for example, words or punctuation marks, make sense only if placed within a global system. It seems impossible to understand them fully without taking into account the sentence, which provides context and connotation, and more generally the language, with its own semiotic constraints. We must also pay attention to the relationship between the text and the reader, to cultural factors in the period in which the text was written, to personal or political context, and to linguistic evolution. That is why a raw list or a single score have no meaning of their own; the analyst needs more than isolated figures to construct a relevant interpretation.

If the research deals with a general theme and includes a diachronic dimension, the corpus may be chosen among a precise period and/or a precise genre. For example, a study of punctuation marks in French poetry at the beginning of the twentieth century will be based on poetry written between 1900 and 1920. This query results in 37 texts, among which we can note the presence of Apollinaire, who in 1912 published a collection of poems, *Alcools*, without punctuation marks. It is thus possible to consider the corpus as helpful for a global study of this topic.

Comparing corpora may instead be done by including contemporary writers so as to maintain some unity between texts from a linguistic point of view. For example, one may study the length of Claude Simon's sentences. Simon is a famous French author who won the Nobel Prize of Literature and is known as a member of a group called "*Le Nouveau Roman.*" His style is very peculiar, in that it includes long sentences and complex syntax but uses surprisingly few punctuation marks. One of the issues at stake is finding out whether the writer followed some contemporary fashion or whether this component of his style is idiosyncratic. The easiest way to determine this is to compare one of his novels, written in 1958, with those of his contemporaries over a period of ten years, such as Duras, Perec, Nathalie Sarraute and Alain Robbe-Grillet. The last two authors are particularly interesting because they belong to the same literary group as Claude Simon.

Compared to his peers, Simon's score is high; the average length of his sentences is 91 words, while it is 10 for Robbe-Grillet, 15 for Nathalie Sarraute, 22 for Perec, and 12 for Duras. We can immediately infer from this that there was no homogeneous style in the *Nouveau Roman* on this particular point, and that Simon does not borrow his stylistic features from a collective aesthetic.

However, the difference is so large that it invites further analysis. It may be relevant to enlarge the comparison corpus by choosing another text written outside of the contemporary period but still well-known for the author's complex syntax and his long sentences. Proust seems a good candidate in this respect; but compared to *Swann,* Simon's score is much higher, since Proust's sentences have an average length of 38 words. These results emphasize Simon's unusual and almost stifling style. An explanation may be found in Simon's poetics, which consists in describing parts of several characters' lives by blending past and present, as if interweaving several streams of consciousness. Like Proust, Simon shows a deep interest in memory and in the way literature succeeds in recreating it, and for this he chooses a never-ending sentence, in the same way memory never stops providing images to consciousness. Thomas N. Corns suggests that "[t]he reader's response to texts may well in part be determined by his or her recognition of deviations from situational norms for such texts; in a historical perspective, such norms, which would include the parameters customarily investigable by stylometrics, are tractable to reconstruction, through computer-based approaches." (Corns 1986, 224)

8. Heuristic problems and perspectives

This kind of database, despite its impressive capacity, raises some specific problems too. In France, almost sixteen years after its introduction on the web, Frantext still is not used as frequently as it should be. The first reason is a complex graphic interface that the team – and especially Gilles Souvay – has been regularly improving since 2006. The grammar writing process is not very intuitive either because it requires a strong logical sense and a basic knowledge of a programming language, which is likely to be, in Henri Béhar's words, "a powerful repellent" (Béhar 1996, 35) for literary scholars. Another explanation for this limited use is that access to the database requires registration: even if the cost remains affordable (30 euros/year), the registration process bans immediate access to the database. Fundamentally, the use of textual statistics still has to fight against a representation in the world of literary studies that implies a feeling of dispossession if a text is transferred and studied in a removable medium, not in a printed version. What is more, as mentioned above, computer-based readings are likely to be seen as too far removed from the subtlety required by literary texts.

The first essays that especially focused on figures, percentages and calculation processes - simply because managing to get such results was at that time a great achievement – were seen as too technical, cold, or worse, esoteric, and sometimes had a negative impact on the further perception of this field. Viprey insists that "one rightly blames lexical statistics for having struggled artwork and the subtle connexions between its components with its massive data"[15].

A large body of work now under development by several researchers at ATILF-CNRS is intended to dispel this false image. Using research dedicated to a single author and precise examples leading to interpretations of literary motives, we are attempting to demonstrate that lexical statistics is neither an end in itself, nor an isolated tool for analyzing texts. It has uses in larger research areas, the basis of which is usually well-established before queries are submitted to the database. But a correct use absolutely requires a reflection about our ways of analysing data; at the same time, this emphasizes the extent to which the interpretation of a text is *highly dependent on* the reader's competence.

Another interesting consideration is our state of mind when we decide to refer to a digitized corpus. We may first note, even if it seems obvious, that more meaningful results are obtained if we already know, if only approximately, what we are looking for. In other words, the user should have an in-depth knowledge of the corpora he is working on. "The point is

---

[15] "On a pu reprocher, à bon droit, à la statistique lexicale, d'avoir écrasé la réticulation de l'oeuvre d'art verbale sous la massivité de ses données". Viprey (1998)

not to read less, but to read better"[16]. As we explained above, a single score alone is meaningless. It becomes relevant not only when compared with other results, but also when connected with the available information about the texts, such as thematic, biographic, genetic, or semantic analyses, depending on the type of readings chosen.

Let's take a simple example: Perec was born in a Polish Jewish family that immigrated to France, and he lost both parents during World War II. His father died during the French military campaign of 1940 and his mother, arrested by the French police, died on the way from Drancy to Auschwitz. That is why studying words naming relatives seems a necessity in this author's case. By writing a grammar, we gathered 28 words and observed the context in which they were employed: first in a corpus made of seven novels, then in an autobiographical text entitled *W ou le souvenir d'enfance*. Some results were surprising: the autobiographical work condenses 46% of this vocabulary, which seems quite normal. But, if we calculate by taking relative sizes into account, this isotopy represents 1.44% of *W*'s vocabulary ... but only 0.1% of the novels' lexicon. This discrepancy is so large that it requires analysis. Some words have almost totally disappeared from the novels, like "cousine" ("cousin") and "tante(s)" ("aunts"). This fact cannot be attributed to chance, since we know that Perec, an orphan, was raised by his aunt Esther with his cousin Ela (Bellos 1997). Once again, lexical statistics reveal Perec's taste for dissimulation and the way he used to conceal several biographic patterns in his literary works. Simultaneously, the novels' vocabulary includes many compounds to express remote family links, like "great-grandfather", "great uncle", and "second cousin". It reveals a strong desire to go back in time when the character's relatives are evoked, to confer them with fictive, but deep familial roots. Maybe it is a way for Perec to counterbalance his loss. What statistics suggest here is confirmed by genetic core studies undertaken by Lejeune on Perec's manuscripts. He gathered tracks of an uncompleted project entitled *L'arbre*, in which the writer attempted to rebuild his family tree. This case confirms what Thomas N. Corns argued in 1986: the statistical approach requires a connection with a comprehensive vision of poetic, thematic, and even meta-textual structure to make fully sense (Corns 1986).

The Frantext team is now (in November 2007) discussing its future. Everyone is convinced that efforts should be made to make Frantext better introduced within the community of literary researchers and linguists. Today, competition from commercial databases and peer-to-peer sites is

---

[16] "Il ne s'agit pas de lire moins, mais de lire mieux." (Bernard 1999, 14).

harsh, and publicly-funded research has a lot to do to prove that its resources are not obsolete. However, no concessions on the copyright issue can be expected, and respecting the intellectual property remains our major preoccupation. The other issues we want to focus on are the digitization processes, the respect of encoding norms, and the quality of editions used: ATILF aims to provide a large choice of works but also wants above all to guarantee reliable texts for use by researchers. In a first stage, the project emphasizes renewing the interface in order to facilitate requests and to offer free-access to some functions. ATILF will try to offer easy ways to constitute corpora and to develop a kind of "basket" which could allow registering queries in order to spare the user the need to repeat them when starting a subsequent session. Another major issue is the enrichment of the corpus. Since Frantext users are either researchers in linguistics or in literature, a balance must be found between different kinds of texts, and various sources have to be entered in the base: recent novels, autobiographical texts, newspapers articles, legal texts, the transcription of screenplays, etc. Another improvement could be the introduction of processes to compose relevant comparisons: once they select one or several works, users could be invited to compare them to others sharing common features, such as genre or period.

Finally, a part of Frantext could be developed as a wiki mode to allow sharing grammars and results, which would enrich the database quite efficiently through external contributions. Frantext's purpose will never be to propose millions of books for downloading, but it will always attempt to offer a representative corpus chosen according to rigorous scientific criteria. The ATILF team tries above all to develop simple and powerful tools for analyzing texts in an empirical way which can greatly enrich the ways to conduct research in literature.

Works Cited

Baudelot, C. 1994. Préface. In *Statistique textuelle,* eds Lebart, L., A. Salem, V-VI, Paris: Dunod.
Béhar, H. 1996. *La Littérature et son Golem*. Paris: Champion.
Bellos, D. 1997. *Perec, une vie dans les mots*. Paris: Seuil.
Bernard, M. 1999. *Introduction aux études littéraires assistées par ordinateur*. Paris: Presses Universitaires de France.
Bernet, C. and Kahn, G. 2007. *Frantext 3, base non catégorisée, exemples de recherché*. (http://cid.ens-lsh.fr/aide, section "Rubriques")
Bernet, C., Pierrel, J.-M. forthcoming. Histoire de Frantext – Constitution d'une base textuelle (1961-2002) et perspectives. In *L'édition*

électronique en littérature et dictionnairique, évaluation et bilan. Paris: Champion.
Bernet, C. 1983. *Le vocabulaire des tragédies de Jean Racine*.Genève: Slatkine.
Brunet, E. 1985. *Vocabulaire de Zola*. Genève: Slatkine.
—. 1987. *Le Vocabulaire de Marcel Proust, avec l'index complet et synoptique de A la Recherche du temps perdu*. Genève: Slatkine.
—. 1993. Peut-on régler son compte à la 'raison'. In *Les Banques de données littéraires comparatistes et francophones*, ed. Alain Vuillemin, 135-145. Limoges: Pulim.
Corns, T.N. 1986. Literary Theory and Computer-based Criticism. Current problems and future prospects. In *En hommage à Charles Brunet. Méthodes quantitatives et informatiques dans l'étude des texts*, ed. E. Brunet, 221-228. Genève-Paris: Slatkine-Champion.
Cossette, A. 1994. *La Richesse lexicale et sa mesure*. Paris: Champion.
Dendien, J. 1986. Un système de gestion de bases textuelles de données. In *En hommage à Charles Brunet. Méthodes quantitatives et informatiques dans l'étude des textes*, ed. Brunet, E. 286-296. Genève-Paris : Slatkine-Champion.
Dosse, F. 1992. *Histoire du structuralisme*. Paris: La Découverte.
Duras, M. 2003. *Un Barrage contre le Pacifique*. Paris: Gallimard, (first published 1950).
Freud, S. 1987. *Introduction à la psychanalyse*. Paris: Payot.
Gicquel B. 1999. *Stylistique littéraire et informatique*. Arras: Artois Presses Université.
Jeanneney, J.-N. 2005. *Quand Google défie l'Europe, plaidoyer pour un sursaut*. Paris: Mille et une nuits.
Magné, B. 1999. *Georges Perec*. Paris: Nathan.
Montémont, V. 2008. Dites voir (sur l'ekphrasis). *Littérature et photographie*. Rennes: Presses Universitaires de Rennes.
Muller, Ch. 1993. *Le vocabulaire du théâtre de Pierre Corneille*. Genève: Slatkine (first edition 1967).
—. 1964. *Essai de statistique lexicale. L'illusion comique de Pierre Corneille*. Paris: Klincksieck.
Perec, G. 1978. *La Vie Mode d'emploi*. Paris: P.O.L.
Queneau, R. 2002. Le symbolisme du soleil. *Œuvres complètes t.2*. Ed. Godard, H., 1338-1339. Paris: Gallimard [1931].
—. 1996. *Journaux 1914-1965*. Paris: Gallimard.
Schaeffer, J.-M. 2001. Les genres littéraires d'hier à aujourd'hui. In *L'éclatement des genres au XXe siècle*. Eds. Dambre M., Gosselin-Noat, M., 11-20, Paris: Presses de la Sorbonne Nouvelle.

Viprey, J.-M. 1998. Une norme endogène. Pour le calcul stylistique du vocabulaire. In *JADT 1998, 4èmes Journées internationales d'Analyse statistique des Données Textuelles.* www.cavi.univ-paris3.fr/lexicometrica/jadt/jadt1998/viprey.htm.

CHAPTER FIVE

UNIGRAMS, BIGRAMS AND LSA: CORPUS LINGUISTICS EXPLORATIONS OF GENRES IN SHAKESPEARE'S PLAYS

MAX LOUWERSE, GWYNETH LEWIS, JIE WU

Abstract

Corpus and computational linguistics could further strengthen the thriving field of empirical studies of literature. This chapter discusses some straightforward corpus linguistic techniques: unigrams, bigrams and latent semantic analysis. The three techniques are then applied to Shakespeare's plays in order to determine how well they can categorize them in genres. In the n-gram analyses frequencies of shared words across the plays are entered in a Multi-Dimensional Scaling (MDS) analysis, in LSA the similarity values between the plays are entered in MDS. With all three techniques two categories emerged: comedies on the one hand, and tragedies/histories on the other. Moreover, a strong correlation was found between the three fundamentally different techniques.

Introduction

The Empirical Study of Literature (ESL) is an interdisciplinary field that draws in researchers from many different fields including Psychology, Sociology, Linguistics, and several others. Since the 1970s, it has attempted to understand the impact of literature on individuals and society. This field has been alluded to as an 'unromantic endeavour' (Cupchik 2007) that demands researchers to consider theories and techniques of a diverse nature in approaching abstract and often challenging problems. Indeed, the ESL endeavour is often less dreamy than the non-empirical approaches one can find in literary studies. And despite the daunting challenges that go hand in hand with understanding the literary phenomena present in ESL research, the field is nonetheless thriving. It has been growing and branching out into new directions, as is evident in the increase in ESL journal submissions, chapters and volumes dedicated to ESL advancement (e.g. Bortolussi and Dixon 2003; Green, Strange and Brock 2002; Louwerse and van Peer 2002; van Peer, Hakemulder and Zyngier 2007), as well as conferences dedicated solely to ESL research contributions (e.g. IGEL, IAEA). The ratio of publications found in databases dedicated to topics in the field of literary studies between the more empirical PsycINFO and the comparatively less empirical Modern Language Association is steadily increasing, twice as much from the period between 1980-1985 and 1990-1995 and tripled between 1980-1985 and 2000-2005. The year 2006 marked not only the 20th anniversary of The Association for Empirical Studies of Literature (IGEL), but also boasted the highest number ever of contributions from studies in literature, linguistics, psychology, sociology, and computer science.

While the field of ESL has developed greatly since the 1970s, it can be considered a hot-bed of opportunities for the introduction and implementation of research methodology from other areas. At the same time, the term 'empirical studies of literature' has slowly but surely become synonymous with psychological and sociological studies of literature (Schram and Steen 2001). Online and offline experiments measuring reader responses are obviously valuable for the field. Questions of how readers understand literature, how they respond to figurative language, how social processes play a role, all undoubtedly are important in the empirical studies of literature. But the field seems to be losing out on important areas of research that form such an obvious match with the empirical studies of literature, namely that between literary studies and areas of research that investigate texts like corpus linguistics and computational linguistics.

This chapter describes and exemplifies three corpus linguistic techniques available to any ESL researcher: unigram analysis, bigram analysis, and latent semantic analysis. In an exploratory study, plays by Shakespeare are computationally categorized on the basis of their content. The purpose of using the three techniques is to better understand the differences and similarities in their ability to cluster text content, as well as to demonstrate how simple corpus linguistic techniques can be applied to the field of ESL.

Unigrams

One of the simplest and most common methods used in corpus linguistics is the unigram analysis. This technique reduces individual words (unigrams) to their lemmata (e.g. *went* becomes *go*) and compares them to dictionary entries. On the basis of the frequency of these unigrams across texts, it is possible to categorize many different kinds of text (Martindale 1975; Martindale and West 2002), poetry by psychopathological versus non-psychopathological authors was categorized by dividing 3000 words into 36 categories of primordial content. The more primordial content, the more drive- and sensation oriented the text would be. Poetry by psychopathological authors was higher in primordial content. Unigrams can also categorize younger vs. older children's expressive narratives on the basis of primordial content (West, Martindale and Sutton-Smith 1985) as well as the speech of schizophrenic versus non-schizophrenic patients, fantasy stories vs. non-creative stories (Martindale and Daily 1996), and varying themes in narratives (Martindale and West 2002).

Unigrams have even shown to be successful to predict the outbreak of war as demonstrated by Hogenraad (2003) who categorized speeches given by George W. Bush, Tony Blair, and Saddam Hussein throughout the conflict prior to the Iraq war. The trends in words related to affiliation (decreasing) and power (increasing) over time predicted the beginning of the war; (see also the contribution by Hogenraad in this volume).

Along the same lines of research, in a previous study (Louwerse 2004) we attempted to categorize eight Modernist and eight Realist texts using a unigram analysis. Using words from semantic fields that form the Modernist code, such as Observation, Consciousness and Detachment, we tested Fokkema and Ibsch's hypothesis (Fokkema and Ibsch 1988) that the Modernist code is more prevalent in Modernist texts. Results showed differences between authors (idiolects) but not between different codes. That is, frequency of semantic fields did not significantly differ between Modernist texts by Joyce and Woolf on the one hand and Realist texts by Dickens and Eliot on the other.

Unigram analysis is a simple and common approach towards text categorization; however, it also has some drawbacks. Text comparison necessitates the difficult and time-consuming task of building dictionaries. The design of new dictionaries as in the studies discussed so far necessitates answering difficult questions such as what words belong to a certain theme and whether or not the chosen words are unique to that theme.

Another option is to consider all words across texts and to not use dictionaries at all. Such a method would consider all unigrams across texts and look at their differences in frequency. Obviously, it is thereby important to place all texts on equal footing by only selecting those words that can be found across all texts, to avoid a situation whereby a literary work is distinguished solely on the basis of a small set of peculiar words it may use. This technique of comparing frequencies of shared words is particularly useful in those approaches where researchers are mining the data to detect patterns, rather than search for predefined patterns in the data. But a problem using unigram analyses is the sheer number of possible comparisons, since many words are shared across texts.

Another disadvantage of unigrams is that disambiguation of homonyms (i.e. *foot* as a body part vs. *foot* as a measurement) is impossible, so is differentiation between homonyms belonging to different syntactic categories (i.e. John will *ditch* you vs. John fell in a *ditch*).

In sum, unigram analyses have proven to be very useful, but there are a number of drawbacks that should be considered when deciding on this type of analysis.

Bigrams

The drawbacks pointed out in unigram analysis are not unique to corpus linguistics. Speech recognition systems, for instance, share similar problems. Word recognition would be a time consuming process if based on the method of matching spoken words with ones in dictionaries. For every word spoken, the system would have to search through a dictionary to match the first letter, then the second, and so on. This would take a long time because of the endless number of shared first few letters between words. A more efficient method is to use probabilities in predicting a word on the basis of a previous word. Such analysis allows prediction because it is based on frequencies of multiple word combinations instead of one word. This is one of the benefits of using n-gram analysis. Because of size constraints, corpus linguistics generally uses bigrams, two-word combinations.

In previous research (Crossley and Louwerse 2007), we used a bigram analysis to categorize nine spoken and two written corpora. The spoken corpora consisted of the London Lund Corpus (broadcast speeches, face to face conversations, telephone conversations, interviews, spontaneous speech, and prepared speeches), the spatial coordination Map Task Corpus, the temporal coordination TRAINS Corpus, the natural face-to-face conversations in the Santa Barbara Corpus, and the telephone conversations of the Switchboard Corpus. These corpora were augmented by two written corpora: the Brown Corpus and the Lancaster Oslo Bergen

Corpus. Frequencies of the bigrams in each of these 11 corpora were entered in the factor analysis to determine underlying dimensions. Four dimensions emerged: (1) Scripted vs. Unscripted Discourse, separating natural dialogues from monologues, written texts, and tasked-based dialogues; (2) Deliberate vs. Unplanned Discourse, separating written and memorized texts from all other spoken texts; (3) Spatial vs. non-Spatial Discourse, separating the Map Task corpus from all other non-spatial discourse; and (4) Directional vs. non-directional Discourse dominated by the directional and temporal discourse of the TRAINS corpus. What this study shows is that bigram analyses are able to categorize corpora solely on the basis of frequencies of word combinations. The numerous applications to literary works, one explored in this paper, are obvious.

One strength of bigram analyses over unigram analyses is that bigram analyses are not only based on semantic differences. They also reveal latent, syntactic and discourse features. Crossley and Louwerse's (2007) bigram analysis was ostensibly based on lexical collocations, but their bigrams also revealed more than just pure semantics. For instance, the bigram analysis showed that natural, spoken dialogues show a preference for using hedges, a high degree of coordinating conjunctions, especially when combined with first and second person pronouns, the expression of opinions, and a lack of prepositional phrases.

In addition to genre classification, bigrams have also been proven useful in detecting speech acts in dialogue, as shown by (Louwerse and Crossley 2006). Applying an n-gram algorithm to transcribed utterances from the Map Task Corpus (Anderson et al. 1991) resulted in the emergence of content features unique to the Map Task scenario. This study demonstrated that out-of-context textual dialogue acts classification, which can be performed traditionally using state vector machine algorithms, is also feasible using bigram analysis. Furthermore, the performance of such analysis is comparable to that of humans.

While bigrams provide more information than unigrams, the argument could be made that trigrams (three-word combinations) are even more powerful. However, the larger the n-gram, the more sparsity becomes a problem: word frequencies are rarer when they include a greater number of words. For example, the content words *be or not* in *to be or not to be* as quoted in Shakespeare's play *Hamlet* is probably unique to Hamlet (or texts that discuss Hamlet), whereas bigrams like *to be*, *or not*, *to be*, *be or*, *not to* are not. Whereas trigrams present the problem of sparsity, unigrams might yield too much meaningless information (differentiating texts by frequency of words like *to*, *be*, *or*, *not*). Bigrams, with their word frequencies of two, are an ideal compromise between the two.

The drawback of using bigrams, or n-grams for that matter, is that they rely too much on using the exact words found in the text. Bigrams consider synonyms (e.g. *sad* and *unhappy*) as completely unique to one another. This could be a problem if a number of texts all shared similar themes yet used different but very similar words. A solution to this problem can be found in techniques that focus on latent semantic similarities.

Latent Semantic Analysis

The advantage of using Latent Semantic Analysis (LSA) over unigrams and bigrams is its ability to capture word meanings the relations between synonyms. Word meaning is captured by mapping words into a high dimensional semantic space. The steps include first associating stimuli (words) and their context (in documents), then pairing the associated stimuli on the basis of their contiguity or co-occurrence, and then transforming them using Singular Value Decomposition (SVD) into a smaller number of dimensions (typically 300). This yields a representation of the words, minus the noise. For example, consider:

1) The girl read a book at school.
2) The boy read a book at school.
3) The teacher taught a lesson to the student.

Girl and *boy* are semantically associated based on first-level co-occurrence because they are presented in the same context (they share *a*, *at*, *book*, *school*, *the*). LSA goes farther than relating *girl* and *boy* based only on context. Even though some words may never ever appear in the same document, LSA is still able to map their relations through their semantic neighbours. For instance, the lexical items in sentence 3 (*teacher, taught, lesson, student*) are absent from sentence 1 (*girl, read, book, school*) and sentence 2 (*boy, read, book, school*) but because *student* in sentence 3 shares semantic content with *school* from both sentences 1 and 3, all sentences are therefore semantically related. Note that n-gram techniques (unigram and bigram analyses) are unable to capture any similarity between such sentences.

Various studies have applied the method of statistical knowledge representation. This method has served as an automated essay grader by comparing student essays with ideal essays (Landauer, Foltz and Laham 1998) and performs at a level comparable to students on the TOEFL (Test of English as a foreign language) (Landauer and Dumais 1997). LSA has also been incorporated in software. Coh-Metrix, a web-based tool capable of analyzing text on over 50 types of cohesion relations and over 200 measures of language, text, and readability (Graesser, McNamara, Louwerse, and Cai 2004; Louwerse, MCarthy, Mcnamara and Graesser 2004; see also Graesser's contribution in the present volume). LSA has also been implemented in intelligent tutoring systems such as AutoTutor, which uses LSA to determine whether a student's answer is more closely related to an ideal, good, or bad answer (Graesser, Lu et al. 2004), and also in iSTART as a basis for appropriate feedback to self-explanations of students (McNamara, Levinstein, and Boonthu 2004).

Recently, Louwerse and van Peer (in press) demonstrated LSA's ability to capture many aspects of cognitive poetics. We took examples from Stockwell (2002) in selecting four topics (figure and ground, prototypes, cognitive deixis, conceptual metaphor) and illustrated how LSA analyses can shed light on the processes of meaning construction.

Although LSA has the advantage of mapping word meanings on many different levels, it has the disadvantage of being less sensitive than unigrams and bigrams to exact words. It also is unable to reveal syntactic and discourse features in text. Bigrams and unigrams, however, reveal such features. Due to these differences, it might be expected that LSA will group text differently than n-grams. The question is, by how much?

Other Techniques

Techniques other than n-grams and LSA can be used to analyse literary texts. The appropriate method to apply should be dictated by features of the text in question. For example, Biber (1988) looked at syntactic information instead of the lexical entries that n-grams and LSA consider. He performed a factor analysis on normalized parts-of-speech (special verbs and linguistic constructions) frequencies. This resulted in six factors that showed relations among texts like involved versus informational production, narrative versus non-narrative concerns, explicit versus situation-dependent reference, overt expression of persuasion, abstract vs. non-abstract information and on-line informational elaboration. It was found that romantic fiction, mystery fiction, and science fiction were categorized under narrative, while academic prose and official documents were categorized as belonging to a non-narrative dimension. As of late, Biber's multi-feature, multi-dimensional approach has become a standard in corpus linguistics (McEnery and Wilson 2001) and has led to extensions on the method (Biber, Conrad, and Reppen 1994; Biber and Conrad 2001).

Linguistic features of a great variety can be identified at word level (e.g. morpho-semantics, syntactic category, frequency) in text. As Biber's 1988 study demonstrates, such identifiable linguistic features serve as powerful determiners of similarities and differences between registers. While such features have yielded persuasive results, we still do not know how effective these are in capturing the nature of a register, because we do not know if it effectively captures the nature of a text. Certainly, linguistic features may betray several register characteristics at a word level, but what does it tell us about the meaning of the text as a whole? Without understanding the structure of words in sentences and sentences in paragraphs etc, we do not have an understanding of the text. How can we then understand the processes behind the text? Readers comprehend text by actively constructing a coherent mental representation of the information presented in it. This coherent representation is built from textual indications that form a text's cohesion (Louwerse and Graesser 2005). This cohesion can not be understood solely at the word level. It instead necessitates understanding at the textual levels of inter-clause, inter-sentence, and inter-paragraph structure.

Text cohesion can be determined by means of the previously mentioned web-based tool Coh-Metrix (McNamara, Louwerse, and Graesser 2002; Graesser, McNamara, et al. 2004). This tool analyses texts on over 230 types of cohesion relations and measures of language, text and readability through modules that use lexicons, parts-of-speech classifiers, syntactic parsers, templates, corpora, latent semantic analysis, and other widely used components in computational linguistics. These other components include WordNet (Miller et al. 1990), which determines underlying lexical concepts; the MRC database (Coltheart 1981) for gathering psycholinguistic information; Latent Semantic Analysis (Landauer and Dumais 1997) for semantic similarities between words, sentences, and paragraphs; the ApplePie parser (Sekine and Grishman 1995); and the parts-of-speech tagger (Brill 1995) for various syntactic categories. For further information about Coh-Metrix's measures, see Graesser, McNamara et al. (2004).

Coh-Metrix is readily available to researchers at http://coh-metrix.memphis.edu. Biber's software is not yet available to the public (see Biber 1988 for a detailed description of the software's algorithm). Louwerse et al. (2004) investigated register variations using Biber's approach in combination with Coh-Metrix.

The focus of this paper is on unigram, bigram, and LSA techniques, as they are most accessible (unigrams and bigrams can be computed using software available at http://www.madresearchlab.org and LSA is available at http://lsa.colorado.edu). Secondly, these methods all focus on one measure (lexical collocations) rather than a multitude of measures. Finally, these measures have been used in our previous work (Crossley and Louwerse 2007; Louwerse and Crossley 2006; Louwerse et al. 2004; Louwerse and van Peer in press). With this in mind, the three methods in question are used to investigate clustering Shakespearean texts.

Categorizing Shakespeare's Plays

We investigated classifications of Shakespearean texts using the three methods described earlier: unigram, bigram and LSA analysis. For this purpose, we used all of the 37 of Shakespeare's plays. These texts were originally (in the Folio of 1623) categorized under comedies, histories and tragedies.

Table 1: *Canonical categorization Shakespeare plays*

Comedy	History	Tragedy
All's Well That Ends Well	Cymbeline	Antony and Cleopatra
As You Like It	Henry IV, part I	Coriolanus
Comedy of Errors	Henry IV, part II	Hamlet
Love's Labour's Lost	Henry V	Julius Caesar
Measure for Measure	Henry VI, part I	King Lear
Merry Wives of Windsor	Henry VI, part II	Macbeth
Merchant of Venice	Henry VI, part III	Othello
Midsummer Night's Dream	Henry VIII	Romeo and Juliet
Much Ado About Nothing	King John	Timon of Athens
Pericles	Richard II	Titus Andronicus
Taming of the Shrew	Richard III	
Tempest		
Troilus and Cressida		
Twelfth Night		
Two Gentlemen of Verona		
Winter's Tale		

It is important to note here that genre clustering in Shakespeare's plays is typically based on plot. Holzknecht (1950) shows that tragedies are tragedies because they start with happiness and prosperity and end with sadness and death; comedies start with all things wrong, and end with all happiness being restored. Historical plays, finally, were an accidental form, closely akin to tragedy (idem, p. 251). Plot, however, is not captured by either n-grams or LSA. Because none of the categorizations are based on Shakespeare's language use (cf. De Grazia 2001), there is no evidence that these techniques can capture genres in Shakespeare's plays.

An additional problem concerns defining the ultimate 'correct' categorization. Comedies like *All's Well That Ends Well*, *Measure for Measure* and *Troilus and Cressida* have been called 'problem plays', or 'black comedies', because they have both happy and frivolous as well as dark and violent elements (Boas 1896; Snyder 2001). Other plays, including *Hamlet*, *The Winter's Tale*, *Timon of Athens*, and *The Merchant of Venice* have also been considered problem plays, because they do not fit the plot of tragedies well. Other plays, like *Cymbeline*, once called tragedies, are later categorized as comedies, but have also been categorized as romance. Additional plays considered romances are *The Tempest*, *The Winter's Tale*, *Pericles* and *Two Noble Kinsmen* (Campbell 1966).

In sum, genre classification of Shakespeare's plays is difficult for the human expert despite the vast contextual and historical resources available to base classification on. Corpus linguistic techniques, which rely on only lexical items to distinguish genres, are therefore expected to pose a degree of challenge.

Unigrams and Shakespeare's Plays

Word frequency lists were computed for all 37 texts whereby only those words that were found across all texts were included. Frequencies were normalized for each text by computing percentiles. This resulted in frequency lists of a total of 174 words. Not surprisingly, this list contained high-frequency items that can be found in typical word frequency lists like Kucera and Francis (1967) and CELEX (Baayen, Piepenbrock, and van Rijn 1993), including words like *a*, *and*, *did*, *in*, *of*, *that*, *the*, *to*. Because we are primarily interested in underlying dimensions of the relationships between the texts, in this and subsequent analyses, these normalized frequencies were then supplied to an ALSCAL algorithm to derive a Multidimensional Scaling (MDS) representation of the stimuli (Kruskal and Wish 1978). That is, from the normalized frequencies we computed a matrix of Euclidean distances. This matrix was compared with arbitrary coordinates in an n-dimensional space. The coordinates were iteratively adjusted such that Kruskal's stress is minimized and the degree of correspondence maximized: High stress and lower correspondence indicates a poor fitting of the data, whereas a low stress and high correspondence indicates a good fitting.

The fitting of the data in two dimensions was satisfactory (Kruskal's stress 1= .28; R^2= .74). For the purpose of this chapter we will focus on one of the two dimensions that emerged from the data and separated Shakespeare's comedies from his tragedies and histories. Coordinates for each text are given in Table 2.

Table 2: *Positioning of Shakespeare text on the dimension comedy versus history/tragedy (unigrams).*

Title	Genre	Coordinates
Merry Wives of Windsor	comedy	-2.445
Much Ado About Nothing	comedy	-2.017
The Two Gentlemen of Verona	comedy	-1.957
The Taming of The Shrew	comedy	-1.913
Twelfth Night	comedy	-1.818
As You Like It	comedy	-1.473
Two Noble Kinsmen	comedy	-1.462
Tragedy of Macbeth	tragedy	-1.391
Measure For Measure	comedy	-1.370
All's Well That Ends Well	comedy	-1.365
The Winter's Tale	comedy	-0.999
The Merchant of Venice	comedy	-0.982
Cymbeline	comedy	-0.485
Hamlet	tragedy	-0.351
Julius Caesar	tragedy	-0.317
Antony And Cleopatra	tragedy	-0.298
The Comedy of Errors	comedy	-0.245
The Tempest	comedy	-0.227
Othello	tragedy	-0.155
A Midsummer Night's Dream	comedy	-0.036
Troilus And Cressida	history	0.064
Titus Andronicus	tragedy	0.070
Henry IV, part II	history	0.096

King Henry V	history	0.109
King Henry VIII	history	0.170
Love's Labour's Lost	comedy	0.353
Coriolanus	tragedy	0.465
Henry VI, part I	history	0.506
King Richard II	history	0.745
Romeo and Juliet	tragedy	1.399
King Lear	tragedy	1.408
Henry VI, part II	history	1.709
King John	history	1.751
King Henry VI, part III	history	1.754
King Richard III	history	1.769
Henry IV, part I	history	1.834
Timon of Athens	tragedy	1.844

As the table shows, the classification of texts according to genre on the basis of frequencies of shared words alone is quite accurate. The two exceptions are *Macbeth* which is erroneously classified as a comedy, and *Love's Labour's Lost* which is erroneously classified as a history/tragedy.

The distinction between comedies on the one hand and tragedies and histories on the other may seem puzzling at first. But when one considers genre classification in Shakespeare's plays, the distinction is not surprising. Snyder (2001), for instance, refers to Francis Meres who in 1598 initially listed *Richard II, Richard III, King John* and *Henry IV* as tragedies, but later classified them as histories.

This classification allows us to determine which plays are considered to be prototypical for the different genres. According to the analysis a prototypical comedy is *The Merry Wives of Windsor*, prototypical histories and tragedies *Henry IV, part I*, and *Timon of Athens*.

What are the unigrams that best distinguish Comedies on the one hand and the Tragedies/Histories on the other? Table 3 presents a list of some of the words indicative for either category. For instance, words like *of, the, and, in, his, to, all, thou, that, there are* most frequent in comedies and least frequent in tragedies/histories.

Table 3: *Unigrams most indicative of comedy versus tragedy/history*

Comedy	Tragedy/History
of, the, and, in, his, to, all, thou, that, their, did, my, thy, o, which, from, was, our, by, thee	with, no, good, if, as, not, have, love, your, be, it, she, me, for, will, her, is, a, you, I

As we argued before, in unigram analyses it is hard to explain why certain words occur relatively more often in one text than another. Tragedies and histories can be marked by a higher frequency of pronouns (*I, you, she, it*) as well as lexical items (*no, good, love*). Grammatical items can be found more frequently in comedies (all indicators of this genre are grammatical items).

What we can conclude from this analysis is that a simple unigram analysis, whereby only the frequencies of words are considered, allows for quite an accurate classification of Shakespeare's plays into two categories that have been considered in the literature: comedies on the one hand and tragedies/histories on the other[74].

Bigrams and Shakespeare's Plays

The drawback of MDS is that it remains exploratory and the current clustering may consequently be coincidental. We therefore extended the unigram analysis to a bigram analysis, otherwise following the same procedure.

The bigram analysis replicated the unigram analysis except that lexical items consisted of two-word combinations. A total of 77 bigrams were

---

[74] At the end of this analysis it may be worthwhile to spend a few words on the MDS method we have used. Because our goal is to detect meaningful underlying dimensions that allow us to explain similarities and dissimilarities between words, and because of the exploratory character of this study, we believe that an exploratory statistical measure like MDS is warranted. It may in fact be worth motivating the choice for MDS over Factor Analysis. Guttman (1977) showed the similarities between factor analysis and MDS. Indeed, when unigram results for a factor analysis (Varimax rotation) are compared with those for the MDS, correlations follow identical patterns, with correlations at $r = .79$, $p < .001$. The advantage of MDS over Factor Analysis lies in the presentation and interpretation and is therefore chosen here.

found that were the same across all 37 texts. Their frequencies were again normalized by text size. Some of the frequent bigrams were *in his, of his, in the, of the, by the, to your, and to, with his* and *I have*. Normalized frequencies for all texts were again entered in an MDS. The fitting of the data in two dimensions was acceptable (Kruskal's stress 1= .29; R^2= .65).

Interestingly, as Table 4 shows, comedies were again quite reliably distinguished from tragedies/histories. Exceptions were *Antony and Cleopatra*, which was classified as a comedy and (again) *Love's Labour's Lost*, identified as a tragedy/history. The similarities in categorizations between unigram and bigram analyses are obvious (r = .6, p < .001, N = 37).

Table 4: *Positioning of Shakespearean text on the dimension comedy versus history/tragedy (bigrams).*

Title	Genre	Coordinates
Twelfth Night	comedy	-2.323
Antony And Cleopatra	tragedy	-1.941
The Taming of The Shrew	comedy	-1.734
The Merchant of Venice	comedy	-1.683
Cymbeline	comedy	-1.599
The Winter's Tale	comedy	-1.588
Much Ado About Nothing	comedy	-1.579
All's Well That Ends Well	comedy	-1.563
The Two Gentlemen of Verona	comedy	-1.459
The Merry Wives of Windsor	comedy	-1.327
As You Like It	comedy	-1.096
The Two Noble Kinsmen	comedy	-1.089
Julius Caesar	tragedy	-0.678
King Henry V	history	-0.555
The Comedy of Errors	comedy	-0.517
Hamlet	tragedy	-0.501
Measure For Measure	comedy	-0.313
The Tempest	comedy	-0.267
Macbeth	tragedy	-0.265
A Midsummer Night's Dream	comedy	-0.150
King Henry VIII	history	-0.054
Henry VI, part I	history	0.142
King Lear	tragedy	0.197

Henry IV, part II	history	0.282
Love's Labour's Lost	comedy	0.677
Titus Andronicus	tragedy	0.718
Romeo and Juliet	tragedy	0.723
Othello	tragedy	0.733
Coriolanus	tragedy	0.828
King Richard III	history	1.037
King John	history	1.082
King Henry VI, Part II	history	1.135
Henry IV, part I	history	1.210
King Richard II	history	1.351
Troilus and Cressida	history	1.431
King Henry VI, part III	history	1.813
Timon of Athens	tragedy	2.219

The most indicative bigrams for the two categories are presented in Table 5. As in the unigrams of the previous analysis, tragedies and histories seem to be more self-centered than comedies. Bigrams like *I had*, *that I*, *I have*, *I am* mark tragedies/histories, bigrams like *of his*, *for his*, *in his*, *with his* mark comedies. One explanation for these findings can come from social psychology. Stirman and Pennebaker (2001) found that suicidal poets use language that was more concerned with the self. The bigram analysis here suggests that we cry about ourselves, we laugh about others.

Table 5: *Bigrams most indicative of comedy versus tragedy/history*

Comedy	Tragedy/History
to the, thou art, with the, of his, from the, my heart, for his, and all, in his, of a, me and, with his, to my, to make, to me, and in, but to, in a , to your, would have	when he, that is , be so, you and, I had, by the, and the, that I , such a, will not, in the , in my, and so, to be, of the, you are, of my, it is, I have, I am

N-gram analyses rely on exact words in the text. The argument can be made that the extreme differences in frequencies of certain words that happen to occur in all texts have supported the categorization into the two genre groups. This argument is not a strong one for a number of reasons: only those words that appeared in all texts were selected and those words were typically high-frequency words. Moreover, the MDS analysis is not sensitive to a small set of differences but scales on the basis of the normalized frequencies of all words. Finally, our previous work, most notably Crossley and Louwerse (2007) and Louwerse and Crossley (2006) have provided evidence for the use of bigrams in categorizations. However, to further support the evidence that corpus linguistic measures can categorize Shakespeare's plays we used the third technique discussed in this chapter, one that is not sensitive to particular words, Latent Semantic Analysis.

Latent Semantic Analysis and Shakespeare's Plays

For the unigram analysis, all texts were computed for frequencies of the unigrams shared across all texts. A Multidimensional Scaling (MDS) algorithm was then applied to the frequencies. In the bigram analysis the method was identical to the unigram analysis, except that frequencies of pairs were used. In the LSA analysis, we used a 37 x 37 cosine value matrix entered into MDS whereby each cosine value represented a semantic similarity between plays.

For the LSA analyses a 'knowledge base' is needed in the form of an LSA space. We used the Touchstone Applied Science Associates (TASA) Corpus. The TASA corpus consists of approximately 10 million words of unmarked high school level English texts on Language Arts, Health, Home Economics, Industrial Arts, Science, Social Studies, and Business. This corpus is divided into 37,600 documents, (averaging 166 words per document) and is considered one of the benchmark corpora in computational linguistics, because it approximates the language familiarity of a college level student (Kintsch 1998; Landauer and Dumais 1997). The immediate argument against this corpus is that it is modern discourse, with expository and narrative texts - not particularly Shakespeare's language. The strength of LSA, however, is its low sensitivity to the semantic space, meaning it can still function adequately despite the mismatch. Besides, if the LSA space were to be a problem, a poor fitting of the data and a classification very different from the previous ones would be predicted.

The matrix of 37 x 37 LSA cosine values was supplied to an ALSCAL algorithm for an MDS representation. The fitting of the data in two dimensions was good (Kruskal's stress 1= .15; R^2= .96). The dimension of interest here is the one we discussed earlier. As with the unigram and bigram analyses, LSA plotted histories/tragedies versus comedies in separate categories. That categorization is not perfect (*Romeo and Juliet* and *Antony and Cleopatra* are considered comedies; *The Tempest* and *Love's Labour's Lost* are considered history/tragedy), but overall the distinction is accurate, as shown in Table 6.

Love's Labour's Lost was categorized all three times (unigram, bigram and LSA) as a history/tragedy. Before we simply label this as a miscategorization, it is interesting to note that the play has many comical events, but does end with a much darker tone.

Table 6: *Positioning of Shakespeare text on the dimension comedy versus history/tragedy (LSA).*

Title	Genre	Coordinate
King Richard II	history	-1.661
King Henry VI, part III	history	-1.651
King Henry VI, Part II	history	-1.478
King Richard III	history	-1.362
The Henry IV, part I	history	-1.317
Timon of Athens	tragedy	-1.053
King John	history	-1.031
Henry VI, part I	history	-0.959
Othello	tragedy	-0.724
Coriolanus	tragedy	-0.597
King Henry VIII	history	-0.560
The Tempest	comedy	-0.482
Henry IV, part II	history	-0.398
Love's Labour's Lost	comedy	-0.397
King Henry V	history	-0.368
Titus Andronicus	tragedy	-0.314
Macbeth	tragedy	-0.186
Julius Caesar	tragedy	-0.148
Cymbeline	comedy	-0.126
Troilus and Cressida	history	0.023
All's Well That Ends Well	comedy	0.067
The Winter's Tale	comedy	0.163

King Lear	tragedy	0.188
Hamlet	tragedy	0.388
Two Noble Kinsmen	comedy	0.391
The Merchant of Venice	comedy	0.400
A Midsummer Night's Dream	comedy	0.461
The Comedy of Errors	comedy	0.536
Romeo And Juliet	tragedy	0.692
Antony and Cleopatra	tragedy	0.865
As You Like It	comedy	0.887
Twelfth Night	comedy	1.003
Measure for Measure	comedy	1.146
Much Ado About Nothing	comedy	1.420
The Taming of The Shrew	comedy	1.479
The Two Gentlemen of Verona	comedy	1.628
The Merry Wives of Windsor	comedy	2.003

LSA analyses do not provide insight in how corpora are clustered, simply because they use higher-order relationships. It is noteworthy that fundamentally different techniques, bigrams and LSA, yield very similar results. The bigram analysis typically includes high-frequency grammatical items (non-lexical items) like *and*, *I*, *have*, *in*. The strength of LSA, on the other hand, lies in not-so-high frequent lexical items. Nevertheless, LSA results correlate with unigram ($r = .86$, $p < .001$, $N = 37$) as well as with bigram results ($r = .59$, $p < .001$, $N = 37$).

Conclusion

The current chapter has provided a brief description of three techniques that have been used frequently in corpus linguistics. We have selected rather straightforward techniques, available to any Humanistic researcher, and have shown how they can be used, for instance, in categorizing Shakespeare's plays into genres.

The field of empirical studies of literature is thriving, with more observable, reliable and valid results being reported, the present volume being an excellent example. At the same time, ESL has moved more and more towards cognitive and social psychology and sociology. Our recommendation for a new beginning for the study of literature is therefore that ESL keeps considering the wide interdisciplinary spectrum of areas and approaches. This should at least include obvious ones like computational linguistics and corpus linguistics: two bigrams, sharing the same unigram, with a high LSA match.

Works Cited

Anderson, A., M. Bader, E. Bard, E. Boyle, G. M. Doherty, S. Garrod, S. Isard, J. Kowtko, J. McAllister, J. Miller, C. Sotillo, H. S. Thompson, and R. Weinert. 1991. The HCRC Map Task Corpus. *Language and Speech* 34: 351-366.
Baayen, H., R. Piepenbrock, and H. van Rijn. 1993. The CELEX Lexical Database. Philadelphia, PA: Linguistic Data Consortium, University of Pennsylvania.
Biber, D. 1988. *Variation across Speech and Writing*. Cambridge: Cambridge University Press.
Biber, D., and S. Conrad. 2001. Quantitative corpus-based research: Much more than bean counting. *TESOL Quarterly* 35: 331-6.
Biber, D., S. Conrad, and R. Reppen. 1994. Corpus-based approaches to issues in applied linguistics. *Applied Linguistics* 15: 169-189.
Boas, F. S. 1896. *Shakespeare and his predecessors*. New York: Charles Scribner's Sons.
Bortolussi, M., and P. Dixon. 2003. *Psychonarratology: Foundations for the empirical study of literary response*. Cambridge: Cambridge University Press.
Brill, E. 1995. Transformation-based error-driven learning and natural language processing: A case study in part-of-speech tagging. *Computational Linguistics* 21: 543-566.
Campbell, O. J. 1966. *The Reader's encyclopedia of Shakespeare*. New York: Crowell.
Coltheart, M. 1981. The MRC Psycholinguistic Database. *Quarterly Journal of Experimental Psychology* 33: 497-505.
Crossley, S. A., and M. Louwerse. 2007. Multi-dimensional register classification using bigrams. *International Journal of Corpus Linguistics* 4: 453-478.
Cupchik, G. 2007. Finding an empirical link between psychology and the humanities. *International Society for the Empirical Study of Literature Newsletter* 2007 no. 17. http://www.arts.ualberta.ca/igel/Newsletter17 Jan 29.
De Grazia, M. 2001. Shakespeare and the craft of language. In *The Cambridge Companion to Shakespeare*, edited by M. de Grazia and S. Wells, 49-64. Cambridge: Cambridge University Press.

Fokkema, D. W., and E. Ibsch. 1988. *Modernist conjectures: A mainstream in European literature*. New York: St. Martin's Press.

Graesser, A. C., D. S. McNamara, M. M. Louwerse, and Z. Cai. 2004. Coh-Metrix: Analysis of text on cohesion and language. *Behavioral Research Methods, Instruments, and Computers* 36: 193-202.

Graesser, A. C., S. Lu, G. T. Jackson, H. H. Mitchell, M. Ventura, A. Olney, and M. M. Louwerse. 2004. AutoTutor: A tutor with dialogue in natural language. *Behavioral Research Methods, Instruments, and Computers* 36: 180–93.

Green, M. C., J. J. Strange, and T. C. Brock, eds. 2002. *Narrative impact: Social and cognitive foundations*. Mahwah, NJ: Lawrence Erlbaum Associates. Inc.

Guttman, L. 1977. What is not what in statistics? *The Statistician* 26: 81-107.

Hogenraad, R. 2003. The words that predict the outbreak of wars. *Empirical Studies of the Arts* 21: 5–20.

Holzknecht, K. J. 1950. *The backgrounds of Shakespeare's plays*. New York: American Book.

Kintsch, W. 1998. *Comprehension: A paradigm for cognition*. Cambridge, UK: Cambridge University Press.

Kruskal, B. J., and M. Wish. 1978. *Multidimensional scaling*. Beverley Hills, CA: Sage Publications.

Kucera, H., and W. N. Francis. 1967. *Computational analysis of present-day English*. Providence, RI: Brown University Press.

Landauer, T. K., Foltz, P. W., and D. Laham. 1988. Introduction to latent semantic analysis. *Discourse Processes* 25: 259-284

Landauer, T. K., and S. T. Dumais. 1997. A solution to Plato's problem: The latent semantic analysis theory of the acquisition, induction, and representation of knowledge. *Psychological Review* 104: 211-240.

Louwerse, M. M. 2004. Semantic variation in idiolect and sociolect: Corpus linguistic evidence from literary texts. *Computers and the Humanities* 38: 207-221.

Louwerse, M. M., and S. Crossley. 2006. Dialog act classification using n-gram algorithms. In *Proceedings of the 19th International Florida Artificial Intelligence Research Society*, 758-763. Menlo Park, CA: AAAI Press.

Louwerse, M. M., and A. C. Graesser. (2005). Coherence in discourse. In *Encyclopedia of linguistics,* edited by P. Strazny, 216-218. Chicago: Fitzroy Dearborn.

Louwerse, M. M, P. M. McCarthy, D. S. McNamara, and A. C. Graesser. 2004. Variation in language and cohesion across written and spoken

registers. In *Proceedings of the 26th Annual Meeting of the Cognitive Science Society*, edited by K. Forbus, D. Gentner, and T. Regier, 843-848. Mahwah, NJ: Erlbaum.
Louwerse, M. M, and W. van Peer, eds. 2002. *Thematics: Interdisciplinary studies*. Amsterdam/Philadelphia: John Benjamins.
Louwerse, M. M., and W. V. Peer. 2006. Waar het over gaat in cijfers. Kwantitatieve benaderuingen in tekst- en literatuurwetenschap. [What numbers are about: quantitative approaches in text- and literary studies]. *Tijdschrift voor Nederlandse Taal- en Letterkunde* 122: 21-35.
Louwerse, M. M., and W. V. Peer. in press. How cognitive is cognitive poetics? The interaction between symbolic and embodied cognition. In *Cognitive Poetics*, edited by G. Brone and J. Vandaele. Berlin: De Gruyter.
Martindale, C. 1975. *Romantic progression: The psychology of literary history*. Washington, DC: Hemisphere.
Martindale, C., and A. Daily. 1996. Creativity, primary process cognition, and personality. *Personality and Individual Differences* 20: 409-414.
Martindale, C., and A. West. 2002. Quantitative hermeneutics. Inferring meaning of narratives from trends in their content. In *Thematics: Interdisciplinary Studies*, edited by M. M. Louwerse and W. van Peer, 377-395. Amsterdam: Benjamins.
McEnery, A. M., and A. Wilson. 2001. *Corpus Linguistics*. Edinburgh: Edinburgh University Press.
McNamara, D. S., H. Levinstein, and C. Boonthum. 2004. iSTART: Interactive Strategy Training for Active Reading and Thinking. *Behavioral Research Methods, Instruments, and Computers* 36: 222 - 233.
McNamara, D. S., M. M. Louwerse, and A. C. Graesser. 2002. Coh-Metrix: Automated cohesion and coherence scores to predict readability and facilitate comprehension. Unpublished technical report: University of Memphis.
Miller, G., R. Beckwith, R. Fellbaum, and D. Gross. 1990. Introduction to WordNet: An on-line lexical database. *International Journal of Lexicography*, 3(4): 235-244. Oxford University Press.
Schram, D. H., and G. J. Steen, eds. 2001. *The psychology and sociology of literature*. Amsterdam: John Benjamins.
Sekine, S., and R. Grishman. 1995. A corpus-based probabilistic grammar with only two non-terminals. *Fourth International Workshop on Parsing Technology,* 260-270. Prague: Karlovy Vary

Snyder, S. 2001. The genres of Shakespeare's plays. In *The Cambridge Companion to Shakespeare*, edited by M. de Grazia and S. Wells, 83-97. Cambridge: Cambridge University Press.
Stirman, S. W., and J. W. Pennebaker. 2001. Word use in the poetry of suicidal and nonsuicidal poets. *Psychosomatic Medicine* 63: 517-522.
Stockwell. P. 2002. *Cognitive poetics: An introduction.* London: Routledge.
van Peer, W., J. Hakemulder, and S. Zyngier. 2007. *Muses and measures: Empirical research methods for the humanities.* Newcastle-upon-Tyne: Cambridge Scholars Publications.
West, A., C. Martindale, and B. Sutton-Smith. 1985. Age trends in the content of children's spontaneous fantasy narratives. *Genetic, Social, and General Psychology Monographs* 111: 391-405.

CHAPTER SIX

THIS WAY TO THE WAR

ROBERT HOGENRAAD

Abstract

It is possible to detect ahead signals of forthcoming conflicts through the analysis of the words contained in political documents describing the moments before a conflict breaks out. Our advanced indicator of risk of war rests on the state of motivation of political decision-makers as drawn from the content of their messages. We present the model used to assess the state of motivation of political leaders. Concretely, we analyse two sets of texts. The first is about the news archives of the Iranian Presidency collated since January 2006. The second is about the remarks and speeches on Iran by Secretary of State Condoleezza Rice since January 2006.

This way to the war

"*Dem Sieg geweiht, vom Krieg zerstört, zum Frieden mahnend*"
(Dedicated to victory, destroyed by war, calling for peace)
—The Victory Arch – *Siegestor* – in Munich

The single red line that traverses this and Graesser's, Louwerse's, and Pennebaker's contributions in this volume is that a simple computer can detect significant patterns in texts. Suitable software and a few semantic filters to go with it is all that is needed. We will get to details in a minute. Two warnings, however, before continuing. First, there is nothing new here. In 1966, the team guided by the late Philip Stone published "The General Inquirer", the first ever published software of computer-aided content analysis (Stone, Dunphy, Smith, and Ogilvie 1966). Hogenraad, McKenzie, and Péladeau (2003) reviewed the major traditions in the practice of computer-aided content analysis since Stone's work. Secondly, none of the procedures to analyse texts is easy to use. Compared with the ease of analyzing questionnaires, the tools to analyse literary texts are complex. Even to these days, not many academic heavies or would-be ones are willing to cross frontiers and risk their careers – and the comfortable salaries that go with it – in the uncertain business of computer-aided content analysis.

The software (PROTAN, for Protocol Analyser) and semantic filters – which we dub dictionaries – we have developed have provided evidence of their power for analyzing literary texts (Hogenraad, Daubies, Bestgen, and Mahau 1995). The software itself is a suite of programs equipped with dictionaries. The latter carry the theories we want to test on literary texts. For example, a question about the emotional change in Pynchon's *"Gravity's Rainbow"* needed using both a dictionary of affect (Whissell 1986) and Martindale's (1979) Regressive Imagery Dictionary (Herman, Hogenraad, and Van Mierlo 2003). Herman et al. (p. 39) found out *"Gravity's Rainbow"* was organized in such a way that every section of the novel tended towards an unsuccessful night journey. In another area, Andrew Wilson (2002) used the Regressive Imagery Dictionary to analyse fictional fetishistic stories. As expected, fetishistic stories contain a significantly higher proportion of primary process content (images) and a significantly lower proportion of secondary process content (conceptual thinking) than the romance and love stories (from the abstract).

But what happens when the texts we need to analyse are not literary ones, but come from the real world? Cognitive psychologists have addressed this question. Stories, they say, are similar in many respects to the real world (Black 1984). When understanding and remembering stories, readers use the same kinds of strategies that they use to understand and remember the real world (p. 235). Memory for an event is much the same whether portrayed in a videotape or in a written description (Lichtenstein and Brewer 1980). Stories of conflicts in the making are cockpits in which we try reality. They provide us with a convenient way to study how words of war change over time: It is simply easier to control stories than it is to control the real world. No doubt war strategies apply in a fictional account as they do in the real world.

In the present chapter, we use the PROTAN software equipped with a new motive dictionary to monitor the risk of war, drawing on news archives of geopolitical conflicts. We confirmed the predictive power of the dictionary when we successfully analysed war stories as well as accounts of real conflicts (Hogenraad 2003). The war stories were Thucydides' *"History of the Peloponnesian War"*, Tolstoy's *"War and Peace"*, and William Golding's *"Lord of the Flies"*. The real conflicts concerned for example the Cuban Missile Crisis of 1962. We then showed evidence of an increased risk of war in Iraq (March 17, 2003-), based on the analysis of the speeches of President G. W. Bush and Prime Minister Tony Blair (Hogenraad 2005). Now we apply the advanced indicator of the risk of war to two sets of political records about Iran. The records concern the Iranian claim to nuclear power. The first set is about archives of the Iranian Presidency collated since January 2006. The second is about remarks and speeches on Iran by Secretary of State Condoleezza Rice since January 2006.

It is possible to detect ahead signals of forthcoming conflicts. We capture these signals through the analysis of the words contained in news archives describing the moments before a conflict breaks out. Our advanced indicator of the risk of war rests on the state of motivation of political decision-makers as drawn from the content of their messages. We present in a moment the model used to assess the state of motivation of political leaders.

With much of social science today, you feel you are walking through a museum after closing time. In the event, our take on predicting war cuts across morals and economics. Morals – wars cause damage beyond repair – because, failing to prevent war, we can predict it, should war come true. And useful too, as for economic planners eager to integrate the risk of war (or its opposite) into their business plans. Koyama and Tanaka (2006), for example, report different possible impacts of the risk of war (or chance of peace) on the oil market.

There is a second big red line that traverses, not a few chapters in this volume, but all of it. It is apt to mention it here. The first victim of ideologies is usually language (Hogenraad 2007). Whether in the press or in political statements, we hear everyday of censorship, propaganda, gagging, misinterpretations, omissions, deceit, half-truths, and sheer lies, well enough, at any rate, to assign a mission to empirical students of literature. That mission is to remediate to man's vulnerability to ideologies by tying back words to their empirical realities, using computers if necessary. When retired U.S. Army Officer Ralph Peters (2006) writes that *"Arab societies can't support democracy as we know it"*, literature scientists have work to do. And follow the steps taken by Victor Klemperer in his 1933-1945 diary. Interned in a Nazi camp during World War II, Klemperer (1975, chapter 9) analysed how, for example, the German word *"Fanatismus"* became more and more positively evaluated in newspapers and in the speeches of the Third Reich leaders. In Orwell (1990), "Newspeak", the Oceania official language made of simple concrete items that everybody can understand, was designed to reduce the range of thought. A cheapened language indeed. Klemperer, Orwell, like

Woolf (Hussey 1992), Revel (1992), Ogden and Richards (1989), even Pound (1973) on economic science (Desai 2006; Joseph 2006), each assigned a role for himself or herself, that of finding and restoring meaning in trouble. A flip role for empirical studies of literature.

The advanced indicator of the risk of war: Solidarity and power, the yin and yang of motivation

McClelland's predictive model of war (1975) involves the need for *affiliation* and the need for *power*. Intimacy, friendship, and positive emotional contacts with a person, define the need for affiliation. The will to exert influence, to have an impact on people or to get control over them, forms the essential of the need for power. These two criss-cross threads, power and affiliation, are always difficult to patch up with each other. What is out there in McClelland's psychological model of war is reasonable enough for the model to survive. The use of one's own power to save others – call it the rage to convince if you want – is often the link between an "imperial motivation pattern" and later wars. That pattern is the gap created by high need for power and low need for affiliation. The wider the gap, the greater the risk of war.

McClelland (1975) argues how reform movements have the unintended outcome of creating *"an action orientation that makes war possible (...). This atmosphere of righteous action has led to war in too many instances in the history of the United States and England for such consequences to be accidental"* (p. 355). Circumstances and opportunities transform local reform movements into pressing needs for regime change in other nations. President Bush's press conference with Prime Minister Blair[1] shows this need for regime change. Indeed, power hates diversity in any of its forms: linguistic, religious, nationality, skin color or sexual orientation (Arendt 2005, p. 5, extracts from her "Denktagebuch" of September 1951). In the words of a world leader, *"You are either with us, or you are with the terrorists"* [2]. Whatever is virtuous in universalism always feeds a non-commendable form of imperialism (Bacevich 2005, p. 75). Universalism replaces whatever was good in the past by something supposed to be even better in the future, blurring differences.

---

[1] April 6, 2002, http://www.whitehouse.gov/news/releases/2002/04/20020406-3.html.
[2] President Bush, September 20, 2001, retrieved March 22, 2007 from http://www.whitehouse.gov/news/releases/2001/09/20010920-8.html).

It seems a bit naive to dissolve war into a couple of psychological motives. But we think that with this advanced indicator of the risk of war, we have put the finger on one of the composites of the chemistry of war. The proof of a method is what happens when we apply it. Until now, our advanced indicator of the risk of war has never produced a false positive throughout the many tests we performed (Hogenraad 2003, 2004, 2005, 2007).

Method

Texts

From http://www.president.ir/eng/, we collated the news archives of the Iranian Presidency since January 1st, 2006 to September 20, 2006. We also collated the interviews and speeches about Iran by Secretary of State Condoleezza Rice since January 12, 2006 to September 19, 2006[3]. Both series of texts are in English. What we record is the number of days on which either the Iranian or the American politician has intervened with a speech, a statement, an interview, or a written announcement (Table 1).

Table 1. The corpus

Texts	Divisions	Total N. of words	N. different words
Iranian Presidency	January 1, 2006- September 20, 2006 (204 days of intervention)	199,627	9,201
Secretary Rice	January 12, 2006 – September 19, 2006 (60 days of intervention)	267,153	7,778

With a language as subtle as Farsi, translation causes some nuances to be lost. One problem occurred, for example, with the words "wiped off the map" used by President Ahmadinejad about Israel[4]. It turns out that a more correct translation would have been "wiped away from the pages of

---

[3] http://www.state.gov/p/nea/ci/ c9604. htm
[4] http://commentisfree.guardian.co.uk/ jonathan_steele/2006/06/post_155.html

history".[5] The archives we collate are the official ones available from the Iranian Presidency web site. When nuances are lost in translation, we may think the translators judged them secondary. Also, the Iranian archives report the Presidential speeches amended, at least in the English translation, by political comments. (On Iran, see Goldstone 2006; Hersh 2006; Jones 2006; Lowe and Spencer 2006).

Content analysis and semantic filters

We analysed the texts using the PROTAN software of computer-aided content analysis (Hogenraad, Daubies, Bestgen, and Mahau 1995). Our purpose is to separate and purify the constituents of a text. Equipped with proper semantic filters, content analysis packs an astonishing amount of information by filtering out the redundancies of speech. Filtering out allows us to keep only what we are looking for. A semantic filter, in content analysis, is a list of words organized into categories, that is, words with a role in a hierarchy. When one applies a semantic filter to a text, one looks for matches between a word in the filter and a word in the text. One then shoves the text words into categories, counts the number of word matches in each category and takes the percentage of the number of word matches.

Table 2. Affiliation and Power categories of the MOTIVE DICTIONARY

Category	Subcategory	N. of entries	Examples
Affiliation		792	
	Affection	105	mate, sweetheart
	Social behavior	79	answer, escort
	Affiliation	448	accompany, courteous
	Affect loss	23	alone, indifference
	Affect participants	59	dad, mistress
	Affect words	44	family, nostalgic

---

[5] See also Juan Cole's http://www.juancole.com/ and, for another view, http://www.nytimes.com/2006/06/11/weekinreview/11bronner.html?ex=1307678400&en=efa2bd266224e880&ei=5088&partner=rssnyt&emc=rss

Positive affect	35	affable, thoughtful

Power		1,440	
	Power	785	ambition, justice
	Power gain	40	emancipate, nominate
	Power loss	56	captive, weak
	Power ends	9	plead, recommend
	Power conflicts	227	adversary, invade
	Power cooperation	64	arbiter, reciprocal
	Power authoritative participants	70	patriarch, detective
	Power ordinary participant	25	emissary, orator
	Power doctrine	24	conservatism, dogma
	Power authority	31	legitimate, reign
	Residual power words	109	colonialism, terrorize

We used two semantic filters for this study, subcategories "need for affiliation" (nAff) and "need for power" (nPow) of the motive dictionary (Table 2). We designed the dictionary so that any word assigned to one category could not be present in another one except in a higher-up category. The present English version 4.0 of March 20, 2007 has 792 entries for affiliation, and 1,440 for power. We measure the risk of war by computing the average difference, we call it gap, between the score for power (nPow) and the score for evaluation (nAff) by day of intervention. The risk of war increases when the gap increases. We controlled the power of the dictionary using fictional texts and historical documents in which the risk of war passed through different phases (Hogenraad 2003, 2005).

Results: No "Google War" for the moment

Results integrate statistical treatments like removing autocorrelations and resampling statistics. To ensure independent observations, as needed in science, we randomize the data. It is impossible to randomize textual data, because the temporal order is part of the information carried by them. There are reasons to believe that, for example, the rate of emotion in chapter 4 of a story depends to some degree on the rate of emotion in the preceding chapter. Such a dependency, when it becomes systematic, creates a seeming change without any genuine change. A systematic dependency in a temporal series is an autocorrelation. It is possible to calculate and to remove the autocorrelation from the rate of emotion in the story. The principle consists of correlating the rate (of emotion) in chapter 1 with the rate in chapter 2, then the rate in 2 with the rate in 3, and so on. We then remove this dependency when we regress the rate of emotion over the chapters of the book (Hogenraad, McKenzie, and Martindale 1997).

Scientists repeat their experiments. Writers cannot, for any literary work is unique and unrepeatable (Hogenraad, McKenzie, and van Peer 1997). But unique events pose a problem about the confidence we can have in a statistical test done on a literary work when there is no real sampling error. Resampling statistics (Diaconis and Efron 1983; Péladeau 1996) consists of simulating what we cannot have. In other words, we treat the scores of each variable of interest, say the rate of emotion in a story, as if they were the population, and recreate several thousands samples from it by sampling with replacement. For example, a particular sample might contain, say, chapter 1, 10 times, chapter 2, none, and chapter 3, 4 times. For each simulated version, we calculate the statistical estimator we have an interest in. Each of the simulated versions of the story is therefore like an experiment – a clone – containing a minor or sometimes major change of the original (Hogenraad and McKenzie 1999).

There is no significant change in the indicator of the risk of war in the archives of the Iranian Presidency, as if the Iranian Presidency was on cruise control. In Figure 1[6], the horizontal axis represents time, while the vertical axis represents power minus affiliation. Thus each dot represents the risk of war on one day on which the Iranian President made one (or several) interventions. The smoothing line in the figure is a moving average that removes the smaller ebbs and flows from the data. If a trend exists in the data, smoothing them will make the trend visible. But we

---

[6] Figure 1 has no regression line in it because there is no significant change in the risk of war.

already know [3] there is no significant change in the risk of war in this case. The smoothing line in Figure 1 merely reflects the unpredictable nature of the data. In each figure, we also tagged in the graphs the Israel-Lebanon conflict, that is, from July 12 to August 14, 2006. The outbreak and end of this armed conflict, as can be seen in Figure 1, did not exert a strong influence. All in all then, as represented in Figure 1, the speeches of President Ahmedinejad do not argue for any warning of a rise in the risk of war.

What about the other side of the potential conflict, the United States? The rate of change in the indicator of the risk of war in the speeches of Secretary Rice increases significantly $[R^2 = .13, F(2, 54) = 4.0, p < .05]$ until August 16. And Figure 2 has a U-shaped regression line in it, in the form of the interrupted line. In Figures 2 and 3, each dot represents one day on which Secretary Rice made one (or several) interventions. After 20,000 resamplings, the average degree of curvilinearity for the linear model is -.08 (95% ci -.15 to -.01), and that for the quadratic model is .002 (95% ci .0003 to .003). This latter result gives weight to the U-shaped regression line. From June 2006 on, yet before the Lebanon conflict, there is a tendency in Secretary Rice's communications to go up towards a higher risk of war (the smoothing line runs up). However, on June 25, 2006, Arab militants abducted Israeli Cpl. Gilad Shalit just before the start of "Operation Summer Rains" on June 28, 2006. The kidnapping of the Israeli soldier may explain in part the change of tone in Secretary Rice's communications. The rate of change in the indicator of the risk of war becomes non-significant when we include Secretary Rice's talks on September 12 and 19. For that reason, there is no regression line in Figure 3. Her three September talks score lower than those of June to August (the smoothing line plummets). These last three scores suggest some degree of thawing on the Iranian question. But they also remind us how data are fleetingly unstable, and how we should always remain suspicious of them.

Figure 1: Rate of change of the risk of war in the news archives of the Iranian Presidency (January 1, 2006 – September 20, 2006).

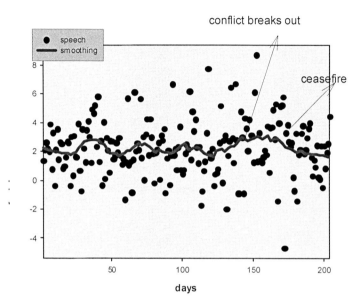

January:	archives 1 to 24	June:	archives 114 to 134
February:	archives 25 to 44	July:	archives 135 to 163
March:	archives 45 to 63	August:	archives 164 to 179
April:	archives 64 to 87	September:	archives 180 to 204
May:	archives 88 to 113		

140 This Way to the War

Figure 2. Rate of change of the risk of war in the speeches and interviews on Iran by US Secretary Rice (January 12, 2006 – August 16, 2006).

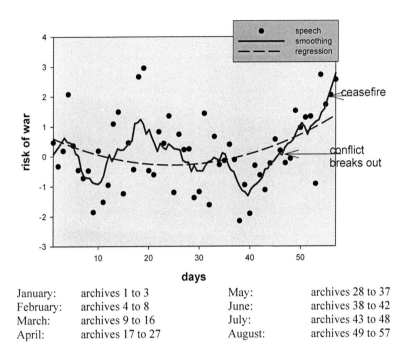

January:	archives 1 to 3	May:	archives 28 to 37
February:	archives 4 to 8	June:	archives 38 to 42
March:	archives 9 to 16	July:	archives 43 to 48
April:	archives 17 to 27	August:	archives 49 to 57

The average value of the risk of war (power minus affiliation) is 2.3 for the Iranian archives, and .2 for Secretary Rice's talk (difference = 2.1). Here we want to ask if these two independent mean values are different from each other over 9 months. They are, the t value is 7.3 ($p < .0001$). After 20,000 resamplings, the t value is 8.2 (95% ci 4.5 to 14.0) and the mean difference is 2.1 (95% ci 1.5 to 2.6). For the period considered (January to September 2006), the overall risk of war is significantly higher in the Iranian statements than in the talks of Secretary Rice.

Figure 3. Rate of change of the risk of war in the speeches and interviews on Iran by US Secretary Rice (January 12, 2006 – September 19, 2006).

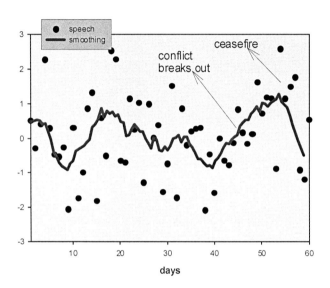

January:	archives 1 to 3	June:	archives 38 to 42
February:	archives 4 to 8	July:	archives 43 to 48
March:	archives 9 to 16	August:	archives 49 to 57
April:	archives 17 to 27	September:	archives 58 to 60
May:	archives 28 to 37		

Closing remarks

Political and economic indicators such as military alliances, economic rivalries, and arms races are also at work in a conflict (Russett and Oneal 2001). The analysis of "the words of war in the making" is no substitute for a political analysis, but it makes it a little more difficult to pass by. The critical test of a model is whether it enables us a better understanding of events. As of September 21, 2006, there is a zero rate of change of the risk of war in the Iranian documents over nine months, as if Iran was sitting out the instability of its neighbourhood. However, on the Iranian side, the threat is steadily high (average risk of war of 2.3 versus .2 for Secretary Rice). That low threat on the U.S. side is open to interpretations, but contrasts with the volatile rate of change of the risk of war in the documents of the US Department of State. Meanwhile another history has been written. We have no competence to decide, let alone to judge. It is not for us to debate the right of nations to increase their security and the right of other ones not to decrease theirs (Jervis 1978). What is for us to analyse, however, are facts, which we cannot afford to ignore. They are evidence that we can predict conflicts because they always break out the same way – because of leaders and nations believing they have been chosen to impose unity on others (Arendt 1985, chapter 7, "Race and Bureaucracy").

Works Cited

Arendt, H. 1985. *The origins of totalitarianism*. New York: Harcourt, Inc. [Original work published 1951].
—. 2005. *The promise of politics*. (Edited and with an introduction by Jerome Kohn). New York: Schocken Books.
Bacevich, A. J. 2005. *The new American militarism. How Americans are seduced by war*. New York: Oxford University Press.
Black, J. B. 1984. Understanding and remembering stories. In *Tutorials in learning and memory*, eds. J. R. Anderson and S. M. Kosslyn, 235-255. San Francisco: W. H. Freeman.
Desai, M. 2006. *The route of all evil. The political economy of Ezra Pound*. London: Faber.
Diaconis, P. and Efron, B. 1983. Computer-intensive methods in statistics. *Scientific American* 248: 96-108.
Goldstone, J. A. March 2006. The return of the radicals in Iran. (Retrieved June 19, 2006, from http://www.project-syndicate.org/commentary/goldstone1.)
Herman, L., Hogenraad, R., and Van Mierlo, W. 2003. Pynchon, postmodernism and quantification: An empirical content analysis of Pynchon's *Gravity's Rainbow. Language and Literature* 12: 27-41.
Hersh, S. M. 2006, April 17. The Iran plan. Would President Bush go to war to stop Tehran from getting the bomb? *The New Yorker*. (Retrieved August 22, 2006 from http://www.newyorker.com/printables/fact/060417fa_fact .)
Hogenraad, R. 2003. The words that predict the outbreak of wars. *Empirical Studies of the Arts* 21: 5-20.
—. 2004. Prognozirovanie razvitiia konfliktov s pomoshch'iu komp'iuternogo kontent-analiza [Predicting conflict development by computer-aided content-analysis]. *Sotsiologiia: Metodologiia, Metody,*

Matematicheskie Modeli [Sociology: Methodology, Methods, Mathematical Models] 19: 158-175. (In Russian).
—. 2005. What the words of war can tell us about the risk of war. *Peace and Conflict: Journal of Peace Psychology*, 11: 137-151.
—. 2007. Perversion and creativity in the language of war. In *Aesthetics and innovation*, eds. L. Dorfman, C. Martindale, and V. Petrov, 161-180. Newcastle: Cambridge Scholars Publishing.
Hogenraad, R., Daubies, C., Bestgen, Y., and Mahau, P. 1995. A general theory and method of computer-aided text analysis: The PROTAN system (PROTocol Analyser). Louvain-la-Neuve (Belgium), Psychology Department, Université catholique de Louvain. (www.psor.ucl.ac.be/protan/protanae.html).
Hogenraad, R., and McKenzie, D. P. 1999. Replicating text: The cumulation of knowledge in social science. *Quality & Quantity*, 33 : 97-116.
Hogenraad, R., McKenzie, D. P., and Martindale, C. 1997. The enemy within: Autocorrelation bias in content analysis of narratives. *Computers and the Humanities*, 30: 433-439.
Hogenraad, R., McKenzie, D. P., and Péladeau, N. 2003. Force and influence in content analysis: The production of new social knowledge. *Quality and Quantity*, 37: 221-238.
Hogenraad, R., McKenzie, D. P., and van Peer, W. 1997: On fact making in empirical studies of literature. *SPIEL*, 16 : 416-421.
Hussey, M., ed. 1992. *Virginia Woolf and war: Fiction, reality and myth*. Syracuse, NY: Syracuse University Press.
Jervis, R. 1978. Cooperation under the security dilemma. *World Politics*, 30: 167-214.
Jones, B. 2006, 22 June. Iran, the West and the bomb. *London Review of Books*, 28: 31-33.
Joseph, J. J. 2006, September 29. Language and the First World War. (Letters to the Editor.). *The Times Literary Supplement, September 29, 2006*, 17.
Klemperer, V. 1975. *LTI – Lingua Tertii Imperii. Notizbuch eines Philologen*. Leipzig: Reclam Verlag.
Koyama, K. and Tanaka, K. 2006. *The analysis of scenarios concerning the Iranian situation and its impact on the international oil market* (Research paper November 29, 2006). Tokyo: The Institute of Energy Economics, Japan. (Retrieved November 29, 2006 from http://eneken.ieej.or.jp/en/data/ pdf/372.pdf.)
Lichtenstein, E. H. and Brewer, W. F. 1980. Memory for goal-directed events. *Cognitive Psychology*, 12 : 412-445.

Lowe, R., and Spencer, C. 2006, 23 August. *Iran, its neighbours and the regional crises. A Middle East Programme report* . London: Chatham House. (Retrieved August 24, 2006 from http://www.chathamhouse.org.uk/ pdf/research/mep/Iran0806.pdf.).

Martindale, C. 1979. The night journey: Trends in the content of narratives symbolizing alteration of consciousness. *Journal of Altered States of Consciousness,* 4: 321-343.

McClelland, D. C. 1975. *Power: The inner experience.* New York: Irvington Publishers.

Ogden, C. K., and Richards, I. A. 1989. *The meaning of meaning: A study of the influence of language upon thought and of the science of symbolism.* New York: Harcourt Brace Jovanovich. [Original work published 1923].

Orwell, G. 1990. *Nineteen eighty-four.* London: Penguin. [Original work published 1949].

Péladeau, N. 1996. Simstat for Windows. User's guide (Version 1.21d, November 1997). Montréal: Provalis Research. (Retrieved December 9, 2006 from http://www.simstat.com/.)

Peters, R. 2006, November 2. *Last gasps in Iraq.* USA Today. (Retrieved March 21, 2007 from http://blogs.usatoday.com/oped/2006/11/post_6.html.)

Pound, E. 1973. *Selected prose, 1909-1965.* New York: New Directions Publishing Corporation.

Revel, J.-F. 1992. *The flight from truth: The reign of deceit in the age of information* (Curtis Cate, Trans.). New York: Random House.

Russett, B. M., and Oneal, J. R. 2001. *Triangulating peace: Democracy, interdependence, and international organizations.* New York: W. W. Norton.

Stone, P. J., Dunphy, D. C., Smith, M. S., and Ogilvie, D. M. (1966). *The General Inquirer: A computer approach to content analysis.* Cambridge, MA: The M.I.T. Press.

Whissell, C., Fournier, M., Pelland, R., Weir, D., and Makarec, K. 1986. A dictionary of affect in language. IV. Reliability, validity, and applications. *Perceptual and Motor Skills,* 62: 875-888.

Wilson, A. 2002. The application of computer content analysis in sexology: A case of primary process content in fictional fetishistic narratives. *Electronic Journal of Human Sexuality,* 5: (June 16). (Retrieved September 19, 2007 from http://www.ejhs.org/volume5/wilson.html.)

CHAPTER SEVEN

READING DIFFERENT TYPES OF NARRATIVE TEXTS: A STUDY OF COGNITIVE AND EMOTIONAL RESPONSES

ALDO NEMESIO, M. CHIARA LEVORATO AND LUCIA RONCONI

Abstract

This paper examines cognitive and emotional responses produced while reading different types of narrative texts. The Italian translation of Borges's short story «La muerte y la brújula» («Death and the Compass») was presented either in the original or in a modified version, which omitted the initial paragraph introducing the two main characters. Readers were asked to evaluate the degree with which they experienced the following responses: coherence, curiosity, emotionality, empathy, facility, imagery, impact, interest, involvement, pleasure, pleasure at the outcome, postdictability, surprise, surprise at the outcome and suspense. A factorial analysis on the scores showed the same three factors found in previous experiments using E.A. Poe's and I.U. Tarchetti's short stories: 1. readers' emotional participation in the story; 2. violation of readers' expectations; 3. cognitive evaluation of the textual features that make the story comprehensible (Levorato and Nemesio, 2005). Differences were found in relation to gender and textual type: a) men showed grater emotional participation in Borges's detective story than women did; b) the two versions of Borges's story significantly influenced responses concerning empathy for the two characters.

Introduction

Reading a narrative text involves cognitive, inferential and linguistic processes through which a Situation Model is built up (Kintsch, 1996), that is: a semantic representation of the meaning expressed in the text. Parallel to this construction based on linguistic processing, aesthetic, affective and emotional responses are produced. Recent research in text comprehension has paid increasing attention to emotional responses to text reading (Levorato, 2000; Miall and Kuiken, 1994, 1995, 1999) and the need to consider the interaction of affective and cognitive components of reading has been discussed in several studies (Gerrig, 1993, 1996; Hidi, 1990; Miall, 1989; Tan, 1996; van Oostendorp and Zwaan, 1994).

This paper examines cognitive and emotional responses produced by students attending various faculties of Italian universities to a Borges short detective story. In order to study the affective-emotional dimension of reading, the following readers' responses were analysed: curiosity, emotionality, empathy, imagery, impact, interest, involvement, pleasure, pleasure at the outcome, surprise, surprise at the outcome and suspense. Interest has been explored in several studies (Hidi, 1990; Kintsch, 1980; Schraw, Bruning and Svoboda, 1995; Wade and Adams, 1990) as has its interactions with pleasure (Cupchik and Gebotys, 1990; Tan, 1996), with pleasure at the outcome (Iran-Nejad, 1987), with curiosity (Loewenstein, 1994), with surprise and suspense (Brewer and Lichtenstein, 1981, 1982) and with imagery and comprehensibility (Sadoski, Goetz and Rodriguez, 2000). In general, these studies have shown that readers' responses are interdependent and that correlations exist between them. Pleasure has also been extensively studied, particularly in relation with pleasure at the outcome (Brewer, 1996; Zillman and Bryant, 1975; Zillman, Hay and Bryant, 1975), with surprise (Iran-Nejad and Ortony, 1985; Zillman, 1996) and with suspense and empathy (Josè and Brewer, 1984; Zillman, 1996). Strict relations between all of these responses have been shown to exist.

In our study we also investigated three aspects of reading which are related to the construction of the Situational Model: coherence, facility and postdictability. Coherence refers to the degree to which the information can be integrated into a global representation. Facility refers to the reader's evaluation of the cognitive resources necessary for comprehension. Both these characteristics facilitate the comprehension process. Postdictability, a concept introduced by Kintsch (1980), refers to the post-hoc integration of every part into the whole: a narrative text, in fact, needs closure (Eco, 1979). We refer to these three features with the term cognitive evaluation, since the reader produces an evaluation of the cognitive resources needed to comprehend the text.

These readers' responses were analysed in previous studies which took into consideration responses to a fantastic mystery story, written by an Italian writer, I.U. Tarchetti, entitled «A spirit in a raspberry» (Levorato, Nemesio and Ronconi, 2004; Levorato and Nemesio, 2005; see also Levorato and Ronconi, 2006). Results showed that readers' responses were described by three dimensions: readers' involvement (which includes emotional responses), violation of expectations (which includes the responses elicited by the story's ending) and cognitive evaluation. The present study is aimed at verifying the hypothesis that the same dimensions identify the reading of a different genre of story: a detective story, narrating deductive inferences produced by a police officer who has to discover a murderer. In both stories a solution has to be found out by a character (and by the reader), but the events that have to be explained are different: in Tarchetti's fantastic mystery tale the events narrated are unnatural or supernatural, whereas in Borges's detective story they are rational, based on reasoning and deduction.

In order to show the differences between these two stories, they were examined by five experts in literature, in addition to the authors of this paper, whose responses agreed that Tarchetti's and Borges's texts belong to different textual types: fantastic tale and detective story, respectively.

The present study also analysed the influence of text structure on reader responses. In order to see if cognitive evaluation and aesthetic-emotional responses vary in function of how the information is organized in the text, the short story was presented in two versions: the original and a manipulated version, where the initial paragraph, introducing the two main characters (the detective and the murderer) was omitted. We decided to modify the initial paragraph of the text because the opening of a text induces the reader to activate the relevant information necessary to fill in the gaps and the blanks of the linear text in front of his eyes (Nemesio, 1990, 2000, 2002). In the manipulated version no new material was introduced: only a segment of the original text (the first paragraph) was deleted: in the new text readers have less information about the two characters and this information is not placed right in the beginning. We expected that by reducing emphasis on the two characters readers would feel less empathy for them.

Method

Participants

Two hundred and seventy-one students (110 males, 161 females) were presented with the Italian translation of Borges' short story. Their age ranged from 18 to 49 (mean age 22 years; SD 4.54; only 3.7% older than 30). They attended either humanistic (Humanities, N=149) or scientific faculties (Engineering, Medicine and Psychology, N=122).

Material

Borges' short story «La muerte y la brújula» («Death and the Compass») was presented to readers either in the original or the modified version (number of words: 3675 and 3547, respectively). The story narrates the investigation of the rational detective Lönnrot, who attempts to solve a series of strange crimes committed in geometrically related places and at periodic intervals of time. Eventually, it turns out that the series of murders is an elaborate plan designed by Scharlach, a gangster who wants to take revenge on him and that all the clues have been carefully faked: Lönnrot finds himself trapped and killed by his opponent.

Procedure

Each participant read either the original or the modified version (original: N = 136; modified: N = 135) in university classrooms during normal classes, without any time limit. At the end of the text, participants found a questionnaire to be answered through a seven-point Likert-type scale. The questionnaire asked the degree with which readers experienced the following 13 emotions: curiosity, emotionality, empathy for L., empathy for S., imagery, impact, interest, involvement, pleasure, pleasure at the outcome, surprise, surprise at the outcome and suspense. The same scale was used to rate cognitive evaluation: coherence, facility and post-dictability. Moreover, three questions were asked to verify readers' comprehension of the text and their previous knowledge of the short story. We did not make use of the answers coming from subjects who were not able to answer the comprehension questions correctly, said they had already read the text before or did not answer all the questions. Nor were the answers obtained from non-native Italian speakers considered.

Results

Table 1 shows mean and standard deviation for each response, starting from the highest. Most of the answers obtained mean scores above the middle point, namely 4, which shows that the short story induced quite intense responses. Only three questions obtained scores lower than 4: two of them regarded the degree of empathy experienced for the two characters and the third one concerned the emotionality induced by the story. This suggests that readers' emotional participation with the facts that involved the two characters was not high.

Table 1. Mean and standard deviation for each response, starting from the highest.

	M	SD
Imagery	5.53	1.25
Coherence	5.17	1.31
Postdictability	5.07	1.53
Curiosity	5.02	1.58
Surprise	5.01	1.40
Surprise at the outcome	4.85	1.56
Pleasure at the outcome	4.77	1.59
Interest	4.75	1.50
Facility	4.61	1.26
Pleasure	4.59	1.54
Involvement	4.40	1.42
Suspense	4.29	1.37
Impact	4.21	1.55
Emotionality	3.86	1.49
Empathy for Lönnrot	3.67	1.66
Empathy for Scharlach	2.58	1.40

The comparison between the two versions of the story showed that only empathy for the two characters was affected by the manipulation at the beginning of the text: Table 2 shows that even though in both versions the murderer induces less empathy than the detective, readers experienced greater empathy for the two characters after reading the original version, whose initial paragraph presented information concerning them. This result suggests that when the characters are presented with a short report of their previous life and their characteristics, the reader is more inclined to feel empathy.

Table 2. Mean scores for responses concerning empathy for the two characters in the original and the manipulated versions (* = p < 0.05).

	Original	Manipulated
Empathy for the detective	3.87	3.47*
Empathy for the murderer	2.77	2.39*

The next analysis was carried out on the scores obtained by the 16 questions, irrespective of the version. A factorial analysis (OBLIMIN rotation) evidenced three factors (see Table 3). The first factor includes pleasure, involvement, curiosity, emotionality, interest, suspense, empathy for the detective, impact, imagery: these responses concern the reader's participation in the story («involvement in reading»). The second factor includes surprise and surprise at the outcome: it synthesizes the psychological condition of the readers whose expectations are not confirmed; we refer to this factor as «violation of the expectations». The third factor includes postdictability, coherence and pleasure at the outcome: it concerns a cognitive evaluation of the structural and textual features that make the story comprehensible («cognitive evaluation»). Facility of the story resulted to be a byfactorial response, belonging both to "involvement in reading" and "cognitive evaluation". Only the responses concerning the degree of empathy experienced for the murderer were not included in these factors: they are not related to the other responses.

Table 3. Factor loadings for the three components.[a]

	Involvement in reading	Violation of expectations	Cognitive evaluation	Empathy for the murder
Pleasure	.86			
Involvement	.86			
Curiosity	.85			
Emotionality	.83			
Interest	.78			
Suspense	.77			
Empathy for the detective	.70			
Impact	.60			
Imagery	.51			
Facility	(.43)		(.30)	
Surprise at the outcome		.70		
Surprise		.68		
Postdictability			.90	
Pleasure at the outcome			.74	
Coherence			.68	
Empathy for the murderer				.94

[a]Loadings lower than .50 are reported in parentheses.

In the present investigation we found the same factors including the same responses as two previous studies using Poe's and Tarchetti's short stories (Levorato, Nemesio and Ronconi, 2004; Levorato and Nemesio, 2005). This shows that this finding is a robust one and allows the tentative conclusion that the psychological dimensions underlying these factors are common to different short stories characterized by a plot in which some cues are given and others have to be inferred by the reader, as it is the case in both fantastic mystery tales and detective stories. Further studies could investigate more deeply which are the features of these short stories that produce the kind of reading described by the three factors we found.

In order to analyse readers' responses at a deeper level, a cluster analysis was conducted on the responses of subjects who read the original version of Borges's short story, using Ward's method. Table 4 shows that two clusters emerge: low evaluators (N=62) and high evaluators (N=67), that have a different composition in relation to participants' gender (chisquare = 6.17; df = 1; p<.05): females are low evaluators, while males are high evaluators. The gender difference is limited to the answers that refer to the first factor: involvement in reading. This means that females in general do not give lower scores than males, but that their tendency to give lower scores is limited to the responses which describe the affective-emotional involvement of the reader. As far as the responses belonging to the factors «violation of the expectations» and «cognitive evaluation» are concerned, the cluster analysis did not show a difference between groups or gender of participants, with the exception of coherence, which obtained a higher score by high evaluators than low evaluators.

Table 4. Cluster analyses on the responses of subjects who read the original version of Borges's detective story (Ward's method).

	Cluster 1: low evaluators N=62		Cluster 2: high evaluators N=67		t(127)	p^a
	Mean	SD	Mean	SD		
Pleasure	3.68	1.35	5.66	0.81	10.18	<.003
Involvement	3.56	1.25	5.33	0.84	9.46	<.003
Curiosity	4.29	1.58	5.76	1.07	6.22	<.003
Emotionality	2.85	1.25	4.76	1.05	9.41	<.003
Interest	3.79	1.45	5.57	0.94	8.32	<.003
Suspense	3.68	1.36	5.00	1.00	6.31	<.003
Empathy (Lönnrot)	2.85	1.58	4.79	1.21	7.85	<.003
Impact	3.24	1.42	5.18	1.00	9.01	<.003
Imagery	5.10	1.28	6.28	0.71	6.58	<.003
Facility	4.03	1.17	5.34	0.96	6.96	<.003
Surprise at the outcome	4.68	1.72	5.00	1.55	1.12	ns
Surprise	4.87	1.45	5.06	1.38	0.76	ns
Postdictability	4.92	1.65	5.42	1.36	1.88	ns

Pleasure at the outcome	4.77	1.53	4.91	1.69	0.48	ns
Coherence	4.68	1.36	5.57	1.08	4.13	<.003
Empathy (Scharlach)	2.48	1.40	2.94	1.36	1.88	ns

[a]alpha (Bonferroni correction) = 0.003

The results of the current study were compared with those obtained in a previous investigation, where a short story written by the Italian writer I.U. Tarchetti was used (Levorato and Nemesio, 2005). Tarchetti's "Uno spirito in un lampone" ("A spirit in a raspberry") is a fantastic short story that narrates the experience of a baron who, after eating a few raspberries picked in a place where a murdered girl's body was buried, is seized by the girl's spirit until the murderer is discovered. From the moment he eats the fruit, his vision of reality splits: at one and the same time he sees and feels with both the girl's spirit and his own senses. Consequently, a conflict arises between the two wills that coexist in his person. The cause of the protagonist's split personality is unveiled at the end of the tale, together with the murderer's confession.

A cluster analysis was carried out on the responses of readers who read Tarchetti's short story, using Ward's method. Also in this case two clusters emerged (see Table 5): low evaluators (N=58) and high evaluators (N=136). In this analysis, as in Borges's one, the two clusters have a different composition in relation to participants' gender (chisquare = 8.51; df = 1; p<.05), but in this case women were higher evaluators that males. In Tarchetti's story, all the questions, not only those included in the first factor, obtained higher scores by females than by males. The unique exception concerns Facility, which did not differentiate the two groups of participants: both groups recognized that the story was very easy to comprehend. In sum, the differences due to the gender of readers seem to be consistent, even though, for different story genres, males and females seem to react following opposite trends.

Table 5. Cluster analyses on the responses of subjects who read the original version of Tarchetti's fantastic tale (Ward's method).

	Cluster 1: low evaluators N=58		Cluster 2: high evaluators N=136		t(192)	p[a]
	Mean	SD	Mean	SD		
Pleasure	3.41	1.20	5.44	0.85	13.37	<0.003
Involvement	3.43	1.04	5.13	0.89	11.51	<0.003
Curiosity	3.71	1.28	5.49	0.93	10.89	<0.003
Emotionality	2.83	1.03	4.68	1.12	10.77	<0.003
Interest	3.76	1.35	5.51	0.91	10.54	<0.003
Suspense	2.83	1.13	4.42	1.18	8.70	<0.003
Empathy	1.90	1.04	3.88	1.77	7.98	<0.003
Impact	3.76	1.48	5.19	1.36	6.55	<0.003
Imagery	4.76	1.45	5.71	1.35	4.39	<0.003
Facility	5.69	1.27	6.16	1.09	2.62	ns
Surprise at the outcome	2.74	1.35	3.99	1.55	5.31	<0.003
Surprise	2.79	1.40	4.32	1.59	6.35	<0.003
Postdictability	4.57	1.64	5.46	0.97	4.72	<0.003
Pleasure at the outcome	3.57	1.50	5.04	1.31	6.82	<0.003
Coherence	4.76	1.35	5.65	1.07	4.91	<0.003

[a] alpha (Bonferroni correction) = 0.003

Tarchetti's and Borges's short stories were compared using the Gulpease index, which rates a text's lexical and syntactical simplicity (Lucisano, 1992; Lucisano and Piemontese, 1988). The index gave values (52.23 and 56.09 respectively) that describe both texts as easy for undergraduate students.[1] In order to evaluate the typological differences between the two short stories, five experts in literature, professors at the Faculty of Humanities of the University of Turin, were asked to compare Tarchetti's and Borges's texts, commenting on differences in textual type. The content of their comments was analysed: in all protocols it was

---

[1] The calculation was done by Èulogos (http://www.eulogos.net/it/censor/default.htm, February 2003 and September 2004).

stressed that two texts belong to different textual types: fantastic tale and detective story, respectively. Tarchetti's text was described as a «tale of mystery and the supernatural» placed «outside the natural order», a «religious-like fable» that «belongs to the category of fantastic tales described by Todorov». Borges's text was considered as an «investigation story», a «thriller» that «takes the form of a detective story». On the basis of these differences we can interpret men's and women's different reactions in relation to textual type. In fact male readers seem to be more involved than females in Borges's detective story whereas women readers seem to experience grater emotional participation in Tarchetti's fantastic tale. Further investigation might explore the consistency of such relationship between gender of the reader and textual type.

Works Cited

Borges, Jorge Luis. 1955. La morte e la bussola. In *Finzioni*, translated by Franco Lucentini, 119-131. Torino: Einaudi.

Brewer, William F. 1996. Good and bad story ending and story completedness. In *Empirical approaches to literature and aesthetics*, edited by R.J. Kreuz and M.S. MacNealy, 261-274. Norwood, NJ: Ablex.

Brewer, William F. and Edward H. Lichtenstein. 1981. Event schemes, story schemes and story grammars. In *Attention and Performance IX*, edited by J.D. Long and A.D. Baddeley, 363-379. Hillsdale, NJ: Erlbaum.

—. 1982. Stories are to entertain: A structural affect theory of stories. *Journal of Pragmatics* 6: 473-486.

Cupchik, Gerald C. and Robert J. Gebotys. 1990. Interest and pleasure as dimensions of aesthetic response. *Empirical Studies of the Arts* 8: 1-14.

Eco, Umberto. 1979. *Lector in fabula*. Milan: Bompiani.

Gerrig, Richard J. 1993. *Experiencing Narrative Worlds. On the psychological activities of reading*. New Haven, CT: Yale University Press.

—. 1996. Participatory aspects on narrative understanding. In *Empirical approaches to literature and aesthetics*, edited by R.J. Kreuz and M.S. MacNealy, 127-142. Norwood, NJ: Ablex.

Hidi, Suzanne. 1990. Interest and its contribution as a mental resource for learning. *Review of Educational Research* 60: 549-571.

Iran-Nejad, Asghar. 1987. Cognitive and affective causes of interest and liking. *Journal of Educational Psychology* 79: 120-130.

Iran-Nejad, Asghar and Andrew Ortony. 1985. Qualitative and quantitative sources of affect: How valence and unexpectedness relate to pleasantness and preference. *Basic and Applied Social Psychology* 6: 257-278.

Josè, Paul and William Brewer. 1984. Development of story liking: Character identification, suspense and outcome resolution. *Developmental Psychology* 20: 911-924.

Kintsch, Walter. 1980. Learning from text, levels of comprehension, or: Why anyone would read a story anyway? *Poetics* 9: 87-98.

—. 1996. *Comprehension: A paradigm for cognition*. New York, NY: Cambridge University Press.

Levorato, Maria Chiara. 2000. *Le emozioni della lettura*. Bologna: Il Mulino.

Levorato, Maria Chiara and Aldo Nemesio. 2005. Readers' responses while reading a narrative text. *Empirical Studies of the Arts* 23: 19-31.

Levorato, Maria Chiara, Aldo Nemesio, and Lucia Ronconi. 2004. Risposta emotiva e qualità del testo nella lettura del racconto del mistero. *Età evolutiva* 79: 60-67.

Levorato, Maria Chiara and Lucia Ronconi. 2006. Cognitive and affective responses to structural variations of an E.A. Poe short story. *Empirical Studies of the Arts* 24: 193-217.

Loewenstein, George. 1994. The psychology of curiosity: A review and reinterpretation. *Psychology Bulletin* 116: 75-98.

Lucisano, Pietro. 1992. *Misurare le parole*. Rome: Kepos.

Lucisano, Pietro and Maria Emanuela Piemontese. 1988. GULPEASE: una formula per la predizione della difficoltà dei testi in lingua italiana. *Scuola e città* 3: 110-124.

Miall, David S. 1989. Beyond the schema given: Affective comprehension of literary narratives. *Cognition and Emotion* 3: 55-78.

Miall, David S. and Don Kuiken. 1994. Beyond text theory: Understanding literary response. *Discourse Processes* 17: 337-352.

—. 1995. Aspects of literary response: A new questionnaire. *Research in the Teaching of English* 29: 37-58.

—. 1999. What is literariness? Three components of literary reading. *Discourse Processes* 28: 121-138.

Nemesio, Aldo. 1990. *Le prime parole. L'uso dell'incipit nella narrativa dell'Italia unita*. Alessandria: Edizioni dell'Orso.

—. 2000. Some Questions for Empirical Research. *Versus* 85-87: 447-460.

—. 2002. *La costruzione del testo. Ricerche empiriche su testi italiani dell'Otto-Novecento*. Turin: Thélème.

Sadoski, Mark, Ernest T.Goez and Maximo Rodriguez. 2000. Engaging texts: Effects of concreteness on comprehensibility, interest and recall in four text types. *Journal of Educational Psychology* 1: 85-95.

Schraw, Gregory, Roger Bruning, and C. Svoboda. 1995. Sources of situational interest. *Journal of Reading Behavior* 27: 1-17.

Tan, Ed S. 1996. *Emotion and the Structure of Narrative Film. Film as an emotion machine*. Hillsdale, NJ: Erlbaum,.

Tarchetti, Igino Ugo. 1967. Uno spirito in un lampone. In *Tutte le opere*, vol. 2, 73-85. Bologna: Cappelli.

Todorov, Tzvetan. 1970. *Introduction à la littérature fantastique*. Paris: Seuil.

van Oostendorp, Herre and Rolf A. Zwaan. 1994. *Naturalistic Text Comprehension*. Norwood, NJ: Ablex.

Wade, Suzanne E. and Robert B. Adams. 1990. Effects of importance and interest on recall of biographical text. *Journal of Reading Behavior* 22: 331-353.

Zillmann, Dolf. 1996. The psychology of suspense in dramatic exposition. In *Suspense: Conceptualizations, theoretical analysis and empirical explorations*, edited by P. Vorderer, H.J. Wulff and M. Friedrichsen, 199-231. Hillsdale, NJ: Erlbaum.

Zillmann, Dolf and Jennings Bryant. 1975. Viewer's moral sanction of retribution in the appreciation of dramatic presentations. *Journal of Experimental Social Psychology* 11: 572-582.

Zillmann, Dolf, T. Alan Hay, and Jennings Bryant. 1975. The effect of suspense and its resolution on the appreciation of dramatic presentations. *Journal of Research in Personality* 9: 307-323.

CHAPTER EIGHT

IMAGE SCHEMAS IN NARRATIVE MACROSTRUCTURE: COMBINING COGNITIVE LINGUISTIC WITH PSYCHOLINGUISTIC APPROACHES

MICHAEL KIMMEL

Abstract

In how readers represent narrative plot-macrostructure extended imaginative gestalts may play a key role (parallel to or instead of more abstract propositions). Image schemas, a notion employed very successfully by cognitive linguists (Gibbs and Colston 1995, Hampe 2005), are an excellent tool for modeling macrostructure in narratives. Applying this hypothesis requires projecting claims about phrases to more extended events and the skeletal representations that readers create of them. As this is methodologically all but trivial, how can we explore if story ontology really involves complex gestalts with image-schematic and sensorimotor properties? Clearly, combining text-linguistic with psycholinguistic methods is highly advisable here. The first major section of this paper summarizes a textual approach to Joseph Conrad's novel *Heart of Darkness*, from which I generated hypotheses about the relation between FORCE, PATH, CONTAINER, and other image schemas on the one and specific "tracks" of event ontology on the other hand. The second section reports on a priming experiment with 40 short stories, which focuses on the "track" of story causality. It was hypothesized that abstract representations of story causality (successful vs. unsuccessful goal completion) involve FORCE-like aspects. In the experiment, readers had to perform dynamic force gestures with their hands that could potentially speed up the comprehension of plots with similar flow contours.

Introduction

I would like to begin this essay on global story representations with a couple of local textual passages, which I culled from Joseph Conrad's famous novella *"Heart of Darkness"*.

„I went a little farther (...), then still a little farther, till I had gone so far that I don't know how I'll ever get back" (p. 90)

„fantastic invasion" (p. 58), "fantastic intrusion" (p. 95); „tear treasures out of the bowel of the land (...) burglars breaking into a safe" (p. 55)

„deeper and deeper into the *Heart of Darkness*" (p. 62); „travelling back to the earliest beginnings of the world" (p. 59)

To see how we can make the transition from local text to global story representation, let us ask what these quotes distributed across the text have in common. First, all passages seem to hold a key status in cueing the reader to understand the story's manifest event structure and - when one goes into interpretation - deeper layers of meaning as well. Second, all use spatial and sensory imagery for abstract facets of the story event (even in the case of the first quote which could be read as spatial, but also refers to a psychic "movement"). Third, it is striking that the imagery of the various text passages seems to amalgamate easily at a conceptual level. The expressions evoke (a) path, which they specify (b) as being covered by applying force, and (c) as leading into some kind of inner-realm or depth. Thus, all the expressions (together with three or four dozen others that I don't mention here for the sake of brevity) seem to hang together in the sense of specifying complementary facets of story progression. They all help the reader create a mental model for understanding the deeper psychological and metaphysical nature of Marlow's disconcerting riverboat journey into the Congo in search of the enigmatic Mr. Kurtz.

This material is drawn from a case study that applies cognitive linguistic methods to literary cognition (Kimmel 2005). In it, I have examined how metaphors and other imagery-imbued words may cue the reader's understanding of the global action and event structure of the novella. I have also looked at how distributed cues of an imagistic sort may reflect subtler literary and aesthetic effects which piggyback on the understanding of the basic event structure. These include symbolic nodes (e.g., the rich symbolism of what "darkness" signifies), megametaphors (e.g., the journey as a parable), and the reader's sensory-motor involvement in the reading process.

In the present chapter, I will use this material as a starting point to illustrate a more general cognitive theory of story macrostructure. In essence, my claim is that a story's macrostructure itself shares with the above metaphors something gestalt-like and imagistic. It is not only in *Heart of Darkness* that the mental model of the overall story ontology may involve the same gestalt aspects (PATH, INSIDE-OUTSIDE, CENTER-PERIPHERY, DEPTH, FORCE-PENETRATION, and the like) found the local text-passages. I claim that gestalt scaffolds, onto which metaphoric and other language may open a window, are a general feature of comprehending and recalling stories. The first purpose of this essay is to explain this hypothesis from a text-linguistic and literary viewpoint and then to go into a discussion of a psycholinguistic experiment with simpler stories that validates the claim.

1. Narrative macrostructure

Before I outline my own theory, I will define the key notion. The term narrative or story macrostructure – related to the terms "theme", "plot" and "storyline" – refers to a compressed representation that arises when a reader selects, combines and makes coherent globally relevant aspects from the text microstructure, usually augmented by schematic knowledge (e.g. of genre schemas) (van Dijk 1980, Vipond 1980). Macrostructures thus create a skeleton-like summary representation of an event's known or expected structure.[1] Generating macrostructures has been described as an inferential process that reduces information (Kintsch 1993). Macrostructures "selectively encode input that addresses the emerging theme [...] an information-rich, compact representation that permits the reader to construct characteristics of the text from multiple perspectives" and produce "adages that succinctly capture conflicts, planning failures, solutions, and resolutions" (Graesser, Pomeroy, and Craig 2002, 30, 26).

Macrostructures fulfil various cognitive functions in story comprehension: First, they let readers represent the theme of a story and its storyline as a more or less coherent meaning structure and allow creating explicit verbal summarisations of a story's gist. Creating this kind of compressed representation is crucial because the recall of long texts never happens as a one-to-one reproduction of the text base, but requires a summarisation process through which microstructures are deleted or reconstructed. The main purpose of successful macrostructures is that they

---

[1] A macrostructure may be conceived of as an extended *situation model* or as a structure developed from a collection of situation models. Situation models are the term chosen by discourse psychologists for mental microworlds whereby readers represent the actions, events, etc. of a text. They result from the integration of episodic text memory with prior domain knowledge (cf. Ferstl and Kintsch 1999, 247).

condense the possible inferences readers may make about a story. Macropropositions that summarise a story well seem to have a special status in event memory (Guindon and Kintsch 1984) and allow of a range of inferences close to those of the complete story (Graesser, Bowers, Olde, White and Person 1999).

Second, in on-line story comprehension the tentative model of a macrostructure at a given moment will guide the reader in selecting, making salient and rendering coherent further input from the text. Thus any macrostructure is an emergent and dynamically evolving model of story ontology, which results because the reader makes an active effort at achieving coherence.

Third, cultural knowledge flows into constructing macrostructures, especially of story genres, of prototypical or "good" stories and of everyday scripts. Readers recognize familiar story models like the *exposition-complication-resolution* structure (Bartlett 1932), but may also elaborate them further or create a salient contrast with them. Familiar schemas like story genres or those of more particular story prototypes facilitate macro-comprehension (Kintsch and Yarborough 1982). Thus, readers are guided by both world knowledge and implicit contextual expectations in their strategy of fitting incoming text into an expected macrostructure (cf. Petterson 2002).

2. Image schemas in narrative macrostructure

After this prefatory sketch, I may now lay out what is a relatively new view of macrostructure. My hypothesis is that readers represent important parts of plot-structure as an extended, dynamic, imaginative and gestalt-like contour. The theory of image schemas (Gibbs and Colston 1995, Kimmel 2002, Peña 2003, Oakley 2004, Hampe 2005) provides the conceptual tools to make sense of various aspects of skeletal event representations with such gestalt-like properties. A benefit of the framework is that both text-linguistic and a psycholinguistic research on image-schematic aspects of events has been done in recent times, although it has not extensively been applied to narrative macrostructure. An exception is my own text-linguistic research (Kimmel 2005) and the experiment I report on below.

My claim that image schemas underlie event/story comprehension counters a long tradition of modelling macrostructures in a non-analogue and propositional format (e.g., van Dijk and Kintsch 1983). This tradition defines macrostructure as a complex hierarchy of propositions, and while it explains well how information is compressed (namely by selecting, deleting and recombining propositions), it has considerable difficulty in explaining both the grounding of story comprehension in percept-near cognition and embodied processes in reading. My alternative to this is the suggestion that macro-gestalts account for global story structure. These macro-gestalts can be described as image schemas.

2.1 Image schemas defined

Image schemas, according to Johnson (1987), are experientially recurrent non-propositional representations which are distinct from rich (= percept-near) images. Rather, they are mere topological scaffolds that inhere as dynamic structuring principles in percepts, conceptual activity, and action patterns. Image schemas are cross-modal and connect kinesthetic, tactile, visual and auditory imagery and interface between the embodied and the conceptual realm. Developmentally, they constitute the embodied protosynthesis of abstract concepts in spatial and kinesthetic experience (Mandler 1992).

Typical image-schematic gestalts, usually written in small caps, include CONTAINER, BALANCE, CYCLE, PATH, CONTACT, UP-DOWN, LEFT-RIGHT, CENTER-PERIPHERY, PART-WHOLE, FORCE, SCALE, NEAR-FAR, STRAIGHT, or MULTIPLEX-MASS. What is important here is that many simple image schemas, when dynamically construed, already represent a minimal event. When a path is followed, something is raised up, a boundary transgressed, a circle traced, an object split, or two objects merged, when the perceptual focus wanders from left to right or from part to whole or "zooms in" from mass to multiplex in each case this constitutes a mini-event with a recognisable gestalt structure. Each gestalt already constitutes a simple conceptual scaffold that otherwise diverse kinds of events share. More complex events involve image schemas in sequence, with a change of manner or direction. For example, a mental representation of "anger" involves a mini-scenario in which a container (the body) comes under pressure from within, which goes to a maximum, upon which a sudden release deflates the container again (Lakoff and Kövecses 1987). This is a sequence of EXPANSION and CONTRACTION of a CONTAINER driven by increasing FORCE from within and thus a scenario constituted by compound and dynamically evolving image schemas.

2.2 Image schematic event structure in cognitive linguistics and cognitive narratology

The reader may by now have guessed that the quotations from *Heart of Darkness* on the opening page in fact were chosen for the fact that all of them exemplify image-schematic expressions which hint at some aspect of how the event of traveling up-river in search of Kurtz unfolds.

That linguistic expressions can be used to infer image-schematic gestalts associated with them is one of the fundamental assumptions of cognitive linguistics. Evidence for image schemas in event cognition comes from linguistic research about word and phrases, some of which I summarise here, as well as a growing number of corresponding psycholinguistic experiments (summarised in Gibbs 2005). First, there is evidence on event shape. The manner of an event is encoded in lexical or grammatical aspect which can be perfective, imperfective, habitual, continuous, progressive or stative. Spivey et al. (2005, 269) suggest that perfectivity has to do with image-schematic boundedness. Parrill's (2000, 20) study suggest that features of verb aspect such as dynamicity (change over time), closure (boundedness in time, or telicity), iterativity (repetition) and durativity (extension in time) "map nicely onto actual observable features of physical motion" in the accompanying gestures used by speakers. Gestural and grammatical aspect apparently share a common origin, e.g. perfectives are frequently accompanied by single emphatic chops and ballistic slaps to mark the clear conceptual boundary that reflects completed action. Studies on cross-modal attunement between mother and child also offer insights about event shapes (Stern 1985). For example, a soothing prosody of "THEre-THEre" shares a cross-modal contour with the way the pressure of the accompanying caress is softened at the end of each movement.[2] A second major aspect that is image-schematic in events is what drives an agent. For example, Sweetser (1990) demonstrated that force-dynamic image schemas underlie modal verbs. In

---

[2] Apparently, image schemas also determine the meaning of some verbs such as *pushing, pulling, resisting, yielding, releasing, dipping, rising, climbing, pouring, falling* (Talmy 2000). Narayanan (1997) claims that verb semantics are defined by "physical motor control primitives such as goal, periodicity, iteration, final state, duration and parameters such as force and effort" (quoted from Zacks and Tversky 2001, 11). The different kinds of processes expressed by verbs can be categorized according to whether they are (1) internally homogeneous or heterogeneous, (2) temporally bounded or unbounded, and (3) involve energy consumption or not. This corresponds roughly to CONTAINER, MULTIPLEX-MASS (or BOUNDEDNESS and CONTAINER) and FORCE schemas.

"root modals" a real person is allowed to or required to do something, such that these modals can be based in prototypical FORCE configurations experienced in space. Sweetser claims that "epistemic modals" that emerge from them by metaphorical extension involve similar force representations. For example, while "may" in "You may be right" denotes the ABSENCE OF AN EXTERNAL BARRIER TO FORCE, "must" in "He must be the Scarlet Pimpernel" denotes an IRRESISTIBLE FORCE MOTION, and "cannot" in "She can't have gone over to the enemy" denotes ENABLEMENT OF A MOTION IS ABSENT.

Some recent approaches in cognitive narratology transpose image-schematic structure to a more extended time-scale and claim that narrative has a temporal "event shape" and other aspects similar to the ones found in sentences. Johnson (1993, 69) claims that narrative tension involves image schemas of balance that gets upset and may be restored. Talmy (2000, 439) suggests that force dynamics in narrative plot "characterize such relationships as two entities opposing each other, a shift in the balance of strength between the entities, and an eventual overcoming of one entity by the other." Most systematically, Turner's (1996) study of literary metaphor and parable claims narrative and poetry is structured by "small spatial stories" that are "routinely held together by one or more dynamic image schemas" (p.19). He suggests that we think of "events in time, which have no spatial shape, as having features of spatial shapes – continuity, extension, discreteness, completion, open-endedness, circularity, part-whole relations, and so on" (p. 18). More specifically, Turner claims that we image-schematically understand an event's internal structure such that it "can be punctual or drawn out; single or repeating; closed or open; preserving, creating, or destroying entities; cyclic or not cyclic, and so on." (p. 28). In addition to this event shape, causal structures are also understood by projecting onto them image schemas of force dynamics and of movement along a path (like in the sentence, 'Fear drove him to a situation he otherwise would have avoided.'). In some instances, causal relations in an event may also be thought of as links, paths, or emergence (p. 18). Furthermore, drawing on Sweetser's work, Turner describes narrative event modality as using force image-schematic. This includes an agent's ability to perform an action, the obligation or necessity to perform it, or the possibility of some condition allowing the actor to perform it (p. 29).

2.3 Towards a typology of narrative image schemas

The recent work on image schemas has prompted me to further systematise the major types of image schemas that may structure narratives at various levels. Authors have overlooked so far that image-schematic models may structure events and literary cognition at various levels, which we need to hold apart (cf. Kimmel, n.d.): (1) Local image schemas recur in local text, most often in metaphors, and thereby become "thematic". Examples would be locally recurrent BALANCE relations or CONTAINERS (e.g. Stockwell 2002, Freeman 1993, 1995) that structure several metaphors that play a major role for the plot. Although these image schemas are repetitive and may of course create major memory pegs for the plot summary they do not genuinely inform the understanding of episodic progression itself. The following three types are more manifestly macro-structural. (2) A second category represents temporal and hierarchical story structure as PARTS AND WHOLES, NESTED subgoal structure, episodic breakpoint INTERVALS, etc. This category is mostly concerned with organising meso-structure. (3) A similar kind of image schemas is used by readers to construe what happens in action-oriented terms (the plot) in terms of causality and protagonist interaction (FORCES). Again, this category is mostly organises the episode level of a story. (4) A high-level type of image schemas holistically captures the changes over the PATH time-line of an event. These arise as emergent structure when then interrelation of local information is globally conceived, much like a melody in music. Such holistic image schemas can be felt by readers in their mind-bodies when they represent the story's affect contour, for example as an arc of tension that ends in a resolution or a restoration of balance.

In developing psycholinguistic experiments we will have to focus on types 2-4, which capture the progression of an episode or entire story, hence a real macro-structural effect (although 4 also seems difficult to deal with because of its highly encompassing nature).

3. A text-linguistic approach to macrostructure based on image schemas

We need to account for how a given story lets several kinds of image-schematic meaning unfold in parallel, because only various "story track" representations together create a full narrative. For example, Zwaan, Magliano and Graesser (1995) assume that readers must encode, monitor and update spatial, causal, intentional, temporal, protagonist, and emotional dimensions during reading, notably – as various studies show – causal, intentional and protagonist information. Although the tracks in my model do not wholly coincide with this framework, I agree that a full macrostructural representation will compress information with regard to several tracks. Predicting which kind of story substructure creates which kind of image-schematic imprint is not only needed for fleshing out the image schema model of reading. It is also a crucial condition for designing experiments, because each experiment can only target one track at a time and it needs to be clear which text cues evoke it.

I will now enter into the details my study of metaphors in *"Heart of Darkness"* with a focus on the data pointing to event ontology (Kimmel 2005). First, some words about the novel's plot. Marlow, a seaman, recounts his riverboat journey into the depths of the Congo to find the enigmatic Mr. Kurtz who has established an irrational reign of charisma and terror at his trading outpost, but now is at the verge of death and madness. The gradual intrusion into the eeriness of the jungle transforms Marlow's senses and the confrontation with Kurtz his soul. He experiences a kind of initiation into "dark" knowledge. Back in "civilisation" Marlow visits Kurtz's fiancée, but keeps the truth about his fall from grace and his last words ("The horror! The horror!") from her.

I will mainly look at the event-ontology related metaphors that characterise the main stage of the journey. These can be grouped into different kinds of ontological aspects. For each type of "track" I will now graphically depict the schematic constituents together with a selection of textual metaphors that cue the representation.

3.1 Ontological story spaces

One kind of image-schematic structuring concerns the spatial layout of a story scene as CONTAINER, CENTER-PERIPHERY, LANDMARK, CONTACT, APART, NEAR or DISTANT etc. Since models of single spaces like rooms, etc. are most characteristic of the single episode level, they tend not to impact the macrostructure too much. The narratively most interesting kind of mental representation concerns spaces in a more abstract or even metaphorical sense. Spaces may conceptualise not only spatial locations, but also psychological and existential states represented as bounded or non-bounded containers (cf. Lakoff and Johnson 1999) superimposed on the time-path a protagonist moves through.

In *Heart of Darkness* Marlow, the protagonist, moves from the European space of restrained passions, enlightenment and "culture" to another deeper space, the jungle wilderness, that is associated with attributes of passion, irrationality, the dark, and the feminine. Here we have a logical pattern of the utter apartness of spheres, of ontological incommensurability (indicated by bundles of opposing attributes). This is bolstered by a moral, metaphysical and sensory opposition (light / dark, ...) between the two spheres.

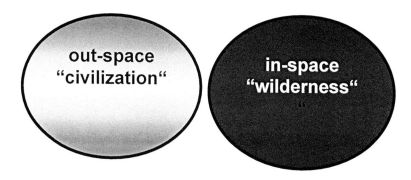

Figure 1
Evaluative and metaphysical opposition as APART, DIFFERENCE
„blank space of delightful mystery" [the Congo] (p. 22); „that great and saving illusion" [the fiancée's naive world] (p. 121); darkness and light metaphors (Kurtz as torch bearer of enlightenment, etc.)
Spheres are related as OUTSIDE-INSIDE or SHALLOW-DEEP
Concentric trip: Outer Station – Central Station – Inner Station
„Mr. Kurtz was in there... a little ivory coming out from there" (p. 49); „deeper and deeper into the *Heart of Darkness*" (p. 62); „traveling back to the earliest beginnings of the world" (p. 59)

3.2 Event modality and temporal texture

The temporal nature and manner of an event is connected to what was earlier said about "aspectual classes" in grammar. Although stories as wholes are, of course, inherently extended and never punctual acts which are during reading construed as imperfective (and after reading as perfective), the manner in which key actions within the whole happen involves "event shapes" of all sorts that contribute incrementally to the whole.

In *Heart of Darkness* Marlow's journey unfolds as a movement along the river from one sphere to the other, and concomitantly from one psychic state to the other. The temporal modality of the movement is gradual and creates a slow continuous transition between states that is accompanied by a gradual accumulation of tension. Note that the slowness in time has to do with other aspects like counterforces being present.

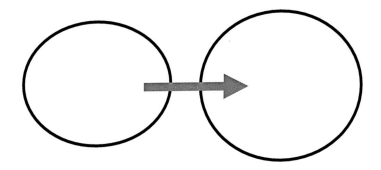

Figure 2
Gradual transition (FORCE-PATH, SCALE)
„The grimy beetle crawled on"; „reality...it fades" (p. 60); „I went a little farther (...), then still a little farther, till I had gone so far that I don't know how I'll ever get back" (p. 90)
Intrusion and transgression (FORCE PENETRATION)
„fantastic invasion" (p. 58), "fantastic intrusion" (p. 95); „tear treasures out of the bowel of the land (...) burglars breaking into a safe" (p. 55)

A further aspect of temporal texture is episodic structure. The breakpoints between episodic meaning units (Zacks and Tvesky 2001) may correspond to container or path-interval image schemas, such that the episode is a part in a story whole. In *Heart of Darkness* this is forcefully expressed in the language of doors, edges and threshold (see below).[3]

3.3 Plot-driving agency and agent intentionality

Protagonist agency pertains to where the impetus for an action comes from. Talmy (2000) specifies that agents have an inherent force tendency. Notably, an agent is conceived of as endowed with a force emanating

---

[3] Event texture over time may produce emergent perceptions of *story "speed", emotional tension, density of action* or the like. A contour over time can be GRADUAL VS. ABRUPT, INCREMENT VS. DECREASE, ACCELERATION VS. DECELERATION, MAINTENANCE. Stories can be STRUCTURED or ERRATIC, as well as STATIC, CYCLIC or CHANGING. However, this kind of effect goes beyond what any metaphor can express.

either from her intrinsic motivation (intrisic force agency) or from an outer or extrinsic causality (external force agency). Intrinsic force agency may be further conceived of as FORCE ENABLEMENT when it is not yet enacted and as FORCE BLOCKAGE REMOVAL when something needs to be done first. Extrinsic force agency can be conceived of as FORCE PULL, FORCE ATTRACTION, FORCE IMPACT, or OBJECT DESTRUCTION BY FORCE that drives the agent entity or enables her actions by removing a blockage, etc.

In *Heart of Darkness*, the protagonist Marlow (and before him Kurtz, whom he emulates) moves into Africa driven not only by his task for the trading company, but, as many metaphors indicate, by a kind of desire and curiosity, a force of internal agency. At the same time, the wilderness is a quasi-agent that actively exerts ATTRACTION, a force of external agency.

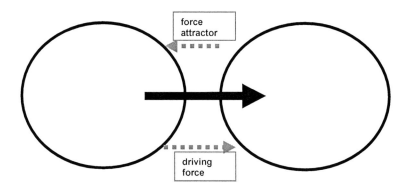

Figure 3
Wilderness [a quasi agent] as seductress and attraction (FORCE ATTRACTOR)
„smiling... inviting, mute with a air of whispering, Come and find out." (p. 29);
„beguiled his unlawful soul beyond the bounds of permitted aspirations" (p. 107)
Desire as impelling force (FORCE DRIVE)
„memory of gratified and monstrous passions ... had driven him out" (p. 107)

3.4 Causality

An aspect related to the previous one is how events are causally connected within and between episodes. This most often concerns how the main goal of a protagonist is attained over various stages and subgoals (cf. Mandler 1984). In terms of image schemas, goals are PATH ENDPOINTS (Lakoff and Johnson 1999, Johnson 1993, 68) and causality consists of maintained, frozen or broken FORCE CHAINS toward this endpoint, which pass on a force impetus. Langacker (1987) calls this the "billiard ball model" of causality. The force-chains are superimposed on the PATH-like timeline. In causal models, hierarchical substructure may issue when a protagonist has to achieve a subgoal. This may be understood as a NESTING-relation, a particular kind of PART-WHOLE schema. Thus, nested force-chains may occur, before the main force-chain can be resumed.

In *Heart of Darkness* explicit metaphors for macro-causality (in the sense of how one event leads to the next) are comparatively absent. However, the continuous FORCE ATTRACTION and FORCE-PULL of agent intentionality that moves Marlow towards the endpoint are established from the beginning on (Kurtz, the Inner Station) and account for the overall action chain without further cues.

3.5 Obstacles and overcoming them

A special facet related to agency/intentionality and causality has to do with the presence (or absence) of obstacles in reaching a protagonist goal. It has to do with FORCE BLOCKAGE and FORCE BLOCKAGE REMOVAL. (In a sense forces that block a story's progress can be more or less treated on a par with antagonists, which I discuss separately here, however.)

Despite the forces that drive the protagonist onward, there are both moral and physical barriers on the journey, the moral ones being related to Marlow's inner turmoil. Yet, the attraction and "gravity" help overcome the barrier (curiosity, captivation with Kurtz), which results in entering the other sphere and a kind of initiation into the 'Other' in a quasi-ritual process.

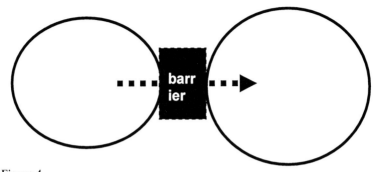

Figure 4
Reaching boundary / threshold (FORCE, PATH, CONTAINER)
„guarding the door of Darkness" (p. 26); „skirts of the unknown" (p. 61); „toiled along slowly on the edge" (p. 62), „peeped over the edge" (p. 119)
Barriers (FORCE BLOCKAGE)
Physical: tropical climate, attacks, death of companions;
Moral: subtly insinuated when Marlow witnesses cruelties;
Psychic: fear and madness
Transgression (FORCE BLOCKAGE REMOVAL)
„beguiled his soul beyond the bounds of permitted aspirations", „driven him out to the edge of the forest" (p. 107); „Transgression, punishment – bang!" (p. 48)

3.6 Protagonist interaction

At an interactional level, what narratologists after Greimas (1966) analyse under the heading of "actant" roles is represented as force configurations between agents. Thus, a protagonist's role at a given time may involve forcing, letting, preventing, helping, hindering, another agent or object as well as acting in vain, each with a specific force-dynamic schema configuration (i.e. FORCE ON OTHER, FORCE RESTRAINT REMOVAL UNTO OTHER, COUNTERFORCE AGAINST OTHER, CONVERGENT FORCE WITH OTHER, FORCE BLOCKAGE OF OTHER'S MOVEMENT and FORCE THAT FAILS TO MOVE AN OBJECT). Patterns of vying forces between protagonists may also change over time, e.g. a shift of the balance of strength, of overcoming the other, or a subsiding antagonism at the end of a story when a complication is resolved and a denouement ensues.

In *Heart of Darkness* a recurrent subtext is the interplay of the Europeans with an antagonist, the wilderness, which has all the attributes of an agent and thus internal force agency. Conrad creates an explicit uncertainty as to whether "white man dominates Africa or the converse". The metaphors used point to an interplay of forces (which is, probably not by coincidence, also the canonical conceptual model for the relation between emotions and rationality, cf. Kövecses 2000).

Figure 5
Wilderness as an agent and enemy (FORCE ANTAGONISM, VYING FORCES)
Metaphors of wilderness dominator, avenger, animal, etc. (see above); „taking possession of an accursed inheritance" (p. 62); „Could we handle that dumb thing or would it handle us?" (p. 49)

Furthermore, there is a process in which Marlow gets taken in by wilderness and is thereby transformed in his soul. This is presumably effected because the wilderness exacts a force on him.

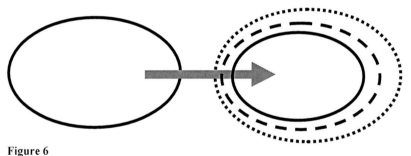

Figure 6
Captivation / being taken in (FORCE ENGULFMENT, CONTAINMENT)
„feel the savagery... had closed around him" (p. 19); „wilderness took him into his bosom again" (p. 45)
„being captured by the incredible which is the very essence of their dream (p. 50)";
„shadowy embrace" (p. 100), „powers of darkness claimed him for their own"

3.7 The compound plot model and the literary effects that it produces

Strikingly, these various metaphor-cued aspects of plot-imagery neatly fit into a single compound image schema. Thus, the conceptual spaces, vectors, and entities arising from several kinds of metaphor can be superimposed imagistically in a single mental substrate where they specify each other. The conceptual base which is responsible for letting aspects of imagery become co-specifying may thus be called a "mental sketchpad" (cf. Baddeley 1986).

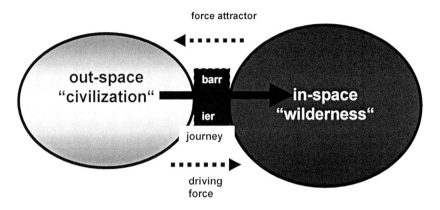

Figure 7

Something interesting may follow from this model of literary processing: When local features become coherent in a global representation by virtue of their image-schematic affinities, further inferences are invited by their combined constraints. In the case of *Heart of Darkness* the compound, integrated and relational nature of this image-schematic skeleton has important inferential and aesthetic properties for literary cognition. For example, the pulling and pushing forces, together with the implied barrier, create a very specific effect of literary tension. Likewise, the mode of gradual transition together with an intensification of attraction make the in-space of the Inner Station as well as Kurtz more and more electrifying. Summing up, I have concluded:

> "readers activate imagery lattices to monitor potential information overlaps between text segments, to link metaphors and cultural models into a higher-level structure, and to produce novel inference. In other words, readers actively search for and mentally simulate matches between imagistic story features they have read" (Kimmel 2005: 233)

What does this metaphor-based case study then reveal about event-related cognition in literature? I do not mean to suggest that every text contains so wonderfully explicit clues of the overall image-schematic event ontology. Some texts do, and others will rely more on the implicit knowledge the reader has about story structure and, in particular, genre knowledge. However, if my image-schematic hypothesis is correct a further-reaching claim can be made: Even where the macrostructure cannot developed in every aspect from metaphor analysis, the underlying mental model that readers eventually construct of the story ontology will share its cognitive features with more explicit cases.

Therefore, I will next take a closer look at stories which lack explicit metaphoric cueing by discussing a psycholinguistic experiment on emergent image schemas in plot-comprehension.

4. An experimental approach to macrostructure

To validate this model of gestalt macrostructures experimentally I chose as a story "track" the force dynamic aspect of causality and goal-attainment. As stimuli I created stories that systematically vary this aspect of plot. The experiment took its inspiration from several related linguistic studies, which I lack the space to summarize here (but see Gibbs 2005: 174-207), but which have produced mounting evidence for the claim that image schemas structure abstract events at the phrase-level.

4.1 Motor priming experiment

The experiment, conducted jointly with Barbara Kaup of the Technical University of Berlin, aimed to find out whether the suggestive phrase-level findings may be extended to the higher level of story macrostructure. A motor priming design was used in the interest of studying the on-line activation of image schemas in short story reading. Because image schemas are believed to be cross-modal,[4] my guiding assumption was this: The cognitive planning effort to carry out a force-dynamic gesture (i.e. activating a motor representation) can interact with a force-dynamic structure that is hypothesized to be part of the reader representation of story goal-attainment. On the basis of this carry-over, a priming design was created such that matches between plot and manifest gestural motor-primes were predicted to let the reader create a macro-representation more quickly than mismatches. The build-up of this representation we were able to deduce from reading times for key sentences. The chosen "story track" agent-driven causality in goal-attainment could manifest itself in three

---

[4] This adds to the assumption that stories have a gestalt-like core. The experimental design implies that this gestalt is also cross-modal and thus not divorced from bodily feeling, but involves substantial sensorimotor and proprioceptive dimensions. This expectation is well rooted in cognitive linguistic research.

kinds of force-dynamic schemas, which in turn reflect three kinds of plot dynamics.

Story stimuli. The stories were "textoids" constructed to ensure that every plot featured a main protagonist with a clear goal, a low number of other agents, no digressions or embedded sub-episodes across test and control conditions. The stories were short, fairly attention-grabbing, and had an invariant kind of plot progression underneath divergent surface structures: (1) A protagonist is introduced in the first sentence with a clear main goal, the achievement or failure of which is at the same time the main topic of the story. Depending on the experimental condition the goal is either reached without trouble, after some difficulty, or not at all. (2) While other agents occur especially in the roles of helper and antagonist, emotion cues and perspectivization devices ensure that the reader takes the perspective of the main protagonist. The rationale for this is that the macrostructure representation may be, to some degree, perspectival in the sense that identification with another person may lead to another kind of causal model, etc. (3) Care was taken that no words evoking strong force dynamic schemas occurred in the text to avoid a priming effect rooted in the manifest microstructure rather than the inferred macrostructure. (4) Although actual spatial movement by protagonists is impossible to exclude, care was taken that the protagonist goal is no genuinely spatial goal and that achieving it did, for the most part, require abstract movement (like a thought-path, etc).

Gestural primes. For each of the 40 stories, one of four simple gestures had to be performed. Beginning from a position of both hands held at elbow-height and at shoulder-breadth one of the following was instructed before each story: (1) the left fist moves forcefully to the clasping right hand, which stops its movement through counterforce; (2) the left fist moves to the right unstopped by anything as far as the impetus goes; (3) the fist is first briefly stopped by the right hand, but then it is pushed away and the movement continued; (4) an outward opening motion of both hands with both palms up is done (filler gesture). Each of these four gestures matched an icon:

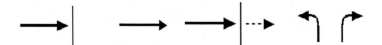

Figure 8

Procedure. The 46 participants were asked to read forty short stories of 10-12 sentences each in a self-paced fashion from a laptop screen, moving forward between screens by pressing the space bar. After familiarising the subjects with the reading and gesturing tasks they read one story after the other. Before a story began one of the four visual icons was displayed so that the subjects could memorise the associated gesture and later carry it out upon hearing a beep during reading. In the final debriefing the participants were asked if they had a clue about the research question and whether they had consciously reflected on a connection between gestures and story plots. (The former was never the case, the latter occasionally.) Each experiment lasted between 20 and 40 minutes.

Test design. Cognitively, the motor memory of the gesture had to be held active in parallel to on-line text comprehension. Our aim was to ascertain whether the (mis-)match between the planned gesture and the story would influence the reading speed of three target sentences in which the story complication occurred. These sentences were located towards the end of each story, but never occurred in last or penultimate position. The reading speed was deduced from the self-paced space-bar presses.

A tri-factorial 2(group) x 2(condition) x 2(match) design was used. Every participant read two different groups of stories (see below for details) and did so including all the conditions. The groups comprised different stories. Twelve stories were included in group 1, another twelve in group 2, and sixteen used as fillers. In an overview, the three factors in which manipulations occurred were:

o The story type (12 stories in Groups 1 and Group 2 each, and 16 additional filler stories):
o The central part of each story sequence (2 plot versions in each story):
o The four gestures could either match the story plot or not.

The following table specifies whether story type and gesture match and provides the number stories used in each test condition (in brackets):

Table 1

STORY TYPE / PLOT VERSION		GESTURE TYPE			
		Source-path-goal (unblocked)	Blockage removal	Folding hands [filler gesture]	Blockage remains
TYPE 1	Goal attainment / no problem	Match (3)	Mismatch (3)		
	Goal attainment after problem is mastered	Mismatch (3)	Match (3)		
TYPE 2	Goal attainment fails / problem persists		Mismatch (3)		Match (3)
	Goal attainment after problem is mastered		Match (3)		Mismatch (3)
FILLER	(gesture early in story)	(3)		(8)	(3)
	(gesture late in story)			(2)	

TOTAL # OF STORIES per gesture type	9	12	10	9

The twelve stories in Group 1 involved plots in which the protagonist either reaches the goal without problems or after overcoming an abstract (non-spatial) obstacle. We predicted that these two plot alternatives would match with an unblocked punch and with a blocked punch gesture, respectively. The twelve stories in Group 2 involved plots in which, again, an obstacle had to be overcome. This was, however, now contrasted with a condition in which the aim is not reached at all and the protagonist "gets stuck". We predicted that these alternative courses of plot development would match with a briefly stopped, but unblocked punch and with a blocked punch gesture, respectively. The two groups thus, all in all, involve three kinds of gestural image schemas that are hypothesised to match with three kind of causal plots: (1) enacted FORCE on a path that reaches its PATH END-POINT OR GOAL (**immediate goal-attainment in plot**), (2) enacted FORCE ON A PATH that reaches its PATH END-POINT, but only after a stage of FORCE BLOCKAGE that has to be overcome actively (**goal-attainment after problem solving in plot**); (3) enacted FORCE on a path that is BLOCKED and that does not reach its PATH END-POINT (**no goal attainment in plot**).

4.3 Results

The dependent variables were the three sentence-reading times, the two sentences that varied with plot version and the reading times for the third target sentence that was constructed in such a way as to be identical in both story plot versions.[5] Reading time analyses were conducted separately for these three dependent variables. This was done only when the participant had actually performed the instructed movement. However, as participants had quite faithfully reproduced the gestures the discarded cases were minimal. Moreover, reading times that were shorter than 500 ms or longer than 10,000 ms were omitted. For determining additional outliers, differences among the story items were considered by converting the reading times of each participant to z-scores and discarding those with a z-score deviating more than 2 standard deviations from the mean z-score of the respective item in the respective condition (3-6% of measures). The remaining data were submitted to 2(group) x 2(condition) x 2(match) ANOVA. This was done (1) with repeated measurement on all three factors in the analysis by participants and with (2) repeated measurement on the last two factors in the analysis by items.

The overall ANOVA in the by-participants analysis produced a significant main effect of the group, with shorter reading times found in Group 1 (GOAL ATTAINMENT vs. BLOCKAGE REMOVAL) than in Group 2 (BLOCKAGE REMOVAL vs. PERSISTING BLOCKAGE), ($F1(1,44)=11$, $p<.05$; $F2(1,22)=1.5$, $p=.24$ The fact of speedier reading in Group 1 than Group 2 does not say anything about the hypothesis, but is noteworthy anyway. There also was a marginally significant interaction of group and match ($F1(1,44)=3.5$; $p=.07$, $F2<1$).

To gain more information with respect to potential interactions, we analysed the reading times separately for the two groups. For Group 1 (GOAL ATTAINMENT vs. BLOCKAGE REMOVAL) no significant effects were found (all $F<1.1$, $p>.30$). However, for Group 2 (BLOCKAGE REMOVAL vs. PERSISTING BLOCKAGE), there was a significant effect in the by-participant analysis, meaning that shorter reading times were found in the match than in the mismatch condition ($F1(1,44)=6.5$, $p<.05$; $F2(1,11)=3.5$, $p=.09$). This effect directly supports the hypothesis. The relative sizes of the effect

---

[5] Because of technical problems with the response time measurement, we only were able to get data from 24 participants for the first and the second variation sentence, slightly limiting the range of what can be said about them. For the target sentences coming last we got data for a total of 46 participants for 19 of the 24 story items of interest, but only got data for 24 participants for the remaining 5 story items.

and direction can be illustrated by comparing match and mismatch conditions in each of the following four pairs of columns:

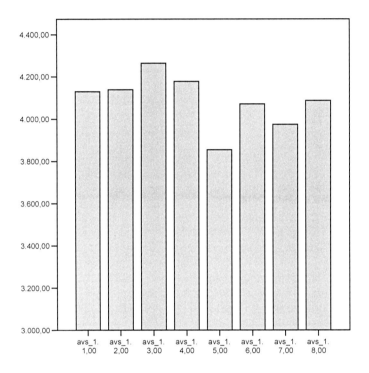

Table 2: The four left columns in the table represent the results for Group 1, whereas columns 5-8 represent Group 2. Here is a summary of the specific conditions involved regarding both the type of force-dynamic schema tested and the condition of match or mismatch:

180 Image Schemas in Narrative Macrostructure

GROUP	FORCE SCHEMA	CONDITION
Group 1	BLOCKAGE REMOVAL	Match
Group 1	BLOCKAGE REMOVAL	Mismatch
Group 1	GOAL-ATTAINMENT	Match
Group 1	GOAL-ATTAINMENT	Mismatch
Group 2	BLOCKAGE REMOVAL	Match
Group 2	BLOCKAGE REMOVAL	Mismatch
Group 2	BLOCKAGE PERSISTS	Match
Group 2	BLOCKAGE PERSISTS	Mismatch

4.4 Interpretation, uncertainties and future directions

The fact that at least for one experimental group (Group 2) a pattern of equivalence between story-plot structure and force-dynamic gestures emerged is suggestive for my hypothesis of image schema structure in plot causality. Two background conditions have to hold for this interpretation: (1) No propositional connections can be derived between gestures and stories. I believe that no such effect is possible. This would require explaining in what way sketchy visual images and subsequent motor planning can call up a propositional representation about a story goal and how transmodal correspondences between movement and linguistic meaning occurs. (2) No distracting microstructural associations are primed by the gesture; e.g. by similarity of the gesture's shape to a single object appearing in the storyworld. Although occasionally subjects reported that they had started reading with searching for microstructural correspondences, this was not only extremely rare, but also apparently unsuccessful, so far as subjects reported in the debriefing.

One theoretical uncertainty relates to the image-schematic modality the obtained effect rests on. Genuine motor-preparation is one possibility, yet the visual icon could also have produced the effect because of a topological correspondence between visual image and plot. The present design thus offers no real measure for the degree that genuine proprioception/kinaesthetics played a role in producing the image-schematic effects. (Many of the participants reported that a visual and not a kinaesthetic image had served as their memory cue. Yet, these self-reports do not exclude that a proprioceptive image of the movement's "feel" was formed subliminally by cross-modal spill-over).

The major problem with the results remains that only one group yielded a significant effect. One possible explanation is that some stories had too irregular and distracting features. This is not likely with twelve different stories in a group, but surely possible. Complexity, embedded sub-goals, overall story length, number of protagonists, and distracting words were largely controlled for, so that the most likely factor to bias the results is the entertainingness of stories. This is a characteristic in which stories differed to some degree, as some participants remarked. An alternative explanation is that features of the planned gestures account for the difference between the two groups. It could either be based on differences in complexity between the gestures (mono, bi- and triphasal) or based on the fact that the gesture's final phase was dissimilar across conditions in one group but not the other. After all ordinary non-blocked FORCE vs. FORCE BLOCKAGE REMOVAL (Group 1) are non-identical in their middle phase, but both end in the same dynamical open swing. These alternatives may not be as distinct as those used in the more successful Group 2, at least for readers to whom a gesture's end state is most salient.

In view of all this, a follow-up study should seek to accomplish three things: (1) Apply a story grammar coding as a prior check of the structural similarity of the story stimuli; (2) devise a control experiment to find out whether the found effect is really due to motor planning or some other mechanism, and (3) understand better why the effect is found only for the target sentence, but not for the two others before it.

Acknowledgments

My thanks go to Barbara Kaup and Jana Lüdke for collaborating in the empirical part of this research.

Works Cited

Baddeley, A. 1986. *Working memory*. Oxford: Clarendon.
Bartlett, F. C. 1932. *Remembering: a study in experimental and social psychology*. Cambridge: Cambridge University Press.
Conrad, Joseph 1995 [1899/1901]. *Heart of Darkness*. London: Penguin.
Dijk, T. A. v. 1980. *Macrostructures: an interdisciplinary study of global structures in discourse, interaction, and cognition*. Hillsdale, N.J.: L. Erlbaum Associates.
Dijk, T. A. v., and W. Kintsch. 1983. *Strategies of discourse comprehension*. New York; London: Academic Press.
Ferstl, E., and W. Kintsch. 1999. Learning from Text: Structural Knowledge Assessment in the Study of Discourse Comprehension. In

The Construction of Mental Representations During Reading, eds. H. van Oostendorp and S. Goldman, 247-277. Mahwah, NJ: Erlbaum.

Freeman, D. 1993. #According to My Bond': King Lear and Re-Cognition. *Language and Literature, 2*(1): 1-18.

—. 1995. 'Catch[ing] the Nearest Way': Macbeth and Cognitive Metaphor. *Journal of Pragmatics, 24*: 689-708.

Gibbs, R. W. 2005. *Embodiment*. Cambridge: Cambridge University Press.

Gibbs, R. W., and H. L. Colston. 1995. The Cognitive Psychological Reality of Image Schemas and their Transformations. *Cognitive Linguistics, 6*(4): 347-378.

Graesser, A., C. Bowers, B. Olde, K. White, and N. Person. 1999. Who Knows What? Propagation of Knowledge Among Agents in a Literary Story World. *Poetics, 26*: 143-175.

Graesser, A., V. Pomeroy, and S. Craig. 2002. Psychological and Computational Research on Theme Comprehension. In *Thematics in Psychology and Literary Studies*, eds. M. Louwerse and W. van Peer, 19-34. Amsterdam & Philadelphia: John Benjamins.

Greimas, A. J. 1966. *Sémantique structurale: recherche et meéthode*. Paris: Larousse.

Guindon, R., and W. Kintsch. 1984. Priming Macropropositions: Evidence for the Primacy of Macropropositions in the Memory for Text. *Journal of Verbal Learning and Verbal Behavior, 23*: 508-518.

Hampe, B., ed. 2005. *From Perception to Meaning: Image Schemas in Cognitive Linguistics*. Berlin & New York: Mouton de Gruyter.

Johnson, M. 1987. *The body in the mind: the bodily basis of meaning, imagination, and reason*. Chicago: University of Chicago Press.

—. 1993. *Moral imagination : implications of cognitive science for ethics*. Chicago ; London: University of Chicago Press 1993.

Kimmel, M. 2002. *Metaphor, Imagery, and Culture*. University of Vienna, Vienna.

—. 2005. From Metaphor to the "Mental Sketchpad": Literary Macrostructure and Compound Image Schemas in Heart of Darkness. *Metaphor & Symbol, 20*(3): 199-238.

—. (n.d.). *The scope of image schemas in narrative and event structure: Towards a typology of functions*. Unpublished manuscript, Vienna.

Kintsch, W. 1993. Information Accretion and Reduction in Text Processing: Inferences. *Discourse Processes, 16*: 193-202.

Kintsch, W. and J. Yarborough. 1982. The Role of Rhetorical Structure in Text Comprehension. *Journal of Educational Psychology, 74*: 828-834.

Lakoff, G. and M. Johnson. 1999. *Philosophy in the flesh: the embodied mind and its challenge to Western thought.* New York: Basic Books.
Lakoff, G. and Z. Kövecses. 1987. The Cognitive Model of Anger Inherent in American English. In *Cultural Models in Language and Thought,* ed. D. a. N. Q. Holland, 195-221. Cambridge: Cambridge University Press.
Langacker, R. W. 1987. *Foundations of cognitive grammar.* Stanford: Stanford U.P.
Mandler, J. M. 1984. *Stories, scripts, and scenes: aspects of schema theory.* Hillsdale, N.J: L. Erlbaum Associates.
—. 1992. How to build a baby: II. Conceptual primitives. *PsychologicalReview, 99*: 587-604.
Narayanan, S. 1997. *Moving right along: A computational model of metaphorical reasoning about events.* University of California, Berkeley.
Oakley, T. (forthcoming). Image Schema. In *The Handbook of Cognitive Linguistics,* D Geeraerts and H. Cuykens. New York: Oxford University Press.
Parrill, F. 2000. *Hand to Mouth: Linking Spontaneous Gesture and Aspect.* Unpublished BA thesis, University of Chicago, Chicago.
Peña Cervel, S. (2003). *Topology and Cognition: What Image-schemas reveal about the Metaphorical Language of Emotions.* Muenchen: LINCOM.
Petterson, B. 2002. Seven Trends in Recent Thematics and a Case Study. In *Thematics: Interdisciplinary Studies,* eds. M. Louwerse and W. van Peer, 237-252. Amsterdam & Philadelphia: John Benjamins.
Spivey, M., D. Richardson, and M. Gonzalez-Marquez. 2005. On the spatial and image-schematic underpinnings of real-time language processing. In *Grounding Cognition: The Role of Perception and Action in Memory, Language, and Thinking,* eds. R. A. Zwaan and D. Pecher. Cambridge: Cambridge University Press.
Stern, D. N. 1985. *The interpersonal world of the infant: a view from psychoanalysis and developmental psychology.* New York: Basic Books.
Stockwell, P. 2002. *Cognitive poetics: an introduction.* London; New York: Routledge.
Sweetser, E. 1990. *From etymology to pragmatics: metaphorical and cultural aspects of semantic structure.* Cambridge: Cambridge University Press.
Talmy, L. 2000. *Toward a cognitive semantics.* Cambridge, Mass.; London: MIT Press.

Turner, M. 1996. *The literary mind.* New York: Oxford University Press.
Vipond, D. 1980. Micro- and Macroprocesses in Text Comprehension. *Journal of Verbal Learning and Verbal Behavior, 19*: 276-296.
Zacks, J. and B. Tversky. 2001. Event Structure in Perception and Cognition. *Psychological Bulletin, 127*(1): 3-21.
Zwaan, R., J. Magliano, and A. Graesser. 1995. Dimensions of Situation Model Construction in Narrative Comprehension. *Journal of Experimental Psychology: Learning, Memory, and Cognition, 21*: 386-397.

Chapter Nine

Fiction and Belief Change: Exploring Boundaries

Melanie C. Green and Jennifer Garst

Abstract

Individuals frequently adopt real-world beliefs from fictional works (e.g., Green and Brock 2000; Slater 1990; Strange and Leung 1999; Prentice, Gerrig, and Bailis 1997). One potential moderator of fictional influence is the realism of the narrative. In the present study, participants in a reading experiment were randomly assigned to read a version of a fictional story that was either 1) realistic, 2) realistic but with blatant factual errors, or 3) science-fiction themed (set in the future and on another planet). A control group responded to belief items before reading the story. Story dialogue contained false belief statements. As predicted, individuals showed belief change in response to the realistic story, but not to the error version. Contrary to expectations, science fiction did not produce belief change; however, individuals rated the science-fiction version as the most plausible. This study suggests that realistic fiction may be most effective at influencing beliefs, but that individuals may have different standards of realism for different genres.

Introduction

Literature scholars – and literature readers – know intuitively that a novel or a short story can change the way readers view the world. But not all stories are created equal – some stories may have characteristics that make them more likely to influence real-world thoughts and beliefs. The work described here explores one possible influence, the plausibility of the story. In particular, our study focused on violations of real-world accuracy, or potentially unreliable authors.

One recent example of an unreliable author is James Frey, who wrote a memoir of his struggle with drug addiction (*A Million Little Pieces*, published in 2003). The book became a bestseller when American talk show host Oprah Winfrey chose it for her book club. However, investigative reporters discovered that several of the key events in the book had not actually occurred. The discovery of his exaggerations not only led to tremendous embarrassment for Frey, but also cast the entire message of his book into doubt. Although Frey's problems arose in part because he claimed that the book was a true account, the same principle may hold true in fictional writings. Even though authors of fiction are permitted and expected to diverge from reality in some ways, "getting it wrong" when it comes to verifiable real-world details may make readers suspicious and less likely to be influenced.

This work is part of a broader research program addressing the question of how narratives, even fictional ones, change individuals' real-world attitudes and beliefs. We approach this question from a social psychological background and perspective. Social psychologists have been interested in persuasion processes for decades, but most of the recent work on attitude change has focused on traditional persuasive messages, such as editorials and advertisements. The study of narratives, and of fiction, has been relatively ignored. The current work attempts to fill that gap and to provide empirical insights for literature scholars.

The power of narrative fiction has been demonstrated empirically in a growing number of studies, with a variety of different kinds of stories. For example, Strange and Leung (1999) found that a short story could influence readers' beliefs about the causes of students dropping out of high school. Slater (2002) discusses the successes of entertainment education programs, which have frequently been used to change health beliefs and behaviours, especially in the developing world. And Marsh and colleagues (Marsh, et al. 2003) found that individuals learned "false facts" from fiction. In short, the mere fact that a narrative is fictional – that it does not report events that actually occurred in the world – does not limit the persuasion that can occur.

An important next step is to come to a deeper understanding of when and how fiction can translate into real world belief change.

Nature of Fiction

Before describing our study, we want to be clear about two important points about fictional persuasion. First, our focus is on fiction that is recognized as fiction. There are certainly cases where individuals might be persuaded by fiction because they believe it to be fact. They might have missed a disclaimer that a program was a drama rather than a documentary (like the famous Orson Welles *War of the Worlds* radio broadcast as a Halloween special on October 30, 1938, where listeners thought that Martians were actually invading Earth and panic ensued). Or, over time, individuals may forget where a particular piece of information came from. They might think that they read it in a factual source, but it was actually fiction. These cases of source confusion are interesting in themselves, but they are not our focus here. Individuals do not have to believe that a story is real to be persuaded by it.

Second, fiction is an unusual category. Fiction refers to a story that is "not necessarily true." Fiction does not mean false. Authors often draw on real-world facts, and authors of historical fiction, for example, often do painstaking research to insure that their settings or plots are appropriate for their era. However, a reader typically does not know what parts of the narrative are made up, and which parts are based on real-world truth. So, determining whether it's reasonable to gain information from fiction can be a difficult question.

Fiction Processing

Our theory has focused on the mental processes that occur when individuals encounter a fictional work (Green, et al. 2004). Specifically, we propose that either fiction or narrative may serve as a cue to a reader to engage in a less-critical, more immersive form of mental engagement. The idea that stories are treated differently from scientific or logical argument, and may be held to different truth standards than rhetorical messages, is not new. For example, Bruner (1986) stated that "A good story and a well-formed argument are different natural kinds...arguments convince one of their truth, stories of their lifelikeness" (p. 11). Along similar lines, Prentice and Gerrig (1999) suggested that fiction tends to be processed non-systematically, and that fiction has its greatest influence when readers respond experientially rather than rationally.

We further propose that this less-critical processing may take an engaged or an un-engaged form. In the un-engaged form of fictional processing, an individual may simply disengage critical or evaluative processing (see Prentice and Gerrig 1999). (This state of mind may be similar to that described in Coleridge's famous dictum "the willing suspension of disbelief", or instead, it may be that individuals automatically believe fictional information, and do not take the extra step to "willingly construct disbelief", as Prentice et al. 1997 argue.) The person may be focused on relaxation, may feel that the material is not particularly important, or may simply wish to be entertained. However, the reader or viewer engaged in this form of processing is not deeply immersed in the narrative. An un-engaged television viewer may be content to flip to another channel; an un-engaged reader might not especially care about the characters or may not devote any effort to imagining scenes or characters. These individuals may simply be looking for an easy way to pass some time. Readers or viewers in this mental state may be passively influenced by the communication.

The engaged form of fictional processing is what Green and Brock (2000) have termed transportation into a narrative world, or getting fully immersed in the content of a story. We define transportation as an integrative melding of attention, imagery, and feelings, focused on story events. We conceptualize transportation as a convergent process, whereby the bulk of an individual's thoughts and attention are focused on the events in the narrative. A transported reader may lose track of time, respond emotionally to events occurring in the narrative, or form vivid mental images of settings or characters, but meanwhile, the majority of the reader's cognitive resources are absorbed by the narrative.

In either the high or low engagement routes to fictional persuasion, the plausibility of the narrative may play a role in its ability to change real-world beliefs. The studies cited above suggest that the important element is whether the narrative feels real and engaging, not whether it reflects actual events. An implausible narrative may reduce readers' transportation, distracting them or making it more difficult for them to remain absorbed by the narrative world. Even in a low-engagement state, readers might be prompted to engage in more critical or elaborative thought if the narrative becomes less plausible, or they may use these narrative elements as a cue for disbelief. The experiment discussed in the current paper focused more directly on plausibility as a factor in fiction-based belief change.

Current Study

In our experiment, we manipulated features of a story that should make it more or less realistic or plausible. The story that we used was called "The Kidnapping," and it was created by psychologists Richard Gerrig and Deborah Prentice (e.g., Prentice et al. 1997). It is about a college student, Brad, who is kidnapped on his way to class. He is held prisoner with his roommate and a professor, who have also been nabbed by the kidnappers. In the end, the kidnapping turns out to be a birthday prank arranged by

Brad's parents. The story is reasonably engaging, but fairly straightforward.

The characters have conversations about various topics, and these conversations suggest false beliefs. Examples include, "eating chocolate helps you lose weight" and "mental illness is contagious." Participants rated their agreement on a scale of 1 (strongly disagree) to 9 (strongly agree). Change in these beliefs will be our primary dependent variables.

Although the *Kidnapping* plot is somewhat farfetched, the original story was written in a fairly realistic style. Our manipulations included two alterations designed to make the story less realistic: an error condition and a science-fiction condition. We also included a no-story control group. This group of participants responded to the belief items before reading the narrative. Thus, the control group provided a baseline comparison for agreement with the beliefs implied by the two experimental versions of the story.

In the first alteration, the error condition, we introduced what we hoped would be obvious or blatant factual errors, such as locating famous landmarks in the wrong cities or misrepresenting well-known historical facts. Several of these errors appeared early in the text. Here are two examples: "Brad loved the sights and sounds of New York City—the White House, the Sears Tower, Rockefeller Center, the Smithsonian—but sometimes it was all a bit too much." and "One of my earliest memories is my mother showing me the *Herald* headline about Mondale's election to the presidency. That was in 1980." In the first sentence, almost all American college students should recognize that the White House is not in New York, but in case they missed that, the Smithsonian and the Sears Tower are also put in the wrong place. In the second example, Mondale lost the election in 1980. We expected that these changes would serve as a wake-up call to readers to be suspicious of what the author was telling them. These types of violations of real world truth should take readers out of a non-critical state and alert them that the text is not a trustworthy representation of real world facts – the author (or possibly the narrator) here is careless or ignorant of the facts. (Another possibility is that the author has reasons beyond what the readers know to disregard these facts.) Thus, belief change should be reduced in this condition.

The second alteration changed the realism in a different way. In this version, we simply altered some of the setting details so that the story took place on a different planet in the distant future: "He looked out the window and saw that it was the beginning of another gray morning on Asimov-6, the first human settlement outside the Milky Way." The names of the towns, newspapers, and the like were changed, but the main characters were still attending a college, the kidnapping was still a birthday prank, and so on. We originally expected that this type of alteration would not affect belief change. Individuals would clearly recognize that some artistic license was being taken, but these diversions from reality occurred within a framework of a recognizable genre, science fiction. Although readers should recognize that the settings are not realistic, they might still suspend their critical thinking and disbelief for more general claims about the world.

Because the effects of plausibility may be related to the extent of critical thinking that readers do, we also included a relevant individual difference measure. We assessed individuals' need for cognition, or their tendency to enjoy and engage in effortful cognitive activity (Cacioppo, et al. 1984). To put it more simply, people who are high in need for cognition – and most academics fall into this category – are internally motivated to think about issues, problems, and ideas. People who are low in need for cognition, on the other hand, prefer to conserve their cognitive resources, and only devote a lot of thought to a communication if there's some external reason to do so – if the topic is personally relevant, for example. Need for cognition is measured with an 18-item scale. Participants rate the extent to which each statement is characteristic of themselves or not. An example item is, "Thinking is not my idea of fun." Low need for cognition individuals would be likely to endorse this item. Individuals who are high in need for cognition might be especially sensitive to violations of plausibility.

We measured perceived plausibility or realism with a 7-item scale which included items such as "the dialogue in the narrative is realistic and believable" and "people in this narrative are like people you or I might really know." Participants rated these items on a 1 (strongly disagree) to 9 (strongly agree) scale.

We had participants list their thoughts about the story (Petty, et al. 1981). After they finished listing the thoughts, they went back and indicated whether those thoughts were positive, negative, or neutral toward the story. Thought listing is frequently used as an index of counter-arguing. A high number of negative thoughts, for instance, might indicate that individuals were in a critical state of mind.

We also had participants rate their transportation into the story. Transportation is measured with a 15-item scale that includes measures of cognitive, emotional, and imagery involvement (Green and Brock 2000). An example item is, "I was emotionally involved in the narrative." Participants rate the items on a scale of 1 (not at all) to 7 (very much). However, our previous research with this narrative suggested that it was only moderately transporting; thus, participants were more likely to be in a "low engagement" state of processing rather than a high-engagement state of processing. So, we included transportation as an exploratory measure, but did not necessarily expect it to play a major role in the results.

Students participated in the study for extra credit toward one of their courses. Our final sample – after dropping a handful of individuals who were not fluent in English (n = 17) or who did not pass a recall test of basic story facts (n = 4) – was 197 people.

Results

The belief results are shown in Figure 1. We took the mean of 6 belief items, statements such as the "mental illness is contagious" items described above. Higher numbers indicate greater endorsement of the beliefs, or a greater shift toward the story content. Only the realistic version of the story led to belief change – the sci-fi and the error versions were not different from the no-story control.

Figure 1: Belief endorsement by condition (higher numbers indicate more story-consistent beliefs)

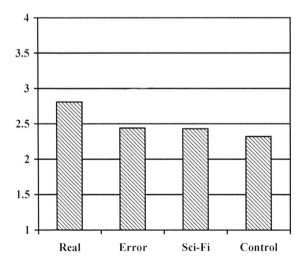

Clearly, individuals were sensitive to discounting cues within the story. The results for the error condition confirmed our expectations, but the results for the science fiction version did not. It appeared that any kind of deviation from reality reduced belief change.

We next examined the plausibility ratings (Figure 2). Here we observed something a little strange: the science fiction version was rated as the most plausible. It appeared that individuals reading a more fantastical story may have been more willing to give the author latitude in what the characters did and said; the suspension of disbelief may have been stronger in the sci-fi world – but only up to a point. Contrary to our expectations, this perceived plausibility did not map on to belief change. Recall that the plausibility measure was geared toward perceptions of the characters and events, rather than the claims or statements made in the story. Nonetheless, this disconnect suggests that different types of plausibility or realism may have different effects.

Figure 2: Perceived Plausibility by Experimental Condition

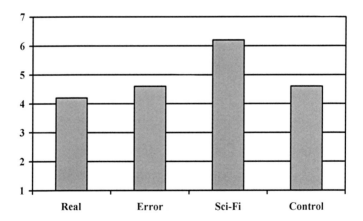

The thought-listing results were consistent with this pattern. To analyse participant thoughts, we used the standard method of creating a "thought positivity" index. We took the number of positive thoughts minus the number of negative thoughts and divided them by the number of total thoughts. Individuals were most negative about the real and the error versions, and were significantly more positive about the sci-fi version. (Further examination of this pattern indicated that it was driven largely by the number of positive thoughts.) This combination of results suggests that sci-fi leads to discounting through a relatively non-thoughtful process.

Did need for cognition, or this general enjoyment of thinking, matter for belief change? The pattern of results was intriguing, but the interaction between condition and need for cognition was not statistically significant. We used a median split to divide our participants into high and low need for cognition groups. The pattern of results is shown in Figure 3.

Figure 3: Belief change by condition and need for cognition

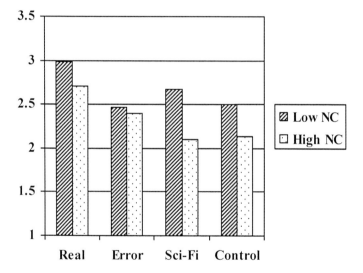

There is a general trend for individuals low in need for cognition to show more story-consistent beliefs, even in the control group. This main effect suggests that low need for cognition individuals might just not be as well-informed or as confident in their beliefs. More interesting is the difference between the error and the science fiction conditions. Low need for cognition people seemed to suspend their disbelief to a greater extent than the high need for cognition individuals for the sci-fi condition. Perhaps for high need for cognition individuals, the outer space setting acted as a cue for them to ignore or dismiss the belief implications of the sci-fi story. However, the interaction between need for cognition and story type did not achieve statistical significance, so these speculations are tentative at best.

Transportation was not significantly affected by the story version; individuals were equally transported into all the stories. Transportation scores were around the midpoint of the scale. Transportation was positively correlated with perceived plausibility ($r = .26$), but was not related to belief change.

Discussion

To summarize, these results suggested that 1) changing features of the story to reduce its plausibility or realism led to reduced belief change, but 2) these changes to surface features of the story did not necessarily reduce perceived realism, at least with the current measure. Furthermore, 3) belief change did not appear to be occurring through a thoughtful process. Where does this leave us? To understand these results, it is helpful to compare the current study to previous research on narrative-based belief change. We suggest that there are different types of belief change that may occur in response to narratives, and the process of change may be different depending on the type of change. In the current study, the beliefs were expressed in the character dialogue, but were not integrated into the plot. One could imagine a story where contagious mental illness, for example, was a key narrative element, but that was not the case here. So, these stories were more akin to the false facts paradigm than the entertainment education or transportation studies.

In other stories that we've used in our research, the belief change arises more naturally from story events; the attitudes are implied rather than stated directly. For example, we have used a story called "Just as I am" about a gay man returning to his college fraternity reunion and encountering discrimination among current fraternity members (see Green 2004). This story implies beliefs about homosexuality and fraternities, relationships between alumni and current fraternity members, and so on. These beliefs and attitudes are never directly stated in the text, however. In studies using this story, measures of perceived plausibility and realism are related to belief change. So, the plausibility of the characters, or the emotional truth of the story, influences belief change when those beliefs emerge out of the experiences of the characters.

Violations of accuracy may then lead to rejection of explicit statements in the text, whereas violations of character plausibility may lead to rejection of story implications. Direct tests of this comparison are a direction for future research.

The manipulations that we used here, particularly the error condition, are somewhat akin to the idea of an "unreliable narrator" (Booth 1961). The unreliable narrator is a literary device in which credibility of narrator is severely compromised, perhaps through psychological instability, bias, lack of knowledge, or intent to deceive.

However, often when there is an unreliable narrator, the attentive reader can, at some point, see beyond the information given. A reader may understand the broader social context of racism in the South even if Huckleberry Finn does not, or see the extent of Lolita's innocence and pain even if Humbert Humbert does not. It is the narrator's credibility or knowledge, not the author's, that is cast into doubt. In our study, we expect that the author's knowledge, rather than the narrator's, was called into question. Whether having an unreliable narrator evokes critical thinking or negative cognitive responding in a way that limits belief change is an open question. At the least, attitude and belief change may be more subtle or complex with these types of narratives.

Works Cited

Booth, Wayne. 1961. *The Rhetoric of Fiction*. Chicago: Chicago University Press.

Bruner, Jerome. 1986. *Actual Minds, Possible Worlds*. Cambridge, MA: Harvard University Press.

Cacioppo, John T., Richard E. Petty, and C.F. Kao. 1984. The efficient assessment of need for cognition. *Journal of Personality Assessment* 48: 306-307.

Green, Melanie C. 2004. Transportation into narrative worlds: The role of prior knowledge and perceived realism. *Discourse Processes* 38: 247-266.

Green, Melanie C., and Timothy C. Brock. 2000. The role of transportation in the persuasiveness of public narratives. *Journal of Personality and Social Psychology* 79: 701-721.

Green, Melanie C., Jennifer Garst, and Timothy C. Brock. 2004. The power of fiction: Persuasion via imagination and narrative. In *The Psychology of Entertainment Media: Blurring the lines between entertainment and persuasion*, ed. L.J. Shrum, 161-176. Mahwah, NJ: Lawrence Erlbaum Associates.

Marsh, Elizabeth J., M.L. Meade, and Henry L. Roediger. 2003. Learning facts from fiction. *Journal of Memory and Language* 49.4: 519-536.

Petty, Richard E., Thomas Ostrom, and Timothy C. Brock. 1981. *Cognitive Responses in Persuasion*. Hillsdale, NJ: Erlbaum.

Prentice, Deborah A., and Richard J. Gerrig. 1999. Exploring the boundary between fiction and reality. In *Dual-process Theories in Social Psychology,* eds. Shelly Chaiken and Yacov Trope, 529-546. New York: Guilford.

Prentice, Deborah A., Richard J. Gerrig, and Daniel S. Bailis. 1997. What readers bring to the processing of fictional texts. *Psychonomic Bulletin & Review,* 5: 416-420.

Slater, Michael D. 1990. Processing social information in messages: Social group familiarity, fiction versus nonfiction, and subsequent beliefs. *Communication Research* 17: 327-343.

Slater, Michael D. 2002. Entertainment education and the persuasive impact of narratives. In *Narrative Impact: Social and Cognitive Foundations,* eds. Melanie C. Green, Jeffrey J. Strange, and Timothy C. Brock, (pp. 157-181)Mahwah, NJ: Lawrence Erlbaum Associates.

Strange, Jeffrey J., and Cynthia C. Leung. 1999. How anecdotal accounts in news and in fiction can influence judgments of a social problem's urgency, causes, and cures. *Personality and Social Psychology Bulletin* 25: 436-449.

PART II

INFLUENCES OF READERS' BACKGROUND ON MEDIA PERCEPTION

CHAPTER TEN

COMPASSION AND DISGUST AS MARKERS OF CULTURAL DIFFERENCES IN READING VIOLENCE IN LITERARY TEXTS

PAUL SOPČÁK

Abstract

In *Upheavals of Thought: The Intelligence of Emotions*, Martha C. Nussbaum develops a theory of the emotions as judgements of value and argues that certain works of literary art may be morally refining, whereas others may elicit destructive behaviour. She focuses particularly on the importance of compassion in moral development and disgust as its impediment. A study of cultural differences in responses to violence in literary texts helps corroborate Nussbaum's claims. Brazilians, Germans, and US-Americans read three excerpts from Latin American literary texts containing graphic descriptions of violence and answered questions assessing their emotional and judgemental reactions. Results showed significant differences between participating cultures as well as between different text passages.

"There, but for the grace of God go I"
—John Bradford on seeing a group of criminals led to the scaffold

Introduction

Violence, like sex, is a touchstone for a culture's double standard. In *Ästhetik der Gewalt: Ihre Darstellung in Literatur und Kunst* (*Aesthetics of Violence: Its Presentation in Literature and Art*), Jürgen Wertheimer points to the paradox of, on the one hand, an increasing taboo on violence within the moral code of our society and, on the other hand, a simultaneous increase in the market share of weapon exports (in the case of Germany) and mass media depicting violence. According to Wertheimer, violence is deeply embedded in our culture in various interdependencies and constellations that society conceals in its attempt to sustain the myth of individual and societal pacifism.

Deeply embedded violence is not merely a contemporary cultural phenomenon. In fact, violence has played a leading role in the Western world's legitimating, identity constituting cultural heritage at least since the *Iliad*. The essentially ambivalent relationship between literature and violence demands an unbiased analysis that defies and demystifies taboos, since one must assume "that through the literary and artistic stylization of violence fundamental, individual, and societal needs are expressed" (Wertheimer 1986, 10).

Martha C. Nussbaum, in her attempt to formulate a normative ethics that incorporates the emotions and stresses the importance of the humanities and the arts in education, touches on this ambivalent relationship. She argues that some works of literary art may be morally edifying, whereas others may elicit destructive behaviour. Furthermore, she emphasizes the importance of compassion in moral development, the socio-cultural factors that influence who will become the object of compassion (Nussbaum 2001, 308, 313-314, and 317-322), and the barrier to compassion that disgust establishes.

In this chapter, I will present the results of a first study that bear out some of Nussbaum's claims. Its main objective was an exploratory cultural comparison – rather than testing particular hypotheses – of responses to violence as portrayed in literary texts. Three groups of students, Brazilian, US-American, and German, read excerpts from Juan Rulfo's short story "Remember", Gabriel García Márquez's *Chronicle of a Death Foretold* (1996), and Julio Cortázar's novel *Hopscotch* (1998), each of which culminates in a death. The first is a case of capital punishment, the second follows social norms and a code of honour, and the last is a consequence of institutionalized torture. The aim was to see whether these violent scenes elicit significant cultural differences.

In the following section, I lay out the design, materials, and procedures of the preliminary study. Next, I present the results, and lastly, I will offer an interpretation of the results within the framework of Nussbaum's account of emotions as judgements of value, with particular attention to her discussion of compassion (2001, 19-85 and 297-441).

Method

Reading Materials

In this study only a small range of the numerous forms of violence was taken into account. The selection of texts was aimed at providing different expressions of violence. Since all three texts were written by Latin American authors, and to counter the chances of participants recognizing the texts, characters' names were changed to common names in Brazil for the Brazilian questionnaire, English names for the English, etc. The rationale behind these changes was also to balance the effect that Latin American stereotyping may have on readers' responses.

The first excerpt stems from Juan Rulfo's short story "Remember." It describes the fate of a man who as a young boy is publicly humiliated by his teachers and fellow students, and severely beaten by his uncle after "playing man and wife behind the lavatories." After this incident, he leaves his village and does not return until twenty years later, now with the authority of a police officer. Out of spite, he slays the village's mentally feeble Mandolin player, is himself severely injured by a bystander, and flees once more. When the police find him, he offers no resistance: "They say that he himself tied the rope around his neck and even picked out the tree of his choice for them to hang him from" (Rulfo 1967, 135-136).

Presentation of the protagonist's history and the potential causes for his violent behaviour provide the opportunity for readers to feel compassion for him. He is not simply portrayed as an unjust criminal. His violence could easily be seen as a consequence of the social segregation he suffered. Whether, and for which cultures, this view holds will be examined in this chapter.

The second text passage, an excerpt from Gabriel García Márquez's *Chronicle of a Death Foretold*, in which the gruesome stabbing of a young man by two butcher brothers is described in vivid detail, stands in stark contrast to the Rulfo passage. Presented out of context, as it was for the purpose of this study, the violent act stands for itself, without explanatory background. The events are related by direct quotations from the brothers' testimony, as well as by the narrator's reconstruction of the scene. The lack of context in which this passage is presented creates ambiguity about the role of social pressure in the crime. Despite the bold and unapologetic descriptions the brothers give of their stabbing, the enormous psychological burden they bear and the role of cultural mores in their crime may be sensed by some readers, even without the explicit context.

The third passage chosen for this study combines a description of horrific institutional violence with musings about the aesthetics of violence. It is taken from the fourteenth chapter of Julio Cortázar's *Hopscotch*, in which the protagonist and a Chinese character contemplate reprints of Polaroid photographs depicting the torture and execution of a victim with knives. The emotionally detached and callous description of the torture scene is chilling; it aptly captures the ambivalent attraction to and abhorrence of violence prevalent in numerous cultures throughout the world.

Questionnaires

In email correspondence, the questionnaires were administered to each of the three groups in their native tongue. The first fifteen questions, given before the texts were read, assessed participants' attitudes towards violence in general, their impression of the degree of violence in their home country, and possible reasons for it. The rationale for these opening questions was to obtain a rough baseline measure of readers' disposition towards violence against which to contrast the situational responses to the violent text passages they subsequently read. I will focus on a subset of five of these questions, which are particularly relevant to the argument made in this chapter. These dispositional measures included questions such as "I am in favour of censoring violence in literature" and "I'm in favour of the death penalty in cases of extreme crimes." Each question was presented with a five point rating scale from 1 (I don't agree at all) to 5 (I totally agree).

Following these general questions, participants first read an excerpt from Juan Rulfo's short story "Remember," then a passage from Gabriel García Márquez's *Chronicle of a Death Foretold*, and lastly, the torture scene from Julio Cortázar's novel *Hopscotch*. After each of these text passages they responded to nine items assessing to what extent the respective passage evoked thoughtfulness, anxiety, helplessness, anger, disgust, aggression, and the desire to actively change something; whether they found the text aesthetically appealing; and whether they were familiar with the text passage.

Apart from the items that were identical for each of the three passages, a number of text-specific questions were asked, such as "The text passage conveys the picture of a just world to me," for the Rulfo text, and "Texts like these glorify violence and should therefore be prohibited," for the Márquez passage. Finally, participants were asked about their reading habits and they provided some demographic information.

Reader Demographics

All participants were volunteers and received no compensation. The group of participants whose mother tongue was German consisted of twenty-seven students of the Ludwig-Maximilian University, Munich, Germany, twenty of whom were women and seven men (mean age 26.81, range = 20–42). The twenty-four English-speaking participants were all students at Ripon College in Ripon, Wisconsin, USA. Fourteen were women and ten men (mean age 20.67, range = 18–31), and the Brazilian group was formed of nine women and seven men studying at the Universidade Federal do Rio de Janeiro, Brazil (mean age 26.06, range = 18–42). Although US-American participants were significantly younger than Brazilians and Germans, there were no significant differences between the three groups in relative socio-economic status and in the proportion of men and women.

Results

Predispositions Toward Violence

To compare these three groups of readers in terms of their dispositions toward violence and its causes we conducted one-way ANOVAs. When the omnibus F-value was significant, we used the Bonferroni Post Hoc test to examine the pattern of differences between groups. Despite the fact that the three groups resembled each other in all assessed criteria but age, they differed significantly in their impressions of violence in their home country. As shown in Table 1, Brazilian participants rated the degree of violence in their home country significantly higher than did the US-Americans, who in turn rated it higher than did the Germans.

The Brazilian and US-American readers were more likely than the German readers to attribute these levels of violence to a hostile global environment. And, the Brazilians especially, but also the US-Americans, were more likely than the Germans to rate such violence as "necessary." While the Brazilians distinctively see violence in their country as broadly "institutionalized" in "everyday life," they share with US-American readers their support for "institutionalized" violence in the form of the death penalty in response to "extreme crimes (sexual murder, child murder)." This pattern may help to explain why the Brazilians and the US-Americans were more likely than the Germans to believe that violence could be justified in some circumstances. In sum, the Brazilian and US-American readers, more than their German counterparts, believe in the *justifiability* of violence, although the Brazilian readers especially are convinced of its *necessity*. Surprisingly perhaps, these three groups of readers did not differ either in their level of trust in the "people in my society" or in their support for censoring violence in literature.

Table 1: Predispositions Toward Violence

		Brazilian (N = 16)	US-American (N = 24)	German (N = 27)
Violence cannot be justified under any circumstances whatsoever.	Mean	2.56[a]	2.50[a]	3.85[b]
	Std. Deviation	1.36	1.32	0.77
In favor of the death penalty.	Mean	2.75[a]	3.13[a]	1.63[b]
	Std. Deviation	1.48	1.75	1.04
Rating of violence in home country.	Mean	4.75[a]	3.67[b]	2.67[c]
	Std. Deviation	0.45	1.09	0.83
The hostile Global Environment is to blame for this violence.	Mean	3.44[a]	3.08[a]	2.11[b]
	Std. Deviation	0.89	1.18	1.12
I trust the people in my society.	Mean	2.75	2.88	3.19
	Std. Deviation	1.18	0.99	0.88
Readiness to be violent is necessary nowadays.	Mean	3.75[a]	2.46[b]	1.69[c]
	Std. Deviation	1.24	1.22	0.93
Institutionalized violence is part of everyday life in my country.	Mean	4.25[a]	2.67[b]	2.19[b]
	Std. Deviation	0.93	1.31	1.04
I'm in favor of censoring violence in literature.	Mean	1.75	1.58	2.22
	Std. Deviation	0.93	0.83	1.12

Note: Cell means with different superscripts differ significantly from each other (at least $p < .05$) as indicated by the Bonferroni Post Hoc test

Responses to Textual Violence

As mentioned earlier, after each of the three text passages participants responded to nine items assessing to what extent the respective passage evoked thoughtfulness, anxiety, helplessness, anger, disgust, aggression, and the desire to actively change something; whether they found the text aesthetically appealing; and whether they were familiar with the text passage. Since almost no one knew the texts, and familiarity did not affect the other responses, I will not return to this item. In what follows, I will begin by reporting the global text effects, that is, to what extent responses to these questions differed across the three texts for all three groups.

Repeated measures ANOVA indicated that there were significant within-subjects effects for the items anxiety, $F(2,128)=4.874$, $p<.009$; disgust, $F(2,128)=11.177$, $p<.001$; helplessness, $F(2,128)=3.302$, $p<.04$; thoughtfulness, $F(2,128)=4.358$, $p<.015$; aggression, $F(2,128)=3.570$, $p<.045$; and the desire to actively change something, $F(2,128)=5.350$, $p<.006$. In general, Text 2 (Márquez) evoked less thoughtfulness and desire to change the situation, and more disgust and anxiety. These results need to be treated with caution, though, since text effects may be confounded by order effects (the order in which the texts appeared on questionnaires was not randomized). Nevertheless, the fact that Text 2 also stands apart from Texts 1 and 3 in its presentation of violence without contextual information and without the dimension of institutionalized violence suggests at least some text effects independent of order effects.

Two of the nine repeated questions also showed significant between-groups differences. Repeated measures ANOVA's indicated that Germans, Brazilians, and US-Americans differed significantly in the level of disgust, $F(2,64)=11.07$, $p<.001$; and anxiety, $F(2,64)=8.194$, $p<.001$; the texts evoked in them. Bonferroni Post Hoc comparisons showed that Brazilian participants reported to have felt significantly less anxiety in response to the texts than both the Germans ($p<.001$) and the US-Americans ($p<.049$) as well as significantly less disgust than the Germans ($p<.011$) and the US-Americans ($p<.001$). As can be seen in Figure 1 below, specifically, in response to the Rulfo passage (Text 1), in which depth is attributed to the protagonist's character and the motives for his violent behaviour, the US-American participants reported higher levels of disgust than did the Brazilians and Germans.

Besides the set of nine questions repeated after each text, additional questions assessed readers' responses to unique aspects of each of the texts. Table 2 below provides a summary of the between-group differences in the responses to these items.

In the excerpt from Juan Rulfo's "Remember," for instance, one villager tells another of how their former classmate, who had been publicly ridiculed and physically abused in his childhood, was recently hung for murdering the village idiot. After reading the passage, participants were asked to indicate their level of agreement with the statement: "I find that [protagonist with altered name] is punished appropriately for his murder." As can be seen in the figure below, the German and Brazilian participants' agreement with this statement is significantly lower than that of the US-American participants, $F(2,64)=10.405, p<.001$.

Table 2: Text Specific Responses

		Brazilian (N =16)	US-America n (N =24)	German (N = 27)
I find that [protagonist with altered name] is punished appropriately for his murder (Text 1: Rulfo).	Mean	1.31ª	2.46ᵇ	1.44ª
	Std. Deviation	0.60	1.22	0.75
The text passage conveys the picture of a just world to me (Text 1: Rulfo).	Mean	1.25ª	1.96ᵇ	1.3ª
	Std. Deviation	0.58	0.91	0.72
Under the circumstances depicted in the text above, I would want to be armed (Text 2: Márquez).	Mean	3.5ª	2.92ª	1.96ᵇ
	Std. Deviation	1.46	1.53	1.16
Texts like these glorify violence and should therefore be prohibited (Text 2: Márquez).	Mean	2.00	1.75	2.44
	Std. Deviation	1.37	1.19	1.28
Descriptions of violence in literature, like the above, are important to increase people's sensitivity toward institutionalized violence (Text 3: Cortázar).	Mean	2.00	1.75	2.44
	Std. Deviation	1.37	1.19	1.28

Note: Cell means with different superscripts differ significantly from each other (at least p < .05) as indicated by the Bonferroni Post Hoc test.

This situational evaluation of the appropriateness of the death penalty also functioned as a measure of potential text effects on attitudes towards the death penalty, with the initial dispositional measure, "I'm in favour of the death penalty in cases of extreme crimes," serving as a baseline measure. Repeated measures ANOVA indicated that there were significant within-subject effects, $F(2,64)=21.725$, $p<.013$; that is, overall participants rated the appropriateness of the death penalty significantly lower in the context of Juan Rulfo's "Remember" than they did when asked about their disposition towards it in general.

Figure 1

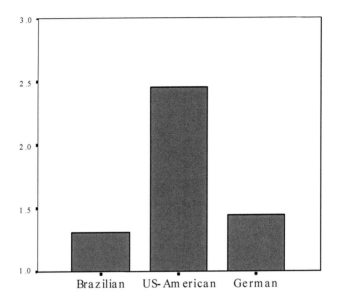

However, there were also significant between-group differences in this text effect, $F(2,64)=9.803$, $p<.001$. Multivariate simple effects analyses showed that the death penalty questions produced a flooring effect[1] in German participants, that is, they strongly opposed the death penalty, both dispositionally as well as in the context of the Rulfo story, $F(2,64)=.542$, n.s. In contrast, there was a measurable text effect for both US-Americans, $F(2,64)=6.243$, $p<.015$ ($p<.045$ after Bonferroni correction) and Brazilians, $F(2,64)=19.352$, $p<.001$, whose endorsement of the death penalty dropped significantly from the dispositional measure to the text-specific measure.

These differences in text effect should not, however, obscure the fact that the endorsement of the death penalty of Rulfo's protagonist was significantly stronger by the US-American participants than by participants of the other cultures as reported in Table 2 and Figure 1.

---

[1] This means that the data cannot take a still lower value, called the 'floor'.

Figure 2

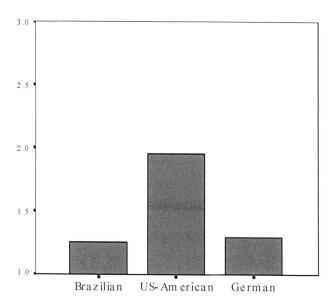

The results for the second question specific to the passage from Rulfo's "Remember," "The text passage conveys the picture of a just world to me." point in the same direction. Differences between groups were statistically significant, $F(2,64)=6.069$, $p<.004$. As can be seen in Figure 2, and as post hoc tests indicated (Table 2), German and Brazilian participants were less likely to agree with this statement than were the US-Americans.

Following the excerpt from Márquez, which graphically portrays the brutal stabbing of a young man by two brothers, participants reported to what extent they agreed with the statement: "Under the circumstances depicted in the text above, I would want to be armed." As can be seen in Figure 3, the German participants' felt need to be armed was significantly lower than that of the other cultural groups.

Figure 3

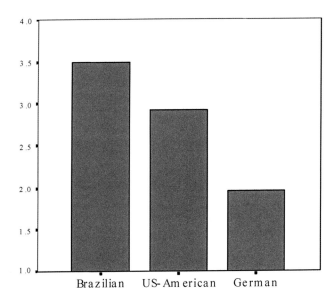

The subsequent question, "Texts like these glorify violence and should therefore be prohibited," which assessed readers' inclination to censor specifically the kind of presentation of violence as it occurs in *The Chronicle of a Death Foretold*, yielded no significant between-group differences. All three groups tended to disagree with the call for censorship.

In order to target responses to the type of violence particular to the excerpt from Cortázar's *Hopscotch*, readers provided their level of agreement with the statement: "Descriptions of violence in literature, like the above, are important to increase people's sensitivity toward institutionalized violence." The level of agreement did not differ significantly between the three groups. They had a slight tendency to agree with the value of such descriptions.

Discussion of Results

Some of the limitations of this study must be acknowledged. First, it must be seen as a preliminary study exploring basic patterns and pathways for further enquiry. The sample size is rather small and not sufficiently homogeneous to allow for confident generalizations. The US-American participants, for instance, are six years younger on average than the Brazilians and Germans. Also, both Munich and especially Rio de Janeiro, from which the German and Brazilian participants stemmed, respectively, are urban areas and most likely expose their inhabitants to violence more frequently and to a higher degree than rural Ripon, Wisconsin. The frequency and extent of violence in Rio de Janeiro, however, is significantly higher than in Munich. Furthermore, all three chosen texts are the works of Latin American authors, and the Brazilian participants may consequently have a greater familiarity with the form of violence described in them, and this may have influenced the findings.

Bearing in mind that the results must therefore be read with caution, I nevertheless would argue that some valuable insights have been gained. The guiding questions in the ensuing discussion will be the following: When does reading violence evoke compassion, and when does it affect attitudes on violence. How does it come about, and does the effect vary across cultures?

As the findings from the first set of questions demonstrate, the three groups of readers in this study approach the selected literary texts with quite different attitudes towards violence. The Brazilians and US-Americans in this study, in contrast to the Germans, thought that violence could not be categorically condemned: some situations called for violent actions. A possible explanation for these differences is that they perceive the societies they live in (and the Global Environment) as much more violent than Germans do theirs. In line with this perception, and the approval of violence in some cases, was their higher acceptance of the death penalty for extreme crimes. Noteworthy, however, is the fact that, while the Brazilian readers agreed with the US-Americans that some crimes call for the death penalty, they do not agree with the US-Americans that Rulfo's protagonist deserved to be hanged for the murder he committed. In fact, they show even more compassion with the protagonist than the Germans do, and the simple poetic justice evident in Rulfo's story does not fit their notion of a just world.

What elements of the text evoke such a discrepancy between the judgments of violence in principle and those of the events related in the story? In order to address this question, I will briefly present a few aspects of Martha C. Nussbaum's views on the importance of emotions and the power of narratives to evoke them.

In *Upheavals of Thought*, Nussbaum develops a theory of the emotions as judgments of value that form an integral part of our intelligence and need to be accounted for (but not privileged) in moral philosophy. In her view, abstract treatises of moral philosophy alone do not lead to the level of self-understanding necessary to see through our often ambivalent and paradoxical relations with the world around us. Furthermore, she proposes that emotions have a temporal dimension and narrative structure in which the imagination plays an important role: "If emotions involve judgements about the salience for our well-being of uncontrolled external objects, judgements in which the mind of the judge is projected unstably outward into a world of objects, we will need to be able to imagine those attachments, their delight and their terror, their intense and even obsessive focusing on their object, if we are ever to talk well about love, or fear, or anger" (Nussbaum 2001, 2-3).

One of the emotions she focuses on as crucial in the moral development of a human being is compassion. She gives an excellent overview of the philosophical discussions that have and still do surround compassion, pity, sympathy, and empathy (pp. 327-35). Although I do not fully agree with Nussbaum's definition of empathy and the way in which she distinguishes it from compassion, I will adopt her terminology here, since my line of argument draws on her work.[2] In the most basic sense, then, compassion is a "painful emotion occasioned by the awareness of another person's undeserved misfortune" (2001, 301). Important to note here is the term "undeserved," since whether or not someone is to blame for his or her plight is dependent on "prevailing social attitudes" (p. 313). Furthermore, compassion "requires the acknowledgment that one has the possibilities and vulnerabilities similar to those of the sufferer," (p. 316) i.e. I must be able to imagine that under different circumstances I could experience the same misfortunes.

Nussbaum also argues for the importance of compassion in the law. By integrating the defendant's history into the sentencing process, the narrative it forms may induce the jury to imagine for a moment the social and personal circumstances of the criminal – not only imagine, but to weigh these within the structure of their own values – and to recognize him or her as a fellow human being (pp. 441-54). On a more general note she describes this as follows: "The claim seems to be that if you really vividly experience a concrete human life, imagine what it's like to live that life, and at the same time permit yourself the full range of emotional responses to that concrete life, you will (if you have had at all a good moral start) be unable to do certain things to that person. Vividness leads

---

[2] For an excellent discussion and overview of empathy and literary texts, see: Suzanne Keen, "A Theory of Narrative Empathy," *Narrative* 14 (2006).

to tenderness, imagination to compassion. The patient effort to see moderates the coarseness of which political horror is made" (Nussbaum 1990, 208).

In the study presented in this chapter, participants were placed in the jurors' seats and asked to decide whether the protagonist of Rulfo's story deserves the death penalty. The reader learns that Urbano Gómez has suffered great injustice and social segregation in his childhood. They also learn that his uncle "gave him such a beating it almost left him paralyzed," implying that his parents are either dead or unable to raise him, and that he grew up in severely adverse conditions. Furthermore, the reader learns that Urbano is injured after committing the crime and that he is in great pain when he flees. His unresisting surrender to the police toward the end of the story, to the point that "he himself tied the rope around his neck and even picked out the tree of his choice for them to hang him from," presents the protagonist as innocuous, helpless, and suffering. Lastly, the fact that a former schoolmate of the hanged man relates these events to a fellow villager in a highly sensational manner increases the ambivalence of the story's moral perspective: "You must remember him, because we were classmates at school, and you knew him just like I did" (Rulfo 1967, 136). Contrasting this to the absence of any information on, let alone history of, the protagonist's victim, there is a large potential for readers to feel compassion for the protagonist. And indeed, most participants did not think the protagonist should have been hanged. What is more, even though on average the Brazilian and US-American participants neither approved nor disapproved of the death penalty in principle (Germans strongly disagreed), the former strongly disagreed that Rulfo's protagonist should suffer it, whereas the latter's opinion remained undecided (see Figure 1).

Thus, it seems that the US-American participants failed to allow themselves "the full range of emotional responses to that concrete life" (Nussbaum 1990, 208), and did not engage with the narrative of Urbano's personal narrative in an imaginative way that would lead to compassion. The Brazilian participants' empathic reaction, on the other hand, seems to imply if not a vivid experience of the protagonist's plight, then at least an imaginative engagement with it.

I will turn to Nussbaum again in the search for an explanation. In *Upheavals of Thought* she discusses the emotions of shame, envy, and disgust as impediments to compassion. Nussbaum draws on Paul Rozin's intriguing studies of the emotion of disgust and extends his conclusions, when she states that: "Disgust thus wards off both animality in general and the mortality that is so prominent in our loathing of animality" (Nussbaum 2001, 203). The emotion of disgust serves as a border police between self and other, which manifests itself in binary pairs such as human/animal; alive/dead (decaying). Moreover, disgust is not an inborn emotion; it first appears around the age of four and is highly influenced by socio-cultural norms and values, as Rozin and Fallon (1987, 33) point out: "The acquisition of disgust is a special case of the acquisition of culture or values and is a prototypical example of the interaction of affect and cognition." Rozin and Fallon further provide convincing examples of how disgust has been employed to create boundaries between cultures and races in order to strengthen one's own identity and submit the disgusting other to non-human treatment (p. 38). Nussbaum explains this as follows: "we see that disgust, which always serves the purpose of setting us at a distance from our own animality and mortality, easily takes as its object other persons and groups, who come to represent what is avoided in the self. So powerful is the desire to cordon ourselves off from our animality that we often don't stop at feces, cockroaches, and slimy animals. We need a group of humans to bound ourselves against, who will come to exemplify the boundary line between the truly human and the basely animal" (Nussbaum 2001, 347).

Within our societies, criminals and psychologically abnormal people often serve as the negative projection plane against which the 'functioning' individual will ensure and define his or her identity. Nussbaum claims that when the emotions of disgust are evoked purposefully, in a court hearing of a murderer, for instance, "[w]e are being urged to see that person as a monster, outside the boundaries of our moral universe. We are urged precisely *not* to have the thought, 'there, but for ... go I'" (p. 452). Within this line of argument, the paradoxical treatment of violence in our society assumes an inner logic. While morally condemning violence, its ubiquitous presence assures a superficially stable identity *ex negativo*.

The results of the study presented here support Nussbaum's claims. I have indicated that the narrative of the criminal's history seems to have affected the Brazilians in such a way that they did not find the death penalty appropriate punishment for the protagonist, unlike the US-American participants (the Germans condemned the death penalty in principle and for Rulfo's protagonist alike). Furthermore, the US-participants agreed far more than the other groups that the short story represented the image of a just world to them.

Looking at the ratings on disgust then, we find that the US-Americans also reported the highest level of disgust as a response not only to the events of "Remember," but to all three text passages. It seems, then, that the US-American participants have a greater tendency to regard violent acts as alien to their self-concept. In my opinion, experiencing the emotion of disgust is less remarkable for the Márquez and Cortázar passage, but it does stand out as a response to Rulfo's story. The US-Americans have placed Rulfo's criminal outside their realm of possible identification, and thus compassion.

This finding is supported by Candace Clark's report in *Misery and Company: Sympathy in Everyday Life*, in which she investigates current (1997) US-American stances on sympathy and compares them to those of other cultures. Her participants all show sympathy only for misfortunes brought upon someone by "bad luck" or "victimization by forces beyond a person's control" (1998, 84). Nussbaum points out that these judgements will vary largely in different cultures: for example, "Americans are on the whole less ready than Europeans to judge that poverty is bad luck, given the prevalence of the belief that initiative and hard work are important factors in determining economic success" (Nussbaum 2001, 313).

In the early 20th century, Max Weber argued in a similar vein. He held that Calvinism with its doctrine of predestination had been established in a secularized form as the USA's national ethics. Of Calvinism and, by extension US-ethics, he wrote: "The elected Christian is in the world only to increase this glory of God by fulfilling His commandments to the best of his ability. But God requires social achievement of the Christian because He wills that social life shall be organized according to His commandments, in accordance with that purpose" (2001, 64). Consequently, the segregation of those visibly cast away by God was justified, and no empathy or compassion was extended.

Focusing on the difference between the Brazilian and US-American participants, the degree of anxiety the text passages elicited may be another factor influencing compassion. For all three passages, the US-Americans reported a significantly higher level of anxiety. Assuming a large overlap of the concepts of anxiety and personal distress, studies regarding the latter's relation to empathy are of interest here. Although the influential empathy investigator Mark H. Davis (1983, 114) considers personal distress as one of the four dimensions of empathy, recent studies in psychology have shown that personal distress must be considered as a separate dimension. Suzanne Keen describes this as follows: "The distinction between empathy and personal distress matters because empathy is associated with the moral emotion *sympathy* (also called *empathic concern*) and thus with prosocial or altruistic action. Empathy that leads to sympathy is by definition other-directed, whereas an over-aroused empathic response that creates personal distress (self-oriented and aversive) causes a turning-away from the provocative condition of the other" (Keen 2006, 208). Thus, besides disgust, the greater anxiety that US-Americans report as opposed to the Brazilian participants may be another factor weighing on their lack of compassion.

The German participants' responses regarding anxiety are more difficult to interpret. Since, as became apparent in the general questions, they are decidedly opposed to any form of institutionalized or practical violence, their condemnation of the death penalty in the case of Rulfo's story and their disagreement that it presents the image of a just world is only consistent. When reading these responses, one must keep in mind that since the end of World War II, Germans are strongly sensitized to institutionalized violence and intolerance in any form through school curricula and the media. The significantly higher approval of censorship that the German participants reported in general and as a response to the text passages is, at least in part, due to their education in the devastating effects of Nazi propaganda materials. Depending how effective these teachings are, it may well be, then, that the factor of social desirability has a stronger impact on the German responses.

Despite the fact that the moderately high levels of disgust and very high levels of anxiety allow for conjecture, they do not warrant any conclusions on whether the seemingly pro-social attitudes of German participants is grounded in a legalistic (external duty), eudemonistic, or Kantian duty ethics (internal duty). A comparison of the grounding ethics of each of the cultures (hedonistic, eudemonistic, utilitarian, legalistic, or Kantian duty ethics), promises to be highly informative in relation to the attitudes toward violence and compassion, and will be examined in a follow up to the study presented in this chapter.

Conclusion

The interpretation of the results may be perceived as a value judgement on the participating cultures. This is not the intent, however. In this chapter, I have attempted to relate the findings of a study on cultural differences in the response to and evaluation of violence in literary texts to Martha C. Nussbaum's notions of compassion and its impeding emotions disgust and anxiety. My cultural bias as a researcher may have led me to focus on particular aspects of each culture. However, despite the fact that the investigation was preliminary, I would argue that some compelling possibilities have been uncovered and some of Nussbaum's claims corroborated. The first set of questions, for instance, showed that the Brazilian, US-American, and German participants differed strongly in their general attitudes toward violence, capital punishment, carrying of firearms, and in their perception of how violent their surroundings were.

Even though Brazilians and US-Americans similarly accepted violent means in certain circumstances, their responses to the text passages also differed. Although Nussbaum claims that the narrative of a criminal's personal and social history may elicit compassion, this seems to have been lost on the US-American participants. Rather, their strong reactions to the text passages in the form of anxiety and disgust indicate that these emotions may have cancelled out the possibility of compassion for Rulfo's protagonist.

The German participants' responses were challenging to interpret, since their categorical rejection of violence seems to have produced a floor effect. I suggested that the education of Germans after World War II might have led to a non-negotiable disapproval of violence. The fact, however, that they scored relatively high on disgust, especially for the Márquez and the Cortázar passages, and higher than the other groups on anxiety, may indicate that social desirability is especially at work for the German participants.

This study indicates several directions for further studies. The most evident, I think, is a psychonarratological investigation of the effects of formal aspects such as focalization, types of represented speech and thought, genre, etc., on the responses to and evaluations of violence in literature.[3] Another possibly worthwhile approach might be to probe further into the deeply rooted ambivalence most cultures seem to exhibit in their treatment of violence, and thus to demystify empirically some of the taboos surrounding it. And lastly, in each of these proposed studies, an inquiry into cultural differences is a necessity to work towards an understanding and eventual bridging of the gap between the factual globalization of market and media, on the one hand, and the continuing fragmentation of cultures in their search for a stable identity on the other.

The present study, then, follows a 'New Beginning' that has dawned on the horizon of the humanities with scholars such as Nussbaum, and is beginning to dawn for the study of literature, with scholars such as Robert Hogenraad (2005), who work toward rendering the machinations of violence transparent, and David S. Miall and Don Kuiken (2002), Don Kuiken et al (2004), and Jèmeljan Hakemulder (2000), in their attempts to lead moral philosophy, ethical criticism, and a focus on the immense importance of emotions back into academia. The corollary of these efforts

---

[3] For an introduction to psychonarratology, see: Marisa Bortolussi and Peter Dixon, *Psychonarratology: Foundations for the Empirical Study of Literary Response* (Cambridge: Cambridge University Press, 2003).

is a regained relevance – through empirical evidence – of "works of art as essential sources of insight and illumination, which could not be taken from human societies without robbing us of a central element in our moral life" (Nussbaum 1990, 196).

Works Cited

Bortolussi, Marisa and Peter Dixon. 2003. *Psychonarratology: Foundations for the Empirical Study of Literary Response*. Cambridge: Cambridge University Press.

Clark, Candace. 1998. *Misery and Company: Sympathy in Everyday Life*. Chicago: University of Chicago Press.

Cortázar, Julio. 1966. *Hopscotch*, translated by Gregory Rabassa. New York: Pantheon Books.

Davis, Mark H. 1983. Measuring Individual Differences in Empathy: Evidence for a Multidimensional Approach. *Journal of Personality and Social Psychology* 44: 113-126.

Hakemulder, Jèmeljan. 2000. *The Moral Laboratory: Experiments Examining the Effects of Reading Literature on Social Perception and Moral Self-Knowledge*. Amsterdam: John Benjamins.

Hogenraad, Robert. 2005. What the Words of War Can Tell Us About the Risk of War." *Peace and Conflict: Journal of Peace Psychology* 11: 137-151.

Keen, Suzanne. 2006. A Theory of Narrative Empathy." *Narrative* 14: 207-236.

Kuiken, Don, David S.Miall, and Shelley Sikora. 2004 Forms of self-implication in literary reading. *Poetics Today* 25: 171-203.

Márquez, Gabriel García. 1996. *Chronicle of a Death Foretold*, trans. Edith Grossman. London: Penguin.

Miall, David S. and Don Kuiken. 2002. A Feeling for Fiction: Becoming what we Behold. *Poetics* 30: 221-241.

Nussbaum, Martha C. 1990. Perception and Revolution: *The Princess Casamassima* and the Political Imagination. In *Love's Knowledge: Essays on Philosophy and Literature*, by Martha C. Nussbaum. New York: Oxford University Press: 195-219.

—. 2001. *Upheavals of Thought: The Intelligence of Emotions*. Cambridge: Cambridge University Press.

Rozin, Paul and April E. Fallon. 1987. A Perspective on Disgust. *Psychological Review* 94: 23-41.

Rulfo, Juan. 1967. Remember. In *The Burning Plain and Other Stories*, trans. George D. Schade. Austin: University of Texas Press.

Weber, Max. 2002. *Protestant Ethic and the Spirit of Capitalism*. London/New York: Routledge.

Wertheimer, Jürgen. 1986. *Ästhetik der Gewalt: Ihre Darstellung in Literatur und Kunst* (*Aesthetics of Violence: Its Presentation in Literature and Art*). Frankfurt a.M.: Athenäum Verlag.

CHAPTER ELEVEN

CULTURE AND READING: THE INFLUENCE OF WESTERN AND EASTERN THOUGHT SYSTEMS ON THE UNDERSTANDING OF FAIRY TALES

YEHONG ZHANG

Abstract

Although cultural thought processes are increasingly compatible with the "flattening" of the globe (Friedman 2006), current research in anthropology and cognitive science shows that tradition and culture still shape cognitive patterns and thinking processes. Cultural approaches in social psychology have shown that there are very different cognitive traditions in the East and West. Starting from the assumption that the analytical European style of thought emphasizes the value of the individual while the holistic Asian style of thought embodies the value of social relations (Nisbett 2003), an empirical research project on reader response to literary texts is undertaken in a German and a Chinese context. The text samples used are traditional fairy tales from Germany and China. The questionnaires are based on typical categories in literary study (figure, plot, spatial semantics). Results show the levels and factors of difference and similarity of perception between the two cultures, thus epitomizing in a concrete way how our cultural traditions influence our perception of narrative texts.

Introduction

In his book The World is Flat, New York Times columnist Thomas L. Friedman draws a picture of the twenty-first century. The globe is "flattening" and the world is getting smaller. With the incredible growth of communication systems and increasing mobility, human thought systems become more and more adapted to the globalization process. People from all over the world enjoy the same books, films and works of art. In the success of globalization it looks like people everywhere in the global village talk about the same stories. However, this is just a first impression. Are these stories also told in the same way? A precise look reveals that cultural differences in our perceptual systems not only continue to exist in this globalized era, but also that additional cultural differences have been produced.

Based on this knowledge, the cultural differences produced by globalization give rise to a problem in the field of literary understanding to be addressed in this research project: if readers from different cultural backgrounds read the same story from either their own or a foreign culture, what will the differences and similarities in their reading responses be? Social psychology pursued universal human cognition two decades ago (Nisbett and Ross 1980), but current research in cultural psychology indicates that no such universal account can be given. A culture-free way of human thinking turns out to be more and more culturally bounded (Peng, Ames, and Knowles 2001). Research findings in psychology illustrate the cultural characteristics of basic thinking processes such as attribution and categorization.

An established cultural psychological theory of cultural difference in thinking systems demonstrates that the Western focus is more on objects while the East Asian focus is more on the whole picture and on the context in which the objects stand. These different thinking models can be traced back to cultural and philosophical traditions in ancient Greece and China, as social psychologist Richard E. Nisbett (2003) demonstrates in detail in his book The Geography of Thought: How Asians and Westerners Think Differently and Why.

My purpose in the present paper is to take these cultural thinking models and examine their influence on literary perception. Taking the Western and Eastern epistemologies as a starting point, I carry out an empirical study to investigate a cultural-comparative sample of the understanding of narrative. Cultural traditions may be strongly linked to readers' understanding models. Tradition can shape perception. More specifically, I hypothesize that different cultural thinking traditions will affect the perception of figure, plot, space and time in a fictional text. However, the causal links between tradition and literary perception are complex. How can the established psychological theory of cultural thinking systems be utilized to work in conjunction with cultural understanding models for literary texts?

Text Corpus: Fairy Tale as Archetype of Narrative

As there are no previous studies of literary understanding in culture-comparative thinking patterns, the text sample for this study should have a simple structure. I chose fairy tales as folk narrative examples for the cross-cultural research. As a narrative form, fairy tales appear world-wide (Bloch 1988, Ueding 1978). In anthropological research, the collections by the Brothers Grimm and Bolte-Polivka and the folkloristic research of Aarne and Thompson (1961), who made a complete index of the types and motifs in folklores from different cultural areas, show an astonishing similarity in subject and structure among the stories from different epochs and cultures again and again (Lüthi 2004, 62-82). The similarity may indicate a common anthropological origin.

Emerging as an original form for the narrative in human culture, the fairy tale is considered to be "real poetry" by German romanticists (Bauman and Briggs 2003, 204). During the Enlightenment, folklorists already understood fairy tales as an art form in which two potentials of human nature join together: the penchant for the wonderful and the love of truth and nature (wahren und natürlichen) (Jolles 1982, 190). The folk narrative derives from archetypes. Stith Thompson describes these magic tales: "A Märchen is a tale of some length involving a succession of motifs or episodes. It moves in an unreal world without definite locality or definite characters and is filled with the marvelous." (Thompson 1946, 8) In this simplified world we find the prototype of daily life through the conceptual structure of narrative patterns in our mind. In reading them we extend the conceptual structure from the experience-based domains to more abstract domains (Lakoff and Johnson 1980, Gibbs 1994).

Fairy Tales for Cultural Interchange

Fairy tales, as the most popular genre in children's literature, serve as a field of exchange between different cultures and for learning 'otherness'. Nowadays globalization leads to a sharing of fairy tales world-wide. The stories of the Brothers Grimm or Hans-Christian Andersen are also the favourite stories of East Asian children and have become the most important works for their literary socialisation. Why does this children's literature transcend cultural differences? In *The Uses of Enchantment: The Meaning and Importance of Fairy Tales*, psychologist Bruno Bettelheim (1976) emphasized that the simple structure of fairy tales is appropriate for children's level of figurative thinking. From the same standpoint, German scholars of children's literature Bettina Hurrelmann and psychologist

Norbert Groeben expound the reason why children's literature is especially suitable for intercultural exchange. Besides the less complex structure, the stories still connect strongly with our living world (Groeben and Hurrelmann 2004).

As Frederic Jameson points out, a literary work delineates a symbolic action (Jameson 1981, 35). A fairy tale describes a symbolic world with a strong pedagogic purpose. With the pedagogic intention, fairy tales function as a chief means of literary socialisation. The authors and collectors of fairy tales attempt to build a dialogue about values, customs and predominant social rules in the stories. Through them children acquire knowledge about the continuous conflicts in social relationships (Zipes 2006, 10). The implication of the stories varies according to different social conditions.

Cultural specifics cannot, however, be conveyed in another culture without some difficulty. The act of translation requires getting under the skin of another culture and communicating its thought and beauty in a new idiom. The translation provokes different perception patterns in the target language. Historical investigation of the reception of the Grimms' fairy tales in East Asia displays a cultural transformation through children's literature. An overview of this historical reception indicates the anthropological constant between cultures on the one hand, and different connotations on the other (Liang 1986). That is to say that the adopted Western fairy tales share similar themes with traditional East Asian fairy tales, stories and legends, which is why they have been imported and subsequently distributed widely. It is fascinating to observe that fairy tales are globalized despite encoded cultural specifics. This phenomenon shows that cultural differences are not so fundamental that people cannot understand one another. However, when a fairy tale is translated from one culture to the other, it will not be understood in the same way. Because the cultural knowledge connected with attributed meaning varies, more or less different meanings will be attributed to the same textual signal.

Inference Theory

This study aims to explore the differences in meaning formation by readers. It is first necessary to find a way to represent the interpretation process of reading. Psycholinguistic research on reading distinguishes between the meaning of a text, which stems explicitly from the linguistic signs, and the inferences, which are derived without such clear signals (Forrester 1996, 43). Literary communication is more than the exchange of 'packages' through information conduits. Meaning formation in a literary reading is far more complicated than in normal communication, because meaning is the result of the inference process (Levinson 2001, 188). A speaker expresses X so that the recipient build Y from X; that is, based on X the recipient forms the meaning Y. Readers bring their presuppositions and world knowledge into the production of indirect meaning.

Literary texts stimulate the reader's imagination by means of a structure of "indeterminacy" (Iser 1974). The blank-point-model in reader-response criticism emphasizes that gaps in literary description are filled in by the reader. According to inference theory, meaning formation of literary texts is not code-based, but inference-based communication between reader and text. Indirect meanings acquired from inferences are therefore crucially important for the interpretation of literary texts. The content of a literary text is dependent on the reader, because understanding of a literary work is structured in such a way as to prefigure the development of the story. Readers use their cultural knowledge and personal experience to make the narrative connections that are needed. Meaning formation may be strongly linked to the reader's cultural background.

Intercultural hermeneutics refers to the reception of literature by foreign receivers. The fundamental idea here is that the view of interpretation is determined by culture. Based on the hermeneutics of H.-G. Gadamer (1975) which states that reception is based on the "fusion of horizons" ("Horizontverschmelzung") of the author, the work, and the reader, the process of understanding a foreign literary work has taken the foreign cultural elements into account. Academic contributions to the cross-cultural study of reading response have not sufficiently considered the empirical evidence involving real readers; nor have they paid sufficient attention to the use of psychological research methods. As model readers, literary critics should also be aware of the response of "normal" readers. The present study aims to provide a new methodological approach to access cross-cultural reading responses investigating in a concrete way of inference-based literary understanding.

Hypothesis

Since the 1990s, cognitive linguistic research has turned against Chomsky's "Universal Grammar", instead emphasizing the Cultural Origins of Human Cognition (Tomasello 1999). Cultural differences reside in embodied thought. The difference between the two thought traditions of ancient Greece and China described above is, in summary that the Western thought model is more analytic and the Asian model is more holistic. In comparison with Western modes of reasoning, East Asian thought draws upon the perceptual field as a whole and relies far less on categories or on formal logic (Markus and Kitayama 1998). How can this theoretical framework from social psychology be concretely transferred to literary understanding? How can reading response to literary texts be measured?

In social psychology, a strong sense of individual identity accompanies the Western sense of personal agency. The Chinese counterpart to Western agency is harmony: there is a sense of collective agency. The Chinese are far more concerned with self-control and implementation of the requirements of others. The European style of thought embodies the value of the individual, while the Asian style emphasizes the value of social relations (Schwartz and Sagiv 1995, Triandis 1995). I therefore speculate that European culture promotes individual struggle much more than Chinese culture does. Although nowadays East Asian societies also realize the importance of individual creativity, they have not reached parity with European societies. Based on the contrast between individualism in the West and collectivism in the East, I assume that Chinese readers use society-oriented principles for their literary perception while German subjects use individual-oriented principles. Through an empirical investigation I want to find out how strongly these traditional thinking models affect the reading response.

Test Objects / Materials

Around the world, Andersen's and Grimms' fairy tales are most popular among children. I preferred Grimms' fairy tales for my empirical study because their origins are much closer to the 'folk' and belong to the genre of "folktales" (Volksmärchen), whereas the stories of H.-C. Andersen are so-called "literary fairy tales" (Kunstmärchen). I thus took one of the Grimms' fairy tales and one fairy tale from traditional Chinese society as text samples to investigate culture-comparative patterns in literary reading.

First, I designed a baseline survey to establish the initial conditions under which the proposed responses to the texts can be compared. My choice of the fairy tales was determined by the general subject areas of the stories after looking for the best-seller lists of the famous publishing houses in China and Germany. Based on the baseline survey, the text sample should deal with the most representative topic in fairy tales, namely love. The fairy tales from both cultures should have similar lengths and comparable structures. As opposed to fairy tales in Germany, fairy tales in China are not clearly distinguished from historical story, myth, legend and fable. Outside of Europe, myth, legend, fable, drollery and fairy tale are close to each other (Lüthi 2004, 37). Therefore, it is not easy to find an original Chinese fairy tale which is built around similar structure comparable to the Grimms' stories. First, I selected several candidate stories from the Brothers' Grimm Kinder- und Hausmärchen. After going through a large assortment of potential Chinese stories, I chose the story "Cowherd and Weaver Girl". Accordingly, I chose the Grimm story "Jorinde and Joringel" as its German counterpart. These two stories have several comparable features. First, the main topic is the same - love. Secondly, in my pilot study I gave participants several fairy tales to read. These two stories were the ones most enjoyed by the participants. The selected stories should be compelling and attract the focus attention of participants. Third, the versions of both stories came from the early 19th century and are not very familiar to the native reader. During the study it was found that most of the participants had not read (the current version of) the stories.

Both stories were presented to the participants in their native language. The translations of both stories were controlled by an independent professional translator who was fluent in both languages.

Here is the synopsis of the Chinese fairy tale "Cowherd and Weaver Girl":

A poor young cowherd was encouraged by his ox and flew to heaven with the help of the ox on the seventh day of the seventh lunar month. In the lake he saw nine fairy sisters bathing. Following the advice of the ox, the cowherd stole the clothes of the most beautiful fairy sister – the seventh daughter of the heaven emperor. She was named "the weaver girl" because she wove colourful clouds in the sky. Only when the weaver girl agreed to his request for marriage, would he return her clothing. The weaver girl told the cowherd that she shouldn't marry without her father's approval, but after asking an old willow tree ashore to act as go-between, she finally agreed to be the wife of the cowherd anyway. After seven days the weaver girl said good-bye to her husband, because she wanted to go back to her former duty of weaving clouds. She left and the cowherd followed her. The weaver girl took out her hairpin and scratched a wide river in the sky to separate the cowherd. But once a year, all the magpies in the world fly up into heaven to form a bridge. The couple could be together for a single night, the seventh night of the seventh month.

Here is the synopsis of the Grimms' fairy tale "Jorinde and Joringel":
A witch lived alone in the woods. She could fix to the ground anyone who came near her castle, and turn innocent maidens into birds and cage them. Jorinde and Joringel, who had promised to marry each other, went for a walk in the forest. They came too near the witch's house; she turned the girl Jorinde into a nightingale and fixed the boy Joringel to the ground. Once she had carried away the bird, she freed the boy. The boy was very sad and went to a distant village to be a shepherd. One night the boy Joringel dreamed of a flower which would break all the witch's spells. The boy sought it for nine days, found it, and carried it back to the castle. He was not fixed to the ground when he approached the castle, and it opened all the doors. He found the witch feeding the birds. She was unable to curse him, and when she tried to take one cage away, he realized it was his lover Jorinde. He touched the witch with the flower, and she was unable to cast any more spells. He touched the bird with the flower and she became his Jorinde again; then he transformed all the other nightingales back to women.

Participants / Sampling

Although fairy tales may no longer be the favourite reading of school children, subjects for fairy tale interpretation should be at least in the 5th grade, according to Piaget's (1974) theory of children's abstract logical thinking stages. Also, the questionnaires had to be developed in accordance with developmental psychologists' demands for this age group. The questionnaires are appropriate for children at the age of 12 who can grasp the text and evaluate the items independently.

Children from different cultural areas have grown up with the same fairy tales. In East Asia, the fairy tales of the Brothers Grimm and Hans-Christian Andersen enjoy the greatest popularity. East Asian means here the region with a historically strong influence of classical Chinese language and ethics such as Confucianism and Taoism. China, Korea, and Japan are the main countries encompassed by this cultural tradition. In this study, Chinese children are chosen as a sample representing the East Asian cultures and German children to represent the Western thinking model. Taking Chinese and German children as samples, the participants who read a story from their own culture were the control group for interpretation. According to the embodied value, the two selected story samples strongly differ from each other. That is why having a control group has an advantage. Participants were 100 German school children from the 6th grade class in the German town of Göttingen and 100 Chinese school children in the same level class in Beijing. These 200 participants were randomly assigned to read either the fairy tale from their own culture or the one from another culture and complete the respective questionnaire. Each participant reads only one story. The German and Chinese participants are representative of an average social group and are comparable in age, gender, and grade point average. The questionnaires for both fairy tales were developed with the same categories in literary study. Under this design, the interpretation of the fairy tales in different cultural areas can be investigated under similar circumstances.

Questionnaires

The questionnaires I developed are the key elements in this empirical reading study. Through a string of pilot tests, I conceived the design of the experiment. The items have been designed to correspond with the main categories of narratology: figures, plot, and spatial / temporal perception. To guarantee the reliability and objectivity of the experiment, there should be sufficient items in each category. The questionnaire for Grimms' story is composed of 27 items, and there are 12, 10 and 5 items each respectively for the three subscales of figure, plot and spatial / temporal perception. In the questionnaire for the Chinese fairy tale, there are 32 items altogether and 15, 11 and 6 items respectively for each subcategory. Each item is administered using a 6-point Likert scale from 1 (completely agree), 2 (mostly agree), 3 (slightly agree), 4 (slightly disagree), 5 (basically disagree), to 6 (completely disagree). The participants responded to each item using this scale. To avoid a situation that often happens when using such scale tests in which participants tend to choose the middle number on the scale, the 6-point Likert scale has no middle point, which thus forces participants to clearly express their preference for or disagreement with each item. The items and scales allow the measurement of readers' responses to the literary categories and presumably reflect cultural differences in literary interpretation.

The construction of the questionnaires is based on the assumption that East Asians read the story with society-oriented tendencies and Europeans orient their perception more in coherence with individual-oriented principles. The collectivism vs. individualism cultural syndrome is illustrated by the results of psychological research (Singelis 1994). This construct of items also tracks back to the interdependent and independent social relationships proposed by Markus and Kitayama (1998). As there were no existing questionnaires of reading response based on Western and Eastern thinking models, I first carried out a few pilot tests with open-ended questions to extract the cultural characteristic in interpreting the figures and reasoning their activities with both text samples. Table 1 summarizes the detailed hypotheses in the categories of figure interpretation. The detailed hypotheses build the basis of the item development.

In both questionnaires, the independent variables are the stories, nation and gender. The dependent variables are the respective interpretation of figures, plot and spatial / temporal semantics.

Table 1 Questionnaire construction for figure interpretation

The society-oriented reading response	The individual-oriented reading response
—respects and adapts to the social rules.	—tends to break the social rules.
—has a strong sense of duty.	—does not have a strong sense of duty.
—keeps social relationships in order.	—tries to create new opportunities.
—Family stands in the foreground.	—Family is not important or not mentioned.
—The world has complicated social relationships.	—The world has simple relationships (good vs. bad).
—Figures stand for their social group.	—Figures stand for themselves.
—Figures act passively.	—Figures act actively.
—Figures stand in self-conflict.	—Figures stand in conflict with the outside world.
—Figures try to keep strong self-control.	—Figures don't try to keep strong self-control.

Results

German fairy tale sample

I first did a reliability analysis to check the correlations between the items. Using Cronbach's Alpha (.669) I estimated the homogeneity of the items. According to the statistical analysis of the quantitative data from the questionnaire of the Grimms' story ($N=100$), among the 27 items there are 11 items with high statistical significance (see Table 2). They are the 8 items for figure understanding and the 3 items for plot interpretation. One interesting finding is that there is no significant difference in response to spatial semantics. The evaluation of the items about spatial imagination by both groups is extremely similar in this story, e.g. the responses of the Chinese and German participants to the item "I can imagine the castle and its surroundings very well" are virtually the same. Another interesting finding is that the Chinese children are more familiar with the motifs of the Grimms' tale. One item of the story "Jorinde" with a highly significant difference between the two cultures is: "I predicted correctly at the beginning of the story that the girl and the boy would have a problem later." (see Table 2: Chinese-Mean=2.0 vs. German-Mean=3.2). The data indicate that Chinese readers are more familiar with the theme of the story. The prediction of the ending of the story is connected with knowledge of the genre. The Chinese children have grown up with the Western fairy tales and have perhaps already developed a good sense for them.

Table 2 Different reading response for the Grimm's story

Questions	Mean: Chinese / German
- The girl only waits for someone to rescue her from the witch.	C 3.7 – G 2.0****
- The boy is really like a hero.	C 3.4 – G 2.3****
- I am very sad for the boy.	C 3.9 – G 2.6****
- If I think of shepherd, I immediately imagine a young man who is unhappy with his love.	C 3.9 – G 5.0****
- I predicted correctly at the beginning of the story that the girl and the boy have problems later.	C 2.0 – G 3.2****
- It would be better if Jorinde and Joringel had gone for a walk into the forest with their parents.	C 5.3 – G 4.6***
- I like the boy very much.	C 2.3 – G 3.1**
- I am very sad for the girl.	C 3.8 – G 3.0**
- The boy has not fought strongly enough for his girl.	C 4.2 – G 4.9**
- I am very sad that the both could not be together any longer.	C 2.5 - G 3.4**
- If I were a boy, I'd like to be the boy in the story.	C 2.0 – G 2.7**
- I find the girl is too incautious.	C 3.7 – G 3.1*

Note. $N = 100$, C = Chinese; G = German. Shown are the items with greatest cultural differences in ratings of the text perception. Ratings can be interpreted with scale labels: 1= completely agree, 2 = mostly agree, 3 = slightly agree, 4 = slightly disagree, 5 = basically disagree, 6 = completely disagree
*$p<.05$ **$p<.02$ ***$p<.005$ ****$p<.001$

For interrelations among the items of the questionnaire for the Grimm story, an exploratory factor analysis, with rotated component matrix, was conducted. The steep screen plot implies the number of factors in which the items are formed. Four factors have been derived. The table 3 shows the items in the four derived factors with loadings larger than .50. The four factors are "evaluation of figures / identification with figures", "spatial semantics / imagination of the space", "plot causality / plot judgement" and "emotion / affection" (see Table 3).

Table 3: Factor analysis for the Grimms' story

Factor	Item	Weight
1. Evaluation of figures (Identification with figures)	- The boy is very brave.	.747
	- I like the boy very much.	.734
	- If I were a boy, I'd like to be the boy in the story.	.716
	- I specially enjoy the ending.	.606
	- I like the girl very much.	.589
	- The boy is really a hero.	.558
	- If I were a girl, I'd like to be the girl in the story.	.539
2. Spatial semantics (Imagination of the space)	- I would not go into the forest alone.	.620
	- I would be afraid of the forest.	.574
	- I would stroll in the forest like the girl and the boy, but I would pay much attention to the boundary of the castle.	.541
	- I don't have a concrete picture of the forest.	.514
3. Plot causality (Plot judgement)	- The boy has not fought strongly enough for the girl.	.562
	- I predicted correctly at the beginning of the story that the girl and the boy will have a problem later.	.535
	- When I think of the shepherd, I immediately imagine a young man who is unhappy with his love.	.521
	- It is very romantic that the boy and the girl stroll in the forest alone.	.496
4. Emotion (Affection)	- I am very sad for the boy.	.776
	- I am very sad for the girl.	.762

Chinese Fairy Tale Sample

In the responses to the questionnaire for the Chinese story "Cowherd and Weaver Girl", I also first analysed individual items and did a Reliability analysis. Using Cronbach's Alpha (.631) I estimated the homogeneity of the items. There are 18 items with high significance among the 32 items (N=100). Under the significant items there are 7 items for figure interpretation, 7 for plot understanding and 2 for spatial/temporal imagination (Table 4).

Table 4 Different reading responses for the Chinese fairy tale.

Questions	Mean: Chinese / German
- If I were a boy, I'd like to be the boy in the story.	C 3.8 – G 5.3****
- It is wonderful that the cowherd flew to the sky and took away the cloth of the weaver girl.	C 4.5 – G 3.3****
- It was very impudent that the cowherd forced the weaver girl to marry him.	C 3.8 – G 2.4****
- I feel very sad that the cowherd and the weaver girl can not be together for ever in the end.	C 1.9 – G 3.2****
- I'm very familiar with the storyline.	C 2.4 – G 4.7****
- I like the cowherd very much.	C 3.4 – G 4.7****
- The weaver girl spent a very long time with the cowherd together in the heaven before she left him.	C 2.8 – G 4.9****
- It's very normal for me that the colour of an ox is yellow.	C 3.0 – G 5.0****
- I am very sad for the cowherd.	C 2.9 – G 4.0****
- The cowherd has a strong own opinion.	C 3.6 – G 2.6***
- It is wonderful that the weaver girl married the cowherd.	C 4.3 – G 3.5***
- It's all his own fault that the weaver girl leaves the cowherd.	C 4.9 – G 3.8***
- The weaver girl virtually wants to marry the cowherd.	C 3.9 – G 4.6**
- I enjoyed the ending very much.	C 3.5 – G 4.5**
- The weaver girl always thinks of her work.	C 3.2 – G 2.3**
- It is very romantic that the weaver girl first consults the willow tree about his approval for marriage.	C 4.1 – G 4.7*
- The world of heaven connects itself with the world of earth.	C 3.0 – G 3.8*
- It is difficult to understand that the weaver girl absolutely obeys the Goddess of heaven.	C 2.8 – G 3.4*

Note. N = 100, C = Chinese; G = German. Shown are the items with greatest cultural differences in ratings of the text perception. Ratings can be interpreted with scale labels: 1= completely agree, 2 = mostly agree, 3 = slightly agree, 4 = slightly disagree, 5 = basically disagree, 6 = completely disagree *p<.05   **p<.01   *** p<.005   **** p<.001

In this Chinese story, the temporal and spatial descriptions strongly embody cultural specifics. To the items concerning spatial and temporal imagination, e.g. "The weaver girl spent a very long time with the cowherd together in the heaven before she left him" and "The world of heaven and the world of earth are connected to each other in the story", the Chinese and German readers answered significant differently (see Table 3).

The highly significant items concentrate on the judgment for the protagonist Cowherd. For instance the items like "It was very impudent that the cowherd forced the weaver girl to marry him"; "If I were a boy, I'd like to be the boy in the story"; "I feel very sad that the cowherd and the weaver girl can not be together for ever in the end"; "I like the cowherd very much"; "I am very sad for the cowherd". The response to these items shows that the evaluation of the cowherd by German children was far more negative than with the Chinese readers (see Table 3). The plot where the cowherd took away the cloth of the weaver girl and asked her in marriage is hardly understandable for European readers. This Chinese story is more of a dreamed-up social life: A boy from the earth flies to the world of heaven and succeeds in marrying a fairy, although they must separate in the end. The present study hypothesized that the cowherd was supposed to be considered a self-realized hero by the Western reader because he crossed the social boundary and went into the upper social layer to marry a woman with absolute higher status (cf. Table 1). But the responses to the items mentioned above related to the cowherd contradicts this assumption. In the pilot study, which included some open-ended questions, Western participants explained the reason for their negative evaluation of the male figure through their lack of familiarity with the motif of taking away the clothes of the girl and then asking her in marriage. Chinese participants, by contrast, show more sympathy with the cowherd because they are familiar with this motif. The statistical results indicate that familiarity with plot and schemata / motifs plays an important role in the interpretation of figure and plot.

An exploratory factor analysis, with rotated component matrix, was conducted for interrelations among the items of the questionnaire for the Chinese story. Four factors have been derived. Based on the items - with loadings larger than .50 - of each of the factors in common, I summarized the factors in Table 5. The four driven factors are "evaluation of figures", "plot familiarity", "motivation of action", "social behaviour" (see Table 5).

Table 5: Factor analysis of the Chinese fairy tale

Factor	Item	Weight
1. Evaluation of figures	- It is wonderful that the weaver girl married the cowherd.	.734
	- I like the cowherd very much.	.679
	- I feel very sad that the cowherd and the weaver girl can not be together for ever in the end.	.678
	- It is the cowherd's own fault that the weaver girl leaves him.	-.641
	- If I were a boy, I'd like to be the boy in the story.	.590
	- The cowherd is very brave.	.555
	- I am very sad for the cowherd.	.551
	- It was very impudent that the cowherd forced the weaver girl.	.517
	- I like the weaver girl very much.	.477
2. Plot familiarity	- The weaver girl spent a very long time with the cowherd together in heaven before she left him.	.781
	- I enjoyed the ending very much.	.665
	- I'm very familiar with the storyline.	.636
	- It is normal for me that the color of an ox is yellow.	.581
3 Motivation of action	- It is understandable that the weaver girl flies back to continue her work.	.613
	- It is understandable that the weaver girl first consults the willow tree for its approval of her marriage.	.531
	- The cowherd has not fought strongly enough to win the weaver girl.	-.503
4. Social behaviour	- It is difficult to understand why the weaver girl absolutely obeys the God of heaven.	.506
	- It is wonderful that the cowherd flew to the sky and took away the clothes of the weaver girl.	.493
	- It's very strange that the weaver girl must follow her father's wish for her to marry.	.467

General Discussion

In the Grimms' story 40% of the items were answered significantly different by German and Chinese readers; in the case of Chinese traditional story 56% of items were responded to significantly. This result not only demonstrates that cultural thought models influence literary understanding, but also illustrates the difference in a concrete way.

In an intercultural context, the reception of texts from two different cultures in terms of interpretation of figures and understanding of plot causality showed both some overlap and some serious differences between readers from German and Chinese culture. Researches in cognitive psychology and cognitive linguistics state that inference is significant in meaning formation of literary texts. The different response in this empirical study doesn't result from the problem of filling in the blanks of the text, which seem incomprehensible to the recipient, but from the different reasoning about the same text element. In the reception of foreign literature, inference plays an essential role. The otherness of the reception comes into being when the behaviour of the protagonists and the reasoning behind their actions differ strongly from the values and life attitudes of the reader. The extended experience of reading literary works further influences the values and life attitudes of readers.

Our mental activities come at least in part from our physical activities. Abstract concepts like danger and freedom are deeply rooted in spatial experience. Linguistic relativism already shows that there are cultural differences on the elementary level: words for the same thing manifest themselves in slightly different brain locations in different cultures (Boroditsky 2000). The language we speak affects the way we think about the world; when sensory information is scarce or inconclusive, languages may play the most important role in shaping abstract thought (Matlock, Ramscar, and Boroditsky 2005). The spatial descriptions in both stories are distinguished from each other, a difference which is reflected in the perceptions of the participants. In the Grimms' story the protagonists move horizontally: from the center to the periphery and conversely (from the castle to the outside world). Chinese readers apparently have no difficulty imagining this horizontal spatial dynamic. In contrast, the protagonist in the Chinese story moves vertically: from the earth to heaven, displaying holistic thinking in spatial imagination. European recipients did not find it natural to construct such a vertical spatial line. The vertical movement displays holistic thinking in the spatial imagination. There is an interesting coincidence between the result described here regarding spatial imagination and recent cross-linguistic studies. For example, Levinson (1996) has likewise suggested cross-linguistic differences in spatial thinking. Slobin (1996) has demonstrated that language may influence thought during "thinking for speaking". The thesis of linguistic relativism shows that different languages and cultures talk about the world differently and consequently shape their members' habitual thought in a different way.

The data of the present study underline such cultural differences: the differences in interpretation of the Chinese fairy tale between German and Chinese readers are very obvious. The plot schemata and spatial semantics in the Chinese fairy tale are unfamiliar to the German recipients. The participants from both cultures had not read the story from the other culture before. By comparison, the Chinese recipients showed far more familiarity with the German story. According to the empirical results in this study, German children lack knowledge of Chinese culture and traditional schemata in Chinese literature. I suggest that familiarity with the schemata, which is closely related to comprehension, has a significant effect on literary interpretation. Bartlett's Schema theory demonstrated the influence of schemata and prior knowledge on interpretation. There are many examples of conceptual thinking in pre-linguistic children. Children have the concept before they can say the word (Bloch 2005). As new findings in the cognitive anthropology have pointed out, there is a deep structure in folklore which serves as the archetype of the narrative traditions of human beings. The recipients recognize the archetype in the narrative stories and identify with the actions of protagonists and construct expectations for the storyline. The results of the study of narrative structure in the structuralistic anthropological tradition reveal that individuals can recognize the deep structure of a narrative text. This deep structure should be intuitive for each reader and closely related to readers' inferences. Already three decades ago R.C. Schank (1976) describes inference as the core of the understanding process. Human beings use inferences to predict the causal consequences of future events. There are rich and wide-ranging connections between culture and human inference.

To discover the connection between text features and reader construction, however, literary studies need to cooperate with other disciplines (Bortolussi and Dixon 2003). I am not trying to reduce to stereotypes of the thinking models for different cultural groups in this study. The results of the analysis give literary scholars evidence of the convergence of the responses of real readers and the concrete factors that influence interpretation. Some of the inevitable questions which emerge from this research are: How can empirical study cooperate with traditional literary study? How can each of these approaches enrich the other in reasoning our understanding of literary work and its effects upon readers and societies? I suggest that the present paper should merely be a modest first step in a series of quantitative and qualitative studies that explore the role of cultural thinking models in the reception of works of art.

Acknowledgement

Thanks are due to Gerhard Lauer at the University of Göttingen (UG) for advice at every stage of this project, to Markus Hasselhorn (UG) and his colleagues for pertinent advice and assistance in developing the concept and questionnaires, to Kaiping Peng and the Culture and Cognition Lab at University of California, Berkeley (UCB), for the skilled help for evaluation of and interpreting the results. Thanks also to Hinrich C. Seeba, Claire Kramsch and Eve Sweetser (UCB) for commenting on earlier versions of the article.

Works Cited

Aarne, Antti and Stith Thompson. 1961. *The Types of the Folktale.* Helsinki: Suomalainen Tiedeakatemia.
Bauman, Richard and Charles L. Briggs. 2003. *Voices of Modernity: Language Ideologies and the Politics of Inequality.* Cambridge, UK: Cambridge University Press.
Bloch, Ernst. 1988. *The Utopian Function of Art and Literature: Selected Essays.* Translated by Jack Zipes and Frank Mecklenburg. Cambridge, MA.: MIT Press,.
Bloch, Maurice. 2005. *Essays on Cultural Transmission.* Oxford: Berg.
Bettelheim, Bruno. 1976. *The Uses of Enchantment: The Meaning and Importance of Fairy Tales.* New York: Knopf.
Boroditsky, Lena. 2000. Metaphoric structuring: understanding time through spatial metaphors. *Cognition* 75: 1-28.
Matlock, Teenie, Michael Ramscar and Lena Boroditsky. 2005. On the experiential link between spatial and temporal language. *Cognitive Science* 29: 655-664.
Bortolussi, Marisa, Peter Dixon. 2003. *Psychonarratology. Foundations for the Empirical Study of Literary Response.* Cambridge: Cambridge University Press.
Forrester, Michael A. 1996. *Psychology of Language: a Critical Introduction.* London: Sage.
Friedman, Thomas L.. 2006. *The World is Flat: A Brief History of the Twenty-first Century.* New York: Farrar, Straus and Giroux.

Gadamer, Hans-Georg. 1975. *Wahrheit und Methode. Grundzüge einer philosophischen Hermeneutik*, 4th ed. Tübingen: Mohr.

Gibbs, Raymond W.. 1994. *The Poetics of Mind: Figurative Thought, Language, and Understanding.* Cambridge, UK: Cambridge University Press.

Groeben, Norbert and Bettina Hurrelmann. 2004. *Lesesozialisation in der Mediengesellschaft: ein Forschungsüberblick.* Weinheim: Juventa.

Iser, Wolfgang. 1974. *The Implied Reader; Patterns of Communication in Prose Fiction from Bunyan to Beckett.* Baltimore: Johns Hopkins University Press.

Jameson, Fredric. 1981. *The Political Unconscious: Narrative as a Socially Symbolic Act.* Ithaca, NY: Cornell University Press.

Jolles, Andre. 1982. *Einfache Formen: Legende, Sage, Mythe, Rätsel, Spruch, Kasus, Memorabile, Märchen, Witz.* 6th ed. Tübingen: Max Niemeyer.

Propp, Vladimir.1968. *Morphology of the Folk Tale.* Trans. Laurence Scott, 2nd ed. Austin: University of Texas Press.

Lakoff, George and Mark Johnson. 1980. *Metaphors We Live by.* Chicago: University of Chicago Press.

Liang, Yea-Jen. 1986. *Kinder- und Hausmärchen der Brüder Grimm in China. Rezeption und Wirkung.* Wiesbaden: Verlag Otto Harrassowitz.

Levinson, Stephen C. 1996. Language and Space. *Annual Reviews of Anthropology* 25: 353-382.

— 2001. *Presumptive Meanings. The Theory of Generalized Conversational Implicature.* Cambridge, MA.: MIT Press.

Lüthi, Max. 2004. *Märchen.* Ed. Heinz Rolleke, 10th ed. Stuttgart: Metzler.

Markus, Hazel R. and Shinobu Kitayama. 1998. The Cultural Psychology of Personality. *Journal of Cross-Cultural Psychology* 29.1: 63-87.

Nisbett, Richard E. 2003. *The Geography of Thought: How Asians and Westerners Think Differently – and Why.* New York: Free Press.

Nisbett, Richard E. and Lee Ross. 1980. *Human Inference: Strategies and Shortcomings of Social Judgment.* Englewood Cliffs, N.J.: Prentice-Hall.

Peng, Kaiping, Daniel R. Ames and Eric D. Knowles. 2001. Culture and Human Inference. Perspectives from Three Traditions. *The Handbook of Culture & Psychology.* ed. D. Matsumoto, 245-284. New York: Oxford University Press.

Piaget, Jean and Bärbel Inhelder: *The Child's Construction of Quantities.* London: Routledge and Kegan Paul, 1974.

Schank, Roger C. 1976. *Conceptual Information Processing*. Amsterdam: North-Holland.

Singelis, Theodore M. 1994. The Measurement of Independent and Interdependent Self-Construals. *Personality and Social Psychology Bulletin*. 20.5: 580-591.

Slobin, Dan I.. 1996. From 'thought and language' to 'thinking for speaking'. *Rethinking Linguistic Relativity,* ed. J. Gumperz and S. Levinson, 70-96. Cambridge: Cambridge University Press.

Schwartz, Shalom H. and Lilach Sagiv. 1995. Identifying Cultural-Specifics in the Content and Structure of Value. *Journal of Cross-Cultural Psychology*. Vol. 26.1: 92-116.

Triandis, Harry C.: *Individualism & Collectivism*. Boulder, Colo.: Westview Press, 1995

Thompson, Stith. 1946. *The Folktale*. New York: The Dryden Press.

Tomasello, Michael. 1999. *Cultural Origins of Human Cognition*. Cambridge, MA: Harvard University Press.

Ueding, Gert. 1978. Schein und Vorschein in der Kunst. *Materialien zu Ernst Blochs ‚Prinzip Hoffnung'*, ed. Burghart Schmidt, 446-464. Frankfurt a.M.: Suhrkamp.

Zipes, Jack. 2006. *Fairy Tales and the Art of Subversion. The Classical Genre for Children and the Process of Civilization*, 2nd ed. New York: Routledge.

CHAPTER TWELVE

TRANSLATING FOREGROUNDING: A COMPARATIVE STUDY OF CHINESE AND CANADIAN READERS

GAO WEI, DAVID S. MIALL AND DON KUIKEN

Abstract

Foregrounding in a literary text, such as special sound effects or a metaphor that draws on local cultural knowledge, presents a specific problem for translation: it risks a diminution of poetic effect, or a kind of entropy. To study this issue we collected empirical evidence for the effectiveness of the translation into English of passages from an early 19th-Century Chinese autobiography, *Six Chapters of a Floating Life*. The passages were presented in segments (usually one sentence) in the original Chinese and in English translation to readers in China and Canada respectively. Readers provided reading times per segment and ratings of segments for strikingness. Overall, a close correspondence of these measures between Chinese and Canadian readers suggest that the stylistic variations in Chinese were largely recreated in the English translation, since readers tended to linger over the same passages and find the same passages striking. In addition, four selected passages were rated on bipolar semantic-differential-type judgements and dimensions relating to stylistic effects. Differences in these ratings indicate that the translated passages were found more formal by Canadian readers, while their ratings also reflected Canadian unfamiliarity with several aspects of Chinese culture. The empirical methods used here help measure the aesthetic comparability of a source and translated text.

Introduction: Foregrounding and Translation

"Like a healthy human heartbeat, which has an intrinsic irregular system, the body of an artwork gets its vitality from a rhythm based in uncertainty" (Howe 2006, vii).

The rhythm of a literary text is influenced by the foregrounding it contains; and foregrounding not only varies from one part of a text to another, but its occurrence is marked by readers' increased uncertainty. Following the work of the Russian Formalists, Mukarovsky, Leech and Short, and van Peer, we (Miall and Kuiken 1994) have proposed that foregrounding is a characteristic feature of literary texts; similarly, Hogan (1997) has argued that the presence of foregrounded features in literature of all cultures is evidence that foregrounding is a cultural universal. Some empirically documented effects of foregrounding include reported defamiliarization, feeling intensification (Emmott 2002), depth of appreciation (Hakemulder 2004), and shifts in literary understanding (Miall and Kuiken 2001).

But, how does foregrounding fare in translation? In an effort to preserve the effects of foregrounding, Venuti advocates what he calls "foreignizing translation" or "abusive fidelity." By foreignizing he means a translation strategy that resists domestication, fluency, and transparency (Venuti 1995, 148 ff.). By abusive fidelity he means reproduction of those very features of the foreign text that "abuse" or resist the prevailing forms and values in the receiving culture, thereby remaining faithful to aspects of the source text while still effecting cultural change through the target language (Venuti 1992, pp. 12-13; 1995, pp. 182-183).

However, because words that "abuse" or defamiliarize in the same dimensions as the source text are not always available, the translation of textual foregrounding risks a certain kind of entropy. Several aspects of foregrounding are vulnerable to loss or degradation in the translation process, especially the effects of sound and rhythm, but also the wording that constitutes a metaphor or the idiom that requires local cultural knowledge. In various ways, then, the translation process is likely to diminish the poetic qualities of the source text, and attenuate aesthetic appreciation. While a translator may aim at the "functional equivalence" of the two texts, in Nida's (1993) words, "This maximal level of equivalence is rarely, if ever, achieved, except for texts having little or no aesthetic value and involving only routine information" (117-8).

For an example (taken from Lodge 2003), consider these lines in a German poem by Rose Ausländer called "Mühlen aus Wind": "Mühlen aus Wind / mahlen sandmehl" – which can be translated, "Mills made of wind / grind sand-flour" (264). The sound progression of *Mühlen, mahlen, -mehl* has no equivalent consonance in the literal English equivalents. The substitute effect of *grind, grains,* and *sand* is striking, but the effect is harsher and not in accord with the original tone of the poem. As Lodge puts it, a translator has little hope of translating the effects of sound in a poem from one language to another: "Alliteration, assonance, rhyme and rhythmic patterns have to be crafted anew during the process of translation" (263). Whether a translator will be as adept as the original author seems, as a general rule, unlikely.

A study by Baker (2004) demonstrates the process of entropy in translation, although it is based on a different premise than is our present concern about foregrounding. Her assumption is that "translators are more conservative in their use of language than the authors they translate; that they tend to prefer more standard forms of the language; that there tends to be a raising of the level of formality in translation; that translated text is 'sanitized' (in terms of translators avoiding certain features such as regionalisms and irregular spelling); and that translators tend to produce more 'uniform' texts, for example by avoiding disruption of tense sequences, etc." (172). According to her, fluency is the main aim of the translator. She carried out a computer-based examination of two bodies of literature: a selection from the British National Corpus, and a corpus she compiled of English texts that had been translated. Her primary measure for comparison of these two text types was lexical repetition: she searched the texts for repeated phrases, on the supposition that greater repetition implies regression to a "normalized" form of English. She found a higher frequency of lexical repetitions in the translated English corpus. As her Table 1 (Baker 2004, 175-6) shows, of the 12 phrases she counted, 2737 occurred in the translated corpus compared with 1134 in the native corpus. Variation across translations was also found, as might be expected, with some translators showing more repetition than others. (Some deliberate repetitions of a phrase were also found, such as "that is to say," used to distinguish a character's verbal style).

Table 1. Frequency of lexical repetitions in two corpora, Baker (2004)

	TEC	BNC
at the same time	669	323
in the middle of the	401	209
from time to time	394	137
on the other hand	347	150
that is	288	119
in other words	161	36
that is to say	129	31
once and for all	120	26
when it comes to	78	35
at the edge of the	67	46
I thought to myself	43	12
in a manner of speaking	40	10
Totals	2737	1134

Note. TEC: Translated English Corpus; BNC: British National Corpus. From Mona Baker 2004. A corpus-based view of similarity and difference in translation. *International Journal of Corpus Linguistics*, 9: 175-6. Reprinted with kind permission from John Benjamins Publishing Company, Amsterdam/Philadelphia. [www.benjamins.com].

The issues raised by translation, then, seem analogous to those raised by empirical studies in which the foregrounded features of literary texts are manipulated: the *unintentional* removal of foregrounding in translation may be comparable to the *deliberate* removal of foregrounding in studies of its effects. For example, Hakemulder (2004) assessed readers' response to two literary texts (an excerpt from a Rushdie novel and a short poem by Nabakov) from which most of the foregrounding had been deliberately removed. Readers' responses indicated a greater depth of appreciation of the original texts than of the manipulated versions. Analogously, when the translator aims, according to Baker, for a target text that will read fluidly but that unintentionally eliminates its poetic qualities, the result will be diminished aesthetic appreciation.

Our goal in the present research was to assess the fate of foregrounding in the process of translation. Rather than attempting critical analysis of a text and its translation, an approach that implicitly assumes an understanding of readers' responses, we adapted the empirical methods used in our earlier foregrounding studies, as we will describe. For this preliminary study we chose a source and target text in languages that are linguistically very different: Chinese and English. The text was a short section from *Six Chapters of a Floating Life*, an autobiography by Shen Fu (1999) written in the early nineteenth century (c. 1805): the main focus of the excerpt we chose is the author's initial acquaintance with his wife Yun and their early marriage; it has a lyrical, elegiac character (his wife was to die young). The translation was by the famous Chinese writer Lin Yutang, who wrote several works of fiction, philosophy, and social commentary. Lin lived for a number of years in the west, acquired native fluency in English, and was the translator of a number of Chinese works into English, including poems by the famous Chinese poets Li Po (699-762) and Tu Fu (712-70). A Chinese scholar writing in 1947 in the USA refers to "his excellent English, certainly the very best any Chinese has ever written, which always holds a spell over his readers" (Chang-Win 1947, 164).

To compare readers' reactions to the Chinese and translated English versions of this text, we adapted measures from our previous foregrounding studies (Miall and Kuiken 1994). In those studies, we observed a strong relationship between the occurrence of foregrounding at the segment level (approximately one sentence) and readers' ratings of how striking they found each segment; in addition, we found that reading times per segment (controlled for segment length) were strongly influenced by level of foregrounding. We used these associations to examine the effectiveness of Lin Yutang's translation stylistically.

Design

We matched an excerpt from the Chinese version of *Six Chapters of a Floating Life* with an English translation of that excerpt by Lin Yutang. The excerpt was divided into 63 segments (approximately one sentence) that corresponded in both languages. For example, here are the opening two paragraphs of the excerpt in English, divided into numbered segments:

1. At this time the guests in the house all wore bright dresses, but Yun alone was clad in a dress of quiet colour, and had on a new pair of shoes.
2. I noticed that the embroidery on her shoes was very fine, and learnt that it was her own work, so that I began to realize that she was gifted at other things, too, besides reading and writing.
3. Of a slender figure, she had drooping shoulders and a rather long neck, slim but not to the point of being skinny.

4. Her eyebrows were arched and in her eyes there was a look of quick intelligence and soft refinement.
5. The only defect was that her two front teeth were slightly inclined forward, which was not a mark of good omen.
6. There was an air of tenderness about her, which completely fascinated me.

The study was carried out in Canada at the University of Alberta, where we recruited 40 university students, and in China at the Tianjin University of Science and Technology, where 28 students participated. The text was presented on computer, segment by segment. In their first reading, participants read the entire excerpt, pacing their reading by pressing the space bar (while the computer calculated reading times per segment). They then read the excerpt a second time, rating each segment for strikingness on a scale of 1 (not at all striking) to 5 (very striking). Finally, four passages selected from the excerpt were presented again, and readers provided ratings on 19 scales for each passage.

Results

The overall pattern of reading times and ratings indicated that Chinese and English readers' responded similarly, suggesting that the stylistic variations in Chinese were largely recreated in the English translation. However, there were also some differences between these two groups of readers, and the source of these differences requires careful examination.

Reading Times

When the reading times and strikingness ratings provided by Chinese and Canadian readers were considered separately, Friedman's test and Kendall's Coefficient of Concordance indicated high interrater agreement, $p < .001$. Therefore, for our primary analyses, we computed the means per segment across all individuals in each data set. We found that, overall, the profiles of mean reading times for Chinese readers and for Canadian readers were highly correlated, $r(61) = .605, p < .001$; given that there was considerable variance in sentence length, this result could be expected. However, the profiles of mean reading times were similar even when corrected for sentence length. That is, reading times per syllable in English and per word in Chinese were still moderately correlated: $r(61) = .389, p = .002$, suggesting that readers in both languages lingered over the same text segments.

At the same time, Canadian readers generally read faster than Chinese readers: mean reading time per segment in China was 8.67 sec; in Canada it was 7.37 sec, $t(62) = 3.405, p = .001$. This implies that Canadian readers may have taken less time to reflect on, or to savour, the story excerpt. Another indication that Canadian readers were less fully engaged with the text was provided by comparing reading times per segment with segment position. It is commonly found that readers tend to speed up during the course of their reading, as though early familiarity facilitates later comprehension. This was indeed the case for Chinese readers: reading times per word were inversely related to segment position, $r(61) = -.284, p = .024$; the Chinese readers read faster as the story progressed. However, for the Canadian readers there was no such effect (the analogous correlation between reading times per syllable and segment position was not significant: $r = -.032$); Canadian readers appear not to have developed the same familiarity with the world of the text as the Chinese readers.

Strikingness Ratings

A similar pattern of results was apparent in the strikingness ratings. The mean segment by segment strikingness ratings for Chinese and Canadian readers were highly correlated, $r(61) = .549, p < .001$. On the other hand, Canadian readers gave lower ratings overall than did the Chinese readers: Canadian: 3.03, Chinese: 3.38, $t(62) = 5.761, p < .001$.

We also expected that reading times would be correlated with strikingness ratings, since in previous studies both of these measures varied in concert with levels of foregrounding. This was partly born out by the analysis. For Chinese readers, mean segment by segment reading times and mean segment by segment strikingness ratings were modestly correlated, $r(61) = .248, p = .025$; however, among the Canadian readers this correlation was not significant, $r(61) = .111$, ns. Moreover, comparing across national groups, the Canadian mean reading times and Chinese mean strikingness ratings showed the expected relationship, $r(61) = .224, p < .05$; however, Chinese mean reading times and Canadian mean strikingness ratings did not, $r(61) = -.035$, ns. These findings, at least for the Chinese readers, are consistent with the foregrounding hypothesis. However, they also suggest that Canadian readers were not responding to foregrounding in the same way as their Chinese counterparts.

Auxiliary Analyses

Overall, the two versions of the text appear to have elicited similar *profiles* of response from Chinese and Canadian readers, even though they produced different *levels* of response on both the reading time and strikingness measures. One possibility is that Canadian readers' response to the translated text was diminished because foregrounded features in the original text were not faithfully rendered in translation. However, another possibility is that Canadian readers were less engaged because even Lin Yutang's finely translated text carried meanings that remained culturally remote.

To examine these possibilities more closely, we located the segments that had been rated most differently by the two groups of readers. The ten segments showing the greatest difference in strikingness can be seen in Table 2. Examination of these segments suggests that the differences can be attributed both to the limits of translatability and to Canadian readers' unfamiliarity with Chinese culture. For instance, segment 49 in Chinese is a sixteen-word sentence made up of four groups of four-word expressions (a formal expression in Chinese for which there is no obvious English equivalent); so, most of the stylistic effect is lost in the English version. Similarly, the original of segment 27 is written in typical classical Chinese, very different from a modern Chinese expression—and very difficult to translate into English. In contrast, in the Chinese version, segments 39 and 40 contain metaphors, antithesis, and some unusual, ancient expressions that would not be at all familiar to Canadian readers. Also, the poetry quoted in the last two segments (62 and 63) contained Chinese idioms that were found more striking by the Chinese readers.

Table 2. Mean Differences in Story Ratings (Chinese minus Canadian)

Diff	seg.	
1.29	62	"When the yellow stork comes again . . .
1.29	7	I asked for the manuscripts of her poems and found that they consisted mainly of couplets and three or four lines, being unfinished poems, and I asked her the reason why.
1.20	49	The light of a rapeseed oil lamp was then burning as small as a pea, and the edges of the bed curtain hung low in the twilight, and we were shaking all over.

1.19	27	All this was done naturally almost without any consciousness, and although at first we felt uneasy about it, later on it became a matter of habit.
1.12	63	"Just look at the white clouds sailing off..."
1.03	39	Then Yun stopped laughing and said, "The citron is the gentleman among the different fragrant plants because its fragrance is so slight that you can hardly detect it; on the other hand, the jasmine is a common fellow because it borrows its fragrance partly from others.
1.01	56	Yun wasn't interested because she did not think much of her, but I was intrigued and composed one on the flying willow catkins, which filled the air in May.
0.98	8	She smiled and said, "I have had no one to teach me poetry, and wish to have a good teacher friend who could help me to finish these poems."
0.84	55	There was a friend of mine, Chang Hsienhan of Wukiang, who was a good friend of Lenghsiang and brought her poems to me, asking us to write some in reply.
0.84	40	Therefore, the fragrance of the jasmine is like that of a smiling sycophant."

In addition to providing ratings for all 63 story segments, readers rated four selected passages on 19 separate 7-point scales, including semantic differential items (e.g., bright-dark, light-heavy, active-passive) and stylistic dimensions (e.g., simple-complex, unformal-formal, unforeign-foreign). Cross-group comparisons of these ratings indicated the following:

Passage 1:
"Do you mean *to tie me down* with all this ceremony?"

For this underlined passage, Chinese readers and Canadian readers reported contrasting connotations: Canadian readers found it relatively fast, hard, dark, dead, and low. Moreover, Canadian readers found the style of this passage less colourful and more formal than did their Chinese counterparts.

Passage 2:
"Therefore, the *fragrance of the jasmine is like that of a smiling sycophant.*"

For this underlined passage, too, Chinese and Canadian readers reported contrasting connotations: Canadian readers found this passage relatively slow, soft, bright, and light. Canadian readers also found this passage more unconventional in its sound, more complex, and (like passage 1) more formal.

Passage 3:
"They softly touch the spring sorrow in my bosom, and gently stir the longings in her heart."

Chinese and Canadian readers did not differ in their ratings of the connotations of this passage. However, like passage 2, Canadian readers found this poetic passage more unconventional in its sound, more complex, and more formal.

Passage 4:
When the yellow stork comes again,
  Let's together empty the golden goblet,
    Pouring wine-offering
      Over the thousand-year green meadow
        on the isle.
Just look at the white clouds sailing off,
  And who will play the jade flute,
    Sending its melodies
      Down the fifth-moon plum-blossoms
        in the city?

Again, Chinese and Canadian readers did not differ in their ratings of the connotations of this passage. However, Canadian readers found this embedded poem more unconventional in its sentence structure and (like passages 2 and 3) more unconventional in its sound, more complex, and more formal.

The greater formality that Canadians attributed to all four of these selected passages echoes Baker's (2004) claim that translated texts tend to be more formal than the original texts. Other ratings, however, help to elaborate the kind of formality that is at issue here. On 3 of the 4 selected passages Canadian readers found the text stylistically more unconventional, especially the sound but also the sentence structure. These ratings suggest that readers were attuned to formal, perhaps especially phonetic or rhythmic, features of the text that were smoothly integrated into the original Chinese version but that became "unconventional" and "complex" when translated into English. Such formal features constitute one of the primary—and perhaps insurmountable—obstacles to effective translation.

However, other contrasts between Chinese and Canadian readers seem to reflect more mundane cultural differences. The contrasting connotations of two of the selected passages seem to reflect Canadian unfamiliarity with aspects of Chinese culture. In one of its forms this involves unfamiliarity with the meaning of idiomatic expressions (e.g., what it may mean to be "tied down" by ceremony); in another of its forms it involves differences that derive from disparate histories with common cultural artifacts (e.g., traditional connotations of the "fragrance of jasmine"). While idiomatic expressions present difficulties in translation that compare, perhaps, with formal (e.g., phonetic, rhythmic) ones, the connotative differences that emerge from different cultural histories with common artifacts present the translator with a somewhat different dilemma. On the one hand, it is possible to construe connotative non-equivalence as a reader deficiency, as though, for example, Canadian readers might be expected to have multicultural understandings of the "fragrance of jasmine." On the other hand, it is possible to see connotative non-equivalence as a mandate for broadening the scope of translation, as justification for (non-literal) elaboration that would ensure equivalent description of the relevant cultural artifacts.

Conclusions

These results indicate that foregrounding – and translations of foregrounding – influence readers in similar ways, as shown by similar profiles of both reading times and strikingness ratings. At the same time, Canadian readers tended to read faster and find the text used in this study less striking. Differences in their rating patterns suggest that the contrast between Chinese and Canadian readers is due in part to the extreme challenge of translating some forms of foregrounding, especially phonetic and rhythmic features, and in part to the unfamiliarity of Canadian readers with Chinese cultural allusions and rhetorical forms.

These findings underline the difficulty of living up to Fu Yan's (1896/1984) three-character translation principles: "faithfulness," "expressiveness," and "elegance." In the preface to his translation of Huxley's *Evolution and Ethics*, Fu Yan (1898/1984) asserts that "Translation has to do with three difficult things: to be faithful, expressive and elegant." However, Fu Yan considered a translator to be a creative writer, at liberty to rearrange the text, and he even thought deletion or addition of necessary information was acceptable – what has been called "hermeneutic translation" (e.g., Wilberg 1999). The Canadian readers' lower strikingness ratings – and their contrasting understanding of the connotations of selected passages – prompt us to ask whether "hermeneutic translation" is required to create connotative equivalence between original and translated texts. Is that style of translation required for readers whose multi-cultural understanding is not well developed? Further study will be needed to clarify this issue, perhaps with more intensive exploration of specific figurative expressions translated from Chinese into English (such as "When the yellow stork comes again . . .").

In the meantime, this preliminary study, drawing on empirical methods with groups of readers, seems to us a promising avenue for beginning the examination of the aesthetic comparability of a source and translated text. Although the "functional equivalence" of a translation, in Nida's (1993) words, "cannot be understood in its mathematical meaning of identity, but only in terms of proximity" (117-8), the measurement of readers' responses, as we have demonstrated, provides a useful method for quantifying the degree of that proximity.

Works Cited

Baker, M. 2004. A corpus-based view of similarity and difference in translation. *International Journal of Corpus Linguistics*, 9: 167-193.
Chang-Win Tsit. 1947. Lin Yutang, critic and interpreter. *College English*, 8: 163-169.
Emmott, Catherine. 2002. Responding to style: Cohesion, foregrounding and thematic interpretation. In *Thematics: Interdisciplinary studies*, ed. Max Louwerse and Willie van Peer, 91-117. Amsterdam / Philadelphia: John Benjamins.
Hakemulder, Jemeljan F. 2004. Foregrounding and its effect on readers' perception. *Discourse Processes*, 38: 193-218.
Hogan, Patrick C. 1997. Literary universals. *Poetics Today*, 18: 223-249.
Howe, Fanny. 2006. Introduction to G. Bernanos, *Mouchette*, trans. J. C. Whitehouse, vii-xxii. New York: New York Review Books.
Lodge, Ken. 2003. Phonological translation and phonetic repertoire. *International Journal of Applied Linguistics*, 13: 263-276.
Miall, David S. and Kuiken, Don. 1994. Foregrounding, defamiliarization, and affect: Response to literary stories. *Poetics*, 22: 389-407.

Miall, David S. and Kuiken, Don. 2001. Shifting perspectives: Readers' feelings and literary response. In *New Perspectives on Narrative Perspective*, ed. Willie van Peer and Seymour Chatman, 289-301. Albany, NY: State University of New York Press.

Nida, Eugene A. 1993. *Language, Culture, and Translating*. Shanghai: Foreign Language Education Press.

Shen Fu. 1999. *Six Chapters of a Floating Life*, trans. Lin Yutang. Beijing: Chinese Translators Association, Foreign Languages Teaching and Research Press.

Venuti, Lawrence. 1995. *The Translator's Invisibility: A History of Translation*. London: Routledge.

—. ed. 1992. *Rethinking Translation: Discourse, Subjectivity, Ideology*. London: Routledge.

Yan, Fu. 1984. Preface to the translation of *Evolution and Ethics*. In: *Essays on Translation Studies*. Beijing: Chinese Translators Association, Foreign Languages Teaching and Research Press. [Original publication 1896.]

Wilberg, Peter. 1999, April. Interlingual Training and Technology. *Humanising Language Teaching*, Year 1, Issue 2 http://www.hltmag.co.uk/apr99/mart1.htm (August 23rd 2007)

CHAPTER THIRTEEN

IS THIS TYPICAL JAPANESE? INFLUENCES OF STEREOTYPES ON TEXT RECEPTION

JAN AURACHER AND AKIKO HIROSE

Abstract

This chapter reports the results of a study conducted to gain a better understanding of the influence of stereotypes when reconstructing the character of a protagonist in a story. Two versions of a fairytale, different only in their claimed cultural origin, were used as materials. When asked to assess protagonists' character traits, subjects who believed the text to be of Japanese origin tended to allocate significantly more (stereo-)typical Japanese traits than subjects who had been made to believe the text to be an Italian fairytale. Moreover, readers who studied either Japanology or Italian philology tended to assess the fairytale as more typically Japanese or Italian, respectively, when compared to students with other majors.

Assessing Protagonists

The interpretation of a literary text hinges – not least – on the interpretation of its protagonists. It is the protagonist who often carries the storyline, whose actions and thoughts cause readers to reflect on issues raised by the story. And, as the contributions by Green and Owen in this volume show, it is not exceptional for readers to draw consequences from the behaviour and/or beliefs of a character. By relating a sequence of actions to the motivation of the protagonists, the author constructs what E. M. Forster calls the 'plot', i.e. a story with "a sense of causality" (Forster 1974, 93; see also Carroll 2001). According to Oatley, the reader, by adopting the protagonist's goals, wishes, or hopes becomes emotionally involved in the story, allowing a deeper understanding of its development

(Oatley 1992, 1994; Oatley and Gholamain 1997). In processing protagonists' motives, readers participate in a narrative rather than just reading it passively, drawing conclusions about past events and anticipating further plot developments.

Without doubt, one important motive for choosing one action over others is the character of a subject. It sounds much more plausible to ascribe a betrayal to the mean and brutal Hook rather than to the innocent and friendly Peter Pan. Consequently, a better understanding of a protagonist's motives demands that the reader draw conclusions about his or her character. Only by categorizing a figure in a plot as a personality with specific traits can the reader meaningfully reconstruct the plot. But what is it that contributes to the assessment of a fictional person? Which measures and information help readers to construct a sometimes complex character out of few 'observations'?

The question of how to interpret a figure in a fictional text is discussed extensively in the narratological literature (for an overview see Margolin 1989, Bortolussi and Dixon 2003, see also http://www.narratology.net/). As Margolin (1990) points out, this task entails a methodological problem arising from the fact that a character is both a semiotic as well as a representational entity, i.e. a textual representation and construction, and a lifelike individual or hypothetical entity analogous to a human being (Fishelov 2004/5, Hochman 1981, 26). Bortolussi and Dixon (2003, 136) relate this duality to two possible approaches, the former focusing on the analysis of the text, the latter bringing the understanding of the reader to the former. This reader's understanding requires the analyst to go beyond the analysis of the text when assessing the way characters are understood. As a fictional person remains "ontologically thin", existing only as "a series of discontinuous states or phases" (Bortolussi and Dixon 2003, 137; Margolin 1989) readers are required to construct the character by filling in informational gaps with their own world knowledge (see also Chatman 1972, 78). Consequently, when interpreting fictional characters the focus shifts from the analysis of the text to that of readers' cognitive processes. In a manner comparable to the construction of the character of individuals in the real world, readers will draw conclusions according to the observations they make by following the plot (Bortolussi and Dixon 2003, 139-140). Hence, the question of how to interpret a fictional character can best be approached by looking at psychological processes when constructing mental representations of other characters in general. One important source upon which readers rely is pre-information, that is, of information, which is, rightly or wrongly, assumed in relation to the person under scrutiny.

In order to formalise this approach, Bortolussi and Dixon rely on Bayes' theorem to assess dependent likelihood, as it is repeatedly used in attribution theory (Bortolussi and Dixon 2003, 146-147). This involves the question: when do people (readers) evaluate a certain trait (T) as likely for a (fictional) person after observing – or hearing/reading about – certain behaviour? According to Bayes' theorem, the likelihood (P) of a trait (T) of a person under a given behaviour (A) (P (T | A)) depends, among other things, on the likelihood that the trait (T) is an actual attribute of the observed person or protagonist (P (T)). This is, of course, always according to the mental construct the observer or reader made of this person or protagonist.

$$P(T \mid A) = \frac{P(A \mid T) P(T)}{P(A)}$$

Without going into details about this formalisation, we want to focus on some points relevant for this paper. The formula tells us that conclusions drawn about a person's character according to his or her doings depend very much on the mental construct the observer already had before the observation. If someone concedes a certain trait as rather unlikely for a person, the product of P (A | T) and P (T) becomes smaller and this means that the likelihood of evaluating the behaviour (A) as a sign for the trait (T) becomes small as well.

If, for example, Prof. Snape in the Harry Potter saga, who is described as a real sod, eventually shows some dignity, this does not prevent the reader to dislike him as such. His willingness to help Harry by teaching him to shut his mind from being read by his enemy is not evaluated as a sign of Snape's good character. The author J.K. Rowling uses this general tendency of her readers to trust everything bad to Prof. Snape by guiding their suspicions towards him, which, however, again and again prove to be biased.

To make this fact even more obvious, one can extend the equation with a term for P (A | T'), where T' symbolizes not-T:

$$\frac{P(T \mid A)}{P(T' \mid A)} = \frac{P(A \mid T) P(T)}{P(A \mid T') P(T')}$$

Bringing the mathematics back into words again, this equation could be transcribed as:

Posterior odds = Likelihood ratio × Prior odds,

which Bortolussi and Dixon explain as follows:

"P (T) / P (T'), is the prior odds, that is, the odds of the characteristic a priori, before observing the behavior."

"P (A | T) / P (A | T'), is the likelihood ratio; it indicates how likely the behavior is when the characteristic is present relative to how likely it is when the characteristic is absent." (Bortolussi and Dixon 2003, 146-147)

With respect to the example above the *Prior Odds* would mean that readers do have already a certain opinion about the character of Prof. Snape or Harry Potter, before they read about a certain event, coming up next in the story. The *Likelihood Ratio* then is the likely evaluation of the behaviour during this event, under the assumption of a certain trait.

Though it is not necessarily the case that humans evaluate their environment based on exact mathematical equations, the empirical data support the predictions made by attribution theory, in accordance with the Bayesian theorem (Ajzen and Fishbein 1975; Trope and Burnstein 1975). In relation to this paper, we want to focus on the 'prior odds'. That is, readers will use their conceptions about the character of a protagonist to evaluate his or her future behaviour. As in most cases, readers will already bring a certain expectation before even starting to read the text; this might cause a strong bias when constructing a mental picture of a character. One source for these expectations could be the genre of a text. Most viewers of a Wild West movie will not be surprised when they discover the hero to be a tough, but sensitive man, who is willing to carry the burden of his fate alone. Quite the contrary, in fact, the viewer might tend to ignore inconsistencies, which could violate the overall impression (see also Ajzen and Fishbein 1975).

Another source for a biased perspective could be a text's cultural origin and the stereotypes a reader has about the respective culture. In what follows, we want to test the relevance of such stereotypes to the evaluation of a fictional character. We hypothesise that readers, when given a (claimed-to-be) traditional Japanese text, will readily find attributes of the protagonists in accordance with common stereotypes about Japan. However, a text presented as from a different culture, will elicit different evaluations of the text, in line with the cultural stereotypes associated with its origin.

Culture and Texts

There is a tradition of regarding literature as a window on culture. Recent publications use the interpretation of literary sources to approach those societies in an attempt to compare cultural traditions (e.g., Corse 1997), to overcome time gaps (e.g., Belsey 2001), or to identify human universals (e.g., Hogan 2003). These attempts are based on two assumptions: on the one hand, the idea that the term *culture* includes all mental and physical products of a society and hence also includes literature, which in return reflects the values and norms of a community (e.g., Leavis 1952; Hoggarts 1957; Gliner and Raines 1971, Assmann and Assmann 1994; Assmann 1995); on the other hand, that the understanding of cultural symbols is comparable to the mental processes of reading a text (Geertz 1973, Eco 1987, Lotman und Uspensky 1978, Bachmann-Medick 1996). In her book *Language and Culture*, Kramsch (1998) points out that texts are part of a discourse community and therefore embedded within the traditions and communication habits of a society. "One of the greatest sources of difficulty for foreign readers is less the internal cohesion of the text than the cultural coherence of the discourse." (p. 59) As a result, several literary scholars emphasise the importance of literary texts for the study of a culture (e.g. Gorman 1989). The interpretation of a text includes an understanding of its cultural background. Literary education, therefore, is repeatedly suggested as being important for the socialisation of children and their multicultural awareness (e.g. Stephens 1992, Harris 1993, Bishop 1997, Livingston and Kurkjian 2005). Moreover, in research of foreign language acquisition, literature is regularly seen as an important source for a better understanding of the target culture (among others: Delanoy 1993; Bredella and Delanoy 1996; Bredella 2000; Kramsch 2000 2003; Burwitz-Meltzer 2001; Rogers and Soter 1997).

To our knowledge, however, little is known about the influence of the stereotypes readers bring from their world knowledge onto their textual interpretations. Lippmann introduced the term *stereotype* as a judgment made about individuals based on their ethnic group membership (Lippmann 1922). Adopting his concept to the reception of literature, this could mean that readers who hold certain stereotypes will be tempted to judge a fictional person according to the nationality of the author.

> "For the most part we do not first see, and then define, we define first and then see. In the great blooming, buzzing confusion of the outer world *we pick out what our culture has already defined for us*, and we tend to perceive that which we have picked out in the form stereotyped for us by our culture." (Lippmann 1922, [italics added])

Similarly, Kramsch argues that "our perception of someone's social identity is very much culturally determined" (Kramsch 1998, 67). This would suggest that German readers, who share common stereotypes about – for example – Japanese, will base their readings on such stereotypes when encountering Japanese texts and, consequently, might interpret certain aspects of the text accordingly. While this already implies two questions, i.e. whether Germans do share common stereotypes about Japanese, and whether these stereotypes do influence their interpretation of a text, we also wanted to know whether such a biased view of cultural artefacts could be relativised through an academic training related to the culture in question. That is, does the extensive involvement with a certain culture enable to attenuate stereotypes in that members from a certain culture can be seen as individuals instead of stereotypes? The focus of our study, therefore, was extended by the dimension of pre-knowledge operationalised through academic education.

Research Design

To carry out this aim we asked subjects to read a text and assess the protagonist's character on a number of given attributes. We expected that differences in the information about the origin of the text would result in significant differences in the answers. To be sure that the background information about the text, and not the text itself, was responsible for any measured differences, all subjects received the same text. As it was one goal of the study to determine the influence of stereotypes about a culture, the given background information about the text's origin, however, differed. That is, the same text was given to two independent groups of readers: in one group the text was labelled as traditional Japanese, in the other as a traditional Italian fairy tale. After reading participants were asked to assess the extent to which certain character traits describe the story's protagonists. Additionally, subjects were asked to rate whether the text was typical or untypical for its place of origin, i.e. Japan or Italy, respectively.

Pre-Study or: What is typical Japanese?

Before we could start with our study we needed some information on German stereotypes about Japanese and Italians. We decided to gather this information empirically, by asking about 20 randomly chosen pedestrians in Munich. Participants were requested to simply name everything which came to mind when they thought about Japan or Italy. After we had a list of frequently mentioned words, we listed them and asked yet another 50 randomly chosen pedestrians to allocate each of these words to either Japan or Italy, or to neither country. We made use of only those attributes which at least 48 out of 50 allocated to the same culture. The typical Japanese properties we found were: polite (höflich), diligent (fleißig), honest (ehrlich), obedient (gehorsam) and self-sacrificing (aufopfernd). Typical Italian characteristics were: passionate (leidenschaftlich), self-confident (selbstbewusst), and open-minded (offenherzig).

Method

Materials

Text

For our text we chose a fairy tale from the collection of the Grimm Brothers called 'Die kluge Bauerntochter' ('the farmer's wise daughter'). In the story, a king marries the daughter of a farmer because of her wisdom, but as she starts to undermine his decisions, he expels her. In the end, however, she wins him back.

The text was presented under two conditions: in one it was claimed to be a traditional fairy tale from Japan, in the other readers were told that it was a traditional fairy tale from Italy. To mask this manipulation, care had been taken to change 'bread' to 'rice' and 'King' to 'Daimyo' in the text presented under the 'Japanese' condition. The texts presented to the two groups were identical in all other respects.

Questionnaire

After reading the text, participant were requested to respond to a questionnaire consisting of three parts, starting with some general questions about the story and whether readers considered the tale to be typically Italian or Japanese, respectively. In the second part, participants were asked to assess the character of all three protagonists in the story, namely the *Daughter*, the *King* (Daimyo), and the *Father*. The attributes that the subjects had to rate were taken from the pre-study and expressed stereotypes about each culture, to be rated on 8-point Likert scales. Additionally, we inserted the items 'wise' (weise) and 'cunning' (listig) as distracters, which, though particularly suited the Daughter, were not related to either culture. Finally, readers were asked some personal questions (gender, age, education) and about their relation to one of the two countries, again in accordance with the text version they read.

Both parts, reading the text and answering the questionnaire, required about 10 to 20 minutes, and most participants completed the questionnaire directly when asked. In what follows, we want to focus on the question whether the text was evaluated as being typical for its claimed cultural origin, and whether these claimed origins had a significant influence on the characterisation of the protagonists. Moreover, we wanted to see whether an academic education concerning the culture in question will help to strengthen these stereotypes.

Participants

Participants were German students at the University of Munich. The 'Japanese group' (Group I) consisted of students of Japanology and students from different departments who were learning Japanese as a foreign language at the University's Japan-Center. The 'Italian group' (Group II) consisted of students from the department of Italian Philology and students from different departments related to intercultural studies, who were learning Italian in language classes. Altogether 139 students participated in this study, out of which 91 read version I (the Japanese version) and 48 read version II (the Italian version). Both groups fell within the age span of 20 to 30 years of age. Nearly all subjects were Germans with German as their mother tongue. The ratio male: female for Group I was 1:1. Group II was predominantly female. However, using sex as a covariate in our analyses revealed no significant influence.

Results

As we regarded most variables as more ordinal than scalar, and as the answers to most questions were not normally distributed, we decided to use the non-parametric Mann-Whitney-U test as a test of significance and to compare the groups according to the medians instead of the means.

Assessing the character of the protagonists

In what follows, we report those cases which showed at least a 1-point difference for the median between the two groups. Group I (Japan) assessed the *Daughter* as more polite, obedient, diligent, and self-sacrificing than Group II. Though these results support the hypothesis, as all of these attributes were regarded as 'typical Japanese', only 'polite' was statistically significant ($p = .028$, $Z = -2.192$) while 'obedient' ($p = .068$, $Z = -1.826$) and 'self-sacrifycing' ($p = .088$, $Z = -1.704$) showed a tendency towards significance. Also, Group I had higher medians for 'polite' when assessing the *King*, for 'obedient' when assessing the *Father*, and for 'honest' in respect to both characters. Among these, 'honest' was significant for the *King* ($p = .023$, $Z = -2,279$) and 'obedient' tended towards significance for the *Father* ($p = .058$, $Z = -1.898$). While all these results pointed in the predicted direction, Group I also assessed 'open-minded', which was originally assigned as being typical for Italy, significantly higher for the *Daughter* and the *King* (Daughter: $p = .006$, $Z = -2.751$; King: $p = .017$, $Z = -2.396$), but not for the *Father*.

As a next step we decided to take averages of each attribute for all three figures and analyse whether there was a general tendency in Group I to assess the stereotypical Japanese traits higher compared to Group II, independent of the actual character of each protagonist. There were significant differences for 'honest' ($p = .033$, $Z = -2.137$) and 'obedient' ($p = .007$, $Z = -2.683$), two stereotypes which are commonly applied to Japanese, but not to Italians. That is, though both groups received the same story and even though the three protagonists, whose characters had to be assessed, represented rather different types, still those subjects who believed to read a Japanese fairy tale showed the tendency to rate some stereotypical Japanese traits on average for all protagonists significantly higher than those subjects who believed to have read a Italian fairy tale. To analyse this even more accurately we decided to conduct a MANOVA with all four (stereo-)typical Japanese traits (i.e. 'polite', 'obedient', 'self-scarifying', and 'diligent') comparing both groups, despite our decision for non-parametric test (as mentioned above). All four traits were rated on average 0.3 points higher by the Japanese Group. However, the differences just failed to be significant ($F = 2.213$; $p = 0.071$).

Evaluating whether the story is typically Japanese or Italian, respectively

The question of whether the text was evaluated as typically Japanese or Italian was meant to give us some insight into the relationship between academic education and readers' recognition of the text as part of the culture (as measured on a 4-point Likert scale: 1 = 'not typical'; 4 = 'very typical'). Participants can be divided into four groups which differ in their relationship to either of the two countries: students who studied either Italian Philology (IP) or who learned Italian in language classes (IL), on the one hand, and students who either studied Japanology [1](JP), i.e. Japanese language and culture, or who learned Japanese at the University (JL)[2]. While two groups can be regarded as 'experts' on one of the relevant cultures, i.e. students of Italian philology and students of Japanology, the other two groups had, though they learned the language as a leisure activity, only a non-academic view on the country in each case. This meant that we had four independent groups.

As can be seen in figure 1, the two 'expert groups' (Japanology (JP) and Italian Philology (IP) – the boxes on the very left and right) tend to assess the texts as being more typical for their respective culture than do the two non-expert groups (JL and IL – two boxes in the middle). However, the medians for all groups were 2 (on the 4-point scale), and only when calculating the means were there differences of about 0.5 points between the 'expert' and the 'non-expert' groups. Still, comparing the averages of the expert to non-expert groups in respect of their assessment of the fairy tale as 'typical' for the claimed culture, reveals a significant difference (Mann-Whitney-U: $Z = -2.136$; $p < 0.05$).

---

[1] We use the term as synonymous with what is called Japanese Studies in North America.
[2] The University of Munich offers language courses for students in all faculties. These classes are free and are often attended by students who plan to complete an internship in a country where the language is spoken, or who have a general interest in the language. The courses take place two times a week during term. Students do not receive credits for participating.

Figure 1: Distribution of answers per subject-group: "Do you consider the text as typical Japanese/Italian?"

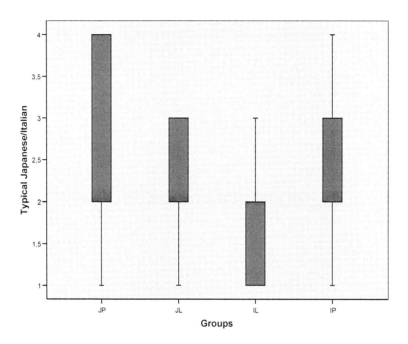

This means that, the more academic education was related to the culture in question, the more readers tended to find corresponding stereotypical aspects in the story. Considering the fact that the tale actually originated in Germany, these differences, though very small, are still highly surprising. Admittedly, it is not impossible that a German fairy tale could look like a typical Italian or Japanese fairytale; however this explanation would raise the question of why the non-expert groups assessed the texts as less typical. It has to be mentioned that, due to the small differences between the groups and the wide range from minimum to maximum on the scale within the expert groups, the results need to be interpreted with care. Moreover, sample size was rather small for some groups. After dividing the two Groups (Japanese version vs. Italian version) into four we had 57 participants in the expert group (Japanology: n = 29; Italian Philology: n = 28) and only 27 in the non-expert group (Japanese: n = 14; Italian = 13). Still, we regard the tendency as very interesting and rather counter-intuitive.

To check within the Japanese group whether the assessment of the text as typically Japanese is in relation to the assessment of the characters, all participants in Group I (Japanese version) were divided into two sub-groups: Those who found the text 'typical' or 'very typical' (→ 'typical') and those who regarded it as 'less typical' or 'not typical' (→ 'non-typical'). This comparison reveals a significant difference in the assessment of the protagonists' attributes, showing that those subjects who assessed the text as 'typical Japanese' also tended to assess stereotypical attributes of the characters significantly higher (Mann-Whitney-U test: 'polite': $Z = -2.279$, $p = ,022$; 'honest': $Z = -1.809$, $p = ,038$; 'obedient': $Z = -1.975$, $p = ,048$). The fact that these differences were calculated with the means of the assessment over all protagonists strongly suggests that a crucial influence is exerted by stereotypes when evaluating characters. All three protagonists had little in common; they represented relatively one-dimensional characters. Though the mean differences between the groups were always between 0.5 and 1 on the scale, whereas the range of answers was always between 4 and 5 points on the scale, the results raise the question of why there is any significant difference between the independent groups at all.

Discussion

The study investigated the role pre-knowledge plays when assessing protagonists in fictional texts. To operationalize this question, stereotypes about Italy and Japan were collected and empirically compared. This revealed that Japanese are regarded as 'polite', 'obedient', 'self-sacrificing', and 'honest', whereas Italians are rather attributed as 'passionate', 'self-confident', and 'open-minded'. In the next step, a German fairy tale was selected and presented to subjects in two versions, which differed only in an introduction claiming the text to be either a Japanese (version 1) or an Italian fairytale (version 2). It was expected that readers, when asked to assess the character of the protagonists, would assess stereotypically Japanese or Italian traits higher, according to the text version they received. Moreover, it was expected that students whose major is closely related to the claimed origin of the text would tend to assess the text as less typical for this culture, which in return would prevent them from finding (stereo-)typical Japanese or Italian characters in a German fairytale.

Results showed that subjects indeed assessed some of those attributes related to the claimed origin of the text significantly higher. This was the case for both the comparison for single protagonists and the average assessment over all protagonists. Surprisingly, the second hypothesis was not only refuted, but the results were actually in the opposite direction: Students who studied the relevant culture tended to find the texts *more* typical than students who did not specialize in one of the two cultures. Additionally, looking only at the 'Japanese' group, the tendency to assess the text as typically Japanese correlated with the tendency to find (stereo-)typical attributes in the characters of the protagonists. (This test was carried out only for Group I (Japanese version), as Group II was too small for an intra-group comparison.)

Although the study involved only a small group of students and wasn't representative at all, the results still raise questions about the usefulness of literary texts in approaching new cultures. It seems that readers tend to find exactly that information in a text which they expected to find. Thus, literature could be seen to be more of a mirror than a window, reflecting an already fixed idea instead of opening up new perspectives on a culture. This seems to be especially true when looking at the comparison between 'expert' and 'non-expert' groups. To repeat, the results were not always clear, but they do suggest that students who become deeper involved with one culture tend to strengthen their stereotypes rather than loosening them up.

A cultural relativistic approach in the humanities is based on the idea that both, the observer and the observed behave and interpret according to their culturally specific socialisation. As quoted above, the 'cultural coherence of a discourse' is regarded as the 'greatest source of difficulties for foreigners' to understand (Kramsch 1998, 59). This is what is mostly taught to students at the University. However, by emphasising mainly the cultural dominance in human interaction, the hermetic aspect of a foreign culture might be overstressed. Though there is undoubtedly some truth in this approach, it includes the danger that students rely too much on theoretical knowledge, not seeing the obvious through their own eyes. When repeatedly told that one's own perspective is necessarily biased according to the socialisation one experienced, the effect might bring about quite the opposite result than was originally intended. From our results we conclude that instead of taking a more relativist approach to a foreign culture, which helps to overcome one's own bias, the fear of becoming trapped in subjectivity might cause an oversimplifying relation to the abstract theoretical discourses that students encounter during their education.

Works Cited

Ajzen, L., and M.A. Fishbein. 1975. Bayesian analysis of attribution processes. *Psychological Bulletin* 82: 21-77.
Assmann, A. 1995. Was sind kulturelle Texte? In *Literaturkanon, Medienereignis, kultureller Text. Formen interkultureller Kommunikation und Übersetzung*, ed. A. Poltermann, 232-244. Berlin: Erich Schmidt Verlag.
Assmann, A., and J. Assmann. 1994. Das Gestern im Heute. Medien und soziales Gedächtnis. In *Die Wirklichkeit der Medien. Eine Einführung in die Kommunikationswissenschaften*, ed. K. Merten, S.J. Schmidt, and S. Weischenberg, 114-140. Opladen: Westdeutscher Verlag.
Bachmann-Medick, D. ed. 1996. *Kultur als Text. Die anthropologische Wende in der Literaturwissenschaft*. Frankfurt a.M.: Fischer.
Belsey, C. 2001. *Shakespeare and the Loss of Eden. The construction of family values in early modern culture*. London: Palgrave.
Bishop, R. S. 1997. Selecting literature for a multicultural curriculum. In *Using multiethnic literature in the K-8 classroom*, ed. V. Harris, 1-20. Norwood, MA: Christopher-Gordon Publishers, Inc.
Bortolussi, M., and Dixon, P. 2003. *Psychonarratology. Foundations for the empirical study of literary response*. Cambridge: Cambridge University Press.
Bredella, L. 2000. Literary texts and intercultural understanding. In *Routledge Encyclopaedia of language teaching and learning*, ed. M. Byram, 382-386. London: Routledge.
Bredella, L., and W. Delanoy, eds. 1996. *Challenges of Literary Texts in the Foreign Language Classroom*. Tubingen: Gunter Narr.
Burwitz-Meltzer, E. 2001. Teaching intercultural communicative competence through literature. In *Developing Intercultural Competence in Practice*, ed. M. Byram, A. Nictiols, and D. Stevens, 29-43. Clevedon: Multilingual Matters.
Carrol, N. 2001. On the Narrative Connection. In *New Perspective on Narrative Perspective*, ed. W. van Peer and S. Chatman, 21-43. Albany: State University of New York Press.
Chatman, S.B. 1972. On the formalist-structuralist theory of character. *Journal of Literary Semantics* 1, 57-79.
Corse, S.M. 1997. *Nationalism and Literature. The politics of culture in Canada and the United States*. Cambridge: Cambridge University Press.
Delanoy, W. 1993. 'Come to Mecca' - Assessing a literary text's potential for intercultural learning. In *Experiencing a Foreign Culture*, ed. W.

Delanoy, J. Koberl, and H. Tschachler, 275-299. Tubingen: Gunter Narr.
Eco, U. 1987. *Semiotik. Entwurf einer Theorie der Zeichen.* [Orig. ed. 1976]. München: Fink.
Fishelov, D. 2004/5. Robinson Crusoe, 'The Other' and the poetics of surprise. *Connotations* 14(1-3): 1-18.
Forster, E.M. 1974. *Aspects of the Novel.* [Orig. ed.1927]. London: Edward Arnold.
Geertz, C. 1973. *The Interpretation of Cultures. Selected essays.* New York: Basic Books.
Gliner, R., and R. Raines, ed. 1971. *Munching on Existence: Contemporary American society through literature.* New York: Free Press.
Gorman, D. 1989. The wordly text: Writing as social action, reading as historical reconstruction. In *Literary Theory's Future(s),* ed. J. Natoli, 181-220. Chicago / Urbana: University of Illinois Press.
Harris, V., ed. 1993. *Teaching Multicultural Literature Grades K thru 8.* Norwood, MA: Christopher-Gordon Publishers, Inc.
Hochman, B. 1981. *Character in Literature.* Ithaca: Cornell University Press.
Hogan, P.C. 2003. *The Mind and its Stories: Narrative universals and human emotion.* Cambridge: Cambridge University Press.
Hoggarts, R. 1957. *The Uses of Literacy. Aspects of working-class life, with special references to publications and entertainments.* London: Chatto and Windus.
Kramsch, C. 1998. *Language and Culture.* Oxford: Oxford University Press.
—. 2000. *Context and Culture in Language Teaching.* 1993. Oxford: Oxford University Press.
Leavis, F.R. 1952. *The Common Pursuit.* London: Chatto and Windus.
Lippmann, W. 1922. *Public Opinion.* Project Gutenberg. http://www.gutenberg.org/ etext/6456 (accessed February 13, 2007).
Livingston, N., and C. Kurkjian. 2005. *Circles and Celebrations: Learning about other cultures through literature.* The Reading Teacher 58(7): 696-703.
Lotman, Y. and B.A. Uspensky. 1978. On the semiotic mechanism of culture. *New Literary History* 9(2): 211-232.
Margolin, U. 1989. Structuralist approaches to character in narrative: The sate of the art. *Semiotica* 75(1/2): 1-24.
—. 1990. The what, the when, and the how of being a character in literary narrative. *Style* 24, no. 3: 453-469.

Oatley, K. 1992. *Best Laid Schemes: The psychology of emotions*. New York: Cambridge University Press.

—. 1994. A taxonomy of the emotions of literary response and a theory of identification in fictional narrative. *Poetics* 23: 53-74.

Oatley, K., and M. Gholamain. 1997. Emotions and identification. Connections between readers and fiction. In *Emotion and the Arts*, ed. M. Hjort and S. Laver, 263-281. New York: Oxford University Press.

Rogers, T., and A. Soter, eds. 1997. *Reading Across Cultures: Teaching literature in a diverse society*. Columbia University: Teachers College Press.

Stephens, J. 1992. *Language and Ideology in Children's Fiction*. London: Longman.

Trope, Y., and E. Burnstein. 1975. Processing the information contained in another's behavior. *Journal of Experimental Social Psychology* 11: 439-458.

Chapter Fourteen

From Sacred to Profane: The Effects of Reading Violent Religious Literature on Subsequent Human Aggression

Robert D. Ridge and Colin W. Key

Abstract

Religious terrorism is ubiquitous today. One source of inspiration for terrorists' actions may be violent religious texts. Previous research in experimental social psychology has documented that exposure to violent media causes increased aggression, but this research has largely ignored exposure to violent literature. We review the social scientific literature on media-induced aggression to explore how and why exposure to violent religious literature may contribute to aggressive behaviour. We argue for a quantitative experimental approach for investigating hypotheses generated from this literature and describe recent research that employed this methodology. Results suggest that quantitative empirical approaches to the study of literature may provide theoretically relevant and practically significant perspectives on pressing social problems.

Religious Terrorism in the Current World

Rejoice, brave warrior, if you live and conquer in the Lord, but rejoice still more and give thanks if you die and go to join the Lord. Blessed are they who die in the Lord. But how much more so are those who die for Him.
—St. Bernard of Clairvaux

In recent years, there appears to have been a marked increase in religious terrorism on a global scale. The typical scenario involves the slaughter of innocent bystanders by religious fundamentalists who kill in the furtherance of their religious and political views. The violence seems to be at odds with religious philosophies that are built on the principles of love, humanitarian concern and tolerance, yet these terrorists frequently justify their behaviour by invoking the name of deity. Such actions are not new in the course of human history, but there is a general feeling, true or not, that intolerance and violence are increasing.

In his book, *Terror in the Mind of God: The Global Rise of Religious Violence*, Juergensmeyer (2003) has proposed three factors that foster religious aggression:

1) Terrorists consider contemporary forms of religion as weakened versions of the true, authentic faith, and therefore embrace a more demanding, "hard" religion that requires sacrifice.
2) They refuse to compromise with secular institutions, critiquing "soft" religions for readily accommodating to the mainstream culture. These activists feel justified in defying laws since they view their responsibilities as citizens as secondary to their faith and religious obligations.
3) The terrorists reject the public-private split whereby faith is considered a private matter to be kept outside the realm of politics. Some even hope that their actions will contribute to the demise of the secular state, ultimately leading to the establishment of a theocracy.

The result of this belief system is a tolerance of violence as an acceptable form of behaviour directed towards those presumed to be in opposition to true faith. Terrorism is an inevitable outgrowth of this ideology.

To what can we attribute the source of these beliefs that produce such hostility? How is it possible for religious extremists to justify their destructive actions? Part of the justification may come from their reading of sacred texts and a culture that embraces their interpretation of these writings. For example, in Christian theology the following verse, attributed to Jesus Christ, appears in the New Testament: *Think not that I am come to send peace on earth, I came not to send peace, but a sword* (Matthew 10, 34). One interpretation of this verse is that violence against others may be warranted if it is necessary for the defence of a religious principle or the subjugation of evil. A verse such as this could be used as justification for terrorism, such as that enacted by Timothy McVeigh, a member of the radical Christian movement called *Christian Identity*, who detonated a truck bomb and killed 167 people in an effort to attack the evils of the U.S. government.

Such extremism, however, is not solely the province of radical Christianity. Jewish faithful believe in the divinity of the Torah, within which is the scripture: *The LORD is a man of war; the LORD is his name* (Exodus 15, 3). Read by one who considers him- or herself to be a victim of religious persecution, it could be interpreted as justification for retaliation. Such may have been the case for Dr. Baruch Goldstein, a Jewish physician who killed 29 Arabs and wounded 125 others in an assault on a religious shrine. He carried out this brutality because his meditation had been interrupted by a group of Arab youths who shouted, "Slaughter the Jews!"

Perhaps most notable in the recent past has been the religious terrorism practiced by militant Muslims. On September 11, 2001, Mohamed Atta al-Sayed and several other followers of Osama bin Laden hijacked four American Airlines airplanes and crashed them into the World Trade Center and the U.S. Pentagon. Two thousand nine hundred seventy-six people were killed in the furtherance of this radical Islamic *jihad*. The words of the Qur'an suggest to some that such an attack is defensible on religious grounds: *Soon shall We cast terror into the hearts of the Unbelievers, for that they joined companions with Allah, for which He had sent no authority: their abode will be Fire: And evil is the home of the wrong-doers!* (Qur'an 3, 151)

In each of these instances of religious violence, believers could claim that there is scriptural justification for the aggressive behaviour. Examples of violence in the service of a divine cause are plentiful in religious canon and exposure to such literature may provide extremists with a blueprint for aggressive action. But how far can one carry the argument? Is it possible that mere exposure to such writings may actually incite readers to violence or elicit aggressive responses from them? Such effects would seem to be counterintuitive given that the objective of religious writing is typically to inspire peaceful contemplation or to motivate individuals to become more caring and compassionate. To what extent is exposure to violent religious literature a *cause* of aggression directed towards other individuals? Answers to such questions may be provided by independent tests carried out in the field of social science.

A Social Scientific Perspective on Religious Terrorism

One approach to answering these questions is to employ a quantitative experimental analysis of exposure to violent literature. This approach permits one to systematically manipulate the literature to which experimental subjects are exposed and examine the effects of the manipulation on valid and reliable measures of aggression. This type of research complements qualitative analyses of violent literature and represents a departure from the more traditional analytic methods employed in the humanities.

There currently exists a large body of social scientific research that investigates the effects of exposure to violent media. This literature provides us with not only a suggested methodology for conducting research with literary sources, but also with theoretical explanations as to how and why such exposure might affect readers. We turn to a brief review of this literature to examine how violence in a variety of media affects consumers, and then we describe recent research investigating how exposure to violence in literature affects readers.

Media Effects on Aggression

For more than 50 years, social scientists have conducted research on the effects of violent media, including TV programs, films, and video games, on consumers. The results of these studies lead to the conclusion that exposure to violent media increases aggression; a summary of these studies may be found in Anderson and Bushman (2002). For example, experiments have shown that exposure to media violence causes people to behave more aggressively immediately after the exposure. Cross-sectional studies (i.e. studies that examine the effects of violent media over the lifespan by comparing people of different ages at a single point in time) have shown that the exposure to media violence is related to societal violence, and longitudinal studies have shown that people who watch higher levels of TV violence early in life are likely to behave more aggressively later in life. This finding holds up even if one controls for differences in initial aggressiveness, intellectual functioning and social class.

The magnitude of this exposure-breeds-aggression effect is surprisingly large, yet is generally unappreciated by or unknown to the lay public. Consider, for example, the relationship between cigarette smoking and lung cancer. It is generally accepted that smoking cigarettes causes lung cancer. Likewise, few would dispute the assertion that using condoms will reduce the incidence of sexually transmitted HIV, that exposure to lead will reduce IQ scores in children, or that calcium intake affects bone mass. These public health "facts" are generally known and believed by the lay public. What is less well known is that, with the exception of the relationship between cigarette smoking and lung cancer, the magnitude of the relationship between exposure to violent media and subsequent aggression exceeds all the aforementioned findings.

In a seminal paper, Bushman and Anderson (2001) presented data comparing the magnitude of the violent media-aggression effect with the effect sizes of these and other relationships in the public health domain; see Figure 1 (from Bushman and Anderson 2001, 481). To estimate this effect, Bushman and Anderson utilized the results of a quantitative meta-analytic literature review conducted by Paik and Comstock (1994). A quantitative meta-analysis is a "statistical analysis of a large collection of...results from individual studies for the purpose of integrating the findings" (Glass 1976, 3). The procedure allows one to statistically determine the magnitude, or size, of the effect of one variable on another across multiple studies. Paik and Comstock combined the results of 217 correlational, experimental, and longitudinal studies and discovered a moderately large effect. Stated in terms of a correlation coefficient, the magnitude of the effect was +.31.[1] This means that, across all the research included in the analysis, increased exposure to violent media was associated with a significant increase in subsequent aggression.

All of the correlations in Figure 1 are significantly different from zero and most are considered sufficiently established to be called "facts". Most, that is to say, except for the violent media-aggression relationship, which is curiously denied by the producers of violent fare who claim that the relationship is miniscule and not causal; Bushman and Anderson (2001, 481). In a manner similar to tobacco companies who, until recently, claimed that smoking does not cause lung cancer, filmmakers, television producers and game manufacturers steadfastly claim that exposure to media violence does not cause people to behave more aggressively. The

---

[1] Bushman and Anderson (2001) explain: "The correlation coefficient measures the magnitude of (linear) relation between two variables. The value of a correlation coefficient can range from -1 (a perfect negative correlation) to +1 (a perfect positive correlation), with 0 indicating no correlation between the two variables. In research, however, virtually no correlations are perfect. According to Cohen (1988), a small correlation is ± .1, a medium correlation is ± .3, and a large correlation is ± .5, respectively. According to Cohen, most of the correlations in the social sciences are small-to-medium in size" (p. 480).

results of this analysis, however, clearly demonstrate that the opposite is the case.

How does exposure to violent media produce this effect? Huesmann and Taylor (2006) reviewed empirical research to identify both short- and long-term processes that may be influential. Both cognitive priming and imitation may produce short-term effects. With cognitive priming, an external stimulus, such as a media depiction of violence, may excite a brain node representing a cognition, emotion or behaviour. For example, the sight of a gun may stimulate the node for the concept of aggression, which may then increase the likelihood of behavioural aggression. With imitation, observance of aggression stimulates social learning in which the observer learns vicariously through the behaviours of the actor. To the extent that the aggressive behaviour can be imitated and appears to be rewarding, the likelihood of imitating the behaviour is increased.

Figure 1. Comparison of the effect of violent media on aggression with effects from other domains (Bushman and Anderson, 2001). Numbered bars refer to the following relationships: 1) Smoking and lung cancer; 2) media violence and aggression; 3) condom use and sexually transmitted HIV; 4) passive smoking and lung cancer at work; 5) exposure to lead and IQ scores in children; 6) nicotine patch and smoking cessation; 7) calcium intake and bone mass; 8) homework and academic achievement; 9) exposure to asbestos and laryngeal cancer; 10) self-examination and extent of breast cancer.

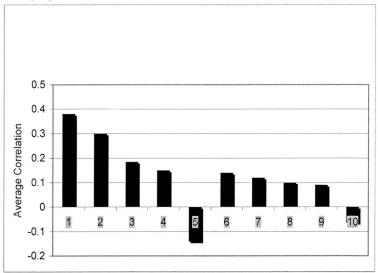

According to social cognitive models, observational learning influences behaviour not only in the short term after behaviour is observed, but also in the long term. The social scripts acquired through observation of family, peers, community, and mass media become more complex, abstracted, and automatic in their invocation. Thus, long-term socialisation effects of the mass media are likely.

In addition to these short- and long-term processes, there are a number of additional factors that may increase the likelihood that an observer of media violence will behave more aggressively. One of the factors is the extent to which the observer *identifies* with aggressive characters. All else being equal, people who identify fairly strongly with an aggressive character (i.e. people who feel a connection to or affinity for the character) are especially likely to have aggressive ideas primed by the observed violence, to imitate the character, or to acquire a variety of aggressive scripts and schemas. Previous research by Huesmann and Eron (1986) has found that aggressive reactions to violent media are intensified when viewers identify with aggressive characters.

Another factor that increases the likelihood of an aggressive response is the extent to which the observer perceives the violence to be *justified*; see Berkowitz (1993). When violence is portrayed as justified (i.e. when the victim of the aggression is portrayed as deserving the treatment because he or she engaged in unprovoked aggression towards the retaliator), observers are likely to conclude that their own aggressive responses to a perceived offence are appropriate, or justified, and are more likely to behave aggressively.

These findings suggest the intriguing possibility that readers of violent literature may 1) behave aggressively after reading violent text and 2) behave more aggressively if they identify with the aggressive characters in the text and/or believe that the aggression is justified. When applied to religious extremists, these findings suggest that such readers may be particularly susceptible to the effects of violent canonical literature because it may represent a type of literature with which they can identify and they may perceive the violent content to be justified. To the extent that religious extremists feel a kinship with or an affinity for the peoples of their scriptures, they are more likely to identify with them. Likewise, to the extent that they believe that deity has sanctioned violent or retaliatory behaviour in the scriptures, they are more likely to believe that such actions are in harmony with divine will and are acceptable. These beliefs may lead them to react with violence in retaliation to perceived threat.

These hypotheses follow from the social scientific literature, but until recently remained untested. Simply put, most of the research on media violence has examined the consequences of exposure to violent movies, television programs and video games. Relatively little, if any, quantitative experimental work has examined the consequences of exposure to violent literature. Yet in an environment where some religious extremists point to literary references to justify their aggression against others, such empirical work is both needed and important. In response to this need, recent quantitative empirical research has investigated the effects of exposure to violent literature on readers' subsequent aggression. We now turn to a discussion of this research.

Exposure to Scriptural and Secular Depictions of Violence

We recently conducted experimental research to investigate how reading violent literature can impact subsequent aggressive behaviour; see Bushman and others (2007) for complete details regarding the methodology. Specifically, our study focused on the effects of reading a violent account that was attributed to either a scriptural source with which Christian subjects might identify (the Bible) or a secular source with which they might identify less (an account from an ancient scroll). Moreover, the violent behaviour in these accounts was alleged to have been either sanctioned by God (justified) or not sanctioned by God (unjustified). Two hundred forty-eight students from a religiously affiliated, Christian university in the United States participated in the study.

Because research participants are often motivated to present themselves favourably, it was necessary to conceal the true purpose of the study so that they would be unaware that their aggressive reaction to violent literature was the focus of the research. As part of a cover story to mask the true intent of the experiment, we told participants that they would be participating in two ostensibly unrelated tasks: the first, a study of reactions to middle-eastern literature and the second, a study on the effects of competition and negative stimulation on task performance. The first "study" was actually conducted so that we could plausibly expose participants to a violent written scenario under socially acceptable circumstances, and the second was conducted so that we could measure participants' aggressive behaviour in a way that was not obvious, but was reliable and valid.

In the first study, we gave participants a story to read under the false pretence that their feedback would impact whether or not a humanities professor would include it in a textbook on ancient middle-eastern literature. The actual story was adapted from several chapters in the Old Testament and was selected both for its violent content and for its relative obscurity, even to participants at a religious institution. By having participants read this story under the guise of evaluating it for a textbook, we were able to expose them to a piece of violent literature without revealing that we wanted to see how aggressively they would behave after reading it. Their subsequent answers to questions regarding the story served the actual purpose of telling us whether or not they interpreted the story as we intended (e.g. Biblical or secular source; behaviour sanctioned or unsanctioned by God). Questions regarding the suitability of the story for inclusion in a textbook were included merely to maintain the cover story and were not analysed.

A basic overview of the story is as follows: a man and his concubine from the ancient Israelite tribe of Ephraim are travelling in the land of Benjamin (another Israelite tribe). At the end of a day, the couple comes to a city and looks for a place to spend the night. An old man, also from the tribe or Ephraim, sees the couple and invites them to spend the night in his home. While they are eating dinner, a mob of men pound on the old man's door and demand that he give them his male guest so they can rape him. The old man refuses, so the mob takes the concubine instead. They beat and rape her all night and then leave her dead body on the old man's doorstep. In the morning, when he is unable to revive her, the visiting man puts her body on his donkey and travels home. Upon his arrival, he chops her body into twelve pieces and sends one piece to each of the tribes of Israel, documenting his loss to them. An assembly of Israelites is called and the man explains what has happened. The assemblage is outraged by what the mob has done, so they form an army to destroy the Benjamites.

What then ensues is a bloody war between the other tribes of Israel and the Benjamites. After much loss of life on both sides, the tribes of Israel eventually defeat the Benjamites and win the war. After the victory, the Israelite army destroys a number of other Benjamite cities, killing all of the men, women, children and animals. This is where the story ends.

The story contains multiple accounts of brutal violence: the unprovoked attack against the Ephraimite concubine, the violent retaliation by the tribes of Israel, and the violence against the Benjamite cities following the war. When participants were queried at the end of the story as to whether or not they were familiar with it, nearly all reported that it was unrecognizable to them.

As noted by Huesmann and Eron (1986) and as mentioned earlier, the degree to which a person identifies with the actors in a violent story impacts his or her level of subsequent aggression. Operating under the assumption that a religious Christian individual might be more likely to identify with a character in the Bible than with a character in a secular text, we manipulated the extent to which participants identified with the literature by leading a randomly selected half of the participants to believe that the story came from the Bible (identification condition) and the other half to believe that it came from an ancient scroll (no identification condition). Manipulation checks confirmed that participants believed the story to come from the source to which it was attributed.

Equally important is the extent to which violent acts are perceived as justified; see Berkowitz (1993, 213-217). Operating under the assumption that a religious Christian individual might perceive violence as being more justified when it is sanctioned by God than when it is not, we manipulated whether or not God was identified as sanctioning the Israelites' behaviour by creating two versions of the story. In one version (justified violence), half the participants received a story that contained explicit references to God sanctioning the violence. This version of the story contained the following verse:

> The assembly fasted and prayed before the LORD and asked, "What shall be done about the sins of our brothers in Benjamin?" and the LORD answered them, saying that no such abomination could stand among his people. The LORD commanded Israel to take arms against their brothers and chasten them before the LORD.

In the other version of the story (unjustified violence), references to and communications with God were removed, making it appear as if the Israelites had decided among themselves to avenge the Ephraimite man's loss. Thus, half the participants were led to believe that God had commanded violent retribution against the Benjamites and the other half were not.

Participation in this experiment took place on computers with all stimulus materials presented on internet web pages. Participants were randomly assigned to one of the four story conditions (story source, Bible or scroll, by story justification, God or no God) using a JavaScript randomization protocol. After completing the story, participants gave feedback to the fictional professor in order to maintain the cover story.

In the second ostensibly unrelated "study", we told participants that a psychology professor was investigating the effects of competition and aversive stimulation on human performance. We told them that they would be competing against other students on a reaction-time task. Their job was to react more quickly to a stimulus on the computer screen than their opponent. They were to observe a box on the screen and click a mouse button as quickly as possible when the box changed colour. If they responded more quickly than their opponent, they would "win" the trial and be permitted to punish their opponent with a blast of white noise delivered through headphones. If they responded more slowly than their opponent, they would "lose" the trial and would have to endure a blast of white noise emitted by their opponent's noise weapon. Before each trial, they were instructed to set both an intensity (0 – 105 dB) and duration (0.5 – 2.5 sec) of noise that would be heard by the opponent. They were also permitted to see the level and duration of noise that was set by their opponent at the end of each trial (25 in all). As a result of this staging, participants believed that the researchers were examining how punishment or the threat of punishment would affect their ability to respond quickly to a computer stimulus. In other words, they believed that the study was focused on human competitive performance.

In reality, the explanation for their participation in this second study was a cover story, masking a behavioural measure of aggression. Participants were not competing against other students and were not punishing or being punished by someone else. The computer simulated the performance of a competitor. They did not win or lose in each of the competitive trials, but "won" and "lost" at a predetermined rate. When they "lost," they were subjected to a blast of white noise of varying intensity and duration. This provided participants with the illusion of competing against another person.

The reason for this elaborate ruse was because the measurement of aggressive behaviour in the laboratory can be problematic. Professional ethics prohibit experimenters from allowing participants to engage in any genuine aggression towards another person. Therefore, reliable and valid surrogates for aggression must be employed. Behavioural aggression was operationally defined as the selection of extremely high noise intensities (levels of 9 or 10 on a 10-point noise level indicator) for the fictional opponent. The number of high intensity blasts selected across the 25 trials was the dependent variable (scores could range from 0 to 25). This task has been used in previous studies of behavioural aggression and is both reliable and valid, as documented in the work of Bernstein, Richardson and Hammock (1987). Furthermore, pilot testing and manipulation checks confirmed that participants believed that the opponent was real and the task was legitimate.

Figure 2. Effect of story source on aggression levels (based on Bushman and others, 2007). Aggression was measured as the number of trials (out of a maximum 25) on which the participant chose to punish a competitor with high levels of noise (9 or 10 on a scale of 10). Aggression scores could range from 0 to 25. The difference was significant, $F(1, 240) = 4.47, p < .04, d = 0.30$.

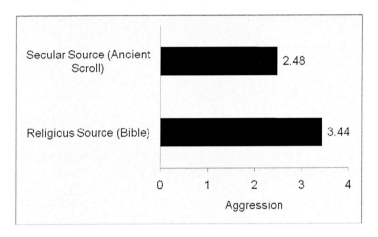

Ninety-nine percent of the participants from this Christian university claimed to believe in God and in the Bible as the word of God. It was hypothesized that these participants would deliver more high-intensity shocks to their opponents after being exposed to the story that was attributed to the Bible than after being exposed to the story that was attributed to an ancient scroll, and results confirmed this hypothesis; see Figure 2.[2] As for justification, we hypothesized that Christian participants would deliver more high-intensity shocks when the violence in the story was justified (i.e. sanctioned by God) than when it was not. Findings supporting this hypothesis were marginally significant (justified violence $M = 3.40$; unjustified violence $M = 2.47$, $F[1,240] = 2.95, p < .09, d = 0.23$[3]).

---

[2] The data were analysed by means of a 2 (character identification: yes [Bible] or no [scroll] X 2 (justification: yes [God sanctioned] or no [not sanctioned by God] X 2 (gender: male or female) analysis of variance [ANOVA]. Detailed results and a discussion of gender are in Bushman and others (2007).

[3] Cohen's d (Cohen 1988) is an index that measures the magnitude of an effect and is defined as the difference between the means, $M_1 - M_2$, divided by standard deviation, s, of either group. An effect size $d = .20$ is considered small, $d = .50$ is medium, and $d = .70$ is large.

Dutch Replication

In order to ensure that the observed effects were not unique to a religious American sample, the study was replicated in the Netherlands. An additional 242 participants were recruited and the same protocol used in the original study was followed (albeit translated into Dutch). The sample in this second study was more religiously diverse. Approximately 40% of participants did not indicate a religious affiliation. Of those remaining, 18% were Catholic, 11% Protestant, 12% Muslim, 8% Christian, 2% Hindu, 1% Jewish and 8% "other". About 50% of participants said they believed in God and only 27% said they believed in the Bible.

The results of the American study confirmed that believers behaved more aggressively when they believed that the aggressive story came from the Bible and when God justified it. The demographic composition of the Dutch sample permitted us to investigate this question again, as well as to compare believers with non-believers to see if the groups would respond similarly or differently to the violent literature. Believers were operationally defined as participants who believed in both God and in the Bible, whereas non-believers were operationally defined as participants who believed in neither God nor the Bible.

With respect to justification, independent of their theological beliefs, Dutch participants behaved significantly more aggressively when they read the story stating that God justified the violence than when they read the story excluding reference to God (unjustified violence). This main effect was qualified, however, by a significant interaction; see Figure 3. The nature of the interaction was as follows: When the sample was divided into believers and non-believers, both behaved significantly more aggressively when the violence in the story was believed to be justified. The magnitude of the effect, however, was larger for the believers than for non-believers. Thus, both believers and non-believers responded more aggressively to justified violence than to unjustified violence, but the effect was especially pronounced for the believers.

Figure 3. Effect of belief in God and the Bible and sanctioning of violence on aggression levels (based on Bushman and others, 2007). Aggression was measured as the number of high-level noise blasts. This effect was significant, $F(1, 225) = 3.99$, $p < .05$, d (nonbelievers) = 0.28, d (believers) = 0.47.

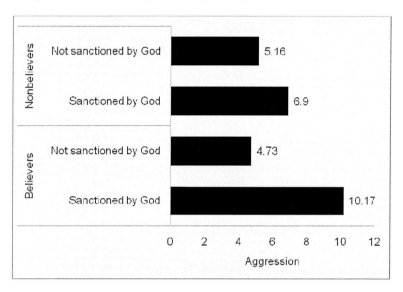

With respect to identification, no significant difference in aggression was found between those who read that the story came from the Bible and those who read that it came from an ancient scroll. However, statistically significant differences were revealed when justification was factored into the equation. Independent of theological beliefs, when the passage was attributed to the Bible, participants behaved significantly more aggressively when the passage mentioned God ($M = 9.77$) than when it did not ($M = 4.20$; $F[1, 225] = 17.47$, $p < .001$, $d = 0.56$). Conversely, when the story was attributed to an ancient scroll, aggression levels were not different. Thus, it appears that believer status did not matter when it came to reading a canonical or secular account of violent retribution; aggression levels were the same between the groups. When God justified the violence, however, source effects emerged. Everyone, believers and non-believers, behaved more aggressively when the source of the story was Biblical as opposed to secular.

Answers to Questions and Questions to Answer

Our results are intriguing and provide answers to some important questions while raising others. Among those questions answered, it is clear that exposure to a written depiction of violence can increase subsequent aggressive behaviour, particularly when the violence appears to have been sanctioned by deity. Participants in the experiment who read about violent retribution that was justified by God retaliated more aggressively towards innocent competitors than did those who read about unjustified violence. This was particularly true for subjects who believed in God and the Bible. For these readers, the approval of God justified the aggressive actions taken by the protagonists in the story and appears to have primed them to respond more aggressively when they perceived provocation from another person.

This result is consistent with Berkowitz's (1993) findings regarding reactions to depictions of justified violence, although in this case justification was operationalized somewhat differently. Berkowitz found that people behaved more aggressively when they believed that the targets of aggression deserved the violence to which they had been subjected. Such a depiction was graphically portrayed in this research and readers may have felt that the initial aggressors in the story (and later the targets of a violent response) deserved their fate. They had provoked the man and, by extension, the other tribes of Israel with their lascivious overtures towards him and their cruel abuse of his concubine. That the tribes of Israel reacted to this aggression with a swift, retributive response appears to have been justified to readers and, as a result, may have motivated them to respond more aggressively when they perceived themselves as being punished by their opponents in the reaction-time task.

But what is unique about our research is that the justification for the aggression was manipulated in a slightly augmented way. Whereas justification in the Berkowitz sense involves retaliation for unprovoked violence, justification in the present sense involved retaliation for unprovoked violence *and* the sanction of an authority figure. In both cases the aggression is justified, but in the former case the actor must decide whether or not it is appropriate, whereas in the latter case an authority figure makes the decision. We found evidence that readers will not only behave more aggressively when exposed to literature depicting justified aggression, but they will behave more aggressively when the aggression is "justified" in this latter sense.

This finding, while novel in the empirical study of religious literature, has empirical precedent. Previous research in social psychology has found that people are vulnerable to justification effects when aggressive acts are sanctioned by an authority. Milgram (1975), for example, observed this in his famous obedience experiments where subjects were asked to shock a "learner" as punishment for failing to master a memory task. Many subjects were fully obedient to the commands of the experimenter, who ordered them to punish the learner by administering progressively higher levels of electric shock until they reached the highest levels on a shock generator. Milgram noted that it was common for subjects to justify their behaviour, not by claiming that the learners deserved to be hurt because of their poor performance, but by "attributing all initiative to the experimenter, a legitimate authority." This was not, he observed, a "thin alibi concocted for the occasion. Rather it [was] a fundamental mode of thinking for a great many people." (1975, 8) Subjects generally justified their destructive behaviour by claiming that it was acceptable because an authority figure (the experimenter) had authorized it. They were no longer responsible for the behaviour or for its consequences.

To religious believers, God (Buddha, Mohammed, Jehovah or whoever) represents not only a legitimate authority, but also the ultimate authority as to what is right and moral. If God sanctions aggression towards another person, it must be right. A person who finds precedent for such behaviour in a canonical source can claim that the aggression is sanctioned by an ultimate authority and that he or she is not only *not* personally responsible for the atrocity, but that the behaviour is actually virtuous and in keeping with divine imperative. In this way, religious literature that is considered to be divinely inspired may induce readers to behave aggressively if they feel that their situation is consistent with historical precedent and is authorized by God.

It should not be overlooked, however, that both believers *and* non-believers were affected by the God manipulation in our research. Although the effect was smaller for non-believers, they nevertheless behaved more aggressively when they were told that an authority figure justified the aggression. That this effect was observed in non-believers may attest to the insidious influence of justified aggression in religious literary sources. A *belief* in God may not be necessary for a *reference* to God to have influence. To the extent that a reference to God conveys a sense of legitimate or ultimate authority, it may be sufficient to induce aggression from readers independent of their religious ideology.

With respect to identification effects, it appears that the religious, American subjects identified with Biblical characters more than with secular characters. Thus, when they read a passage attributed to the Bible, they behaved more aggressively in the subsequent competitive task than when the passage was attributed to a scroll. Similar identification effects have been observed in other research with other media, as reported by Huesmann and Eron (1986). This was not the case, however, in the Dutch sample. Constituting a less religious sample, they responded more aggressively to the biblical text only when God was referenced in the story, but not when he was absent. This result may seem to reflect a justification effect, but Dutch subjects were no more aggressive when God was mentioned in the secular text than when he was absent. There is no parsimonious theory to explain this finding, suggesting the need for additional research to investigate this intriguing effect.

Based on this discussion, it appears that several conclusions can be drawn from our research. First, exposure to violent religious literature can elevate subsequent aggression levels in readers. Second, an element of justification in literary depictions of violence appears to be an important factor contributing to readers' aggressive responses. It appears that the type of justification need not be limited to violent retaliation for unprovoked aggression, but may also reflect aggressive behaviour in response to divine injunction. And third, identification with the characters in an aggressive episode is implicated as an important contributing factor to subsequent aggression, but further research is needed to clarify its role in the overall process.

It is noteworthy that our results were not obtained in a sample of religious extremists poised to exterminate a "profane" enemy, but emerged from average university students of varying religiosity across two continents. This suggests that readers of violent literature need not be especially religious or hostile to be vulnerable to the influence of aggressive religious literature. Granted, aggression measured in the laboratory is a far cry from violence in the streets of Baghdad, but our results suggest a medium by which aggressive behaviour may be induced: the reading of violent religious literature.

Does this then suggest that people should not read violent religious canon for fear that it will cause them to become more aggressive? We do not believe so. Such a dim view of exposure to violent literature is unwarranted for several reasons. In the first place, there is an instructive parallel between exposure to violent media and cigarette smoking. As Bushman and Anderson (2001) point out, smoking a single cigarette is unlikely to cause an individual to contract lung cancer. It would take a repeated, prolonged pattern of smoking to make one terminally ill, and even then lung cancer might never result. Similarly, sporadic exposure to aggressive literature is unlikely to make an individual more violent, but a steady diet of such reading over a long period of time could increase the likelihood of one behaving more aggressively. To the extent that religious extremists engage in a pattern of prolonged, selective reading of violent canonical literature, one might expect to observe a more aggressive stance towards perceived provocation and threat.

In the second place, context is important. Religious accounts of violent retribution and holy warfare are not recorded in a vacuum. Many violent episodes are but smaller parts of larger stories that have broader messages. Some teach the tragic consequence of sinful behaviour (e.g. being subjected to violent retribution), whereas others warn against aggression because it is sinful in and of itself (e.g. engaging in unprovoked aggression). As Bushman and colleagues note, "Violent stories that teach moral lessons or that are balanced with descriptions of victims' suffering or the aggressor's remorse can teach important lessons and have legitimate artistic merit." (2007, 207) Aggressive episodes taken out of context may have pernicious effects, whereas those understood in context may be laudable. It is the selective reading of violent religious literature, out of context, that may contribute to terrorists' violent behaviour.

Finally, one must remember that the overall theme of many religious works is the promotion of peace and love, not hatred and intolerance. It would be naïve to suggest that religious canon, or religion in general, is primarily responsible for the terrorism practiced by extremists. As Nepstad has argued, "Religion has historically played a significant role in curbing violence, constraining aggression, and promoting reconciliation and understanding between groups." (2004, 297) Violent religious text, a very small proportion of scriptural content, is only one of many potential factors that may contribute to the aggression engaged in by terrorists.

Ultimately, it is the violent religious literature with which one identifies and which appears to be justified that may be problematic. Further research is needed to investigate whether and how the results from a laboratory investigation map onto life in the real world. The social scientific literature suggests that there is a link between reading violent literature and engaging in subsequent behavioural aggression. Further work in this area can enlighten not only students of media and aggression, but also students of the humanities, religion, and international relations. A collaboration of theory and method from all these fields would go a long way towards understanding the complex phenomenon that is religious terrorism.

Works Cited

Anderson, Craig A. and Brad J. Bushman. 2002. The Effects of Media Violence on Society, *Science* 295: 2377-2378.

Berkowitz, Leonard. 1993. *Aggression: Its Causes, Consequences and Control.* New York: McGraw-Hill.

Bernstein, Sandy, Deborah Richardson, and Georgina Hammock. 1987. Convergent and Discriminant Validity of the Taylor and Buss Measures of Physical Aggression. *Aggressive Behavior* 13: 22-23.

Bushman, Brad J. and Craig A. Anderson. 2001. Media Violence and the American Public: Scientific Facts vs. Media Misinformation. *American Psychologist* 56: 477-489.

Bushman, Brad J., Robert D. Ridge, Enny Das, Colin W. Key, and Gregory L Busath. 2007. When God Sanctions Killing: Effect of Scriptural Violence on Aggression. *Psychological Science* 18: 204-207.

Cohen, Jacob. 1988. *Statistical Analysis for the Behavioral Sciences* (2nd ed.). Hillsdale, NJ: Erlbaum.

Glass, Gene V. 1076. Primary, secondary, and meta-analysis of research. *Educational Researcher* 6: 3-8.

Huesmann, L. Rowell and Leonard Eron. 1986. *Television and the Aggressive Child: A Cross-National Comparison.* Hillsdale, NJ: Erlbaum.

Huesmann, L. Rowell and Laramie D. Taylor. 2006. The Role of Media Violence in Human Behavior. *Annual Review of Public Health* 27: 401-407.

Juergensmeyer, Mark. 2003. *Terror in the Mind of God: The Global Rise of Religious Violence.* Berkeley, CA: The University of California Press.

Milgram, Stanley. 1975. *Obedience to Authority: An Experimental View.* New York: Harper Colophon.

Nepstad, Sharon E. 2004. Religion, Violence and Peacemaking. *Journal for the Scientific Study of Religion* 43: 297-301.

Paik, Haejung and Comstock, George. 1994. The Effects of Television Violence on Antisocial Behavior: A Meta-analysis. *Communication Research* 21: 516-546.

CHAPTER FIFTEEN

NARRATIVE COMPREHENSION AND ENJOYMENT OF FEATURE FILMS: AN EXPERIMENTAL STUDY

BRADFORD OWEN

Abstract

Study objectives were to apply Graesser's constructionist theory of narrative comprehension to motion pictures; to examine the affective aspects of understanding of narrative; and to test whether individual differences (in cognitive ability, need for cognition and experience with challenging films) impact enjoyment of story comprehension.

The feature film *Memento* was re-edited to produce three experimental treatment versions with varying levels of cognitive challenge. In a 2 x 4 experimental design, these three versions plus the original were shown to four experimental groups of undergraduates.

Analysis of variance showed no main effects of treatment group on comprehension or enjoyment. Analysis of variance also showed no interaction effects between cognitive ability, need for cognition, or experience with challenging films. A stepwise regression showed that only liking for the protagonist was a significant predictor of enjoyment. This suggests that feelings for the characters may outweigh narrative comprehension in producing viewer enjoyment.

Introduction

Narrative, both internal and public, is ubiquitous in human existence. Scholars across the disciplines argue for its centrality in individual minds and aggregate culture. The present study is an investigation of construction of narrative comprehension and enjoyment of a public narrative, a feature motion picture, based on two strands of theory and research: narrative discourse psychology and entertainment theory. These theories offer to explain, respectively, cognitive and affective aspects of the reader's or viewer's engagement with public narratives.

The present research departs from most current practices in the field of film studies by not focusing on textual analysis, post-structural theory, or the wider cultural contexts of film production and consumption. However, it does share the examination of the individual viewer's engagement with audio-visual texts with two very different current film studies approaches: philosophy-oriented cognitive film theory, and the audience analysis technique of ethnographic participant observation of viewers' encounters with films or television programs. This study differs from these two approaches in its experimental psychology-based quantitative method.

The research questions investigated in the present study are:
RQ1. Do theories of narrative comprehension based on oral and printed verbal narratives apply to narrative comprehension of movies?
RQ2. How does the level of a feature film viewer's narrative comprehension affect the viewer's enjoyment of the film?
RQ3. Do individual differences play a role? More specifically: do characteristics which are thought to make cognitive processing of a challenging feature film narrative more efficient (high cognitive ability, need for cognition, and experience with challenging films) mediate a viewer's enjoyment of the film?

Theoretical Background - Discourse Psychology and Constructionist Theory

In empirically-oriented communication and psychology research, only the cognitive-oriented sub-field of discourse psychology has sought to theorize and investigate how we construct understanding of narratives "online" (while we read them). Graesser's constructionist model of narrative comprehension embraces the three assumptions of the search-after-meaning principle, which has a long history in experimental psychology; see Graesser, Singer and Trabasso (1994). This principle has, according to Stein and Trabasso (1985), three critical assumptions: first, the reader constructs meaning representations that address the reader's goals. He or she will build quite different meaning representations of the narrative if his or her goal is to proofread it, rather than to be immersed in and entertained by it. Second, the reader attempts to construct a meaning representation that is coherent at both the local and global levels. Third, the reader attempts to explain why actions, events, and states are mentioned in the text; he or she uses contingent, provisional theories of psychological and physical causality to explain why characters do what they do and feel what they feel, why events occur, and even why the author has included these elements in the story.

What are the means by which the reader seeks to establish coherence and explain actions and events in what he or she is reading? Constructionist theory (and most theories of narrative discourse psychology) holds that the explicit text to be comprehended by the reader does not itself contain all or even most of the meaning representations the reader will create in the search for meaning. Rather, the explicit text stimulates the reader to make inferences drawn from his or her existing knowledge; this active interplay between the words on the page and the reader's world knowledge is the key to building meaning. Overlapping sources of knowledge the reader draws upon include the information pool shared by members of the reader's culture, experiences in the reader's life, and previous encounters with other narratives and other media.

The central goal of Graesser's constructionist theory is to specify the set of knowledge-based inferences that are routinely activated and encoded during the process of narrative comprehension. Knowledge-based inferences are inherited from generic knowledge structures such as scripts and stereotypes and from specific episodic structures previously created in the reader's mind by encounters with other media texts, oral discourse, and life experiences. A generic script has typical information about an activity or story that a person has enacted or witnessed. Similarly, a generic stereotype contains typical information about a class of people. In contrast to generic knowledge structures, episodic structures are associated with episodes that a person has experienced at a particular time and place. The knowledge-based inferences in the situation model are inherited from both generic and episodic knowledge structures; see Graesser, Singer and Trabasso (1994). Constructionist theory predicts that the reader makes these two types of inferences online in an effort to establish local and global coherence in the situation model, and to explain story events, character actions, and authorial intent.

Constructionist Theory and Film

The constructionist theory of narrative comprehension, like other theories of discourse processing, was developed through cognitive psychology-oriented experimental research using verbal discourse, both printed and oral. Despite this, the theory's author holds that its predictions should be valid for narrative across all media, including live oral storytelling, print, radio, theatre, television, and film (Graesser, Olde and Klettke 2002). However, little empirical work on constructionist theory and non-print media has been done. This chapter tests some of its predictions of narrative comprehension on film viewers.

Constructionist Theory and Affect

In the tradition of cognitive science, constructionist theory is concerned primarily with comprehension of narratives, rather than affective aspects of experiencing them. However, one of the key assumptions of constructionist theory opens the door to enquiry into affect and narrative comprehension: that the reader constructs meaning representations that address the reader's goals. If these goals are diversion, pleasure, and entertainment, as they often are in the consumption of fictional public narratives, then an investigation of the relationship between cognition and affect is warranted.

Affect is indeed central to our choices and enjoyment of public narratives. According to mood-management theory (Bryant and Zillman 1984; Zillman 1988), public narratives like movies and television programs are an important part of the symbolic environment we arrange to maximize pleasure and minimize pain. I argue that comprehension of a narrative typically plays an important role in enjoying the experience of that narrative. A narrative which is challenging enough to be interesting but not too challenging to be understood presents the optimal level. I will thus argue and test empirically that cognitive challenge is itself a source of positive or negative affect during the experience of a narrative.

Constructionist Theory and Differences among Viewers

Constructionist theory "focuses on the similarities more than the differences among comprehenders" of narrative, as can be seen in Graesser, Olde and Klettke (2002, 232). This is understandable in the attempt to build a theory that explains what we tend to have in common in the way we process stories. However, constructionist theory also supports Vorderer's (1996, 242) assertion that

> "readers or viewers not only choose a certain text according to their current needs and interests, but they also process this text subjectively…[they] construct a text that is not identical with the text that has been described objectively (e. g., by content analysis)."

In other words, differences among readers and viewers are important both in selection of narrative texts and in the way they understand and enjoy those texts.

Entertainment theory research has found empirical support for the notion that individual differences impact both the experience of narratives and the strategies used to moderate moods (Raney and Bryant 2002, Zillman 2000). For example, Vorderer, Knobloch, and Schramm (2001) found that cognitive ability mediated feelings of entertainment toward an interactive television program. Discourse psychology research too points towards the importance of individual differences: for example, the rate of narrative comprehension decreases at unequal rates among individuals when elements which increase cognitive load are introduced into the narrative, such as change of scene, new characters, and illogical actions (Zwaan, Magliano and Graesser 1995). Further, Graesser's constructionist theory of narrative comprehension (as proposed in Graesser, Singer and Trabasso 1994) argues that the reader's or viewer's varying levels of relevant world knowledge deployed "online" during comprehension of the narrative will have differential effects on cognitive load. In the present research, I hypothesize that the level of cognitive challenge which optimizes pleasure in experiencing a film narrative varies among individuals, and is influenced by individual differences which make online cognitive processing more efficient and reduce cognitive load.

In expectation of an interaction between viewer characteristics and the degree of cognitive challenge presented by different narratives, I also hypothesize differences of enjoyment of film narrative based on individual viewer differences in cognitive ability, need for cognition, and experience with challenging films.

Hypotheses

To extend constructionist theory's predictions to film and test hypotheses on the relationships between viewer comprehension, viewer enjoyment, and viewer characteristics, this study will use as experimental treatments three versions of *Memento* (Nolan 2001). These versions will vary in cognitive challenge presented to the viewers, with two re-edited versions presenting the least and greatest challenge, respectively, and the original theatrical version presenting an intermediate level of challenge.

The theories and research cited above suggest that lower levels of cognitive ability may impact the formation of a coherent situation model while watching a film, and so affect comprehension of the narrative. A film that is less challenging should be able to be translated into coherent situation models than a more challenging film. The first hypothesis tests this idea:

> H1. Viewers with lower cognitive ability will have higher comprehension of a film with lower levels of cognitive challenge than of a film with higher levels of cognitive challenge.
>
> I also propose that lower levels of need for cognition (the degree to which a person likes mental challenge) and less experience with challenging films will also have a diminishing impact on comprehension:
>
> H2. Viewers with lower need for cognition will have higher comprehension of a film with lower levels of cognitive challenge than of a film with higher levels of cognitive challenge.
>
> H3. Viewers with lower levels of experience with challenging films will have higher comprehension of a film with lower levels of cognitive challenge than of a film with higher levels of cognitive challenge.

Viewers with higher levels of cognitive ability, need for cognition, and experience with challenging films are expected to have equal comprehension of films with lesser and greater levels of cognitive challenge. As no variance is expected, no hypotheses on these relationships are proposed.

Based on constructionist's theory's tenet that we read or watch narratives that serve our goals, and on mood management theory's idea that we seek pleasure in the media we choose, I propose that the experiment should reveal the following relationships between cognitive-related viewer characteristics, cognitive challenge presented by a film, and enjoyment of that film:

> H4. Viewers with higher cognitive ability will enjoy a film with higher levels of cognitive challenge more than they will a film with lower levels of cognitive challenge.
>
> H5a. Viewers with a higher need for cognition will enjoy a film with higher levels of cognitive challenge more than they will a film with lower levels of cognitive challenge.
>
> H5b. Viewers with a lower need for cognition will enjoy a film with lower levels of cognitive challenge more than they will a film with higher levels of cognitive challenge.

H6a. Viewers with more experience with challenging films will enjoy a film with higher levels of cognitive challenge more than they will a film with lower levels of cognitive challenge.

H6b. Viewers with less experience with challenging films will enjoy a film with lower levels of cognitive challenge more than they will a film with higher levels of cognitive challenge.

Method

In order to test the hypotheses, an experimental study with a 3 x 2 between-subjects design was conducted.

Participants

Sixty-nine participants for the pilot study and an additional 37 participants for the main experiment were recruited from lower division communication courses at a large American university. All interested students were offered an information form which asked for the student's contact information, availability, and history of viewing a list of challenging films. Christopher Nolan's (2001) *Memento* was one of the films on this list; only students who did not report having seen *Memento* were contacted to participate in the study. The contacted students all received extra credit for their participation in the courses from which they were recruited.

Design and Independent Variables

The participants were randomly assigned to four experimental conditions in the pilot study and three experimental conditions in the main study. These conditions varied in the level of cognitive challenge presented by the treatment film in each experimental group. The treatment was the feature film *Memento* and three re-edited versions of *Memento*. The re-edited versions changed story chronology and/or completeness of story information of the original film (see below). Besides cognitive challenge, the independent variables were subject traits:

- cognitive ability (a composite of self-reported high school grade point average, SAT, and university grade point average),
- need for cognition,
- and experience with viewing challenging films.

Subjects were grouped into high and low levels of each of these traits not during the experiment but during analysis. Experience with challenging films was measured through an ad-hoc self-report scale asking which of 24 films made between 1960 and 2004 the subject had seen (Table 1).

Table 1. Experience With Challenging Films Instrument.

Please put a check mark beside each film that you have seen.	
Being John Malkovich (1999)	Pulp Fiction (1994)
L'Avventura (1961)	House of Flying Daggers (2004)
Adaptation (2002)	Capturing the Friedmans (2003)
Eternal Sunshine of the Spotless Mind (2004)	Before Sunset (2004)
8 1/2 (1963)	Fargo (1996)
Memento (2000)	Donnie Darko (2001)
Kinsey (2004)	Bad Education (2004)
Dogville (2004)	21 Grams (2003)
Fahrenheit 9/11 (2004)	Mulholland Drive (2001)
The Machinist (2004)	Last Year at Marienbad (1961)
Lost in Translation (2003)	Trainspotting (1996)
Monster (2003)	The Usual Suspects (1995)

Need for cognition was measured through Cacciopo, Petty, and Kao's (1984) 18-item self-report scale (Table 2).

Table 2. Need for Cognition Scale.

1. I would prefer complex to simple problems.
2. I like to have the responsibility of handling a situation that requires a lot of thinking.
3. Thinking is not my idea of fun.
4. I would rather do something that requires little thought than something that is sure to challenge my thinking abilities.
5. I try to anticipate and avoid situations where there is likely chance I will have to think in depth about something.
6. I find satisfaction in deliberating hard and for long hours.
7. I only think as hard as I have to.

8. I prefer to think about small, daily projects to long-term ones.
9. I like tasks that require little thought once I've learned them.
10. The idea of relying on thought to make my way to the top appeals to me.
11. I really enjoy a task that involves coming up with new solutions to problems.
12. Learning new ways to think doesn't excite me very much.
13. I prefer my life to be filled with puzzles that I must solve.
14. The notion of thinking abstractly is appealing to me.
15. I would prefer a task that is intellectual, difficult, and important to one that is somewhat important but does not require much thought.
16. I feel relief rather than satisfaction after completing a task that required a lot of mental effort.
17. It's enough for me that something gets the job done; I don't care how or why it works.
18. I usually end up deliberating about issues even when they do not affect me personally.

Perceived cognitive challenge was measured as a treatment check to confirm that the proposed variation in cognitive challenge among the versions of the film was in fact achieved (Table 3).

Table 3. Cognitive Challenge Scale.

Sometimes movies' stories are challenging for viewers to follow. Overall, how challenging was it for you to follow this movie's story?
Overall, how much did you have to think to understand what was going on in this movie?
Overall, how confusing did you find this movie?

Experimental Materials

I chose Christopher Nolan's 2001 feature film *Memento* because it presents a moderately high level of cognitive challenge through a unique narrative strategy: the telling in reverse order of its main story line, wherein each succeeding scene as the film unfolds actually comes earlier in story time. In effect, the viewer is moving backwards in time scene by scene to the beginning of the story.

More even than most mysteries, *Memento* is a puzzle film. Because of its highly original narrative structure, the viewer (like the main character) is forced to rethink causality and try to re-determine the relevant facts after almost every scene. *Memento*'s manipulation of story chronology thus presents an ongoing cognitive challenge to viewers' attempt to establish coherence in their situation model. The writer-director Christopher Nolan has intentionally made determining cause-and-effect relations during viewing difficult; those relations are tentative and change from scene to scene.

Chronological irregularities in a narrative have been shown empirically to increase cognitive load during narrative comprehension, as demonstrated by Zwaan (1996). The importance of chronology in narrative comprehension is suggested by its frequent manipulation in discourse studies (Graesser, Kassler, Kreuz and McLain-Allen 1998, Radvansky, Zwaan, Federico and Franklin 1998). Further, the reverse chronology used in *Memento* disrupts the other dimensions in which the viewer tries to establish coherence: action causality, story spatiality, and character motivation.

Perhaps most importantly for the experimental nature of this research, *Memento*'s overt manipulation of story time also presented an opportunity to create alternative treatments through re-configuring the film's chronology and leaving out key story information. Such manipulations, according to constructionist theory, should make the film easier or harder to understand in comparison to the original version by lessening or increasing the challenge in creating a coherent mental situation model.

The treatment versions of the film are as follows:
1) The original theatrical release version, hereafter "original version" (O);
2) A re-edited version in which all the scenes have been re-arranged into chronological story order, hereafter "version 1" (R1);
3) A re-edited version in which scenes appear in chronological story order but with shots and scenes that contain key story information deleted, hereafter "version 2" (R2);
4) A re-edited version in which scenes appear in reverse chronological order (as they do in the original version) but with shots and scenes that contain key story information removed, hereafter "version 3" (R3).

The last two versions should present the viewer with more lapses in local coherence of causality, temporality, and character motivation through omission of original material than the first two complete versions. The order of increasing cognitive challenge is proposed to be R1, O, R2, R3.

Procedure

Pilot study. As a manipulation check, groups of eleven to seventeen students each watched one of four treatment versions of *Memento*. The pilot study was predicted to show that self-reported cognitive challenge would increase as follows: complete chronological recut (R1) < original version (O) < chronological recut with key story information removed (R2) < reverse chronological recut with key story information removed (R3).

Main experiment. In each session, subjects assembled in a computer lab in groups of five to 20 and were briefed on the experiment. They were informed that the film was R-rated and contained much profanity, some sexual situations, and some explicit violence, and they were told that they could leave the screening at any time without any penalty. The subjects then signed the experimental consent form.

The lights in the lab were turned off and the subjects watched one of the four treatment versions of *Memento* video-projected from a source VHS tape onto an eight-foot screen. The original (O) and first recut (R1) versions of the film ran 113 minutes; the second (R2) and third (R3) recut versions ran 108 minutes. Immediately following the conclusion of the treatment film and the turning on of the lab lights, subjects filled out a paper questionnaire with need for cognition (Table 2), cognitive challenge (Table 3), enjoyment (Table 4), liking of protagonist (Table 5), and comprehension items (Table 6).

Table 4. Enjoyment Scale.

How redundant did you find this movie (how much did it repeat information unecessarily?)
Overall, did this movie seem too slow to you?
Overall, how much did you enjoy the movie?
Overall, how frustrated did you feel watching this movie?
Overall, how bored did you feel watching this movie?
How strongly would you recommend this movie to a friend?

Table 5. Liking of Protagonist Scale.

How much did you like the main character, Leonard?
How unpleasant did you find the main character, Leonard?

Table 6. Comprehension Items.

If you think about the events of the movie in the order in which they would have happened in real life, would the scene in which Leonard (the main character) talks to Natalie (the dark haired bartender) in the bar come before or after the scene in which her late boyfriend's associate Dodd shoots at and chases Leonard?
If you think about the events of the movie in the order in which they would have happened in real life, would the scene in which Leonard reads "Don't believe his lies" about Teddy (the annoying self-described policeman), come before or after the scene in which he tattoos a license plate number on his (Leonard's) thigh?
If you think about the events of the movie in the order in which they would have happened in real life, would the scene in which Leonard kills Jimmy come before or after the scene in which he spends the night at Natalie's house?
Why did Leonard (the main character) shoot and kill Teddy (the self-described policeman)? What was the information and logic that led him to do this? Please explain fully, and use the back if you need to.
Why did Leonard (the main character) kill Jimmy Grants (the drug dealer that Leonard strangles in the isolated building)? What was the information and logic that led him to do this? Please explain fully, and use the back if you need to.
Why did Natalie provoke Leonard into hitting her? What was the information and logic that led her to do this? Please explain fully, and use the back if you need to.

Subjects were then de-briefed through information on the purpose of the experiment, and they were told about the re-editing of the film versions being used.

Dependent Measures

Enjoyment in viewing the treatment film was measured through a six-item self-report scale (Table 4) that was incorporated with the other questionnaire items to be answered after viewing. Comprehension was measured through three before/after items that asked about plot chronology and three open-ended items asking the subject to describe character motivation and logic for a particular action (Table 6).

Results

Treatment Check

After an initial round of experimental runs using the four treatments, a one-way analysis of variance was performed to evaluate whether subjects who viewed each of the four versions of *Memento* experienced the predicted different levels of cognitive challenge. The difference among mean reported levels of cognitive challenge was significant: F (3, 65) = 7.79, p = .000, η^2 = .26. The strength of the relationship between the versions of the film and the reported level of cognitive challenge as assessed by η^2 was strong, with the treatment condition accounting for 26% of the variance of the dependent variable.

The means of the cognitive challenge reported by each group were in the expected relationship, with the group seeing version 1 of the film (the chronological complete version) reporting the least cognitive challenge (M = 5.90). The next two groups reported an intermediate level of cognitive challenge: the group who saw the original version of the film (reverse chronology, complete information) (M = 6.98), and the group who saw version 2 of the film (the chronological version with missing information) (M = 7.36). The group who saw version 3 of the film (reverse chronology, missing information) reported the highest level of cognitive challenge (M = 8.07).

Follow-up tests were conducted to evaluate pairwise differences among the means. There was a significant difference in means between the group seeing version 1 of the film (the least challenging version) and the group seeing version 3 of the film (the most challenging version). There were no significant differences between other pairs of means. Because the extremes of the range of cognitive challenge were represented by versions 1 and 3, because of the similarity in reported levels of challenge presented by version 2 and the original version of *Memento*, and because it was desirable to include the original source film in the study, version 2 was eliminated as a treatment after the pilot study.

An analysis of variance was performed on the main experimental groups after all data was collected to determine whether the variance among perceived cognitive challenge in the three versions of the film which had been confirmed by the treatment check still held in the main experiment. The difference among means was again significant, F (2, 103) = 7.71, p = .001. The relationship among mean perceived cognitive challenge in each group was again as predicted (means here are expressed in terms of factor analysis beta values, see "Reliabilities," below): version 1 (M = -.431) < version 0 (M = -.043) < version 3 (M = .488). Post-hoc tests again showed that the only significant pairwise difference was between version 1 and version 3. Thus, because the hypotheses all predict relationships based on different levels of cognitive challenge presented by the treatments, only subjects who saw version 1 or version 3 were included in subsequent analyses to evaluate the hypotheses.

Descriptives

The treatment groups for the original version ($N = 38$), version 1 ($N = 32$), and version 3 ($N = 30$) overall had an age range of 18 to 23 ($M = 19.4$), 88 % were female; 93% listed communication as their major subject; and 100% got extra credit in an undergraduate communication course for participating in the study. For all subjects, mean values of enjoyment and liking for the protagonist were 5.87 and 6.62, respectively. Analyses of variance found no significant difference among treatment groups in age [$F(2, 103) = 1.04, p = .356$], gender [$F(2, 103) = .907, p = .407$], cognitive ability [$F(2, 103) = .076, p = .927$], liking for the protagonist [$F(2, 103) = .744, p = .478$], or enjoyment of the film [$F(2, 103) = .176, p = .839$].

Data Preparation

Data was entered from the hand-written paper questionnaires into SPSS and items were reverse-coded as appropriate.

After completion of the experiment, three of the six items of the comprehension scale were removed due to ambiguity or measurement bias. Specifically, the second before/after comprehension item asking about Leonard reading "don't believe his lies" on the Polaroid of Teddy was judged to be ambiguous because there are two points in the original and first recut (chronological) versions of *Memento* where Leonard reads this writing; based on viewer interpretation, either "before" or "after" could be correct.

Two of the open-ended comprehension items ("why did Leonard shoot and kill Teddy" and "why did Natalie provoke Leonard into hitting her") were judged to be unequal measures across the two treatments. Viewers of Version 1 were presented with explicit information that allowed them to answer these questions. Version 3 lacked some of this explicit information, which required viewers to make inferences or guesses to answer the questions. Thus, these two open-ended items and the second before/after item were excluded from the composite measure of comprehension.

A mean variable was created from the 18 items comprising the Need for Cognition scale. Grouping variables by upper and lower halves split at the median were created for each of the following independent variables: cognitive ability (a composite variable of self-reported high school grade point average, SAT score, and university grade point average), experience with challenging films, and mean need for cognition.

During preliminary analysis, a statistically significant correlation between liking for the main character and mean overall enjoyment of the film was noted [$r(106) = .538, p = .000$]. As the hypotheses in this study address the relationship between understanding of story and enjoyment of the film, rather than the relationship between feelings toward the main character and enjoyment, the liking of the main character variable was used as a covariate in all analyses of variance dealing with mean enjoyment as a dependent variable, in order to remove the impact of affect towards the protagonist from the overall enjoyment of the film.

Reliabilities

Coefficient alpha internal consistency estimates of reliability were computed for the other four scales used in the study: an ad-hoc scale measuring perceived cognitive challenge presented by the film (3 items); an ad-hoc scale measuring enjoyment during viewing of the film (6 items); an ad-hoc scale measuring the viewer's liking of Leonard, the main character (2 items); and the Need for Cognition scale (18 items). Values for coefficient alpha of the scales were .81 (perceived challenge scale), .86 (enjoyment scale), .76 (liking of Leonard scale) and .87 (Need for Cognition scale), each indicating satisfactory reliability. However, to further improve measurement accuracy, factor analyses was performed on the challenge, enjoyment, and liking of the protagonist scales, and a single factor variable was created for each.

Hypotheses

Two by two analyses of variances were conducted on each of the relationships among variables proposed in the hypotheses. Independent variables were cognitive challenge presented by Versions 1 and 3, cognitive ability (assessed as a composite of self-reported high school grade point average, combined SAT score, and university grade point average), need for cognition, and experience with challenging films. Dependent variables measured were comprehension of the film's story and enjoyment of viewing the film.

For each relationship among variables proposed by the hypotheses, possible main effects and possible interaction effects were calculated. None of these possible main or interaction effects among the six hypotheses were statistically significant (see Table 7).

Table 7. Summary of hypotheses results

Hypothesis	Independent Variable	Dependent Variable	F value	p value
1	Cognitive Challenge	Comprehension	$F(1, 44) = 1.15$	.289
	Cognitive Ability	Comprehension	$F(1, 44) = .310$	.581
	Cognitive Challenge x Cognitive Ability	Comprehension	$F(1, 44) = .069$	.793
2	Cognitive Challenge	Comprehension	$F(1, 62) = .173$	.146
	Need for Cognition	Comprehension	$F(1, 62) = .043$	.837
	Cognitive Challenge x Need for Cognition	Comprehension	$F(1, 62) = .427$	.516
3	Cognitive Challenge	Comprehension	$F(1, 55) = 2.08$	.156
	Experience With Challenging Films	Comprehension	$F(1, 55) = .151$	.699
	Cognitive Challenge x Experience With Challenging Films	Comprehension	$F(1, 55) = .000$	.988
4	Cognitive Challenge	Enjoyment	$F(1, 43) = .763$	.388
	Cognitive Ability	Enjoyment	$F(1, 43) = .044$	.834
	Cognitive Challenge x Cognitive Ability	Enjoyment	$F(1, 43) = .486$	.490
5	Cognitive Challenge	Enjoyment	$F(1, 61) = .355$	.554
	Need for Cognition	Enjoyment	$F(1, 61) = 1.75$	.191
	Cognitive Challenge x Need for Cognition	Enjoyment	$F(1, 61) = .119$	.731
6	Cognitive Challenge	Enjoyment	$F(1, 55) = 1.18$	.283
	Experience With Challenging Films	Enjoyment	$F(1, 55) = 1.14$	.291

	Cognitive Challenge x Experience With Challenging Films	Enjoyment	$F(1, 55) = 1.24$	.270

Because none of the six hypotheses were supported, an exploratory stepwise regression analysis was performed to see if any of the measured constructs would be predictive of the main dependent variable of interest, enjoyment. Factors submitted for stepwise regression were age, gender, cognitive ability, need for cognition, experience with challenging films, and liking of the film's protagonist. The results of the regression show that only one measured construct, liking for the protagonist, was significantly predictive of enjoyment.

Discussion

The results in the previous section show that this study's experiment successfully manipulated the level of cognitive challenge reported by subjects across two re-edited versions of *Memento*. However, this variance in reported cognitive challenge did not result in significant main effects on measured comprehension or enjoyment. That is, none of the paired subject groups compared to each other were significantly different in the levels of comprehension or enjoyment experienced: the two film version treatment groups; the higher and lower cognitive ability groups; the higher and lower need for cognition groups; or the greater and less experience with challenging films groups.

Neither were there the significant interaction effects on comprehension and enjoyment between cognitive challenge presented by each treatment film and the higher/lower levels of subject cognitive ability, need for cognition, or experience with challenging films predicted by the hypotheses.

There was one significant interaction effect in the results: subjects with lower need for cognition had significantly higher comprehension of version 3 than did subjects with higher need for cognition. The explanation for this could be that the viewers with higher need for cognition felt frustrated with the incoherence of the missing-information version of the film they watched, and so lost interest and focus. Perhaps more likely is that this result reflects this study's methodological problem in measuring comprehension in this study, namely that the construct finally was measured by only one item.

Another methodological issue that could contribute to the lack of anticipated main and predicted interaction effects is the lack of variance in subjects: most were female undergraduates between the ages of 18 and 21 at a selective university who participated in the experiment for extra credit in a course in communication, the major subject for most of them. The differences between the upper and lower halves of the groups created for data analysis in cognitive ability and need for cognition are relatively small. A more diverse population and a larger sample would perhaps provide more variance in this experiment's data, and thus possibly different outcomes in the results.

Bearing in mind the methodological issues in this research, we turn to the more abstract implications of the results: what conclusions relevant to the theory applied in this research can be drawn from the dearth of main and interaction effects predicted by the hypotheses?

As explained earlier, Graesser's constructionist theory of narrative comprehension proposes that the reader or viewer attempts to integrate information about setting, events, and characters streaming from the narrative source into a situation model, a coherent mental construction by which the reader or viewer comprehends the narrative. Lapses in local coherence in the narrative's chronology, place, or character motivation impede the construction of this situation model.

The variance in reported level of cognitive challenge by viewers of versions 1 and 3 in this experiment is consistent with Graesser's constructionist model. Version 1 re-arranged all of the original *Memento*'s scenes into conventional chronological order; version 3 kept the reverse chronology of the original but deleted information. The much higher level of cognitive challenge reported by the latter's viewers, whose efforts to construct a coherent situation model were impeded both by the challenge of the reverse chronology and by missing information that would explain events and character motivation, provides clear support for the constructionist model.

The tested hypotheses' proposed relationships among cognitive challenge presented by the narrative, viewer traits (cognitive ability, need for cognition, and experience with challenging films), and enjoyment are not predicted directly by Graesser's constructionist model, but were my attempt to link cognitive-oriented constructionist theory to the affect- and behaviouralist-oriented entertainment theory of mood management. The former theorizes little about affect, but proposes that readers and viewers construct meaning representations from narratives which address their goals; the latter states that entertainment narratives are a significant part of our symbolic environment which we arrange to maximize pleasure. Bringing these two strands of theory together, I argued that the comprehension of narratives is an important part of the pleasure we get from them. However, the results seem to provide no support for the notion that a viewer's understanding of a film story determines enjoyment. In this experiment, even though viewers found the chronological re-edit of *Memento* much easier to understand than the reverse-order, missing information version, they enjoyed both of these versions, as well as the original version, equally.

Perhaps this may be explained in part by the high quality of the original *Memento* and its effectiveness as a puzzle film and suspense story. Responses to an open-ended item on this experiment's questionnaire ("What did you most like about this film?") which were not coded for the quantitative analysis suggest that viewers of the incomplete Version 3 enjoyed the challenge the story presented in spite of not attaining full understanding of the plot by the end of the film. This may speak to the robustness of *Memento* – the pleasures of its story held up despite the ten or so minutes of missing vital story information.

Another explanation of the lack of measured linkage between comprehension and enjoyment is indicated by the outcome of the final exploratory stepwise regression analysis: the only variable of those measured which predicts enjoyment of the film is the level of liking of the film's protagonist. This finding is consistent with affective disposition theory (Zillman and Cantor 1976), one of the three theories along with mood management and excitation transfer which are sometimes bundled as "entertainment theory." Affective disposition theory proposes that in dramatic entertainment, as opposed to comedy, "enjoyment increases ... the more we like characters that prosper or succeed" (Raney 2003, 72); and that we like characters in drama whose actions we judge to be morally correct (Zillman 2000). In the present research, this theory explains the high correlation of liking of Leonard, *Memento*'s protagonist, and enjoying any version of the film. Affective disposition theory provides an account for the finding that understanding the story is literally insignificant compared to feeling towards the main character in influencing our film-watching pleasure.

Finally, the viewer's experience of psychological immersion in the world portrayed on the screen should not be underestimated as a factor in enjoyment of films. The research construct "presence," defined by Lombard and Ditton (1997) as "the perceptual illusion of non-mediation in mediated environments," or the viewer's sensation of actually being present in an onscreen world, is often associated with theory and research on various forms of digital new media such as videogames and virtual reality, but can also be fruitful for investigations into the pleasures of watching films. Interrelated facets of presence relevant to this study's research include presence as realism (the sense of accurate representation of places, events and people); presence as immersion (the viewer's sense that he or she is submerged in a virtual environment); and presence of social actors within a medium (the viewer's feeling that onscreen characters are with them; this is related to the concept of parasocial interaction).

It seems likely that the experience of presence relates strongly to the process of mental situation model construction in narrative comprehension. Perhaps the pleasure derived from the various aspects of presence, which viewers experience without a complete understanding of the story, helps explain the lack of observed causality between comprehension and enjoyment in the present research. The hypotheses tested in this study thus do not account for important factors in the viewer's enjoyment of movies, or at least of *Memento*.

These speculations suggest directions for future empirical research on enjoyment of movies in the context of narrative understanding:

- Would a larger and more diverse subject sample provide different results for the proposed relationships between narrative comprehension and enjoyment which were unsupported in this research?
- What is the relationship among affective disposition toward the protagonist, narrative comprehension, and enjoyment? Would a film with a less attractive protagonist or a less robust narrative than *Memento's* yield insight?
- What is the relationship among understanding of a film narrative, the experience of aspects of presence while watching a film such as realism, immersion, and parasocial interaction, and enjoyment?

Further research in these directions may help us achieve a more complete understanding of both cognitive and affective aspects of experiencing and enjoying motion pictures.

Works Cited

Primary Sources

Nolan, Christopher. 2001. *Memento*. Distributed by Newmarket Films,

Secondary Sources

Bryant, Jennings and Dolf Zillman. 1984. Using Television to Alleviate Boredom and Stress: Selective Exposure as a Function of Induced Excitational States. *Journal of Broadcasting* 28: 1-20.
Cacioppo, John T., Richard E. Petty, and Chuan F. Kao. 1984. The Efficient Assessment of Need for Cognition. *Journal of Personality Assessment* 48: 306-307.
Graesser, Arthur C., Brent Olde, and Bianca Klettke. 2002. How Does the Mind Represent and Construct Stories? In *Narrative Impact: Social and Cognitive Foundations*, ed. T. C. Brock, 229-262, Mahwah, NJ: Erlbaum.
Graesser, Arthur C., Max A. Kassler, Roger J. Kreuz, and Bonnie McLain-Allen. 1998. Verification of Statements About Story Worlds That Deviate from Normal Conceptions of Time: What is True About *Einstein's Dreams*? *Cognitive Psychology* 35: 246-301.
Graesser, Arthur C., Murray Singer, and Tom Trabasso. 1994. Constructing Inferences During Narrative Text Comprehension. *Psychological Review* 101: 371-395.
Lombard, Matthew, and Theresa Ditton. 1997. At the Heart of it All: The Concept of Presence. *Journal of Computer-Mediated Communication* 3, http://jcmc.indiana.edu/vol3/issue2/lombard.html
Radvansky, Gabriel A., Rolf A. Zwaan, Todd Federico, and Nancy Franklin. 1998. Retrieval from Temporally Organized Situation Models. *Journal of Experimental Psychology: Learning, Memory, and Cognition* 24: 1224-1237.
Raney, Arthur A. 2003. Disposition-based Theories. In *Communication and Emotion: Essays in Honor of Dolf Zillman,* ed. J. Cantor, 61-84, Mahwah, NJ: Erlbaum.
Raney, Arthur A., and Jennings Bryant. 2002. Moral Judgement and Crime Drama: An Integrated Theory of Enjoyment. *Journal of Communication* 52: 402-415.
Stein, Nancy L., and Tom Trabasso. 1985. The Search after Meaning: Comprehension and Comprehension Monitoring. In *Applied*

Developmental Psychology (vol. 2), ed. D. Keating, 33-58. San Diego, CA: Academic Press.
Vorderer, Peter, Sylvia Knobloch, and Holger Schramm. 2001. Does Entertainment Suffer From Interactivity? The Impact of Watching an Interactive TV Movie on Viewers' Experience of Entertainment. *Media Psychology* 3: 343-363.
—. 1996. Toward a Psychological Theory of Suspense. In *Suspense: Conceptualizations, Theoretical Analyses, and Empirical Explorations*, ed. M. Friedrichsen, 233-254, Mahwah, NJ: Lawerence Erlbaum Associates.
Zillman, Dolf and Joanne Cantor. 1976. Affective Responses to the Emotions of a Protagonist. *Journal of Experimental Social Psychology* 13: 155-165.
Zillman, Dolf. 1988. Mood Management: Using Entertainment to its Full Advantage. In *Communication, Social Cognition, and Affect,* ed. E. T. Higgins, 147-167, Hillsdale, NJ: Lawrence Erlbaum Associates.
Zillman, Dolf. 2000. Basal Morality in Drama Appreciation. In *Moving Images, Culture, and the Mind*, ed. I. Bondebjerg, 53-63, Luton, U.K.: University of Luton Press.
—. Mood Management in the Context of Selective Exposure Theory. In *Communication Yearbook* 23, ed. M. E. Roloff, 103-123, Thousand Oaks: CA: Sage.
Zwaan, Rolf A., Joseph P. Magliano, and Arthur C. Graesser. 1995. Dimensions of Situation Model Construction in Narrative Comprehension. *Journal of Experimental Psychology: Learning, Memory, and Cognition* 21: 386-397.
Zwaan, Rolf A. 1996. Processing Narrative Time Shifts. *Journal of Experimental Psychology: Learning, Memory, and Cognition* 22: 1196-1207.

CHAPTER SIXTEEN

OF MEN WHO READ ROMANCE AND WOMEN
WHO READ ADVENTURE STORIES...
AN EMPIRICAL RECEPTION STUDY
ON THE EMOTIONAL ENGAGEMENT
OF MEN AND WOMEN WHILE READING
NARRATIVE TEXTS

ÖZEN ODAĞ

Abstract

Against the background of feminist literary theory and based on a number of German representative survey studies about reading practices, it is assumed that women are more emotionally involved during reading than men, especially so when reading *fiction* and texts with a focus on the *inner world* of characters. Hypotheses are tested as part of an experimental between-subjects-design with *category of work* (fiction/non-fiction), *thematic focus* (inner world/outer world) and *biological sex* (male/female) constituting the independent variables and *emotional involvement* constituting the dependent variable. The emotional involvement of readers is assessed by both questionnaire and the *reminding method*. Results show that, contrary to expectation, and as opposed to both feminist theory and widespread survey results, male participants score higher than females on questionnaire scales assessing emotional involvement. At the same time, the personal remindings of readers disclose no differences in how closely men and women approach characters. Likewise surprisingly, the *category of a literary* work seems of negligible importance for the two sexes while the *thematic focus* of a text appears to have an impact on *female* reading in particular. Exploratory results indicate a sex difference in the *valence* of reading experiences as well as differential *foci* of men and women during reception.

Introduction

If there is one thing that German scholars of literature and literary reception are certain about, it is the alleged difference between men and women in both reading behaviour and the ways in which men and women read! The certainty with which sex differences in reading are promulgated in the German academic community usually rests on either of the following grounds – (1) feminist literary theory and (2) results of representative surveys.

The basic theoretical assumptions of feminist literary scholars concerning sex differences in reading resemble the concept of an *écriture féminine* put forward for the production of texts (for an overview of *l'écriture féminine*, see Osinski 1998, chapter II.3; for a critical review, see Jones 1981). Klüger (1984), for instance, investigates the 'otherness' of a female reading, and some scholars have gone as far as to evaluate a female reading as 'deficient' or 'privileged' (for an overview, see van Heydebrand and Winko 1995). In addition, and on the basis of psychoanalytic reasoning (by, e.g., Chodorow 1978), a few researchers have pointed to a particularly engaged as well as emotional type of female reading, resting upon the communal desire of women to establish close relationships – as opposed to an individualistic desire of men for separateness and autonomy (Garbe 1993; 2002; see also Schweickart 1997).

The majority of publications within the framework of feminist literary theory mention no empirical evidence for their assumptions at all. A few articles (such as those of Garbe 1993; 2002) are exceptional, however, in that they draw upon representative survey results to corroborate their theory of sex differences in reading. And interestingly, feminist assumptions of a particular female reading have so far been confirmed by survey data – even though feminist theory and surveys are rooted in completely different research traditions and have, for the most time, been clearly detached from each other[1].

---

[1] While feminist literary theory seeks to critically unravel a male dominance in both writing and reading texts (overview in Moi 2002), survey studies serve to display an overall and superficial snapshot of reading practices in a given country, at a given time (overview in Bonfadelli 1999).

A closer look at the aforementioned representative surveys, carried out by major German foundations such as the *Bertelsmann Stiftung* or the *Stiftung Lesen*, shows that (in line with feminist theory) women have a much stronger affinity to reading than men: Women apparently read and enjoy reading more than men do (e.g. Hurrelmann, Hammer, and Nieß 1993; Bonfadelli and Fritz 1993), they read more frequently than their male counterparts (Gilges 1992; Bonfadelli and Fritz 1993), they prefer higher levels of literary quality (Garbe 1993), and score higher on reading literacy in terms of comprehending, interpreting and evaluating textual material (Franz and Payrhuber 2002; Stanat and Kunter 2001). Properties of the reading material itself, however, seem to also come into play, here: Again in line with feminist assumptions (see, for instance, the chapter on 'Gender and Genre' in Eagleton 1996), women appear to read fictional novels, men prefer non-fictional texts (Gilges 1992; Stiftung Lesen 2001). And among products of *fiction*, women appear to be more drawn to romance and love stories, while men are more interested in adventure-type stories, Western or science fiction[2]. Among products of *non-fiction*, men seem to be more curious about economy, politics, or contemporary history, whereas women tend to choose reading about health, counselling or psychology (Bonfadelli 1999; Gilges 1992; Stiftung Lesen 2001). In sum, survey studies suggest that – irrespective of the category of a literary piece (*fiction* or *non-fiction*) – differences between men and women are quite profound: Women are more interested in interpersonal issues and the inner world of protagonists, men are more focused on the complexities of their outside world. In addition, women seem to be attracted by issues that are life-like and compatible with their real lives, whereas men prefer to read about things that diverge from their own lives.

Much less is known about differences in the quality of reading, i.e. the ways in which men and women read. Feminist assumptions of an especially engaged type of female reading are again met, however, by first findings of surveys and a very small number of reception studies (e.g., Andringa 2004; Oatley 1994). These findings also point to differential reading styles and indicate that women seem to be more able than men to become absorbed into literary worlds, get deeply immersed or even lost in the time and space of the literary piece. Women appear to be more emotionally engaged when reading and to derive a sense of satisfaction and relaxation from it. In contrast, men appear to read more rationally, often for the purpose of broadening their knowledge (e.g., Hurrelmann et

---

[2] A seminal empirical study investigating the affinity of women to romance novels was conducted by Radway (1984) within the framework of feminist literary criticism.

al. 1993; Oatley 1999; Köcher 1993). Also, women are shown to be more inclined to come to terms with real life issues by means of reading, while men seem to prefer quite the opposite: They like to distance themselves from their everyday life through reading (Garbe 1993; Andringa 2004; Charlton, Burbaum, and Sutter 2004; Charlton, Pette, and Burbaum 2004.) In short, a review of the literature about *biological sex and reading* conveys the impression that women and men are profoundly different with respect to several aspects of reading practices. And much of what representative surveys disclose is very much in line with feminist assumptions of a female reading. Yet, despite the plausibility of feminist literary theory and despite the validity of empirical findings, I would like to point to at least three aspects in research on sex differences in reading that need be criticized (for a more elaborate discussion, see Odağ 2007): Firstly, most of the research places the emphasis clearly on the side of the reader (and his or her biological sex) without taking into account the specific qualities of the preferred narratives themselves, which on their part most likely impact the reception as well. Secondly, representative surveys merely focus on a reader's retrospective account of reading practices (such as the remembered amount of time spent on book reading, remembered types of reading etc.), thereby largely neglecting the process of reading per se and producing crude and undifferentiated data. Thirdly, and most importantly, the feminist approach to literature lacks direct empirical evidence, and the empirical evidence, at the same time, lacks a theory! As mentioned earlier, hardly any feminist critical assumptions concerning biological sex and reading have so far been tested empirically, within the framework of a controlled experimental design. And vice versa: Most surveys on female and male reading lack theoretical assumptions for any differences found – differences between men and women are rarely predicted by theory-based hypotheses, and most often interpreted post hoc as related to or even caused by the biological sex of readers.

In the following reception study[3], the main goal is to expand upon previous research on *biological sex and reading* by taking into consideration both the properties of the media products (i.e. narrative texts) themselves and the biological sex of readers. More precisely, this project is designed to predict differences in the reading experiences of men and women on theoretical as well as empirical grounds, assuming that in addition to the biological sex of readers, certain text characteristics – such as the category of the piece of literature or its thematic focus will have

---

[3] This study is part of a larger PhD project completed at Jacobs University Bremen (Odağ 2007).

specific effects on the reception as well – most likely in interaction with the biological sex of readers. Several hypotheses about the impact of reader characteristics as well as their interactions with textual features on the reception of narratives are tested – aiming to see whether the 'received opinion' about sex differences in reading, portraying women as the more engaged readers, will eventually stand up against a controlled experimental investigation. And it is precisely these characteristics that make the present study a further example for a new beginning of the study of literature.

Hypotheses

Where the impact of *biological sex* on the reception is concerned, research has demonstrated a tendency for women to become more emotionally involved when reading narratives than men. Women are therefore expected to display higher degrees of emotional engagement than their male counterparts (hypothesis 1).

Yet, many findings have also pointed out implicitly that much of what women and men feel when they read can also be traced back to properties of the narratives that women and men prefer. None of these implicit findings concerning the interaction between textual features and reader characteristics have, however, been put to the test so far. As illustrated above, men and women have frequently been shown to differ in what they enjoy reading: While women appear to be drawn to fictional narratives, men seem to prefer non-fictional texts. This leads me to assume that women are more emotionally engaged when reading *fiction*, and men more so when reading *non-fiction* (hypothesis 2). In addition, and as indicated above, while women are shown to be more interested in narratives focusing on relationships (e.g., a romance novel), men appear to be more drawn to stories about unexplored worlds and like to read science fiction, thrillers, or Western-type stories. A second interaction hypothesis is thus put forward: Women display higher degrees of emotional engagement if the narrative focuses on socio-emotional issues and on the 'inner world' of protagonists. Men, on the other hand, are more likely to become emotionally engaged if the story concentrates on the 'outer world', i.e. the environment or more generally the physical properties of the setting (hypothesis 3.)

Procedure

The hypotheses were tested within the framework of an experimental between-subjects design that comprised two (experimental) independent textual variables (i.e. *category of narrative* as well as *thematic focus*), one (quasi-experimental) reader variable (i.e. *biological sex*), and one dependent variable (*emotional engagement*)[4]. The dependent variable (*emotional engagement*) in turn comprised the two broader realms *experiential states* and *emotions*.

As one purpose of this study was to explore the effect of the category of a narrative on the emotional involvement of men and women, *category of work* with the levels *fiction* versus *non-fiction* was the first independent variable. A second purpose was to test the relationship between emotional engagement and biological sex, assuming that men and women are interested in different topics and in turn become emotionally involved with different kinds of narratives. This necessitated the variation of the focus of the narrative, resulting in the inclusion of *thematic focus* with the levels *focus on the inner world* versus *focus on the outer world* of protagonists as a second independent variable. Four narrative texts resulted from a full combination of these levels:

(1) a fictional narrative that focuses on the inner world of the protagonists (text 1),
(2) a non-fictional narrative with a focus on the inner world of the protagonists (text 2),
(3) a fictional narrative that focuses on the outer world (text 3),
(4) and a non-fictional one that focuses on the outer world (text 4).

Selected texts were not in any way manipulated so as to match the respective factors – instead, the present study was based on *natural* texts which already comprised the intended variations: Text 1 – *The woman at the gas station*[5] – is a story by *Bernhard Schlink* depicting the relationship of a married couple, where the male protagonist eventually decides to break out and start a new life. Text 2 is *Matt Seaton*'s epilogue to *Before I*

---

[4] While not the focus of this paper, it should be mentioned here that in addition to the above-mentioned factors (biological sex, category of work and thematic focus of text) some further reader characteristics, i.e., *gender*, level of *empathy*, ability to *distinguish fact from fiction*, were considered relevant mediators and were therefore assessed as well. They were included in the study design as covariates.

[5] German title: *Die Frau an der Tankstelle*; the English title was suggested by the author of this paper

say goodbye[6] in which he portrays his pain and awe during the cancer disease of his wife *Ruth Picardie*. Text 3 – *Ananke*[7] – is a science fiction story by *Stanislaw Lem* about a space-shuttle crash on Mars and a team of experts trying to clarify the accident. Text 4 – *635 days in the ice*[8] – is *Klaus Bachmann*'s report about *Shackleton*'s crew trapped in the Antarctic for 635 days.

In order to make sure that the texts did in fact exemplify the intended variations, and in order to assess the intended variations in the natural texts inter-subjectively, a *text analysis study* was carried out. Selected texts were content analysed by 12 experts from literary studies. This study served as a manipulation check as well as to identify potentially confounding variables in the texts of choice. Without going into much detail here, it should be mentioned that the manipulation check turned out to be successful – indicating that the selected texts clearly represented either the *fiction* or the *non-fiction* category, as well as either the *inner* or the *outer* world of protagonists (i.e. the values of the independent variables on the side of the texts).

In order to assess the reception of the four narratives (with respect to potential impacts of textual features, reader characteristics and their interactions), *a reception study* was carried out. 99 readers (49 male and 50 female) participated in this study, their age ranging between 19 and 61 with an average of 26 years. The sample of females was homogeneous in that nearly all of them were students of Literary Studies in their first semester. Their response rate was sufficiently high – 80 % of the women asked returned their questionnaires. Men, however, were much more difficult to convince to take part in this study. The sample of males was thus heterogeneous in that it drew upon several sources of sampling, i.e. contacts to student councils at German universities, online journals, and professors as well as colleagues. Participants were instructed to read the narratives in their natural reading environment, fill out the questionnaires and send the material back in a stamped and addressed envelope which was also enclosed in the study material. Participants were given a narrative text as well as a questionnaire assessing their emotional engagement during reading.[9] Final questions comprised socio-demographic information.

---

[6] German title: *Es wird mir fehlen – das Leben*; the English title is the original one.
[7] German and English titles are identical.
[8] German title: *635 Tage im Eis*; the English title was suggested by the author of this paper.
[9] This questionnaire was complemented by three further instruments assessing the readers' *gender, empathy* and *ability to distinguish fact from fiction*.

As mentioned earlier, *emotional engagement* in this study is conceptualized as both *basic emotions* (such as fear, guilt, pity, joy etc.) and free floating *experiential states* (such as flow, transportation, parasocial interaction, identification, etc.). The overall emotional engagement was assessed by (1) a standardized questionnaire (the *Experiential States During Reading Questionnaire*, Appel, Koch, Schreier, and Groeben 2002) as well as (2) a qualitative method (the *reminding*-method, Seilmann and Larssen 1989). The questionnaire integrates various theoretical conceptualizations of reading experiences and serves to identify the degree of intensity on 14 potentially distinct state-dimensions which are termed: *focusing of attention* („While reading I noticed that I was thinking of something else."; inverse item), *immersion in a text* („I forgot about the world around me while reading."), *vividness* („I had problems visualizing what I was reading about."; inverse item), *being there* („It felt as though I was actually in the world described by the text."), *ending of reception* („When I finished reading it felt like I had just returned from a long journey."), *suspense* („I was curious to find out what would happen next."), *emotional involvement* („I felt touched by the text."), *pleasure in reading* („I enjoyed reading this text."), *identification* („I felt sorry for the main protagonist."), *parasocial interaction* („At least once I felt the impulse to say something to the main protagonist."), *cognitive involvement* („I kept on thinking about the text."), *thematic interest* („I would like to read another text on the same topic."), *analytic mode of reception* („I noticed the language used in the text."), *and ease of cognitive access* („I found the events easy to follow."). For preparation of further analysis, the overall emotional engagement of readers was summed across all statements assessing emotional aspects of experiential states, resulting in one index termed *involvement*.

In the *reminding*-method, readers were asked to mark the text during reading, whenever they had a feeling, a thought, or a memory. Furthermore, they were requested to elucidate their marks in written form after reading. Readers submitted 1261 written comments altogether. These comments were then content analysed on the basis of yet another category scheme comprising deductive categories for the assessment of experiential states (e.g. the *proximity of readers to story elements*) as well as deductive categories for identifying basic emotions (e.g. *fear, pity, shame, joy* etc.). The following report limits itself to these two dimensions of the coding scheme: The category *proximity of readers to story elements* captured how closely readers approached story elements. It in turn comprised four sub-categories: *strong proximity* (identification according to Oatley 1994) was coded if readers related the story events to their own experiences; *medium proximity* (empathy according to Zillmann 1991) was coded if they observed the events from the perspective of an outside spectator, without mentioning any resemblances to their own lives; *distance* was coded if readers employed a distant mode of reception and were, for instance, bored or distracted; a fourth subcategory captured *miscellaneous* aspects which could not be assigned to any of the other sub-categories.

The second dimension that will be touched upon in this paper is the *basic emotions* dimension comprising 14 different emotions (such as suspense, pleasure, fear, sadness, pity etc., based on Renaud and Unz 2006), that were coded with two subcategories each – the first subcategory was selected, if the respective emotion was in fact described in the reader's comment; sub-category 2 was coded, if the emotion was not mentioned. By applying both of these categories to each emotion, the coding scheme accounted for the possibility that different emotions could simultaneously be referred to. Inter-rater agreement scores for both *proximity* as well as *basic emotions* were sufficiently high with *kappa*-coefficients ranging between 0.86 and 0.88 which, according to Landis and Koch (1977, 165), can be considered 'almost perfect'.

The quantitative and qualitative methods employed in this study were combined in order to cover the phenomenon under study in greater detail. In this, the two methods complemented each other (see Tashakkorie and Teddlie 1998, for the risks and benefits of combining qualitative and quantitative methods): Both of them were employed to assess experiential states during reading (see above). While the quantitative method captured the type of an experience during reading as well as its degree, the qualitative method helped to dig deeper into the subjective aspects of reading experiences and facilitated a better understanding of readers' individual meanings of the events in the story world. It thus helped to carve out a person's position on a continuum of proximity versus distance to the story-elements (with *identification*, i.e. *strong proximity* forming one pole of this continuum, a *distant* mode of reception forming the opposite pole, and *empathy*, i.e. *medium proximity* located in the centre). In addition, as already indicated, by using the qualitative method of data collection, several *basic emotions* were identified as well.

In order to test the impact of the independent variables on the degree of engagement during reading, univariate analyses of variance (as well as regression analyses) were calculated with *category of narrative*, *thematic focus* and *biological sex* as the independent variables (i.e. *predictors* in the regression model) and *emotional engagement* (as represented by the *involvement* index) as the dependent variable (i.e. *criterion* in the regression model). The data collected by the reminding method were content- and frequency-analysed. Chi-squared tests were calculated for contingency tables including category of work, thematic focus and biological sex (and possible interactions) as the independent variables and the categories of the coding scheme (and, more precisely, the *proximity of readers to story elements* and *basic emotions*) as the dependent variables. In order to discover underlying dimensions in the categories of the coding scheme for the reception analysis, a multiple correspondence analysis was carried out (categories inserted into this analysis are mentioned below).

Results

Surprisingly, the first main effects hypothesis concerning biological sex, expecting women to be more emotionally involved in narratives than men could not be confirmed. The results were absolutely counterintuitive in that they did not only refute the hypothesis, but suggested quite the opposite: As far as the questionnaire scales are concerned, it were the men who were clearly more engaged than women – and with a level of significance that leaves hardly any doubt as to its meaning, contradicting both feminist literary theory as well as results of representative surveys ($M_{males} = 49.09$; $M_{females} = 44.59$; $F = 5.304$; $df = 1$; $p = 0.024$; $\eta^2 = 0.061$).

A closer, and exploratory look at the various scales of the questionnaire showed that there were hardly any differences between male and female readers on scales assessing an engagement with particular literary characters (e.g., *identification*: $M_{females} = 3.441$; $M_{males} = 3.515$; $F = 0.119$; $df = 1$; $p = 0.731$; $\eta^2 = 0.001$, or *parasocial interaction*: $M_{females} = 2.386$; $M_{males} = 2.563$; $F = 0.633$; $df = 1$; $p = 0.429$; $\eta^2 = 0.008$). There were, however, (marginally) significant differences on scales assessing an engagement with the overall story (e.g., *suspense*: $M_{females} = 3.700$; $M_{males} = 4.244$; $F = 4.448$; $df = 1$; $p = 0.038$; $\eta^2 = 0.052$, *ease of cognitive access*: $M_{females} = 4.155$; $M_{males} = 4.648$; $F = 6.377$; $df = 1$; $p = 0.014$; $\eta^2 = 0.073$, and *pleasure*: $M_{females} = 2.995$; $M_{males} = 3.745$; $F = 7.135$; $df = 1$; $p = 0.009$; $\eta^2 = 0.081$). More precisely, men derived a greater sense of *suspense* from reading, as well as a greater sense of pleasure. They reported a greater ease of cognitive access to the stories and elaborately reflected upon what they read – more so than women. There were no sex differences, however, in the level of engagement with particular *characters*.

As far as reader comments are concerned, and again surprisingly so, there was hardly any difference in the frequencies with which readers of different sex mentioned *strong* or *moderate proximity* towards the story-elements (*strong proximity*: $OF_{females} = 312$; $EF_{females} = 269.5$; $SR_{females} = 0.9$; $OF_{males} = 258$; $EF_{males} = 273.5$; $SR_{males} = -0.9$; *medium proximity*:

$OF_{females} = 328$; $EF_{females} = 333.5$; $SR_{females} = -0.3$; $OF_{males} = 313$; $EF_{males} = 307.5$; $SR_{males} = -0.3$; $\chi^2 = 10.319$; $df = 3$; $p = 0.016$)[10]. Both women and men tended to either establish strong links between their own lives and the story (in an identificatory mode of reception), or observed the happenings as from the perspective of an outside spectator (in an empathic mode of reception). Men and women appeared to be quite similar in these respects. And once more, these counterintuitive findings can count as further – and strong – evidence against hypothesis 1, contradicting the above-mentioned assumptions of feminist literary theory as well as survey results. Only a minor difference between men and women appeared in the sub-category *distance*, with men mentioning this mode of reading more often than women did ($OF_{males} = 33$; $EF_{males} = 23.5$; $SR_{males} = 2.0$; $OF_{females} = 16$; $EF_{females} = 25.5$; $SR_{females} = -1.9$; $\chi^2 = 10.319$; $df = 3$; $p = 0.016$). In view of the strong evidence *against* hypothesis 1, however, this finding cannot count as much of an evidence *for* it, either.

Hypothesis 2, predicting an interaction between the biological sex of readers and the category of narratives, could also not be confirmed. The data collected by questionnaire showed that the category of a narrative does not have a significant effect on the emotional engagement of men and women ($M_{females*fiction} = 42.18$; $M_{males*fiction} = 47.25$; $M_{females*non-fiction} = 47.00$; $M_{males*non-fiction} = 50.92$; $F = 0.087$; $df = 1$; $p = 0.769$; $\eta^2 = 0.001$). The data collected by the reminding method disclosed a similar result with respect to reading *fiction* – where differences between men and women turned out to be not significant ($\chi^2 = 3.347$; $df = 2$; $p = 0.188$). At the same time, the latter method revealed some differences between men and women when reading *non-fiction* – with men reporting a *distant* mode of reception more frequently than women did ($OF_{males} = 19$; $EF_{males} = 12.8$; $SR_{males} = 1.7$; $OF_{females} = 7$; $EF_{females} = 13.2$; $SR_{females} = -1.7$; $\chi^2 = 11.001$; $df = 2$; $p = 0.004$[11]). Taken together, the category of a narrative (as *fiction* or *non-fiction*) appeared to be of limited importance for the reading experiences of men and women, while the higher frequency of *distance* in the men's accounts of reading *non-fiction* can count as further evidence against hypothesis 2 – once again, a highly astonishing result opposing both feminist literary theory and survey results.

Interaction hypothesis 3 assumed that women would be more involved in stories about the inner world of protagonists, while men were assumed to become more engaged in stories about their outer world. Results of the questionnaire yielded partial evidence for this hypothesis (see figure 1). It

---

[10] OF = observed frequencies; EF = expected frequencies; SR = standardized residuals
[11] This *p*-score falls below the Bonferroni-corrected α of 0,025.

were, more precisely, women who were highly engaged when reading the inner-world narratives, and not involved at all when reading the outer-world stories. Men, however, seemed to be unaffected by the thematic focus of a story; their emotional participation was moderate to high, independent of whether they read about the inner or the outer world of a story-character ($M_{females*inner\ world} = 52.96$; $M_{males*\ inner\ world} = 51.55$; $M_{females*outer\ world} = 36.22$; $M_{males*outer\ worldt} = 46.63$; $F = 9.164$; $df = 1$; $p = 0.003$; $\eta^2 = 0.102$)[12].

Figure 1: The interaction between *thematic focus* and *biological sex* on emotional involvement (endpoints represent mean values)

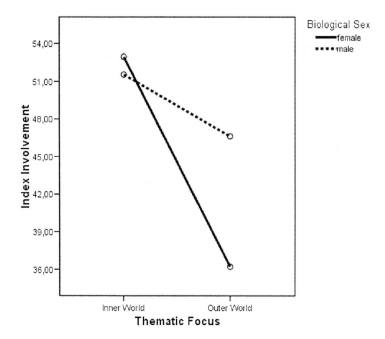

$F = 9.164$; $df = 1$; $p = 0.003$; $eta^2 = 0.102$

---

[12] Pairwise comparisons (with Bonferroni-correction) indicated that differences between men and women are not significant with respect to reading *inner-world*-narratives ($F = 0.253$; $df = 1$; $p = 0.616$). Mean differences turned out to be significant, however, with respect to reading *outer-world*-narratives ($F = 11.506$; $df = 1$; $p = 0.001$).

In addition to the joint impact of *biological sex* and *thematic focus*, the separate impact of the *thematic focus* of texts on the reception was very striking, too: *Inner-world* texts – as opposed to *outer-world* texts – were read with both higher intensities of involvement (as measured by the questionnaire scales: $M_{inner\,world} = 52.25$; $M_{outer\,world} = 41.42$; $F = 30.738$; $df = 1$; $p < 0.001$; $\eta^2 = 0.275$) and more frequent accounts of *strong proximity* to the story-events (as indicated by the reader comments: $OF_{inner\,world} = 407$; $EF_{inner\,world} = 344.0$; $SR_{inner\,world} = 3.4$; $OF_{outer\,world} = 163$; $EF_{outer\,world} = 226.0$; $SR_{outer\,world} = -4.2$; $\chi^2 = 77.820$; $df = 3$; $p < 0.001$). By comparison, and as indicated by the β-coefficients of a linear regression, the effect of the *thematic focus* of texts appeared to be the strongest of all factors involved: Its effect was stronger than the effect of the category of a narrative, the biological sex of readers, or possible interactions ($\beta_{category\,of\,work} = -0.197$; $\beta_{thematic\,focus} = 0.423$; $\beta_{biological\,sex} = -0.284$; $\beta_{category\,of\,work*biological\,sex} = -0.035$; $\beta_{thematic\,focus*biological\,sex} = 0.200$)[13].

Apart from results concerning the hypotheses, the study yielded a number of exploratory results that are worth mentioning: First, women and men appeared to be slightly different concerning their points of reference in the narratives. While there were no differences in the frequencies with which women and men referred to the *characters* of the story ($OF_{women} = 457$; $EF_{women} = 453.1$; $SR_{women} = 0.2$; $OF_{men} = 414$; $EF_{men} = 417.9$; $SR_{men} = -0.2$; $\chi^2 = 0.225$; $df = 1$; $p = 0.636$), men commented on the *plot* and *happenings* of the story significantly more frequently than women did ($OF_{women} = 497$; $EF_{women} = 528.0$; $SR_{women} = -1.9$; $OF_{men} = 518$; $EF_{men} = 487.0$; $SR_{men} = 1.9$; $\chi^2 = 19.477$; $df = 1$; $p < 0.001$). In view of the assumptions of feminist literary theory mentioned above, portraying women to invest more in relationships and men to invest more in autonomy and separateness, it appears surprising that men and women equally often refer to the story characters. At the same time, and based on the feminist approach, it seems plausible that men refer to the story world more often than women.

---

[13] with $\beta_{category\,of\,work}$, $\beta_{biological\,sex}$, and $\beta_{thematic\,focus*biological\,sex}$ being significant at the α-level of 0,05, $\beta_{thematic\,focus}$ being significant at the α-level of 0.001, and $\beta_{category\,of\,work*biological\,sex}$ not being significant. Detracting the influence of the three trait characteristics (*gender, empathy, distinguishing fact from fiction*) from the impact of the independent variables on the reception (i.e. partialling them out by means of regression analysis) did not entail any changes in the impact of the independent variables under study – their impact appeared to be stable and robust irrespective of any covariate effects.

Further important findings – discovered by means of multiple correspondence analysis – pertain to both the *proximity of readers to story elements* and their *basic emotions* when reading. As mentioned earlier, a multiple correspondence analysis was carried out in order to identify underlying dimensions in the data collected by the reminding method. Selected categories of the coding scheme were inserted into this analysis.[14] The analysis yielded two dimensions, with the first one interpreted as the '*proximity versus distance*'-dimension (explained variance 16.2 %) and the second one interpreted as the '*positive versus negative emotions*'- dimension (explained variance 12.6 %).[15] Figure 2 illustrates where men and women are located on these dimensions: While men and women are rather close to each other on dimension 1, they appear further apart on dimension 2. Women and men are thus hardly any different from each other in how far they approach the characters and events in the story and in how far they relate the narratives to their own lives (dimension 1). Differences between men and women are not significant on this first dimension (*Mean Rank$_{females}$* = 622.53; *Mean Rank$_{males}$* = 640.18; Z = -0.860; p = 0.390, as indicated by a non-parametric Mann-Whitney-U-test[16]). Men and women are, however, different in perceiving their emotional engagement as either positive or negative – women report a greater number of negative emotions (such as fear, guilt, shame, etc.), whereas men report a higher number of positive ones (such as interest, suspense, pleasure etc.). These differences on the *positive / negative emotions dimension* of the multiple correspondence analysis in fact turn out to be marginally significant (*Mean Rank$_{females}$* = 650.60; *Mean Rank$_{males}$* = 609.75; Z = -1.990; p = 0.047, as indicated by a non-parametric Mann-Whitney-U-test[17]).

---

[14] Categories included in the analysis were: *proximity of reader to story elements* (sub-categories: strong proximity, medium proximity, distance), *point of transportation* (sub-categories: transportation into one's own world, transportation into the story-world, transportation into both, transportation into neither), *basic emotions* (sub-categories: interest/suspense, pleasure/joy, surprise/irritation, sadness/pity, anger, disgust, fear, shame/guilt, fascination/being personally touched by the story, relief, pride, sympathy/liking, rejection/contempt, boredom), and *valence* (sub-categories: positive experience, negative experience).
[15] Criteria for identifying these dimensions were based on those listed in Ibsch and Schreier (2001).
[16] Due to a lack of homogeneity of variance, a Mann-Whitney-U-test was carried out instead on an analysis of variance, here.
[17] See footnote 16.

Figure 2: Location of men and women on the two dimensions of the multiple correspondence analysis – women and men are circled

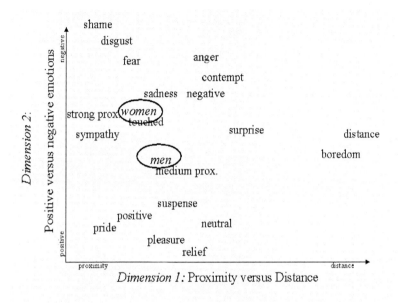

Dimension 1: Proximity versus Distance

Discussion

In contrast to feminist assumptions of a distinctively *female* reading and raw survey findings that to date pervade the German language literature, the emotional participation of men and women while reading narratives turned out to diverge from expectations in several ways: Astonishingly, and contrary to the central hypothesis of the present study (hypothesis 1), men were *more* involved than women on the scales of the questionnaire. Furthermore, in their personal comments, men unexpectedly reported being as close to the characters as the women of the sample did. These counterintuitive findings, resting upon a controlled experimental manipulation, here, go directly against many feminist academic theories of reading differences between men and women and contradict the crude picture of men and women portrayed in representative surveys. They illustrate quite straightforwardly, and at high levels of statistical significance, that neither the somewhat intuitive assumptions of feminist literary criticism nor the rudimentary findings of representative surveys can be upheld when put to the test empirically. The present study in fact posits a remarkable tendency in the opposite direction – men are more involved than women! – which certainly shakes what has been taken for granted in research on sex differences in reading up to now. It may well be that the central hypothesis of the present study, namely that women experience greater amounts of emotional engagement during reading, is simply not true – and that quite the opposite is the case. And this will of course have to be investigated further with different texts as well as different samples.

Yet, the results of the present study are worthy of a more differentiated analysis: How is it possible, for example, that men were clearly more involved than women while reading, yet, at the same time, hardly any different from women in terms of their reported proximity to characters?

A first explanation for this seeming paradox may be that men and women focus on different aspects of the stories when reading. In the reader comments, men frequently referred to the plot of a narrative and its characters. Women, however, focused their attention primarily on the characters. In addition, the scales on which the men's degree of involvement outscored that of the women's were mostly those that relate to the whole story and its plot – i.e. scales such as *suspense*, *pleasure* and *ease of cognitive access*. There were no differences between men and women on scales concerning the characters – i.e. scales such as *identification* or *parasocial interaction*. It is thus likely that due to their increased focus on the plot and story-events, men experienced more suspense and pleasure and accessed the stories with a greater ease than women did. This line of reasoning will of course have to be tested again, employing different samples and texts.

One other explanation is that women and men obviously have different types of feelings when reading the same stories – women experienced a greater amount of negative feelings (such as sadness, fear, shame etc.), men a greater amount of positive ones (such as suspense, interest, pleasure). The experience of negative feelings in the sub-sample of women might in turn have diminished the women's overall emotional involvement as measured by the scales of the questionnaire. This is yet another finding of the present study that will certainly have to be tested again – using different samples and texts.

A third possible post hoc explanation for the finding that men and women differed with respect to their intensity of involvement and were highly similar with respect to their proximity to characters is that men and women may *evaluate* their experiential states differently – when asked to estimate the degree of their experiential state on the scales of the questionnaire, men scored higher and evaluated their experiences as more intense. When asked to describe their experiences in greater detail and without any evaluation thereof, however, men and women spoke of similar things. It could thus be that men evaluated the same experience as more intense than women did. And again, this will have to repeatedly be put to the test by using different samples and texts.

The surprising results of the present study might, however, also be traced back to sampling issues involved: While it turned out to be quite easy to collect a sample of female participants, setting up a male sample required much more effort. It is likely that during the effortful recruitment of men, a certain stereotype like 'men are usually not involved while reading, and therefore not interested in a study about the emotional reception of stories' was brought across. Men who decided to eventually participate, were hence likely to be exceptional in that they were willing to face a 1½ hour study on reading and emotions and ready to deal with a 'woman's business' right from the start. In addition, it is likely that these 'exceptional' men were keen to prove that they were at least as 'good' as women in reading, too. Their effort might then have been mirrored in their scores on the scales assessing experiential states, since – as is widely known – a self-report questionnaire is more susceptible to impression management. Their effort to portray an 'emotional male reader' was, however, not reflected in their personal comments, since these are more descriptive, less evaluative and thereby less open to the participant's impression management. This line of reasoning once again renders it highly important to repeat the present study with different samples (while at the same time being aware of the difficulties of having men participate in studies on reading practices).

Coming back to expected interactions between the category of a narrative and the biological sex of readers (in hypothesis 2), results were again not in line with the hypothesis, pointing to the fact that the category of a narrative does apparently not affect the experiences of men and women in different ways. In view of feminist critical arguments, postulating a strong affinity of women for *fiction*-products, the present finding startles the researcher once more. The study unmistakably demonstrates that the category of a narrative is less crucial for an emotional reception than a narrative's thematic focus. Whether or not a story depicts the inner world of a character appears to be particularly vital for an emotional engagement during reading – especially that of women.

Expected interactions between the thematic focus of a narrative and the biological sex of readers (in hypothesis 3) were accordingly partly confirmed, indicating that women were in fact highly affected by the focus of the narrative, while men were less so. Women read with high levels of inner engagement if – and only if – what they read was about the inner world of story characters. Men read with high levels of inner engagement irrespective of what the story was about. These results might in turn be explained in light of the said 'plot-focus' of men and 'character-focus' of women mentioned above: Men appeared to not have any difficulties getting involved in outer-world stories, as the plot of narratives was highly thrilling for them. Women, however, obviously lacked their favourite point of reference when reading about the outer world of protagonists, i.e. when characters' feelings, thoughts and motives were not an issue.

In this study, textual features – such as the thematic focus of a narrative – in fact influenced the emotional reception much more than did characteristics of readers. At the same time, this study disclosed several perspectives for future research on biological sex and reading – one of them being *differential foci* of men and women on plot and characters, a second one being differences in the *valence* of the reading experience.

Most importantly, however, it became clear that (certain) men can in fact be more engaged during reading than (certain) women. And it became evident that men and women are not always different from each other but astonishingly similar in how closely they approach characters in a narrative. Central assumptions of feminist literary theory as well as unpolished data from representative surveys were hereby seriously questioned. Whether, and to what extent, the common literature on sex differences in reading is wrong remains to certainly be investigated in further studies. At present, however, it is quite evident that new and empirical beginnings for literary studies are particularly vital in shaking speculations about the nature of male and female reading – which do apparently not hold when tested in a controlled experimental investigation.

Taken together, one might conclude that the relationship between biological sex and reading as portrayed in feminist literary theory and many survey studies is not as clear-cut and simple as researchers would like to have it – several features of narratives, numerous characteristics of readers, and possible interactions between the two constituents do in fact complicate the picture to a large extent, and can only be disentangled within the framework of meticulous experimental studies.

Works Cited

Primary Sources

Bachmann, Klaus. 1998. 635 Tage im Eis. [635 days in the ice.] *GEO. Das neue Bild der Erde*, Okt.: 110-130.
Lem, Stanislaw. 1988. Ananke. In *Die phantastischen Erzählungen*, by Stanislaw Lem, 34-89. Frankfurt am Main: Suhrkamp.
Schlink, Bernhard. 2000. Die Frau an der Tankstelle. [The woman at the gas station.] In *Liebesfluchten*, by B. Schlink, 283-308. Zürich: Diogenes.
Seaton, Matt. 1999. Nachwort. [Epilogue.] In *Es wird mir fehlen, das Leben*, by Ruth Picardie, Matt Seaton, and Justine Picardie, 147-174. Reinbek bei Hamburg: Wunderlich Verlag.

Secondary Sources

Andringa, Els. 2004. The Interface between Fiction and Life: Patterns of Identification in Reading Autobiographies. *Poetics Today* 25: 205-240.
Appel, Markus, Erik Koch, Margrit Schreier, and Norbert Groeben. 2002. Aspekte des Leseerlebens. Skalenentwicklung. [Aspects of reading experiences. Scale development.] *Zeitschrift für Medienpsychologie* 14: 149-154.
Bonfadelli, Heinz, and Angela Fritz. 1993. Lesen im Alltag von Jugendlichen. [Reading in the daily life of adolescents.] In *Lesesozialisation. Leseerfahrungen und Lesekarrieren. Lesesozialisation*, Bd. 2. Eds. Heinz Bonfadelli, Angela Fritz, and Renate Köcher, 215-310. Gütersloh: Verlag Bertelsmann Stiftung.
Bonfadelli, Heinz. 1999. Leser und Leseverhalten heute - Sozialwissenschaftliche Buchlese(r)forschung. [Readers and reading practices today – social science research on reading and readers.] In *Handbuch Lesen*. Eds. Bodo Franzmann, Klaus Hasemann, Dietrich Löffler, and Erich Schön, 86-144. München: Saur.
Charlton, Michael, Christina Burbaum, and Tilmann Sutter. 2004. Lesen Frauen wirklich anders? Oder lesen sie nur andere Literatur als Männer? [Do women really read differently? Or do they merely read different literature than men?]. *Siegener Peridocum zur Empirischen Literaturwissenschaft SPIEL* 23: 3-22.
Charlton, Michael, Corinna Pette, and Christina Burbaum. 2004. Reading strategies in everyday life: Different ways of reading a novel which make a distinction. *Poetics Today* 25.2: 241-263.

Chodorow, Nancy. 1978. *The Reproduction of Mothering: Psychoanalysis and the sociology of gender.* Berkeley, CA: University of California Press.

Eagleton, Mary, ed. 1996. *Feminist literary theory. A reader.* Oxford, Malden: Blackwell Publishers.

Franz, Kurt, and Franz-Josef Payrhuber, eds. 2002. *Lesen heute. Leseverhalten von Kindern und Jugendlichen und Leseförderung im Kontext der PISA-Studie.* [Reading today. Reading behaviour of children and adolescents in the context of *PISA*.] Baltmannsweiler: Schneider Verlag Hohengehren.

Garbe, Christine. 1993. Frauen – das lesende Geschlecht? Perspektiven einer geschlechtsdifferenzierten Leseforschung. [Women – the reading gender? Perspectives of a gender-differentiated research on reading.] *Literatur & Erfahrung* 26/27: 7-33.

—. 2002. Geschlechterspezifische Zugänge zum fiktionalen Lesen. [Gender-specific approaches to reading fiction.] In *Lesen in der Mediengesellschaft. Stand und Perspektiven der Forschung.* Eds. Heinz Bonfadelli, and Priska Bucher, 215-234. Zürich: Pestalozzianum.

Gilges, Martina. 1992. *Lesewelten. Geschlechtsspezifische Nutzung von Büchern bei Kindern und Erwachsenen.* [Reading-worlds. Gender-specific uses of books by children and adults.] Bochum: Brockmeyer.

Heydebrand, Renate von, and Winko, Simone. 1995. Arbeit am Kanon: Geschlechterdifferenz in Rezeption und Wertung von Literatur. [Work on the canon: gender-difference in reception and evaluation of literature.] In *Genus. Zur Geschlechterdifferenz in den Kulturwissenschaften.* Eds. Hadumod Bußmann, and Renate Hof, 206-261. Stuttgart: Kröner

Hurrelmann, Bettina, Michael Hammer, and Ferdinand Nieß. 1993. Leseklima in der Familie. [Reading-climate in the family.] In *Lesesozialisation. Studien der Bertelsmann Stiftung,* vol. 1. Ed. Bertelsmann Stiftung. Gütersloh: Verlag Bertelsmann Stiftung.

Ibsch, Elrud, and Margrit Schreier. 2001. Reading Holocaust Literature: An Interview Study. *Empirical Studies of the Arts* 19: 65-84.

Jones, Ann Rosalind. 1981. Writing the Body: Toward an Understanding of 'L'Ecriture Feminine'. *Feminist Studies* 7.2: 247-263.

Klüger, Ruth. 1984. *Lesen Frauen anders?* [Do women read differently?] Heidelberg: C.F. Müller – Juristischer Verlag.

Köcher, Renate. 1993. Lesekarrieren – Kontinuität und Brüche. [Reading careers – continuities and breaks.] In *Lesesozialisation. Leseerfahrungen und Lesekarrieren*, vol. 2. Eds. Heinz Bonfadelli,

Angela Fritz, and Renate Köcher, 215-310. Gütersloh: Verlag Bertelsmann Stiftung.

Landis, J. Richard, and Gary G. Koch.. 1977. The measurement of observer agreement for categorical data. *Biometrics* 33: 159-174.

Moi, Toril. 2002. *Sexual/Textual Politics: Feminist Literary Theory.* New York, NY: Routledge [1985].

Oatley, Keith. 1994. A taxonomy of the emotions of literary response and a theory of identification in fictional narrative. *Poetics* 23: 53-74.

—. 1999. Meetings of minds: Dialogue, sympathy, and identification, in reading fiction. *Poetics* 26: 439-454.

Odağ, Özen. 2007. *Wenn Männer von der Liebe lesen und Frauen von Abenteuern... Eine empirische Rezeptionsstudie zur emotionalen Beteiligung von Männern und Frauen beim Lesen narrativer Texe.* [When men read romance, and women read adventure... An empirical reception study on the emotional engagement of men and women when reading narrative texts.] Lengerich: Pabst Science Publishers.

Osinski, Jutta. 1998. *Einführung in die feministische Literaturwissenschaft.* [An introduction into feminist literary studies.] Berlin: Schmidt.

Radway, Janice A. 1984. *Reading the Romance.* Chapel Hill, NC: University of North Carolina Press.

Renaud, Dagmar, and Dagmar Unz. 2006. Die M-DAS – eine modifizierte Version der Differentiellen Affekt Skala zur Erfassung von Emotionen bei der Mediennutzung. [The M-DAS – a modified version of the Differential Affect Scale for the assessment of emotions during media use.] *Zeitschrift für Medienpsychologie* 18.2: 70-75.

Schweickart, Patrocinio. 1997. Reading ourselves: Toward a Feminist Theory of Reading. In *Feminisms. An anthology of literary theory and criticism.* Eds. Robin R. Warhol, and Diane Price Herndl, 609-634. New Brunswick, NJ: Rutgers University Press.

Seilmann, Uffe, and Steen Larssen. 1989. Personal resonance to literature: a study of personal remindings while reading. *Poetics* 18.1/2: 165-177.

Stanat, Petra, and Mareike Kunter. 2001. Geschlechterunterschiede in Basiskompetenzen. [Gender-differences in basic competences.] In *PISA 2000. Basiskompetenzen von Schülerinnen und Schülern im internationalen Vergleich*, 249-269. Ed. Deutsches PISA-Konsortium. Opladen: Leske und Budrich.

Stiftung Lesen. 2001. *Leseverhalten in Deutschland im neuen Jahrtausend.* [Reading behaviour in Germany in the new millennium.] Hamburg: Spiegel-Verlag.

Tashakkori, Abbas, and Charles Teddlie. 1998. *Mixed Methodology: Combining qualitative and quantitative approaches. Applied Social Research Methods Series, 46.* Thousand Oaks, CA: Sage Publications.

Zillmann, Dolf. 1991. Affect from bearing witness to the emotions of others. In *Responding to the screen: Reception and reaction processes*, 135-168. Eds. Jennings Bryant, and Dolf Zillmann. Hillsdale, NJ: Lawrence Erlbaum Associates.

Part III:

The Personal in Literary Response

CHAPTER SEVENTEEN

THE MORE YOU SEE, THE MORE YOU GET: HOW SPECTATORS USE THEIR LIMITED CAPACITY FOR ATTENTION IN RESPONSES TO FORMAL ASPECTS OF FILM

JÈMELJAN HAKEMULDER

Abstract

The present chapter explores which factors may help us predict spectators' use of cognitive resources to process formal aspects of artefacts, more in particular movies. It will be argued that being familiar with story content allows viewers' attention to focus on other aspects of the representation, most likely the way in which narrative information is presented. In addition, there are reasons to believe that deviation from 'usual' ways of presentation stimulates viewers to pay attention to form. The results of four studies are discussed here to clarify the way in which spectators use their cognitive resources in an aesthetic response.

Introduction

A small movie house hidden somewhere in the city centre screens Radford's adaptation of *The Merchant of Venice* (2004). The audience is dead silent. Shakespeare's poetry obviously requires concentration. In addition, the movie consists of two major almost independent story lines. One concerns Antonio, who borrows a large sum of money to help his good friend Bassanio. Unfortunately his ships are wrecked at sea, which brings him into serious trouble with his moneylender, Shylock the Jew. Their contract states that the fine for not paying back in time is one pound of flesh cut from Antonio's body. The court decides against the Jew, though, and Antonio is saved. It is Portia, a rich heiress, who saves him from certain death in court. The second major plot line revolves around

Bassanio. He is in love with Portia. To be able to compete with his rivals poor Bassanio needs to seem wealthy. He overcomes the other suitors, and marries Portia.

Strangely, both stories receive an equal amount of attention. Shylock is a surprisingly well-developed character, almost more so than Antonio, the merchant of the title, and more than Bassanio, whose happy end concludes the film. Another remarkable aspect about the movie is that the screenplay seems to be aimed at making Shylock's position morally acceptable. In Act 1, Scene iv of Shakespeare's play Shylock reminds Antonio of the denigrating way he treated him in the past. The adaptation dramatizes this part of the dialogue, and places it at the beginning of the screenplay, showing Antonio involved in an ugly mob molesting Jews. Shylock speaks to him in the crowd, only to be met with his spitting. Before this scene the spectators are introduced to the context of the story. The following text appears: "Intolerance of the Jews was a fact of 16th Century life even in Venice, the most powerful and liberal city state in Europe." Some details follow about discriminating laws of the time. This is clearly not Shakespeare. Subsequently we see shots of the torching of Hebrew books, alternated with shots of prostitutes with uncovered breasts, and shots of praying men. The Gregorian singing in the soundtrack adds a dramatic effect. It seems the tone is set for what is to come. Radford thematises anti-Semitism rather than that he reads Shakespeare's play as expressing such an attitude, as some critics believe it does.

As people start leaving the movie house, a perfect opportunity arises for some innocent eavesdropping, especially for those among us with an interest in audience responses. Would it be possible to predict what we would hear people say? Does it seem likely that some spectators wondered about the structure of the scenario, that is, about the significance of the combination of the two stories? Were they puzzled by the prominent role of the Jew? As for the differences between the play and the movie, how would the adaptation affect those who already knew the play?

Some of these aspects of Radford's movie seem likely to draw spectators' attention, and in them they will experience an appeal to come to some coherent interpretation of what they have witnessed. In other words, formal aspects such as narrative structure and the choices made in the adaptation, invite spectators to search for meaning. The present chapter is an investigation of those factors that cause such a focus.

What would such examinations contribute to our understanding of responses to art? Some scholars in the humanities propose that form is crucial. Others would say it is utterly irrelevant. Briefly consider how the community of professional readers, listeners, and viewers respond to artefacts. Art disciplines are characterized by a wide variety of approaches. In several text-oriented approaches formal aspects are considered a key to understanding the work. Narratology, for instance, aims at the development of instruments that help to describe the way stories are told. Think of the typologies of speech and thought representation in narratives that are based on formal linguistic description. It is certainly the form of the texts that is focus of attention here. As to the study of the visual arts, certain approaches attempt to catch some underlying mathematical principles in the composition of paintings, statues, and architecture. Attention paid to form is also evident in the description and classification of style, ever since Vasari, to enable reliable attributions of paintings to their artist. Characteristically also, music scholars focus on formal aspects as well. The role individual composers played in the development of composition techniques is considered a deciding factor for their place in the history of music. Finally, in film studies too, it is not the narrative content of the scenario that dominates, but rather the way the material is organized that forms the object of research.

As this overview of research in some part of the humanities suggests, the work of academic readers, listeners, and viewers often begins by paying attention to form. The choice of examples is biased, however. In several fields of research formal aspects are not the focal point of attention, at all. There are too many aspects in artistic artefacts that are ignored by a strictly formal approach, such as ideology criticism, gender matters, or the nature of fictionality. The position of form in the perception of art, therefore, is not self-evident.

How would this be outside academia? In the evaluation of contemporary literature, critics sometimes aim to determine how well-made texts are, for instance, in examining the effectiveness of an author's style. In some widely held opinions about art education, students should learn to look beyond the surface of a work and uncover more profound levels of interpretation. Consequently, this attitude is also likely to be found among many readers, spectators, and visitors to museums. Art, literary texts, and 'serious' movies hide some message, in most cases one, that can only be discovered through reflection, close reading, and in general a careful study of formal aspects. It may therefore be argued that understanding response to form is essential to understanding of response to art and literature. However, form is not omnipresent in art criticism and education. Rather than training close textual analysis, some approaches to literary education foster the development of readers' personal responses.

Another matter to consider is whether spectators' or readers' attention to form is exclusive to the perception of art. Is it relevant in responses to non-aesthetic, or popular genres as well? In film studies, to mention just one example, formal analyses of shot patterning (i.e., the alternation and repetition of shots) is a method that can be used to analyse both 'serious' and popular genres, as the work of Bellour illustrates (see Stam et al. 1992). Although such analyses result in explicit claims about effects on spectators, it remains an empirical question whether form does influence audience perception. Average spectators of Hitchcock's *The Birds* are perhaps unlikely to note the subtleties that Bellour detects in his frame-by-frame analysis.

Intuitively, it could be assumed that form cannot be the sole incentive for spectators to search for meaning. At least one other possible factor should be mentioned here: personal relevance. It seems plausible that a perceived parallel between the fictional world and that of the spectator or reader makes the story meaningful. This is what some would call personal resonance, the "feeling a literary work (is) deeply relevant and meaningful," and that "occurs when knowledge of personal experience is mobilized while reading" (Larsen and László 1990, 427). Two comments should be made in this respect. First, research suggests that also here form can be a catalyst. Studies by Miall and Kuiken (e.g., 1994, 1998) have shown that the occurrence of deviation or foregrounded text features correlates with moments of reflection in which readers ponder on relations between the story and their own world. The researchers demonstrate that unusual aspects of style draw readers' attention, generating a sense of defamiliarization, and prompting them to reflect on the meaning of the phrasing. Such responses to deviation eventually result in a "modification or transformation of an existing concept or feeling" (Miall and Kuiken 1998, 2) and thus "…literary response has a critical function to play in alerting us to alternative perspectives on our self and on our social and natural environment." (4) The second comment pertains to the question whether personal resonance is unique to literary responses. It seems that the experience may also ensue in reactions to non-literary narratives (e.g., stories shared in support groups) or non-literary expository genres (e.g., newspaper columns). The effects are therefore probably not typical of responses to 'literariness'.

Understanding the role of form would help explain some of the most important phenomena in the production and reception of symbolic artefacts. One aspect relevant to the purposes of this chapter is the surprising amount of recycling of narrative material throughout the history of art and literature. The theatres of Ancient Greece entertained audiences with stories they probably already knew very well. The myth of King Oedipus, for instance, was known to the men who saw Sophocles' tragedy.

Moreover, through the ages the misfortunes of Oedipus were told and retold, albeit each time in a different way. It seems safe to assume that also after Antiquity many of the readers and spectators who were confronted with the tragedy were well aware of the basic plot. Nevertheless, over the past centuries the theatres were filled over and over again, to the present day. Apart from the recycling of the myth of Oedipus by playwrights, we also see the material turn up in films (e.g., Pasolini, Woody Allen), music (e.g., Gabrieli, Purcell, Strawinsky) and the visual arts (e.g., Ingres, Moreau, and Ernst, but also of course in Greek, Etruscan and Roman art).

What attracts readers and viewers to stories they already know? Aristotle (1986) says that humans characteristically enjoy representation: "inborn in all of us is the instinct to enjoy works of imitation" (35). It is in the execution that we find pleasure, not so much in the content. In several other places Aristotle emphasizes the importance of a style that is 'distinguished', by the use of unfamiliar terms, metaphors, strange words, or lengthened forms (cf. Van Peer and Hakemulder 2006). The aesthetic pleasure, then, that Sophocles' audiences may have experienced can be assumed to have been caused by *how* the stories were represented rather than by *what* was represented. A related argument can be found in the works of the Russian Formalists. Take, for instance, the distinction between *fabula* (i.e., the chronological sequence of story events) and *syuzhet* (the order and manner in which the events are represented in the narrative; Tomashevsky 1965). Knowing the *fabula*, it could be argued, audiences can use their cognitive resources to process the particularities of the *syuzhet*, and in understanding the purpose of choices made in the representation they find meaning and aesthetic pleasure. The present chapter explores spectators' uses of their limited capacity for information-processing when watching a movie. We will examine factors that may determine when they focus their attention on, or in other words allocate their cognitive resources to the processing of the *way* things are represented rather than *what* is represented.

Today an obvious place to examine whether these processes do occur is film adaptations of literary works. In terms of audience size film is certainly an important medium. Within the medium, adaptation of novels, especially bestsellers, makes out an easily underestimated share of the productions. Corrigan (1999, 2) refers to research that states that 20% of the movies are based on novels and 80% of bestsellers are adapted to film. Naremore (2000) mentions research that shows that of the movies produced in Hollywood 40% are based on books, theatre plays, television shows, or newspaper articles. It therefore may often occur that a part of film audiences already read the book in question. Adaptations are thus a potential gold mine for researchers of cognitive resource allocation. Surprisingly, however, few scholars have looked at responses to adaptations. Also, among the many theories of adaptation (Stam and Raengo 2005), we find few that may actually help us develop insight, by generating hypotheses about possible effects of story knowledge on responses. Whelehan (1999) is one exception. She predicts that viewers familiar with the story will be more involved in the choices made in the adaptation. One could argue that the abundance of theoretical reflection on adaptation by film and literary theorists is in itself evidence that knowledge of the story entices comparison of formal aspects in the representation. For example, many have analysed how certain formal aspects of (literary) narrative are transposed into film (e.g., Chatman 1980). Film theorists commonly analyse adaptations in terms of Genette's hypertextuality (his fifth form of transtextuality), looking at the relation between hypertext and hypotext, detecting processes of selection, amplification, concretisation, actualisation, etc. (Stam, Burgoyne, and Flitterman-Lewis 1992, 209). The output of such 'postprocessing' shows that professional spectators do relocate their resources the way suggested here. How would this be for other audiences?

To my knowledge there are only two empirical studies that are directly relevant to this question. In an experiment by Wardetzky (2000) one group of children was read a fairytale and then saw a film adaptation of the same story. The control group saw the adaptation only. Results showed that in comparison to the control group the experimental group had higher expectations, experienced more disappointment, but also that participants' retellings of the story were more coherent, referring to the written version rather than to its adaptation. Hakemulder and Ten Velde (2006) conducted a survey among the audiences of Jackson's adaptation of Tolkien's *The Return of the King* (Jackson 2003). Participants were asked to answer a number of questions concerning their appreciation of the movie. In the analyses of the data a comparison was made between respondents who had read the book and those who did not. It was found that Tolkien's readers did not differ from the other spectators in their appreciation of the movie. However, they did make significantly more comments on the movie when asked about aspects that had disappointed them. Most of their criticism pertained to differences between book and film (mainly concerning scenes that were deleted *or* added). On the other hand, participants who had not read the books made more comments on the complexity of the story (e.g., too complicated, too many side-stories, too much happening at the same time), and about the story itself (e.g., expressing their preferences for other outcomes). It seems that Tolkien's readers had the opportunity to use their resources in a different way than non-readers. Instead of having to try to distinguish the host of characters in Tolkien's complex mythology, they could focus on other aspects of the representation, mainly the choices that were made in the adaptation (cf. Whelehan 1999).

Relevant to our understanding of the role of resource allocation in aesthetic responses are also those studies in which participants are exposed more than one time to the same materials. In an experiment by Dixon et al. (1993) participants read a text twice, rating their appreciation after first and second reading. It was expected that the literary text read in this study, Borges' *Emma Zunz*, would reveal an increase in appreciation after the second reading. Based on the researchers' analysis of the text, they expected such an effect to be due to one essential aspect of the story, namely the ambiguous narrator. Therefore, erasing this aspect would not result in an increased aesthetic appreciation from the first to the second reading, referred to by the authors as an emerging effect. The results of the experiment suggest three factors that are relevant in aesthetic response. First there is the repeated exposure itself. The second time participants read a text their understanding of its literary qualities emerged. Second, particular textual qualities are responsible for this effect; if there is nothing extra to be discovered in the structure or formulation, a second reading will not yield any surplus value. Third, some readers will be more likely to detect such text qualities: in this study the emerging effects observed were restricted to frequent readers. Two other studies replicated the findings of Dixon et al. for other literary texts (Hakemulder 2004; Zyngier, van Peer and Hakemulder 2007). In Hakemulder (2007) the approach was used to examine responses to movies. Interestingly, the effects of rereading were examined in other research domains as well. Millis and colleagues (Millis, Simon, and ten Broek 1998; Millis and King 2001), for instance, showed that information that had been encoded during the first reading of an expository text did not need to be processed again, allowing readers to use their resources to incorporate new information into their representation of the text (i.e., their situation model). However, this held especially for experienced readers, just like the rereading of the literary text in Dixon et al. (1993) only affected frequent readers.

In sum, the rereading approach supports the idea that during the initial reading of the (literary) text, readers process only part of all the information they are exposed to (e.g., the narrative content), allowing them to pay more attention to other aspects (e.g., form) during a second reading. Although the results seem to correspond with the present predictions concerning the role of resource allocation in aesthetic response, it is unclear what readers and spectators actually do during second reading or screening. What is it they think they have seen the second time around? Which aspects of form did the participants in these studies actually notice, and which were ignored? In the study by Dixon et al. (1993), for instance, it remains unclear whether participants did notice the ambiguity, let alone how they interpreted it, and whether it was their interpretation that caused the increase in aesthetic appreciation. Moreover, conclusions in terms of causality require control over all intervening factors; but even careful rewriting of Borges' text, trying to manipulate only the narrating agent's level of knowledge, unavoidably causes many more changes. Consequently, we do not know which of these changes affected participants' aesthetic appreciation.

The lack of information about participants' use of cognitive resources during a second exposure allows room for alternative explanations. One is that they are an artefact of the rereading procedure itself. In a research procedure known as the 'mere exposure paradigm' stimuli (e.g., a piece of music) are repeatedly presented to participants. The studies show that participants systematically preferred stimuli that they had been exposed to a number of times over those they saw or heard for the first time. Zajonc (1968, 2001) attributes this effect simply to familiarity with the stimuli. This 'mere exposure effect' is a robust phenomenon, occurring across different cultures, and in responses to a wide variety of stimuli (e.g., the repeated exposure to Chinese characters, foreign words, human faces, classical music, etc.). The sting this research bears for our conceptualization of aesthetic responses as a relocation of cognitive resources is that the effects do not require participants to be aware of the stimuli. It is a fact well-known among advertisers, and it may have very little to do with aesthetics, at least not in terms of reflection or close reading (cf. Cutting 2006).

The present research

It could be, however, that the mere exposure effect of Zajonc (1968, 2001) and the increased appreciation for literary text qualities from first to second reading found by Dixon et al (1993) are two different things altogether. To find out whether this is the case we need to know whether participants do really consciously reflect on the aspects that researchers suppose makes the text relevant in a literary way. Four studies were conducted using film as stimulus material. Central to all the experiments is the notion that spectators of film cannot process all information at once. It is hypothesized that after second exposure they will use their cognitive resources to focus on the *way* a narrative is represented, simply because they already know what happens. In the following section the results of two studies are presented examining this prediction. Section 3 discusses the results of two further experiments that test the hypothesis that deviations draw spectators' attention to formal aspects.

1. Response to adaptation

In this section two hypotheses will be put to the test. First, it was expected that knowledge of narrative content allows viewers to focus their attention on formal aspects in the representation. Second, it was assumed that spectators' responses are guided by dissimilarity between the original that they know, and the way it was adapted (cf. Genette's concepts of hypotext and hypertext). Considering the arguments put forward in the introduction, including the results of previous studies, it seems plausible that differences between adaptation and original will draw viewers' attention.

Study 1

In this study seventy-five students of the Faculty of Arts of Utrecht University were asked to participate in an experiment as an introduction to empirical approaches to the Arts. They were randomly assigned to an experimental or a control group. In the experimental group participants read a Dutch translation of the first chapter of *Solaris*, a pioneer Science Fiction novel by the Polish author Stanislaw Lem (1961). The control group conducted a task unrelated to the purpose of the experiment – reading a story by Borges and underlining passages they considered remarkable. All participants then saw one of two sequences, from either Tarkovsky's *Solyaris* (1972) or Soderbergh's *Solaris* (2002). Both sequences represent the events describing the events of Lem's first chapter. The two adaptations differ greatly in the degree of fidelity. Tarkovsky stays very close to Lem's text, while Soderbergh takes a number of liberties with dialogue, setting, and the order of the events. It should be stressed that with so many different factors at play, it is impossible to make strong claims about the role of fidelity in spectators' responses. The two adaptations vary on many more variables than just the degree of fidelity. Soderbergh's *Solaris* is in English, a language probably more familiar to participants, and therefore more accessible than Tarkovsky's movie, which is Russian spoken. In addition, Soderbergh casts popular actor George Clooney as Chris Kelvin, the main character. Few participants will recognize Donatas Banionis in the Tarkovsky adaptation. Obviously, these potentially intervening factors prohibit causal conclusions about the role of fidelity. Nevertheless, considering the large role that fidelity criticism plays in debates about adaptation, a first attempt to examine the effects quasi-experimentally does seem worthwhile.

After the screening of one of the two adaptations, participants were asked to fill out a questionnaire consisting of open and closed questions. Respondents were asked to respond to a number of statements by indicating the degree to which they agreed on a five-point scale. Primarily the following statements are relevant in the present context: "I found this scene beautiful"; "I have watched the movie with interest"; "I noticed that I paid attention to how the movie was made." It was expected that on all three of these variables the experimental group (the one that had read Lem's first chapter) would score significantly higher than the control group (the one that did something unrelated to the film version). Furthermore, participants described what they liked and disliked about the scene they had watched. Here it was assumed that viewers of Soderbergh's liberal adaptation would be more inclined to comment on formal aspects than those who saw Tarkovsky's. Also, it was expected that participants who had read Lem's story would focus more on formal aspects.

The results revealed that the manipulation did not have the expected effect on aesthetic appreciation. Also, the groups did not differ in the level of interest for the movie. But of those participants who commented on the choices made in the adaptation we find 70% in the experimental group and 30% in the control group ($p < .037$). The groups that had read Lem's text made more observations about the mise-en-scene, the acting, the ratio between image and texts, also made more general remarks about the style of filming and the use of special effects. Knowledge of the story information apparently stimulated spectators to focus on formal aspects. However, this held for the Tarkovsky adaptation only (78.6% of the respondents in the experimental group made comments of formal aspects, and 21.4% in the control condition ($p < .05$). In the responses to the Soderbergh adaptation we see the same pattern (62.5% versus 37.5%) but the difference is not statistically significant. This was contrary to expectations. It must have been other factors than the level of fidelity that caused participants to pay attention to formal aspects. Possibly the way Tarkovsky imagines a trip to outer space was less familiar to participants than the way Soderbergh did.

Unexpectedly, an effect was registered on another variable, one that does not seem directly relevant to cognitive resource allocation. Two main effects occurred on a variable measuring participants' empathy ("Did you imagine yourself into the situation shown in this sequence?"). It appeared that the Russian adaptation caused less empathic responses (M=2.21, SD= .98) than the American one (M=2.97, SD= .89; F (1,64)= 13.5, p < .001). Again it could be that this effect is due to participants' familiarity with the more modern representation in Soderbergh's adaptation. Moreover, the focalization in the sequence seems to stimulate identification with the main character. The camera often shows close ups of Clooney as he explores the seemingly deserted space ship. Tarkovsky's arguably outdated depiction may have obstructed participants' empathy for the character (on the whole, participants' aesthetic appreciation of the Soderbergh adaptation was higher than that of Tarkovsky's).

The second main effect was found for condition: independent of the adaptation that was shown, the experimental groups scored significantly higher on empathy (M= 2.81; SD= .95) than the control groups (M=2.25; SD=1.00; F(1,64) = 5.61, p < .021). A similar result was found for the degree to which participants indicated they felt curious about what was to come in the rest of the movie. Again, independent of the adaptation that was shown experimental groups scored significantly higher (M= 3.36, SD=1.2) than those of the control condition (M=2.93, SD=1.2; F(1,64)=5.33, p < .022). It seems that the cognitive advantage of the experimental groups was not only used to focus on the way of representation, but also allowed them to be more absorbed in the fictional events.

As said before, working with existing materials invites a host of potentially intervening variables. However, one way to be more certain about causal relationships is replication. To start work on this, a second study was conducted using different materials. The choice for a different genre seemed important. In Study 1 the analyses of variance revealed time and again a role for one of the covariates. The degree to which participants indicated they liked the genre (Science Fiction) in general was shown to affect scores significantly throughout the data. Few students actually enjoyed watching this type of movies. In the next study, therefore, materials were selected that I hoped would be appreciated more by participants.

Study 2

In the second study ninety-one students were asked to participate in an experiment as an introduction to empirical approaches to the Arts. They were randomised across several conditions. The experimental condition read Paul Auster's 'Christmas story'. Participants then saw either the last seventeen minutes or just the last five minutes of the movie *Smoke* (Wang

1995). In the final seventeen minutes the character Auggie tells his friend Paul Benjamin a Christmas story. His monologue is exactly the same as Auster's text. In the interchange after the narration, some doubts emerge in Paul's mind as to the truth of the story. Auggie, for his part, does not do much to make him believe that it is indeed a true story. During the last five minutes of the movie, we see a representation of the same story in black and white images. This combination makes this material ideal for the present research. Wang presents an adaptation within his own movie. Moreover, it was expected that this cult movie would be appreciated by the students of the Faculty of Arts, at least more than the Science Fiction movie used in Study 1.

After the screening of either the images-only or the full version, participants filled out a questionnaire. They were asked to respond to the following statement on a seven-point scale: "I found this sequence very beautiful", "I noticed that I mainly paid attention to how the sequence was filmed." and "I watched this sequence with much interest". As in Study 1, it was predicted that participants who had read the story would score higher on all these scales. Also, participants who were shown the full version were expected to score higher than those who saw the image-only version.

The results show that the experimental manipulation did not affect scores on the first question: contrary to expectations, having read the story did not enhance scores on aesthetic appreciation. However, it was found that the groups who saw the full version scored significantly higher on the second scale (M= 4.22, SD=1.86) than the groups who saw the black-and-white images only (M=3.37, SD=1.89; $F_{(3, 89)} = 2.9$, $p < .037$). It seems that knowledge of the story did indeed stimulate a relocation of attention in favour of the formal aspects of the representation. However, contrary to expectations, there was no interaction between the version that was shown (full version or image-only) and the condition (having read the story first or not). The hypothesis predicted that participants who read the story before watching either of the versions would also score higher on this scale. However, this is not what happened. Maybe it is due to the fact that there were actually very few things that the participants could observe about the representation, since the sequence is filmed rather soberly.

Responses to the statement "I watched this sequence with much interest" did show an interaction effect ($F_{(1, 89)} = 6.9$, $p < .010$). Post hoc analyses revealed that only the difference between the two experimental groups was significant at the .05 level: scores of the participants who had read the story were less interested in the full version of the story than the participants who read the story and saw the images only version. This effect may be due to boredom, since the first group was exposed three times to approximately the same story events.

Both studies show indications that spectators' knowledge of the movie narrative stimulates them to use their cognitive resources to focus on formal aspects of the representation. However, the results only partly confirm the expectations. It seems that a more comprehensive model is needed to predict the effects. One suggestion already formulated in the introduction is that the level of deviation in a representation may determine how resources are used. In the following section two more studies are presented to shed some light on the subject.

Deviation

In this section we will look at the effects of deviation on the allocation of spectators' attention. In the introduction to this chapter it was argued that deviation from 'normal' representations focuses resources on those deviations. Two different approaches will be used to put this hypothesis to the test. First, materials will be selected depicting a similar situation, but differing in the level of deviant elements, as determined by the researcher previous to the experiment. The second approach used here attempts to manipulate participants' awareness of convention. Before watching a highly unconventional, foregrounded sequence, participants see a conventional depiction of a similar situation. In a control condition participants see a sequence showing events unrelated to that particular situation. It is expected that awareness of the relevant conventions would stimulate participants to focus on formal aspects in the foregrounded sequence. Combining the two methods should increase the reliability of the study.

Study 3

In an earlier experiment (Hakemulder 2007) a dinner scene from the movie *E la nave va* (Fellini 1983) was used. There are a number of devices used in this sequence that are likely to draw spectators' attention. For instance, the first half is in fast motion, and makes a rather slapstick-like impression, enhanced by hectic music and the abrupt movements of the characters. In second half we see character movements in slow motion, simultaneous eating their soup to the elegant music of the soundtrack. These and other peculiarities were expected to stand out more when spectators are aware what a dinner scene looks like in a more conventional movie, for instance in *Moulin Rouge* (Huston 1952). Here there is hardly any aspect in the representation that draws away attention from the conversation between the dinner guests.

In the experiment sixty-six students participated. In the experimental condition participants first saw the conventional dinner scene from *Moulin Rouge*. In the control condition participants saw an unrelated scene, a shootout from the movie *Witness* (Weir 1985). After this scene all participants filled out the first part of the questionnaire constisting of three open questions: "Please describe what you saw"; "What struck you most in this sequence?" and "What else struck you?" Then all participants saw the foregrounded dinner scene from *E la nave va*. After the screening they were again asked to answer the three open questions. In addition they compared the two sequences they had seen on a number of ten-point scales. The items concerned the degree to which they found the scenes striking, beautiful, interesting, poetic, surprising, artful, and the degree to which it drew their attention.

The results of repeated measures t-tests provide support for the hypothesis. The dinner scene from *E la nave va* was considered more striking ($p < .000$), beautiful ($p < .018$), interesting ($p < .006$), surprising ($p < .000$), and artful ($p < .000$), and it caught participants' attention more than the *Moulin Rouge* sequence ($p < .000$). Also, analysing the open responses revealed that participants mentioned more formal aspects to *E la nave va* than to *Moulin Rouge*. It seems that deviation in a representation of a particular event (a dinner in this case) causes spectators' to use their resources to focus on those formal aspects.

Second, to test the effects of awareness of conventions (an external deviation), the results for the control and the experimental conditions were compared. The results are not as pronounced as expected. Participants who evaluated Fellini's dinner scene after seeing Huston's conventional scene considered the former more interesting ($p < .020$) and indicated it drew their attention more ($p < .004$) than the participants of the control condition who had seen the shooting scene from *Witness* before they saw Fellini. Also, the group that was probably more aware of conventional representations made more comments about formal aspects than the control group.

The results suggest that deviation stimulates spectators to relocate their resources. Unconventional ways of representation draw their attention, and even more so when they are made aware of convention. Because this outcome may be due to specific aspects of the materials rather than a common phenomenon, an attempt was made to replicate the findings, running the same experiment but using different materials.

Study 4

For Study 4 a scene from Oliver Stone's *Nixon* (1995) was selected, staging a conversation between Nixon and Hoover. They meet at the horse races, which are clearly fixed. The montage seems to suggest a parallel between what happens on the tracks and among the two characters. Shots of the races interrupt the shots of the conversations. Some of the shots are in black and white. Some show extreme close-ups of the horses. Some are taken from odd angles. We see images of horses shifting over the tracks, and disappearing without a trace. It was expected that spectators' attention would be drawn toward these aspects, and even more after seeing a more conventional scene of a similar situation. In the Bond movie *A View to a Kill* (Glen 1985) we also have a fixed horse race. However, here it is an integral part of the *fabula*, while in *Nixon* the shots of the setting obstructed the direct understanding of the plot. Having seen the conventional horse race first, it was expected, spectators would focus more on the peculiarities of Stone's horse race.

122 students were asked to participate in an experiment. The procedure was similar to that of Study 3. Participants were randomly assigned to two groups. In the experimental group they first saw the conventional horse race from *A View to a Kill*. In the control group participants saw an unrelated scene (the discovery of the extraordinary gifts of Will in the movie *Good Will Hunting* (Van Sant 1997). After answering a set of open-ended questions, the same as in Study 3, they all saw the scene from *Nixon*. After this they again answered the same questions. In addition, they compared both movies, rating them on a ten-point scale for strikingness, beauty, interest, surprisingness, the degree to which they thought the sequences well made, and to what degree it drew their attention.

Participants' comparison of *A View to a Kill* and *Nixon* revealed that the latter was considered more striking ($p < .000$), beautiful ($p < .001$), interesting ($p < .012$), surprising ($p < .000$), well made ($p < .000$) than the former. This means we again can confirm the hypothesis. An unconventional representation of a horse race causes a relocation of resources. Analysis of the open responses also showed that spectators paid more attention to form when watching the unconventional horse race. On all three open-ended questions participants mentioned more formal aspects in response to *Nixon* than to *A View to a Kill* (all p-values $< .000$).

To test the effect of awareness of conventions, scores on the rating scales and the number of mentions of formal aspects were compared for the experimental and control groups. The analyses showed that both conditions revealed more mentions for *Nixon* than for either of the first sequences participants saw. Both the contrast between, on the one hand, *Nixon* and *A View to a Kill* or *Good Will Hunting* on the other, revealed highly significant differences (all p-values < .000). However, scores on the scale for attention led to significantly higher results for the experimental group (M = 6.68, SD=1.8) than for the control group (M=5.65, SD=2.1; t=2.6, df=119, p < .010). Apparently, being aware of the conventions did make participants more alert, though this did not result in *more* observations in the experimental condition than in the control condition. The lack of significant effect for the manipulation may be due to a floor effect: the number of mentions of formal aspects was excessively low for both *Good Will Hunting* and *A View to a Kill*.

General discussion: A new beginning

A small movie house in the inner city screens Radford's adaptation of *The Merchant of Venice* (2004). The audience is dead silent, partly because it is hard to keep up with all the mixture of story lines in the movie. One concerns Antonio. It is obvious that Antonio's love for Bassanio is more than that for a friend. Bassanio knows this, but still he wants more and more money from Antonio. This time his mind is set on an expensive courtship of a rich woman, Portia. When Antonio agrees to finance all the luxuries that Bassanio thinks he needs to win Portia's heart, Bassanio thanks him by kissing him, full on the mouth (obviously this is not in Shakespeare's stage directions). Bassanio does marry Portia in the end, but almost at the cost of Antonio's life.

We can infer much from how stories are told and retold, for instance about the norms and intentions of the narrator. After the brief synopsis at the beginning of this chapter, readers will notice differences in the retelling here, and hopefully, infer the purpose of the repetition. The research presented here shows that knowledge of a narrative stimulates a relocation of resources (Study 1 and 2). Spectators pay more attention to formal aspects of the representation when they are already familiar with the contents of the story. A second factor that was shown to be relevant is deviation (Study 3 and 4). Aspects that differ from conventional ways of representation stand out in spectators' perception, especially, it seems when they are aware of such conventions.

However, these conclusions were not supported on all fronts. One possible explanation for this can be found in the complexity of the material. Using existing movies enhances the ecological validity of empirical research, but because it is difficult to isolate one independent factor, the unpredictability of the outcomes increases. A related problem was that it was impossible to find materials without any (perceived) deviation at all. Participants frequently pointed out more deviation in the alleged conventional materials than expected by the researcher. To avoid such problems, the present studies need to be complemented with fundamental research, using experimenter-generated and -controlled materials.

Nevertheless, the present approach did provide more details about the effect of story knowledge on the perception of representations. It seems that the results favour one of the interpretations of the rereading experiments: rather than a mere familiarity effect (Zajonc 1968) it is more likely that aesthetic appreciation increased due to a better understanding of formal aspects (e.g., Dixon et al. 1993). These issues are far from resolved, though. It seems impossible to exclude the possibility that the mere exposure is at least part of the cause of emerging effects.

We now know a little more about how people's cognitive resources are used in dealing with artistic products, but we have also seen they can be used for other purposes as well: some of the results show the advantage of being aware of the story content. In such a situation cognitive resources can be used to allow the reader or spectator to be more immersed in the fictional world. However, we do not know what it is exactly that interests people in retellings. They may pay more attention to formal aspects during a retelling, but it is uncertain whether this motivates a fascination for retellings. Children who are read bedtime stories often cannot get enough of hearing the exact same story over again. We can hardly expect that for them the repetition results in new discoveries about formal aspects. However, it may be that this holds for children only. In a survey among students of literature, respondents were asked whether they could mention a book that they had read more than once. In their responses to the question to explain their motives for rereading, the largest category corresponds with the notion of resource allocation. Of the 74 students that responded, 59 (82%) mentioned a title of a book. Of these students 22 (37%) explained that they reread the book to discover new aspects. These results may be particular to the sample, of course. Further research should examine motives for rereading in other populations.

All in all, a step has been taken toward a comprehensive model of aesthetic response. Some of the evidence presented here suggests that resource allocation should be added to the available attempts to describe aesthetic response in terms of common processes of information processing (e.g., Berlyne 1974; Leder, Carbon and Ripsas 2006, Millis submitted). Perceived deviation should be part of such a model. This requires that one conceptual problem is avoided, namely that of a text-based operationalisation of deviation.

In the introduction it was briefly illustrated how widespread the phenomenon of adaptation is. The history of art and literature frequently shows the re-use of materials, within one medium, and taken from one medium and transformed into another. We have seen that in responses to adaptations, story knowledge affects subsequent information processing. There is no consistency in theory nor in the research results as to the effects this may have on appreciation. Keeping in mind the extent and variety to which adaptation occurs in several arts and media, but also the magnitude of the film industry, a systematic investigation of responses to adaptation may be relevant to parties inside as well as outside academia.

Finally, consider, again, the centrality of the issues at hand, by going back to the audience, quietly watching the film adaptation of *The Merchant of Venice*. What was it that brought them to the movie theatre? What do they bring home? If it is true that their attention for formal aspects is the key to their understanding, that it is the appeal to interpret what they see in terms of the world outside the movie theatre, and their own life, empirical studies of literature and the arts should contribute to a better understanding of such processes.

Works Cited

Aristotle. 1986. On the Art of Poetry. In *Classical Literary Criticism*. Ed. T.S. Dorsch. Harmondsworth: Penguin.
Berlyne, Daniel. E. 1974. *Studies in the New Experimental Aesthetics.* New York: Wiley.
Chatman, Seymour. 1980. What Novels Can Do That Films Can't (and Vice Versa). *Critical Inquiry* 7: 121 – 140.
Corrigan, Timothy. 1999. *Film and Literature: An Introduction and Reader.* Upper Saddle River, NJ: Prentice Hall.
Cutting, James E. 2006. The Mere Exposure Effect and Aesthetic Preference. In *New Directions in Aesthetics, Creativity and the Arts.* Eds. Paul Locher, Colin Martindale, and Leonid Dorfman, 33-46. Amityville, NY: Baywood Publishing.
Dixon, Peter, Marisa Bortolussi, Leslie C. Twilley, and Alice Leung. 1993. Literary Processing and Interpretation: Towards Empirical Foundations. *Poetics* 22: 5 – 33.
Fellini, Federico. 1983. *E la nave va.* Motion Picture. Italy.
Glen, John. 1985. *A View to a Kill.* Motion Picture. United Kingdom.
Hakemulder, Jèmeljan, and Ankie Ten Velde. 2006. Was het boek beter

dan de film? Verwachtingen, teleurstellingen en interpretatie bij de receptie van *The Return of the King*. [Was the Book Better Than the Film? Expectations, Disappointments and Interpretation in the Reception of *The Return of the King.*] *Tijdschrift voor Communicatiewetenschap* [Journal of Communication Studies] 34.1: 48 – 68.

Hakemulder, Jèmeljan. 2004. Foregrounding and Its Effects on Readers' Perception. *Discourse Processes* 38.2: 193-218.

—. 2007. Tracing Foregrounding in Responses to Film. *Language and Literature* 16:2: 125-139.

Huston, John. 1952. *Moulin Rouge.* Motion Picture: United States.

Jackson, Peter. 2003. *Return of the King.* Motion Picture.

Larsen, Steen. F., and Janos László. 1990. Cultural-Historical Knowledge and Personal Experience in Appreciation of Literature. *European Journal of Social Psychology* 20: 425-440.

Leder, Helmut, Claus Ch. Carbon, and Ai Leen Ripsas. 2006. Entitling Art: Influence of Title Information on Understanding and Appreciation of Paintings. *Acta Psychologica* 121.2: 176-198.

Lem, Stanislaw. 1984. *Solaris* (Orig. 1961). Utrecht: Het Spectrum.

Miall, David S. and Don Kuiken. 1994. Foregrounding, Defamiliarization, and Affect: Response to Literary Stories. *Poetics* 22: 389-407.

Miall, David S. and Don Kuiken. 1998. What is Literariness? Empirical Traces of Reading. Paper presented at the 4th Biennial IGEL Conference, Aug. 26-29, at Utrecht University, the Netherlands.

Millis, Keith, and Anne King. 2001. Rereading Strategically: The Influences of Comprehension Ability and a Prior Reading on the Memory for Expository Text. *Reading Psychology* 22: 41-65.

Millis, Keith, Seymore Simon, and Nicholas S. ten Broek. 1998. Resource Allocation During the Rereading of Scientific Texts. *Memory and Cognition* 26: 232-246.

Millis, Keith. submitted. Semantic Activation and Aesthetic Response: Applying the Construction-Integration Framework to Art. *Discourse Processes*.

Naremore, James, ed. 2000. *Film Adaptation.* London: Athlone.

Radford, Michael. 2004. *The Merchant of Venice.* Motion picture. United States.

Soderbergh, Steven. 2002. *Solaris.* Motion Picture. United States.

Stam, Robert, and Alessandra Raengo, eds 2005. *Literature and Film. A Guide to the Theory and Practice of Film Adaptation.* Oxford: Blackwell.

Stam, Robert, Robert Burgoyne, and Sandy Flitterman-Lewis. 1992. *New Vocabularies in Semiotics: Structuralism, Post-Structuralism, and Beyond*. London: Routledge.
Stone, Oliver. 1995. *Nixon*. Motion Picture. United States.
Tarkovsky, Andrei. 1972. *Solyaris*. Motion Picture. Soviet Union.
Tomashevsky, Boris. 1965. Thematics. In *Russian Formalist Criticism*. Eds. Lee T. Lemon, and Marion J. Reis, 61-95. Lincoln: University of Nebraska Press.
Van Peer, Willie and Jèmeljan Hakemulder. 2006. Foregrounding. In *Encyclopaedia of Language and Linguistics*, Vol. 4. Ed. K. Brown, 546-551. Oxford: Elsevier.
Van Sant, Gus. 1997. *Good Will Hunting*. Motion Picture. United States.
Wang, Wayne. 1995. *Smoke*. Motion Picture. United States.
Wardetzky, K. 2000. Märchen als Erzählung und Trickfilm: Eine rezeptionspsychologische Vergleichsuntersuchung. [Fairy tales as narration and cartoon: A comparison of psychological responses.] In *Märchen, Kinder, Medien: Beiträge zur medialen Adaption von Märchen und zum didaktischen Umgang* [Fairy Tales, Children, Media; Contributions of the study of adaptation of fairy tales in education.]. Eds. Kurt Franz, and Walter Kahn, 121-130. Hohengehren: Baltmannsweiler Schneider.
Weir, Peter. 1985. *Witness*. Motion Picture. United States.
Whelehan, Imelda. 1999. Adaptations: The contemporary dilemmas. In *Adaptation: From text to Screen, screen to text*. Eds. Deborah Cartmell and Imelda Whelehan, 3-19. London: Routledge.
Zajonc, Robert B. 1968. Attitudinal Effects of Mere Exposure. *Journal of Personality and Social Psychology* 9.2: 1-27.
—. 2001. Mere Exposure: A Gateway to the Subliminal. *Current Directions in Psychological Science* 10.6: 225-228.
Zyngier, Sonia, Willie van Peer, and Jèmeljan Hakemulder. 2007. Complexity and Foregrounding: In the Eye of the Beholder? *Poetics Today* 28.4: 653-682.

CHAPTER EIGHTEEN

REMINDINGS, UNDERSTANDING AND INVOLVEMENT: A CLOSE READING OF THE CONTENT AND CONTEXT OF REMINDINGS

CECILIA THERMAN

Abstract

This study re-examines the role of remindings in literary reading through a close analysis of the content of remindings and the context that elicited them. A new category system is proposed for analysing remindings. The analysis shows that the relationship between remindings, understanding and the reader's attitude towards a story is more complex than, for example, the theories of Schank (1986) and Seilman and Larsen (1989) suggest. It is argued that in the context of literary reading, imagination may be more important for understanding and responding to a text than connecting story events with personal experiences.

Introduction

It is a common assumption that a person's experiences influence the way he or she interprets the world. Popular psychology has taught us to believe that experiences mould our personality, our interests and our attitude towards phenomena in the world. It thus seems plausible to assume that also when reading literature, our experiences influence the kinds of things we pay attention to, the way we understand aspects of a text and the way we respond to it.

In empirical literary scholarship some attempts have been made to examine how personal experiences function in a reading experience.

Seilman and Larsen (1989)[1] and Halász (1991) were among the first to explore role of personal experiences in reading by studying the conscious remindings of experiences that occur while reading literary and expository texts. Seilman and Larsen argued that in the context of literary reading, remindings can facilitate understanding as proposed by Schank (1986), but most importantly, they contribute to a sense of personal resonance (Seilman and Larsen 1989, 167). Since Seilman and Larsen (1989), personal experiences have been discussed in many other empirical studies of literature. For example, it has been suggested that foregrounded language can prompt readers to think about personal experiences in an effort to create novel meanings (Miall and Kuiken 1994, 395). Green found that transportation into a narrative world was greater for readers who had personal experiences relevant to the theme of a short story (2004, 257). When examining how literary texts can deepen a person's self-understanding, Kuiken, Miall, and Sikora suggest that a metaphor-like identification is more important than a simile-like recognition of correspondence with previous personal experience (2004, 187-193). Thus, it seems that the way in which personal experiences influence reading continues to intrigue researchers.

In this paper I hope to provide some new tools for examining the role that remindings have in literary reading by proposing a new category system for analysing remindings. My approach has been inspired by the studies of Seilman and Larsen (1989) and Halász (1991), research on autobiographical memory (Berntsen 1998; Berntsen and Hall 2004; Conway and Pleydell-Pearce 2000; Singer and Salovey 1993) and a theoretical examination of the assumed connection between personal experiences, understanding and involvement. In addition to theoretical considerations, the category system is based on empirical data collected with a modified version of the self-probed retrospection method by Seilman and Larsen (1989).

My main argument is that in order to properly understand the role of remindings in literary reading, the content of the remindings has to be considered as well as the context in which they occur. An analysis of this kind reveals that remindings do not unambiguously serve understanding but can be irrelevant or even distracting. It is also difficult to establish clear patterns between remindings of personal experiences and the readers' attitude towards a story. This suggests that the relationship between remindings, understanding and perceived meaningfulness of a text is much

---

[1] See also Larsen and Seilman (1988)

more complicated than Seilman and Larsen (1989) and Schank (1986) propose.

I will begin by recapitulating the method and findings of Seilman and Larsen (1989) and Halász (1991) and examine the points for further developing in these approaches. I will then discuss Schank's (1986) view of the relationship between remindings and understanding. Finally I will introduce a new category system for analysis, and show what this framework reveals about remindings.

The retrospective self-probing protocol in previous studies

In the self-probed retrospection framework, readers were asked to make a mark in the text each time they "come to think of something [they] experienced at some time" (Seilman and Larsen 1989, 172). When they had finished reading, they were to indicate on a questionnaire whether they were an *actor*, *observer* or *receiver* in the remembered experience using multiple choice or rating scale options (ibid. 171-2).

Seilman and Larsen's main finding was that the number of remindings elicited by a literary text and an expository text was approximately equal, but the literary text evoked more remindings in the *actor* category. The researchers considered this finding to support their assumption that *actor* remindings are related to a feeling that the text is meaningful. In addition, they observed that the frequency of the remindings was highest in the first third of the text. Their explanation for this finding was that in order to get an understanding of the story world, readers try to recall helpful background information (ibid. 172-5).

Halász (1991) criticised Seilman and Larsen (1989) for the fact that in their investigation the readers classified the remindings on scales and categories that did not provide information on the content of the reminding. Therefore he asked his readers to describe the remindings in their own words. In his analysis, Halász (1991) created some new categories for the remindings. He found that readers would be reminded of other fictional works (*fiction* category) or world knowledge (*non-fiction* category). The readers might also tell something about their feelings and psychological states (*self-reflection*), talk about their views related to the text (*reflection*) or report their free associations or future imaginings (*imagery*) (ibid. 254-5). One of the main findings in Halász's study was that a literary text elicited mainly remindings of other fictional works (almost 50 % of the remindings) while a scientific text reminded readers mainly of other non-fictional works (also almost 50 %) (ibid. 255).

Thus, based on these previous studies we would predict that readers who find a text deeply meaningful have a lot of *actor* remindings, and that the number of remindings is larger at the beginning of the text. Moreover, almost half of the remindings evoked by a literary text are related to other fictional works.

Personal experiences and meaningfulness

The first issue I would like to address in Seilman and Larsen's approach is the ambiguity of the concept of personal resonance, which is defined as the feeling that a text is "deeply relevant and personally meaningful" (1989, 167). It seems that a text can be meaningful on two levels: it can provide insight into some world phenomena, or it can relate to a matter of personal concern. I believe it is quite common to feel that a literary text has something meaningful to say about a phenomenon of general concern, such as poverty or inequality; it is much rarer that a text addresses a topic of intense personal concern, such as a particular kind of triangle drama. Presumably the ways in which readers connect a text with their personal experiences and the *kinds* of personal experiences they think about is different in each case.

The second, and most serious problem in Seilman and Larsen's study (1989) is that because they did not measure subjects' sense of personal resonance, their data does not actually give grounds for any conclusions on how the *actor*, *observer* and *receiver* remindings relate to the perceived meaningfulness of a text. Similarly, because they did not know the content of the remindings and the way they relate to the context which evoked them, they could not know whether the remindings in fact facilitate understanding.

Finally, it seems that the categories of *actor*, *observer* and *receiver* may not capture the relevant distinction between remindings that can contribute to a feeling of personal relevance. A reader could be reminded of a routine action such as driving a car, while another reader is reminded of being told that his father has deserted the family. In the former reminding the reader is an actor, in the second a recipient. Yet the emotional charge of the experience and its impact on the person is presumably much stronger in the recipient reminding. Most likely a reminding of an unusual and personally relevant experience is going to influence the reading experience differently from a reminding of a routine action. Therefore it seems that the relevant aspect to monitor in the remindings is not whether the person is an actor but whether the remembered experience is likely to be important for the person.

Singer and Salovey argue that important personal experiences are marked by strong emotions (1993, 6), it would thus seem sensible to expect that highly emotional memories will have a stronger impact on the reading experience. The extent to which a reminding relates to the central content of the story also seems relevant. If one is reading a text that describes driving when performing daily chores, being reminded of one's own experiences of driving might add to a feeling that the text is personally relevant more than the memory of a disappeared father.

Hence, I propose that when examining how remindings of personal experiences influence a reader's sense that the story is meaningful, it is useful to distinguish between *ordinary* and *special* experiences and see whether these experiences are *repeated* or *single*. It is also important to note whether an experience is *emotionally charged* and how closely it is related to the theme of a text.

Understanding of fictional texts and remindings

The core assumption of Schank's theory is that "[u]nderstanding means being reminded of the closest previously experienced phenomenon" (1986, 24). A reminding occurs in a new situation that does not fulfil expectations, and its function is to provide information that will help to generate more accurate predictions (ibid. 28-9). Story understanding involves comprehending the motivations and goals of the characters. The "point" of stories is to reveal why an agent failed in achieving his or her goals (ibid. 30). The prediction that we can formulate from Schank's theory is that readers are likely to have remindings at points where something unusual happens, and that the remindings should help them to understand the motivations of characters.

When discussing understanding as an act of connecting new information with previous *experiences*, the first distinction that seems important is whether "experience" refers to a *lived experience* or an understanding produced by generalising from lived experience and other sources of knowledge, such as other people's testimonies. Schank stresses that his theory of scripts tries to explain how people generalise and abstract from lived experience, and how they create an understanding also of situations they have not experienced (ibid. 8-9). Hence, it seems "background knowledge" may be a more accurate term than "experience".

It is easy to agree with the idea that understanding happens in relation to background knowledge. I would, however, like to stress one activity that is central when people try to understand phenomena they have *not* lived through. When the relationship between *understanding* and *experience* is emphasised, it is often forgotten that our understanding of various phenomena is based on *imagination*.

In a discussion of the way in which literary texts are understood, it seems particularly important not to forget imagination. By definition, fictional texts are not testimonies of anyone's lived experience but *descriptions of imagined experience*. Although authors might incorporate accounts of lived experience in fictional works, they usually create multiple characters with different gender, background, and attitude, which means that they are no longer describing something they *can* know from lived experience. If the author cannot know the things he or she describes from lived experience but is using imagination to create a particular representation, then it follows that imagination must be a central tool also in understanding the description. From this perspective, connecting a literary text with lived experience seems less important for understanding it than is often assumed.

This brings us to the question of what it means to understand a story. I would argue that when the text has a mimetic function, i.e. is a representation of human existence, then very often it can be seen as an *invitation to imagine* what it might be like to be in the described situation, and to *reflect* on that reality. It is not so relevant whether one "knows" from personal experience what a particular situation is like but that one reflects on a depicted situation *from the point of view of those experiencing it* in the story world. When trying to understand a situation as it is experienced by someone else, connecting it very closely with one's own experiences may even be distracting. Moreover, it seems that comprehending the goals and possible failures of characters as Schank (1986, 30) proposes is only one preliminary step in understanding literary narratives.

I propose that remindings can have at least the following functions when they occur during the reading of a literary text. This proposal is based both on theoretical considerations and the data I have collected.

A reminding can most clearly facilitate understanding in the sense suggested by Schank (1986) when a reader is reminded of a familiar situation that shares an aspect with an unfamiliar one. For example, if one tries to understand what it is like to feed hedgehogs, it might be helpful to think about one's experiences of feeding other wild animals. I call instances of this type *mediating* remindings.

A reminding can also direct the reader to make a connection that goes beyond the context at hand. Members of this category I call *enriching* remindings. A reminding can also be completely *irrelevant* in a given context, for example, a reader might be reminded of the meaning a word has in another context. In some cases remindings can be *distracting* in a way that prevents the reader from considering the function that a passage has in a text. Finally, a reader can be reminded of an experience very similar to the depicted one. I call members of this category *knowing from lived experience*.

The experimental setup

Data collection method and participants

Participants in the present study were asked to read a short story and mark parts of the text that "catch your attention or remind you of something". They were told that once they had finished reading, they would be asked to list the expressions they had marked and give a brief description of their observations. Hence, the method was a modified version of the self-probed introspection first introduced by Larsen and Seilman (1988). I chose this method because it seems less intrusive and guides readers' attention less than, for example, think-aloud methods where readers have to comment on every segment of a text.

In addition, participants were asked to complete a questionnaire with open-ended questions on, for instance, the characters, themes and aspects of the text they found noteworthy. They were also asked "what feelings does the text evoke in you", and "did the text remind you of personal experiences, and if so did they influence your understanding of it?" The questionnaire was used because it allows one to examine possible relationships between the observations made during reading and the final conclusions. It also turned out that the separate question about the role of remembered personal experiences gave very valuable information that could not have been inferred from the self-probed retrospection protocols.

The participants were Finnish university students of comparative literature who are in their first years of their studies. The students' ages were between 19 and 25 years (mean 21.4 years). In this paper I am analysing the responses of ten participants, six females and four males. The participants completed the task in class as the first event on a lecture series on reader-response.

The story

The short story is "Aunt Elsie" (Elsie-täti) by the Finnish author Kjell Westö (2004)[2]. In the story, a male narrator tells his recollections of a summer in his childhood when his favourite aunt, Elsie, had a mental breakdown, and as a result disappeared from his life. The story is set in a very typical Finnish summer cottage surrounding. The setting is most likely familiar to the readers and might evoke a lot of memories of activities at a summer cottage. The story is 14 pages long (approximately 3,500 words). The text was presented without the author's name, though this was revealed at the end of the questionnaire.

The story ends in a passage where the narrator reflects on how the event influenced his family and uses a metaphor of weaving carpets. Many of the readers' comments that I will discuss are related to this passage, therefore I quote it in full. Henceforth this passage is referred to as the *carpet metaphor*. The narrator notes that

[i]n some cultures, I know that now as an adult, only God has the right to be perfect. When a believer weaves a carpet, he deliberately makes a mistake to make sure he is not boasting with his work. Whoever weaved us into a carpet had done the same. [...] Elsie, whoever she was, was the weaver's prayer.

What I would like to know is if, after that August evening when we found Aunt Elsie and the Aaltonens' daughter on the rock near the green house, any of us stopped accepting the carpet's small mistake, or if we all really did what we could.

Method of analysis

The main objective of the study was to do a qualitative close reading of the remindings in the context in which they appear, and to compare the insight produced by a new category system with the results of previous studies. Therefore I analysed the data both with the category systems proposed by Seilman and Larsen (1989) and Halász (1991) and the one developed in this study. The category labels and descriptions of them are summarised below.

Often an observation falls into several categories and has been placed in all the relevant ones. For example, the expression 'Her eyes looked like a perch's,' prompts the following associations from one reader "perch is

---

[2] English references to the story are from a professional translation by David McDuff.

some kind of national symbol, Juhani Aho? A symbol of anxiety." This chain of associations seems to evoke *world knowledge* (the fish is a national symbol) and *fiction* remindings (the works of Juhani Aho, a canonical Finnish author). The idea that the fish is a symbol of anxiety can be seen to *mediate* the reader's understanding of Elsie's deranged state, but the connection with Juhani Aho may also bring ideas that *enrich* the interpretation beyond the given context.

Table 1: Categories proposed by Therman

Closeness to the content of the text	Description
Close	The observation is closely related to the content of the text.
Intermediate	The observation is not directly related to what is happening in the story at that point but relates to the setting or another aspect of the story.
Distant	The observation has very little to do with the content of the text.
Role in relation to understanding	
Mediating	The reader is reminded of something that is different from what is represented in the text but seems useful in understanding an aspect of it.
Enriching	The observation adds a dimension that goes beyond the given context.
Irrelevant	The observation does not seem to be related to the given context.
Distracting	The observation seems to distract the reader from considering the meaning of an expression in the given context.
Knowing from lived experience	The reader is reminded of a similar personal experience.
Remindings related to personal experiences	
Repeated ordinary	An ordinary repeated experience.
Repeated special	A special but repeated experience.
Single ordinary	A particular ordinary experience.
Single special	A particular experience that is unusual, emotionally charged or otherwise special.

Table 2

Categories proposed by Seilman and Larsen (1989)	Description
Actor	The reader is an active participant in the event.
Observer	The reader observes an event.
Receiver	The reader has heard the information from someone.
Additional categories proposed by Halász (1991)	
Fiction	A reminding of another fictional work.
Text reflection (originally called reflection)	Reflection on the text or the described world.
World knowledge (originally called non-fiction)	A reminding of world knowledge gained from newspapers, school etc.
Self-reflection	Report on feelings, emotions or psychological states.
Imagery	Report on free associations and imaginings related to the future.

Results

Overview and general connections with previous studies

The ten participants made a total of 152 observations. The number of observations made by a reader ranged from four to thirty, with three readers making 4–5 observations, four making 13–17 observations and three making 20–30 observations. Observations belonging to the category of *text reflection* were made mainly by two participants: readers 2F[3] and 13M who made very few observations of other types. (The distribution of the remindings between the different categories used in previous studies is summarised in Table 3.)

Seilman and Larsen asked ten students to read a text of about 3,000 words and collected a total of 135 remindings. In this experiment, the corresponding numbers are 3,500 words and 152 remindings. Thus the results should be comparable. In Seilman and Larsen's study the proportions of the remindings were 61.5 % for the *actor* category, 13.9 % for *observer* and 24.6 % for *receiver*. Table 3 shows that when the

---

[3] In the reader labels F refers to female and M to male.

additional categories of *fiction, world knowledge* and *text reflection* are used, the corresponding portions are 13.8 % for *actor*, 19.7 % for *observer* and 1.3 % for *receiver* in this study. It is possible that some aspect of the text used by Seilman and Larsen explains why it evoked more *actor* remindings than the story used in this experiment. Another option is that when the readers had only three options from which to choose, many remindings which did not comfortably fit into any of the categories were placed somewhere nevertheless, and as a result the *actor* category grew much bigger than it does with a more fine-grained category scheme.

Table 3 also shows that the portion of *fiction* remindings is much higher in Halász's data (approximately 50 %) than in this study (19.1 %). One obvious difference in these studies is that Halász used a very short text of only 250 words. If one calculates the average number of remindings per person in Halász's study, the result is 4.4 per participant, whereas it is 15.2 in this study. Possibly the fiction remindings became accentuated by the fact that the story was short and did not evoke very many remindings per person.[4]

Table 3

Categories proposed by Seilman and Larsen	Actual number	Percentage in this study	Percentage in Seilman and Larsen 1989	Percentage in Halász 1991
Actor	21	13.8	61.5	~20
Observer	30	19.7	13.9	
Receiver	2	1.3	24.6	
Additional categories proposed by Halász				
Fiction	29	19.1		~50
Text reflection	35	23.0		
World knowledge	38	25.0		~20
Self-reflection	0	0		
Imagery	4	2.6		

---

[4] Another obvious difference is the age of the participants. Halász's participants were 17 year-old high school students whereas my participants were university students with a mean age of 21.4 years.

Remindings and understanding

Schank (1986) proposed that memories during reading assist comprehension by reminding the reader of a familiar situation that helps to understand a new, unexpected situation. We would hence expect the number of *mediating* remindings to be very high. Moreover, the remindings should be more frequent when something strange happens in the text. The data fulfil neither prediction.

I will first discuss the frequency of different types of remindings and then look at how the remindings are distributed over the story. The different types of remindings are summarised in Table 4.

Table 4

Categories proposed by Therman	Actual number	Percentage in relation to total number of *all* remindings	Percentage in relation to total number of *remindings of personal experiences*
Closeness to the content of the text			
Close[5]	53	43.8	
Intermediate	29	24.0	
Distant	38	31.4	
Role in relation to understanding			
Mediating	6	4.0	
Enriching	51	34.0	
Irrelevant	24	16.0	
Distracting	2	1.3	
Knowing from lived experience	50	33.0	
Remindings related to personal experiences			
Repeated ordinary	33	21.7	62.3
Repeated special	10	6.6	18.9
Single ordinary	5	3.2	9.4
Single special	5	3.2	9.4

---

[5] Observations in the category of *text reflection* are not included in the *close* category or the calculation of the percentage because they are obviously closely related to the text and mainly done by only two readers.

From Table 4 we can see that there are in fact only six remindings in the *mediating* category, corresponding to 4 percent of the total. It is more common that readers make connections that go beyond the immediate context of the text, which is shown by fifty-one observations (34 %) in the *enriching* category. The remindings can also be *irrelevant* (16 %), and in a few cases even *distracting* (1.3 %). Most of the remindings are very *close* to what is being described in the text (43.8 %), and when readers are reminded of personal experiences, the experience is usually in the *repeated ordinary* category (62.3 %).

Thus it seems that the remindings do not unambiguously only serve understanding, but have different roles. I hope to illuminate these roles with some examples, which also indicate relationships with the other categories, such as *fiction* remindings and remindings of *repeated ordinary personal experiences*.

In relation to Halász's (1991) finding that fictional texts primarily reminded readers of other fictional works, it is interesting to note that according to these data, *fiction* remindings tend to contribute to the reader's understanding of the story either in a *mediating* or *enriching* role.

A good example of a *mediating* fiction reminding is the fact that five of the ten readers connected the story with fairy tales, fantasy, or *The Lord of the Rings*. Four of the remindings were prompted by the capitalized names in the story, such as "The Land of the Tall Pines". The story itself is realistic, thus a reminding which connects it with fantasy may seem misleading. However, the capitalized names that have prompted most of these fantasy remindings are a key device in signalling focalization through the narrator's childhood self. Although connecting the text with fantasy may set up the wrong kinds of expectations, it is appropriate for building a sense of the child's way of perceiving things.

Recollections that enrich interpretation usually refer to other *fictional* works or *world knowledge*. For example, reader 2F connects the *carpet metaphor* with another fictional work (*Poltettu oranssi* by Eeva-Liisa Manner 1968) and "the symbolism of weaving, cultures where women have for centuries woven symbols and meanings into textiles." According to my interpretation the main function of the carpet metaphor is to illustrate that Elsie's fate caused the narrator to realise how important tolerance towards difference is. Connecting the metaphor with cultural practices of weaving thus goes beyond the most relevant context, but it seems an interesting addition to it.

An analysis of the *irrelevant* remindings reveals that usually they refer to another meaning of a word appearing in the text. For example, the metaphorical description "shook her head so energetically that the black surge [of hair] fell down over her eyes like a curtain" reminded reader 12F that "I should buy a curtain".

I believe that in most cases the irrelevant remindings do not inhibit the readers from grasping the contextually relevant meaning as well. However, there are two occasions where an association does seem to *distract* the reader from noticing the function of an expression in the text. In both cases the reader connects the text with religion. For example, the *carpet metaphor* prompts the following observation from reader 3M: "reminds me of my atheism and inability to believe in this type of text." Apparently the reference to religion triggers rejection. Yet it can be argued that the function of the metaphor is not to preach religion but tolerance, i.e. a goal that an atheist could presumably accept, if he fully considered it. Religion is often an emotionally loaded issue, and it seems plausible that associating a text with something that one feels very strongly about can be distracting.

Finally, we come to remindings in the *knowing from lived experience* category. Reader 1F's observation is a good example. It is related to the following exchange between the narrator and his grandmother:

'When are you going to tell me where Aunt Elsie lives in the winter, and how she's related to us?' I ventured.

'When you're a bit older. Now off you go down to the shore and fetch some water for your old grandmother.'

Reader 1F indicated that fetching water from the shore at the summer cottage is a familiar task for her and thus an example of an *ordinary repeated* experience. Although it may be tempting to suggest that this reminding helps the reader to understand the text, if one considers the matter carefully, it seems unlikely that the reader needs to search her memory for a corresponding experience in order to understand the description in the text. Furthermore, if one considers the function of the detail in the text, it is irrelevant whether one knows what it is like to fetch water. For understanding the story, it is much more important to notice that the water is a pretext with which the grandmother evades the narrator's question.

But, even if recalling familiar actions may not be *necessary* for understanding a particular detail, might they not facilitate understanding in some other way? It seems plausible that connecting a text with ordinary personal experiences can contribute to interest towards the text and a positive or negative attitude depending on the emotional colouring of the remembered experiences. Thus I am not arguing that remindings of ordinary experiences should be ignored. Rather, I believe that we need more detailed studies of remindings of ordinary personal experiences in different contexts before we can determine how, and under what conditions, they influence comprehension or attitude.

When the distribution of the remindings over the text is examined, we note that remindings are more frequent in the beginning and at the end of the story. The pattern of decrease after the first segment reported by Seilman and Larsen (1989) is thus repeated, but in this study the decrease in remindings is sharper, and there is another peak at the very end of the story. The number of remindings per text segment are summarised in Table 5.

Table 5

Segment	Number of remindings in this study	Number of remindings reported in Seilman and Larsen 1989
First (1,000 words)	74	~60
Second (1,000 words)	26	~48
Third (1,000 words)	23	~28
Fourth (**500 words**)	22	

Seilman and Larsen thought the large number of remindings in the first segment was an indication that readers were recruiting knowledge that would help to understand the story (1989, 174). It is plausible that some of the remindings function in this way. However, the first segment has also evoked *irrelevant* remindings, and as Halász pointed out, habituation and exhaustion probably are an important reason for the decrease in the number of remindings (1991, 248).

In relation to Schank's (1986) proposition that remindings are likely to occur when a person encounters an unusual situation, it must be noted that it is difficult to observe such patterns in the distribution of the remindings. For example, towards the end of the story, Elsie is spotted standing at the tip of a distant island howling like a wolf. This is the point where Elsie's actions deviate most clearly from any script of normal behaviour, but the whole page has evoked only one reminding.

In sum, the data suggest that the functions of remindings in literary reading are more manifold than, for example, Schank (1986) and Seilman and Larsen (1989) proposed. Remindings do not only serve understanding, but can be irrelevant or even distracting. Even in cases where readers acknowledge that they know a detail described in the text from experience, familiarity with the detail may be irrelevant for grasping its relevance in the story.

Remindings and involvement

Based on Seilman and Larsen's (1989, 173) theory, the hypothesis is that people who find a text deeply meaningful have many remindings of personal experiences where they have been an actor. The data collected in this experiment do not include precise measurements of perceived meaningfulness, but participants' comments do give an indication of their attitude towards the story. Some of them clearly expressed a positive attitude: "The critique of society was valuable and it felt good to see that someone else is thinking about these things" (2F), while some had a negative tone in their comments: "I doubt that texts of this type are needed" (3M), and some seemed neutral: "The setting reminded me of summers at my grandmother's place. It raised a longing for summer" (1F). Hence we are in a position to examine relationships between different types of remindings and participants' attitude. These are summarised in Table 5. The data are organised according to the attitude expressed by the reader.

Table 6

Percentage of personal remindings in relation to total number of all remindings						Percentage of *actor* remindings in relation to total number of personal remindings					
Neutral		Positive		Negative		Neutral		Positive		Negative	
1F	53	13M	6	3M	38	1F	50	13M	0	3M	17
12F	52	14M	15	6M	20	12F	38	14M	0	6M	0
		2F	0					2F	0		
		4F	75					4F	33		
		5F	100					5F	80		
		17F	38					17F	40		

The first thing that can be noted from the table is that it is difficult to find any clear patterns between personal remindings[6] and the reader's attitude. Low as well as high figures of personal remindings are found among those who have a positive attitude. For example, out of the readers who express a positive attitude, reader 2F has no personal remindings whereas reader 5F has nothing but personal remindings (although it should be noted that reader 5F only made a total of five observations). The readers who express a neutral attitude (1F, 12F) both made many observations (30 and 25 respectively), and approximately a half of their observations relate to personal experiences. Readers with a negative attitude also have personal remindings, the percentage is 38 for 3M and 20 for 6M. Hence it seems that the fact that readers have personal remindings while reading a story is not a sufficient indication that they find the story personally relevant.

The number of remindings in the *actor* category does not seem related to readers' attitudes either. Several readers who expressed a positive attitude towards the story have no remindings in this category (13M, 14M, 2F) although they did have a large total number of remindings (17, 20 and 17 respectively). The figures are low also for the readers with a negative attitude (17 % for 3M and 0 % for 6M). An analysis of the content of the *actor* remindings reveals that they mainly refer to rather ordinary experiences such as school and the kinds of activities performed at a summer cottage. It seems that connecting the text with ordinary past actions may not be enough to create a feeling that a text is *deeply* meaningful.

Readers' reflections on how memories of personal experiences influenced their reading suggest one possible source of personal resonance. Readers 2F and 17F indicate that they have experience of mental illness. Reader 14M says his godmother is "a lot like Elsie". Reader 4F mentions the feeling of "being left out from adult world" and the disappearance of a person. Reader 5F indicates that the story reminded her of how she inquired after her father when he had disappeared from her life. Reader 13M says he identifies with Elsie. In all of these cases the readers connect *a central theme with an emotionally charged personal experience*. It seems quite sensible that if one feels the main content of a text to be related to some important personal experience, then the text is likely to feel personally relevant.

---

[6] I use the term "personal reminding" as a shorter version of "reminding of personal experience".

Methodologically it is very interesting that four of the readers (14M, 2F, 4F and 17F) express the connection with their personal experience and a central theme in the text *only in the questionnaire* as a response to the whole text rather than in the self-probed retrospection protocol as an observation related to a particular passage. This suggests that although a detail might prompt an immediate response, readers may suspend judgement on their preliminary impression until they have read a longer passage and see how the detail relates to the whole.

These data suggest that readers who have a positive attitude towards the text have connected it with an emotionally charged personal experience that is close to the central theme. An intriguing question for future research is whether people can find texts deeply meaningful also when they do not primarily connect them with personal experiences. Research on autobiographical memory suggests one important methodological consideration for such research. Conway and Pleydell-Pearce (2000) suggest that conscious retrieval of memories is always guided by the person's current goals. Therefore the instruction to consciously recall, for example, the most memorable reading experiences is likely to emphasise memories related to the self. Thus it seems the best way to compare the characteristics of trivial or meaningful reading experiences would be to ask readers to record impressions soon after reading[7].

Discussion

The main finding that emerges from the analysis is that remindings seem to be a less orderly and purposeful activity than theorists such as Schank (1986) assume. Rather than appearing consistently in certain kinds of situations, for example points where expectations are unfulfilled, remindings seem to occur here and there, as something in the text happens to cue a memory. The process is not haphazard, because even the irrelevant remindings typically have a semantic relation to their cue words, but they can be coincidental in relation to the comprehension task. In this sense the data offer support for Kintsch's (1998) assumption.

The power of literary texts to cue memories also seems one potential way of changing a person's self-understanding. Accounts that have tried to define self-modifying reading experiences often emphasise the distance between the reader and the text (e.g. Iser 1978, 132; Kuiken, Miall, and

---

[7] I am grateful to Margrit Schreier and Elizabeth Long for comments that set me thinking about methods for further research.

Sikora 2004, 187-193). Typically such theories stress the aesthetic dimension of these experiences. However, the finding of the present study that readers who had a positive attitude towards the story connected it with an emotionally charged experience close to the theme suggests that simile-like identification is an important ingredient in meaningful reading experiences (see also Andringa 2004). It seems simile-like recognition can change self-understanding by giving the reader a chance to reconsider past experiences.

However, when considering the findings, it must be taken into account that the sample is small and a specific one: the participants were literature students and people with a different background might follow another pattern of remindings. The instructions given to the participants and the experimental set-up have also influenced the data, although it is difficult to know specifically what their impact has been. It seems the instruction to record two kinds of things; ones that either catch one's attention or remind one of something may have accentuated either category at the expense of the other. But, if there is such an influence, it may be evened out by individual differences as some readers have recorded a bigger amount of personal remindings and others have mainly made other types of observations. The fact that the story described actions familiar to the readers may have increased the number of remindings of *ordinary repeated* experiences, and the data need to be complemented with observations related to a story set in unfamiliar circumstances. I also assume that the number of remindings produced in the experimental situation is higher than in a natural reading situation. Finally, this study only examines conscious remindings. Below the threshold of consciousness, prior experiences and knowledge may influence reading differently from the way suggested by conscious remindings.

In addition to the empirical analysis, I hope to have shown that also from a theoretical point of view it is problematic to emphasise the connection between understanding and lived experience. If fictional texts are conceptualised as representations of imagined experience, then it seems imagination may be an even more important activity in understanding literary texts and being emotionally involved in them than a process of establishing connections with lived experience. I would therefore encourage a new openness in thinking about the relationship between previous personal experiences, understanding and involvement.

Works Cited

Andringa, Els. 2004. The interface between fiction and life: Patterns of identification in reading autobiographies. *Poetics Today* 25.2: 205-240.
Berntsen, Dorthe. 1998. Voluntary and involuntary access to autobiographical memory. *Memory* 6.2.03: 113-141.
Berntsen, Dorthe, and Nicoline Marie Hall. 2004. The episodic nature of involuntary autobiographical memories. *Memory and Cognition* 32.5: 789-803.
Conway, Martin A., and Christopher W. Pleydell-Pearce. 2000. The construction of autobiographical memories in the self-memory system. *Psychological Review* 107.2: 261-288.
Green, Melanie C. 2004. Transportation into narrative worlds: The role of prior knowledge and perceived realism. *Discourse Processes* 38.2.09: 247-266.
Halász, László. 1991. Emotional effect and reminding in literary processing. *Poetics* 20.3.6: 247-272.
Iser, Wolfgang. 1978. *The act of reading: A theory of aesthetic response*. London: Routledge and Kegan Paul.
Kintsch, Walter. 1998. *Comprehension: A paradigm for cognition*. Cambridge: Cambridge University Press.
Kuiken, Don, David S. Miall, and Shelley Sikora. 2004. Forms of self-implication in literary reading. *Poetics Today* 25.2: 171-203.
Larsen, Steen F., and Uffe Seilman. 1988. Personal remindings while reading literature. *Text* 8.4: 411-429.
Manner, Eeva-Liisa. 1968. *Poltettu oranssi: Balladi sanan ja veren ansoista; tapahtuu pikkukaupungissa kymmenluvulla ennen I maailmansotaa*. Helsingissä: Tammi.
Miall, David S., and Don Kuiken. 1994. Foregrounding, defamiliarization, and affect: Response to literary stories. *Poetics* 22.5.8: 389-407.
Schank, Roger C. 1986. *Dynamic memory: A theory of reminding and learning in computers and people*. Cambridge: Cambridge University Press.
Seilman, Uffe, and Steen F. Larsen. 1989. Personal resonance to literature: A study of remindings while reading. *Poetics* 18.1-2.4: 165-177.
Singer, Jefferson A., and Peter Salovey. 1993. *The remembered self: Emotion and memory in personality*. New York: Free Press.
Westö, Kjell. 2004. Elsie-täti. In *Rennot suosikit: Kertomuksia 1989-2004.*, 11-26. Helsinki: Otava.

CHAPTER NINETEEN

MEDIA RECEPTION, LANGUAGE ACQUISITION
AND CULTURAL IDENTITY AS SEEN
BY MIGRANT MINORITY CHILDREN
AND THEIR PARENTS

PETRA WIELER AND JANINA PETZOLD

Abstract

The goal of our qualitative study was to analyse processes of reading socialisation and media reception as well as related narrative activities of school children from different districts in Berlin, living in German and migrant families with varying social and educational backgrounds. Data are based on interviews with twenty-six eight-year-old children and their parents. Our results show similarities as well as differences in the values and norms about education and media socialisation between German-speaking and migrant families. Differences exist insofar as migrant parents carefully pay attention to the (second) language acquisition of their children and to the coherence of media experiences and cultural identity. At the same time, migrant families should not be considered to be a homogeneous group. We will argue that the success of minority parents' efforts to use and monitor media reception in order to sustain children's language acquisition and to secure cultural identity depends less on their specific cultural/language orientation than on their socioeconomic background and/or their ability to activate specific resources compensating social disadvantages.

1. Introduction

The original focus of our research project, analyzing children's reactions to the changing formats of the 'new' in comparison with the 'old' media, was complemented by a socially comparative perspective, taking into account the highly diverse social structure of a city like Berlin. Particularly schools situated in socially deprived neighbourhoods have a significantly higher than average proportion of children coming from migrant families, as our school survey demonstrated. Therefore, our family survey focuses on differences in socio-cultural orientations of parents, especially in families with a migration background. Children as well as their parents were interviewed as 'experts' concerning their media experiences. Furthermore, social interactions between family members in different contexts of media use and reception have been documented. From a total of twenty-six children involved in the family survey, we will, in this article, concentrate on the seven children with a migration background, which means that the German language for one or both of their parents is not his or her mother-tongue – Umutcan, Ayda, Metin, Kalina, Majida, Dana and Noah. Umutcan's and Ayda's parents come from Turkey, Metin's mother, a second-generation Turkish migrant was born in Germany; Kalina's parents come from Poland, Majida's parents from Afghanistan, Dana's mother comes from Croatia, the father of Noah from Ethiopia.

There are similarities between German and migrant families. German as well as minority children demonstrated great interest in all of the children's media offered to them during the project, and all of them mentioned specific preferences according to their gender. Besides, most of the children knew quite well about their parents' different evaluation of their preferred media use. Furthermore, all of the eight-year-olds seemed to be rather conscious of the fact that the parents' estimation of their children's media reception activities often differed considerably from their own – the children's – point of view. The parents of most families also paid special attention to their children's use and reception of television; some of the German and minority parents correspondingly mentioned their uneasiness about the children's reception of TV violence. In addition, all the parents agreed to the project's special interest in their children's computer-games.

However, the children in our study cannot be regarded as a homogeneous group at all. We found relevant differences in the domain of the children's language and cultural socialisation, especially in the group of minority families. These differences relate to the special status of 'German' as the second language for communication in the families, the cultivation of the parents' language of origin, the emphasis on their own cultural identity, the formal education of the parents, and the socioeconomic status of the families.

2. Research Design and Guiding Questions

The above-mentioned similarities and differences are supported by the results of thematically connected projects, e.g. the so-called FABER-projects, analyzing the consequences of work-migration for educational processes (Folgen der Arbeitsmigration für Bildung und Erziehung). In these projects neither of the following two hypotheses could be verified:

Firstly, the hypothesis that there is a fixed 'set of characteristics', which unmistakably highlights the origin of the migrants as an ethnic group (Gogolin 2000, 17).

Secondly, the hypothesis that differences of participation in educational processes could be explained by different ethno-cultural orientations (Ibid., 21). Rather, one has to suppose that differences of participation in educational processes are much more influenced by the particular social and educational conditions of the socialisation in the family (Ibid.).

As a consequence, our project is based on a similar premise, namely that reading and media experiences of school children are mainly influenced by the specific conditions of family socialisation. This affords a comparative perspective, analyzing on the one hand the processes of children's media socialisation both in the context of school and within the family, and on the other hand comparing German with migrant families as well as families with different social backgrounds. This is reflected in the research design of our family case study, based on ethnographic documentation and qualitative interviews, guided by the following research questions:

o What kind of media (beyond those offered by the project) are the children using during their leisure time? How are the media experiences shaped thematically and how is this articulated in children's dialogues with their siblings and parents?
o How do parents evaluate their children's media use and reception processes, and on what kind of educational concept are these judgements based?
o What do the children's recounts of their media experiences look like, and how do the children think about their media reception?

These research questions emphasise the decisive influence the family's interaction has for the children's media experiences. At the same time they take into account the possibility of any different perspectives of parents and children, and not least a possible tension between the participants' subjective lay theories on the one hand and the reality of familiar media reception on the other hand. With regard to these research questions, processes of minority children's media reception have been reconstructed, closely connected to the linguistic-cultural socialisation within the multilingual family contexts.

3. Language acquisition and enculturation of minority children

Studies of language and cultural socialisation of minority children are primarily focused on differences in the form and results of education in more than one language (see Siebert-Ott 2000; also Ehlers 2002). All these studies mention, for instance, the evident contrast between the high prestige of individuals' bilingualism on the one hand, and the potentially conflicting multilingual situation of minority groups on the other (Jeuk 2003, 50). A constant source of disturbance is the failing school careers of most children with migration backgrounds, especially documented for Turkish children with "insufficient German language skills" – a fact which has been well known for decades (Steinmüller 1987). This problem was documented once more in the recent international comparative studies on pupils' reading proficiencies. In the context of German as well as international research, it is of specific interest that the encounter with the culture of written language is seen as having a determining influence on the further development of the minority children´s language skills, e.g. their ability of story-telling in the second language (Knapp 1997; Knapp 1998, 225-244) or their sustained ability of reading in the first language.

Similar to our project, Ehlers (2002, 46) regards the family context as predominantly important for the process of (language) socialisation. She discusses several factors which are considered to have a key influence on reading proficiency in the first and second language. As a dominant parameter, she mentions the socio-economic status and the formal education of the family and its further influence on the prestige of a minority language. A study by Nakip (1997) demonstrates the important influence of the 'prestige' of a minority language for the linguistic enculturation of children from multilingual families – many Turkish-German families abstain from teaching their children Turkish because they fear social and educational disadvantages. Oddly enough, this observation conflicts with the widespread notion of many Germans that migrant families themselves – and particularly those of Turkish origin – tend to look for ethnic isolation, a behaviour for which cultural differences are assumed to be the decisive reason. According to Jeuk (2003, 50), this contradiction raises the question "to what extent the landscapes of meaning for members of a certain culture are the same or similar after all." In this context he refers to the problem already discussed by Diehm and Radtke (1999, 63) that "the concept of culture implies a unity of social interpretations which constructs and evaluates social, political and personal determinants hierarchically." Diehm and Radtke pronounce, moreover: "When cultural 'unities' are determined and 'foreigners' are 'labelled', an idea of homogeneity is attached that ignores a broad 'intracultural variation', which characterises not only simple communities but even more societies that are socially layered and functionally differentiated" (Ibid.).

The argumentation outlined above sheds light on the complexities of the reading and media socialisation (of a by no means homogeneous social group) of migrant children, which our project "Media Reception and Narration" is analyzing. The very fact of the 'diversity of languages' alone (Turkish, Polish, Croatian, Persian and Amharic), which characterises the socialisation of children with migration background in just seven families, points to this fact. Given the broad language range, one can also expect highly diversified processes of linguistic and cultural socialisation of these migrant children in their individual family contexts.

In addition to the socio-economic family context, Ehlers (2002, 47) mentions the cultural orientation of the family (as varying identification with the majority- or minority culture) and the aspiration to move up in the social hierarchy as most important for the bilingual-reading socialisation of minority children. With reference to seven and eight-year-old Turkish children, another study confirms that multiple contacts with Germans (children in the school yard and playground, but also with adults while shopping) are most important for the successful acquisition of two languages. According to Röhr-Sendelmeier (1985, 301), the frequency of language contacts is actually independent of a 'positive orientation towards the minority culture' and there is no relationship between language abilities of minority families and their orientation towards the culture of origin. These divergent results are of special interest for the present project, insofar as the preservation of the culture of origin is probably accompanying the cultivation of the language of origin, an undertaking which primarily has to be fulfilled by the families themselves and this mostly without any support of educational institutions like kindergarten and school. In contrast, empirical studies on learning processes at school come to the conclusion that disregarding the first language of minority children has persistent and negative effects on their 'language-self-awareness' (and also their 'self-esteem') which plays a dominant role in the explanation of differences in proficiency and success at school.

The appreciation of their own language and culture, which minority parents integrate as a part of their personal identity into family life – along with an open orientation towards the majority culture – will probably determine the self-esteem ('Selbstwertgefühl') of their children as well (Jeuk 2003). Not least the media reception in the family, the educational concepts of the parents, and the media theories of the children as well promise some deeper insights into how much support children get in developing (linguistic and cultural) self-esteem and becoming aware of "what they know and what they do not know" (Jeuk 2003, 55). Of decisive influence on the process of media socialisation are the literal practices and resources (starting a long time before children go to school) established within the family, as well as the accordant resources parents and children have at their disposal. Ehlers illustrates the precursors of this acquisition of literacy by processes of 'making meaning' with still very young children: "If children grow up in a milieu where multiple parent-child interactions take place, where stories are told and picture-book reading is a shared activity, then they can build up a conceptual basis which facilitates their learning to read and their development of mental concepts through reading <...> The literal practice in the family and an environment where plenty of printed material is on offer are important preconditions for learning to write. These are not only preconditions for recognizing and understanding words; but children also become conscious that print is meaningful, that in the process of reading, letters acquire a meaning, and that written and spoken language are not the same" (Ehlers 2002, 47f.). Ehlers sees only a limited realization of these preconditions in most migrant families. Especially in families with a low socio-economic status, not enough reading materials are available. It might also be that the promotion of the child's linguistic and cognitive development is insufficient if the manner and amount of the literary practice itself is insufficient.

Of additional interest for our study is the question of which language is used during media reception in migrant minority families. In this context Ehlers (2002, 48) states: "Not only do the literal resources and interactions influence the reading socialisation but also the choice of the language one reads and listens to. Therefore, one has to examine what kind of materials (books, newspapers, magazines, religious texts) is read and in which language." – Therefore, our project 'Media Reception and Narration' expands this perspective further by investigating which language migrant minority families are choosing when using audio-visual and digital media, such as narrative computer games.

4. Social circumstances of the participating migrant minority families

The children participating in our family survey go to schools in districts of Berlin with diverse social structures and neighbourhoods. This is also indicated by the socio-economic status of their families. Some of the families (Dana, Noah) do live in privileged districts, others in deprived neighbourhoods (Kalina, Majida, Ayda, Metin and Umutcan). But it has to be mentioned that those families who live in deprived neighbourhoods and under financially limited circumstances also take special care and make extraordinary efforts to make their lives as comfortable as possible – especially in relation to the interests and education of their children. With the exception of Umutcan (whose family has seven members), all of the children have their own personal rooms. The parents of Ayda and Kalina have reconstructed former storage-rooms as 'media-rooms' for themselves and their children. In all of the households there was at least one TV *and* one computer which could be used by the children as well.

There are obvious differences in the formal education and actual occupation of the parents in migrant families, ranging from finishing elementary school in the country of origin up to academic studies. Some of the parents are presently occupied in jobs below the level of their formal education, but some of them also work above this level: formerly: midwife, at present: doctor's assistant (Kalina); formerly: accountant, at present: job at a post office (Umutcan), another father, who formerly worked as a factory worker now works independently as a cameraman. (Ayda). – This spectrum underscores an observation of Jeuk (2003, 48), according to which especially Turkish families are socially deprived by low formal education, low income and/or unemployment. At the same time it illustrates that "migrated families in these situations develop special resources, which serve to compensate complex and insecure living circumstances" (Gogolin 2000, 22).

5. Education with more than one language and media reception in the family

There are also marked differences in minority families' behaviour towards living with more than one language. The fact that the project offered several children's media (books, videos, narrative computer-games) in the 'German language' to children who lived in families using more than one language provides a possible explanation for the detailed consideration of language education in most of the interviews carried out with minority parents and their children. At the same time it should be noted that in some of the interviews – which were generally focused on media reception alone – the two-language-situation was not mentioned at all, while it formed the 'leitmotif' in discussions of normative principles of (media) education and practices of media reception in other interviews. The spectrum of discussed principles and ways of promoting spoken language and literacy of the children ('mother-tongue', 'language of origin', 'language of the majority culture') is so wide that in some cases the boundary between 'first' and 'second' language can hardly be reconstructed. Some insights were gained into the status of German as the second language for the families by the language parents used during the interviews of our project. The Polish family (Kalina) and two of the Turkish families (Ayda, Umutcan) used the opportunity to talk in their mother-tongue during the interviews. Another mother (Metin), second-generation Turkish migrant, born and brought up in Germany, spoke German. During the interview with the German-Ethiopian family the mother-tongue of the father, Amharian, and the child's (Noah) abilities in two languages weren't mentioned at all. In this family just the forenames of the children hinted at a migration background.

All of the children chose to speak 'German' during the interview. When the children were busy with the books, videos and computer-games offered to them, they spoke German as well. The language of the media themselves or the language skills of the communicative partner seemed to determine the language of media-oriented communication. Moreover, there was no problem in communicating in two languages about a book or computer game in German. All the families use media in two languages, as the interviews document.

All of the parents – especially when both the father and mother are migrants – believed that well-based language skills for their children, above all those concerning the German language, were very important. However, the strategies used to promote the children's language abilities – in German and in the language of origin – differ a lot. Only in the Croatian and the Polish families was the parents' mother-tongue highly appreciated. In these families the parents also actively supported the children's acquisition of literacy in two languages.

"I have been reading this for nearly half a year" – Kalina
Kalina 8;7 years old; Marcin 11;6 years old; father: taxi driver, mother: doctor's assistant (trained as midwife)

Kalina's parents come from Poland, whereas Kalina and her brother were born in Germany. The children grow up with both languages, which is important for their mother: *"Though she speaks more German, she is a child who masters both languages"*.[1]

The parents mainly focus on promoting their mother-tongue, Polish, presumably taking into account the dominance of the German language. Accordingly, Kalina's mother does not worry about her daughter's German skills: *"If she ... reads a lot of books in German, then she talks better, she can express herself ... I can see that. For example, I have talked to her teacher and she said the same. So, she has no problems at all with the German language, which is also important"*.

The intensive use of media in both languages is one of their means of developing their children's bilingualism. Kalina's mother ambitiously learned German when she came to Germany, and she characterizes herself as an enthusiastic reader. She makes a point of encouraging her children to read books in both languages. Regular visits to the public library provide them with the books required. This reading though, is an exhausting and challenging activity for the eight-year-old daughter, which the following section from the interview shows: *"Yeah, he [the brother] reads better in Polish than me. And actually, he has already read a really big book [...]. And I am no further than ... page 145. [I: That's quite a lot.] No, I've been reading this for almost half a year"*. As well as books, other media are used in order to promote language acquisition in this family. Asked for her favourite program on TV, Kalina talks enthusiastically about a South American daily soap Milagros, which she watches in a Polish synchronisation. However, her mother's attention is directed towards the children's reading experiences – and Kalina knows about the hierarchy concerning the appreciation for the different media: *"My mother loves it when I read a lot. She's happy then. When I'm at the computer, too. Or, not so much. But she doesn't like me watching TV"*.

However, despite her mother's rather strict reading regime, Kalina considers reading first and foremost as a source of communication with her mother. The quality of their conversations is also apparent in the documents showing the family's interaction while dealing with the project media. Her brother on the other hand seems to have his own opinion about his mother's strict reading rules. His sister reports: *"My brother would rather risk his life than read"*.

"Sometimes she'll read Croatian on her own" – Mother of Dana
Dana 7;4 years old, Lukas 9;9 years old; both parents: psychologists

---

[1] For the sake of comprehension the interview transcripts are not literally translated.

Dana's mother comes from Croatia, her father is German. Similar to Kalina's mother, Dana's mother has a strong interest in her daughter's learning her mother-tongue Croatian, and she also strives for a bilingual literalisation. Through their Croatian housekeeper Milka, who takes care of the children in the afternoon, they come into contact with the Croatian language in everyday situations so that the support in this family doesn't appear as forced as in Kalina's family. Dana's mother describes the housekeeper's function as follows: *"What is important about her [Milka], is that she speaks my mother-tongue, namely Croatian. [...] She is a bit like a grandma. [...] After Dana has been to school she speaks Croatian at home and she gets something to eat, something warm"*.

The family's language-support concept is evidence of the privileged circumstances of an academic family, and comes close to the "elite-bilingualism" as described by Jeuk (2003, 43). Although Dana's mother describes Milka as an important partner for media-reception and playing, Dana herself emphasises the significance the mother has for her: *"With mama I speak the most. [I: And what about Milka who takes care of you? Not so much?] No"*.

Books play an important role in this family; however, reading in Croatian is not a rule – another characteristic which distinguishes them from the Polish family, as the following statement from the mother shows: *"She [Dana] also has [books] in Croatian, but she is not so interested. She has books in the second language, the bible for example, the bible for children, but, well, I also encourage her to read in my language, so that she learns how to read. [...] I don't push her though because I have heard that it is better if one language is basic and well-learned, both writing and reading. And then you introduce the second one. [...] And so I just leave her the books and she sometimes reads Croatian on her own"*.

Dana affirms her mother's estimation and refers to Croatian fairy tales as her favourite book: *"[I: What is your favourite book?] ++ Croatian fairy tales"*. Dana's mother has a strong appreciation for cultural assets. She emphatically emphasises the high quality of Croatian films and criticises German synchronisations: *"What shocked me was how mild this German version was. [...] It [the Croatian version] is much more dramatic and intensive and// [...] it really is full of drama and passion and the German version is somehow so shallow and flat so ( ). [...] For Goodness sake! No indication of a disaster and it's not true that he is fighting evil. Those [...] bridges between cultures. This is highly interesting"*.

"It's just that German seems to be easier for her" – Father of Ayda
Ayda 9;4 years old; Ismet 15;0 years old; father: cameraman, mother: housewife

Ayda's parents come from Turkey. The interview with the parents is held in Turkish, the one with Ayda in German, her preferred language. Her parents approve of their children speaking German amongst each other. They even sent Ayda to a confessional (Catholic) German kindergarten in order to expose her to German at an early age. Her father explains Ayda's preference for German with the fact that she is exposed to German at school: *"The child learns reading and writing in German. [...] And so throughout her life German will thus be easier for her"*. He knows that Ayda's Turkish is not perfect but he does not seem to worry: *"She asks questions in Turkish but she is not able to construct sentences in the right way. [...] These sentences are then quite amusing"*. Moreover, the father makes this observation: *"I have noticed this. She always told fairy tales to her dolls in German. [...] She never told the stories in Turkish. How about that? When a child tells something from its own imagination, it's just that German seems to be easier for her. Therefore she shouldn't be pressed too much to [learn] Turkish"*.

Stories play a major role in the family's everyday life. Parents and daughter regularly visit a large bookshop with *"seating accommodation"* where they forage *"for hours"* and where *"the ice cream parlour is right around the corner"*. Whereas the intensive reading practice of the family is described with a fullness of detail, the situation of living with two languages, or even the promotion of language skills are scarcely mentioned. Most characteristic for this family is that the daughter's interests and needs take a central role for her parents: *"I just wonder what she could be interested in"* (father). At the same time the parents do have a decided concept of education concerning media reception, in which books are especially considered important. Watching television is less appreciated by the parents, an evaluation Ayda is conscious of, too: *"She [the mother] doesn't want me to watch TV, but they like it when I read"*. The parents provide their daughter with the media to suit her needs, for example with her preference for specialised books on philosophical questions for children etc. That Ayda is a critical and ambitious reader becomes apparent during her interview. Asked about her favourite book she talks about a book she got from her teacher. Asked why she likes this book most, she answers: *"I like this book most because the other books are more for little children"*.

Also noticeable about this family is the relation between Ayda and her parents, which in some areas seems to be on an equal footing. One recording of a situation from our project, where father and daughter play a computer game, shows how Ayda teaches her father how to play a computer game after he asked her how it worked.

Although the parents do not explicitly promote an awareness of the Turkish culture, Ayda does concern herself with Turkish identity as the following interview sequence shows: "*[I: Do you have a favourite TV series?] Well, it's actually for grown ups: 'Alarm for Cobra 11'. [I: And do you have a favourite character?] There are two men who are policemen. [...] There is a Turkish man. [...] And another who is German*".

„At school you read to get a grade, but at home, too" – Metin
Metin 9;0 years old; father: unemployed (presently acquires a taxi driver's licence), mother: shop assistant (presently not working because she is expecting her second child)

Metin's father comes from Turkey and speaks little German. His mother was born in Germany but has Turkish parents; she speaks German with a Turkish influence. Throughout the interview she emphasises the importance of acquiring and promoting the dominant language German: "*But Metin and I we generally speak German at home anyway. We also generally read in German because we say he goes to a German school. ( ) You cannot get around it. So he has to learn German. [...] And if one day he learns Turkish but I mean really well [...], why not, he can read Turkish as far as I'm concerned*". Speaking the father's mother tongue, Turkish seems to be more of a necessity than an advantage for her son. The mother notes that Metin has to speak Turkish with his father and does not acknowledge the potential the Turkish language has to offer.

The mother describes herself and her husband as versatile readers: "*But as I already said, well, me and my husband, we are more occupied with reading. Everything that is new, that ought to be read from newspapers, magazines, from novels, well, autobiographies, well, we always read. [...] That's why we don't understand why he doesn't resemble us. [Interviewer: Everyone is different after all.] I'm afraid so. [...] Well, I'll put it this way, he's not a keen reader*". This evaluation is a clear contrast to Metin's fondness for stories on dinosaurs and not least his distinct interest for scary ghost stories "*because I love reading them*". Metin's preferences could be interpreted as a response to the strong concern of his mother when it comes to violence in media, a big issue which at times even dominates the interview. The mother has a very protective attitude, and very much fears the impact of potentially violent media content, which she even sees in Pippi Langstrumpf and Tom and Jerry.

Asked the question, which sort of media reception mother and son shared together, the mother answered that she *"would prefer reading"* and she explains this as follows: *"On the one hand he should read this, because whatever you are reading, you will remember it. You will always keep it in mind. Even a few years later you can say, oh, I've read this book. This is the same for adults, too"*. In this family reading is closely connected with the intention of promoting the child's cognitive (and linguistic) development – and encouraged with some pressure. *"Well to be honest, I have been reading a lot to him. <...> Today, to be honest, I did, because he won't do it himself. If I say, I insist you do it, I want you to read once more, then he will read, then it's okay. [I: And then he likes to do it.] Then it works. Then I'll ask him, what he has been reading, whether he understood this, and he is able to repeat it for me. It works, for heaven's sake"*. Reading to the child does not seem to be important any longer: *"Now we've changed roles of course. Now he reads to me"*. Metin, who says that he sometimes reads with his mother, but less with his father, prefers reading at school because *"they help you there"*. A characteristic sign of the reading socialisation in Metin's family is the mother's particular concentration on reading skills, which are promoted vigorously.

The mother's other main concern is that her son gets on and works his way up in Germany: *"I expect him later to give me back what I give to him now, when he's old enough. Well, I would like my son to get a better education than me. He can be an engineer or doctor as far as I'm concerned .. so that he could .. how can I say it that he becomes someone who is accepted instead of someone where they say: 'Ugh! Piss off!'"*. Her concept of learning becomes apparent at several points in the interview, which could be exemplified by the following statement: *"Yes, there are words he doesn't understand, of course. Then I say: 'Keep them up there, remember them, because you'll hear these words again'"*. For someone who thinks like this, processes of learning and reading are primarily a sort of storing of linguistic data, which are always recallable. Metin's statement that „*At school you read to get a grade, but at home too*" illustrates how he perceives his mother's concept of reading.

"**We normally watch German television series so that […] the children's German keeps up to scratch**" – **Mother of Umutcan**
Umutcan 9;0 years old; Ilknur 15;7 years old; Onur 13;8 years old; Betül 11;6 years old; Kevser 5;8 years old; father: works at a post office (formally educated as tax advisor), mother: housewife.

Umutcan's parents come from Turkey and speak only a little German. The interview is held in Turkish. Among themselves the children predominantly speak German. This too confirms one of Jeuk's observations (2002, 198), according to which the acquisition of German language skills is especially easier for younger children whose older siblings already have introduced and established German as the family's main language in place of the parents' language of origin. The parents pay attention to the children's German skills, whereas Turkish skills are not an issue; no special promotion of that language is mentioned. Although the parents proudly emphasise Umutcan's good reading skills, the book, in this family, is a rather separating medium. His mother notes: *"Well, we watch the telly together, but don't read books together. [...] Television, because the books I read he doesn't understand anyway. They're in Turkish"*. Umutcan is also proud of his reading skills, however, he seems to be especially enthusiastic about the latest technical equipment: *"Yes, but I want a laser (computer-)mouse like Tolga [cousin]. A laser keyboard and a laser mouse. [...] What I hate most about my computer is because it's Windows 98. [...] My cousin has Windows XP"*.

TV is the shared medium which the mother regards as helpful for promoting their children's German skills: *"[...] although to be honest I don't switch the TV on when they're at home. Or only for a certain time because I think otherwise their German may suffer, and I don't want that. Every now and then or when their father is at home, we normally watch German TV series so that [...] the children's German doesn't suffer"*. The parent's way of promoting their children's language skills appears a little awkward and clumsy, yet it has to be considered against the background of their own inability to promote the children's German skills.

The importance the parents attach to the acquisition of German becomes apparent when they talk about the German kindergarten. In terms of cultural values the father judges the kindergarten rather critically, in terms of language acquisition positively: „*In kindergarten there's only one good thing: Their German has improved. [...] Yes! We have to show them certain things then which have to do with our own culture. If we don't do this there will be a break*".

6. Conclusions

The reconstructive analysis of our data demonstrates that media reception and language enculturation (in both languages) are closely connected in migrant minority families, while cultural identity is not necessarily regarded as an integral part of this relationship. All of the observed families use media in order to promote the language skills of

their children. At the same time there are different modes of promoting them.
- o   In some cases the language of origin is absolutely necessary for the communication of the family and its cultivation is primarily a 'necessary evil'; the reception of German media is reduced to the desired effects for promoting the acquisition of the second language (compare Umutcan, Metin).
- o   In other cases the acquisition and the improvement of the first and second language of the children, including the acquisition of literacy in both languages, is promoted in a very goal-oriented, sometimes rather strict way; the media are consequently used in both languages (compare Kalina).
- o   Another type could be labelled conceptual promotion of first and second language acquisition, including the encounter with literacy in both languages; efforts of promotion principally pay regard to the child's development and try to take her or his needs and wishes into account, but also to establish 'shared interests' (compare Ayda, Dana).

One may argue that especially the last two mentioned modes of promoting children's language skills are more likely to be successful, because they include the use of stories, the appreciation of their specific content as well as their aesthetic composition. Furthermore, parents demonstrate a self-confident attitude towards their own culture and language of origin, while sharing reading and media experiences from this culture with their children (compare the comments of Dana's mother on the specific aesthetics of Croatian fairy-tales). However, none of these modes can be unambiguously recommended or discarded. In addition, our categorisation of these modes relating to the children is only provisional. In order to describe more precisely the extent to which the various processes of media reception will be decisive for the successful promotion of children's language skills, one has to take further data into account. In this respect the (quality of) parent-child-interaction during media reception, which also has been documented, promises some deeper insights. Defining the 'quality' of this type of parent-child-interaction in terms of 'symmetry', one finds multiple indices in the communication of Ayda's family, but just a few ones in Dana's family. In a similar way, the enjoyment which Kalina and her mother show when talking about books illustrates the girl's motivation to read more convincingly than the rather rigorous reading promotion concept of her mother.

In all of the families, the parents' educational concepts (concerning the relationship of media reception and promoting children's language skills), the 'media theories' of the children and the families' actual practice of media reception – whether congruous or not – nevertheless seem to show a dynamic and mutual relationship. This insight also sheds light on the previously mentioned factors of influence on reading and media socialisation, e.g. the 'socioeconomic status', the 'cultural orientation' of the families, or the 'language chosen during media reception'. Any of these factors – including the parents' German language skills, which highly vary in all of the families, independent of their socio-cultural orientation – have a determining influence on the children's skills in two languages. Consequently, the spectrum of these factors should be regarded as an interactional system of flexible entities. This is accomplished by every family's individual capacity of activating special resources in order to compensate social disadvantages. According to the certainly limited data of our qualitative case study that should be treated cautiously, the most decisive factor of influence on the socialisation of children with migration backgrounds is the parents' consciousness of the child as the subject of learning in processes of language-skill acquisition and the development of cultural identity as well. In this respect the two following comments of a Turkish father, a former factory worker, allow a certain optimism:

> "And we just try by doing these things Ayda is interested in, what she likes, to get her used to these reading habits"

> "She get's on, when she goes to the library, goes swimming, you know, mixing with people".

This implicit educational concept underlines migrant minority families' ability to activate specific resources compensating educational deficits and social disadvantages. Contrary to common belief, we may conclude, at least, that migrant minority parents' language skills in their mother-tongue, or the majority language, are scarcely so bad that they should avoid talking and reading to their children.

Works Cited

Diehm, Isabell, Radtke, and Frank-Olaf . 1999. *Erziehung und Migration* [Education and Migration]. Stuttgart: Kohlhammer.

Ehlers, Swantje. 2002. Lesesozialisation zugewanderter Sprachminderheiten [Reading Socialisation of Immigrant Language Minority Groups]. In *Ergebnisse soziologischer und psychologischer Forschung. Impulse für den Deutschunterricht* [Results of Sociological and Psychological

Research. Incentives for Teaching German], ed. Michael Hug, Sigrun Richter, 44-61. Baltmannsweiler: Schneider Hohengehren.

Gogolin, Ingrid. 2000. Minderheiten, Migration und Forschung. Ergebnisse des DFG-Schwerpunktprogramms FABER [Minorities, Migration, and Research. Results of the DFG priority programme FABER]. In *Migration, gesellschaftliche Differenzierung und Bildung* [Migration, Social Differentiation and Education], ed. Ingrid Gogolin, Bernhard Nauck, 15-35. Opladen: Leske & Budrich.

Jeuk, Stefan. 2002. Überlegungen zur Untersuchung des Zweitspracherwerbs bei türkischen Kindergartenkindern [Considerations About Second Language Acquisition of Turkish Kindergarten Children]. In *Empirische Unterrichtsforschung und Deutschdidaktik* [Empirical Teaching Research and German Didactics], ed. Clemens Kammler, Werner Knapp, 186-199. Baltmannsweiler: Schneider Verlag Hohengehren.

—. 2003. *Erste Schritte in der Zweitsprache Deutsch. Eine empirische Untersuchung zum Zweitspracherwerb türkischer Migrantenkinder in Kindertageseinrichtungen* [First Steps In Second Language German. An Empirical Study about Second Language Acquisition of Turkish Migrant Children in Kindergarten]. Freiburg im Breisgau: Fillibach.

Knapp, Werner. 1997. *Schriftliches Erzählen in der Zweitsprache* [Written Narration in the Second Language]. Tübingen: Narr.

—. 1998. Lässt sich der gordische Knoten lösen? Analysen von Erzähltexten von Kindern aus Sprachminderheiten [Can The Gordian Knot Be Unravelled? Analyses of Written Texts of Children from Language Minority Groups]. In *Pfade durch Babylon. Konzepte und Beispiele für den Umgang mit sprachlicher Vielfalt in Schule und Gesellschaft* [Paths Through Babylon. Concepts and Models for Dealing with Language Diversity in School and Society)], ed. Katharina Kuhs, Wolfgang Steinig, 225-244. Freiburg im Breisgau: Fillibach.

Nakip, Susanne. 1997. '*...und irgendwie habe ich mein deutsches Leben gelebt.' Zweisprachige Kindererziehung in deutsch-türkischen Partnerschaften* ['...And Somehow I Have Lived My German Life.' Bilingual Education of Children in German-Turkish Partnerships]. *Deutsch Lernen* [Learning German] 22: 291-316.

Röhr-Sendelmeier, Una-Maria. 1985. *Zweitsprachenerwerb und Sozialisationsbedingungen* [Second Language Acquisition and Conditions of Socialisation]. Frankfurt: Peter Lang.

Siebert-Ott, Gesa. 2000. 'Elitebilingualismus' und 'Konfliktzweisprachigkeit' (folk bilingualism). Über den Umgang mit Problemen und Chancen von Mehrsprachigkeit auch in der Lehrerausbildung ['Elite-Bilingualism' and 'Folk Bilingualism'. About Dealing with Problems and Chances of Multilingualism, also in Teacher Training]. In *Jenseits von Babylon. Wege zu einer interkulturellen Deutschdidaktik* [Beyond Babylon, Ways to an Intercultural German Pedagogy], ed. Norbert Griesmayer, Werner Wintersteiner, 89-105. Innsbruck; Wien; München: Studien Verlag.

Steinmüller, Ulrich. 1987. Sprachentwicklung und Sprachunterricht türkischer Schüler (Türkisch und Deutsch) im Modellversuch 'Integration ausländischer Schüler in Gesamtschulen' [Language Development and Language Classes/Lessons of Turkish Pupils (Turkish and German) in the Model Experiment: Integration of Immigrant Pupils in Comprehensive Schools']. In *Modellversuch "Integration ausländischer Schüler in Gesamtschulen"*. Abschlussbericht der Wissenschaftlichen Begleitung, Bd. 1., ed. H. Thomas, 207-315. Berlin: Pädagogisches Zentrum.

CHAPTER TWENTY

VIRTUAL COMMUNITIES – REAL READERS: NEW DATA IN EMPIRICAL STUDIES OF LITERATURE

MACIEJ MARYL

Abstract

The internet revolution brought about an increased interest in "virtual communities" of different kinds. Empirical studies of literature may benefit from the material produced by groups of literary readers exchanging their experiences via the internet.

Materials bearing on literature found on the internet raise several questions about their validity and general importance for empirical studies. On the other hand, given easy access at relatively low cost and readers' spontaneity, such materials are highly attractive for the study of literary reception.

This chapter discusses some of the methodological aspects of internet research, proposing some solutions based on a pilot study of the Polish book-recommendation system biblioNetka.pl.

Introduction

I would like to start with this short passage taken from a reader's diary found on the internet:

> I force myself to finish this page and my organism fights against it. One of the muscles starts to shudder and an intrusive thought appears: 'hey girl, buy yourself some magnesium'. And the other one: 'with vitamin B6'. And another: 'or aspargine'. Nice potassium is not so bad either. However, I remember why do I [sic!] sit here with this book, so I force myself to return to the last sentence I read. My ambition tells me so. But it is not an

ambition of my mind, which is turned off right now. I'm reaching the desired end of the page, realising that I don't have a clue what I have just read.[1]

This naturalistic description of the reading process introduces the core question of this chapter, namely the question of usefulness of this kind of material in the study of literature. What is the research value of such material? In what way, if at all, do this pill popper's confessions contribute to the advancement of our understanding? How should we treat such material? Should we consider such statements valid research material? If so, how should we classify this material? What kind of data treatment should be applied in such a project? Finally, the core question in every research is: why should we do it? Is this material worthy of being examined carefully? In the course of my discussion I will address these questions and propose possible answers. My remarks are based on a pilot study of biblioNETka.pl, a Polish portal dedicated to literature. In the following parts of this article I will give an overview of this research, its methodology and findings. Finally, I will raise the question of the possible usefulness of internet material for empirical investigations.

Virtual Communities

The internet revolution brought about, among other things, people's increased interest in gathering in "virtual communities" of various kinds. Numerous discussion forums, specialised portals, or newsgroups on Usenet, dedicated to various topics (e.g. books, movies, computers, fishing…), attract manifold users interested in a particular subject, in sharing their experience and obtaining some desired information. The idea of analysing material available there originates from marketing research. Nowadays many firms specialised in online monitoring sell their services to companies for vast sums of money (Mącik 2005, 90).

The phenomenon of internet communities can be regarded as something completely new, especially when we focus on the novelty of non-real-time communication (see Wallace 1999). It is possible to log on and take part in a discussion anytime and to have access to previous statements in that particular discussion. Some of these could have been posted several days or months earlier. However, it is the medium that has changed, not the specific relation between people who share the same

---

[1] All quotations from the internet sources are taken from the study of an internet portal BiblioNETka.pl, unless indicated otherwise. All passages were translated from Polish by the author.

interests. The new medium gave them new opportunities and tools to establish, maintain and develop this communication. Online discussions can be viewed as an extension of natural face-to-face contact.

In her extensive study of women book-clubs in Houston, Elizabeth Long (2003, 210-213) makes some interesting points regarding differences between real-world groups and the virtual ones. As Long observes, on-line book-clubs tend to gather largely upper class participants, who are more likely to have internet access. Such groups are usually cross-national, within one language group, (e.g. English speakers). On-line book clubs tend to have less clear boundaries, and their moderators bear more responsibility to keep the discussion going. Moreover, such groups concentrate less on analysing and commenting on the interpretations of other users, which in turn can serve as an indicator of higher subjectivity of on-line utterances.

Yet, the medium takes the advantage of an established genre of communication (i.e. discussion on literature) and transforms it according to its own capabilities. In other words, all differences stem from the nature of this medium. As Pietrowicz (2006, 360) points out, every research project run on the internet has to take into account three interlacing contexts: social, technological, and informational. When using the internet as a tool in any research one must bear in mind the specificity of internet discourse.

Having that in mind, we should consider material from biblioNETka.pl as a sort of record of discussions on literature. Around 2,000 users registered on this portal exchange opinions about books they read. Basically, biblioNETka.pl is a book-recommendation system, similar to those run by online bookstores (e.g. Amazon.com), where users are encouraged to express their opinions about a book and recommend it to others. Recommendations of this kind are very influential in business, since readers who are not keen on professional criticism prefer to take advice from ordinary people similar to themselves. Yet, an important question arises, whether encouraging users to create a positive 'word of mouth' – all of the submitted utterances are potential means of advertisement – does not affect reader responses published online. As Elizabeth Long puts it, „Amazon.com encourages readers to comment on books for the company's own commercial purposes". (2003, 206).

Yet, all internet discussion forums and recommendation systems provide a vast amount of data for reader response analysis. Hence, the findings presented in this study – although dedicated to a single internet community – should be considered valid for other online resources of this kind. Amazon.com, as a commercial recommendation system, will serve as a context for the study, whenever it will be useful to point out some interesting comparisons.

In general, actual readers investigated online are common readers, who read for aesthetic pleasure, or to escape, or to fulfil their individual goals. Eva Maria Scherf (1990, 492) distinguishes three kinds of reception: reception as an action, activity and operation. The last type refers to a research activity, which "is not determined by a sensory cognition motive, but by a scientific cognition motive". This type of reading is subject to institutional norms of literary criticism. Hence, one rarely finds testimonies of such reading in discussion groups of ordinary readers. Moreover, as Long observes, sometimes readers' goal is to submit a personal and by no means 'academic' interpretation (Long 2003, 145-146). What the researcher does encounter is evidence of two other types of reading. Reading as an action is that

> type of reception which is founded on the need for physical and psychological reproduction, in which reception functions as an action which, incorporated to a greater or lesser extent into practical everyday forms of activity, aims to stimulate this activity emotionally, i.e. to dynamize it or to break down particular internal tensions (for example, by laughing). (ibid., 491)

In other words, literature approached in this way serves as an emotional tuning. The third type of reception, reading as an activity, serves different purposes:

> The hierarchically superior motive is the desire to (re)cognise oneself and the world in appropriating a text; what makes this a special kind of activity is the knowledge that such (re)cognition will be accompanied by a highly emotional experience ... the reader/viewer/listener seeks to take from the text whatever s/he can relate as directly as possible to personal practice. (ibid.)

Internet material is therefore a source of highly personal accounts of reading as an action and activity. This kind of reading, as I shall discuss in a minute, requires a specific kind of literature, which will enable readers' self-implication and highly emotional reactions. Therefore, participants in biblioNETka.pl concentrate mostly on realistic prose, which enables immersion into the fictional world. The virtual absence of poetry in their discussions may be caused by a general belief that poetic texts are "difficult" and "incomprehensible".

BiblioNETka.pl, as a non-profit community, not only recommends books but also provides the space for discussions about literary experiences. Various forums at biblioNETka.pl resemble ordinary discussions about literature one can hear in a book club, in the subway or on the street. Therefore an empirical researcher in the field of literature has the unique opportunity to explore the ordinary behaviour of actual readers. However, the question arises: is it really so simple? Does the internet give researchers a magic tool to explore their field of interest? Let me complicate this picture, by pointing out several problems the researcher should be aware of when working with this material.

Basically, we can divide the internet material into two groups: requested material and "fresh" material. (Mącik 2005 proposes a different terminology calling these categories respectively primary and secondary material. Being confused about which category should be in fact called primary I will use my own terminology). Each of these groups contains different kinds of data, which may serve different research purposes. Requested material generally consists of data submitted in reaction to a researcher's enquiry. This group therefore comprises all surveys distributed online (either via e-mail, or on websites), online focus groups moderated by a researcher, and all other forms of data gathering in which a researcher encourages subjects to express their opinions. A researcher can, therefore, influence the form of the response from the very beginning. In general, this kind of research does not differ much from a standard research procedure (e.g. surveys). The researcher treats the internet as a *tool* for standard data collecting. In the case of "fresh" data, however, the internet serves as a *source* of data. The main difference is that data are not requested but only collected by a researcher. Hence, subjects' opinions are more spontaneous and not biased by a research situation. Fresh material can be found on various internet forums and websites where users express their personal views and react to statements submitted by others.

Disadvantages of the internet material

Typical problems that occur in internet research are closely linked to the specific nature of the medium. First of all, we do not know much about the subjects, who remain largely anonymous on an internet forum. Secondly, internet research is, by definition, narrowed down to a small but constantly growing population of people using the internet and taking part in online discussions. That in turn raises the question whether those groups are representative of the population at large. Thirdly, an online community of any kind influences its members, which affects their individual responses, especially when we take into account the commercial basis of some recommendation systems. Fourthly, internet material is not coherent

– the researcher has to deal with various types of expression. Finally, the core problem of every qualitative research is this: what if the data collected on the website show a low degree of relevance to the research topic? I will discuss these disadvantages in detail and try to suggest some solutions to avoid them.

Subjects in an internet study are anonymous. All that the researcher obtains is a text signed – if at all – with a nickname. If one deals with registered users it is sometimes possible to see their personal data, edited by users themselves in the form of a short presentation. Needless to say, relevant data from such statements is hard to obtain, and its reliability is questionable. Hence, it is difficult to judge subjects' gender, age, education and social background, to name just a few characteristics one is generally interested in. Lack of such data is the strongest disadvantage of such internet research.

Although the situation is problematic there are still some indicators a researcher may employ in order to deduce something about subjects. This procedure is based on the analysis of language, the only thing the researcher has access to. First of all, in some languages it is easy to tell the gender from the verb form used by a subject. For instance, in most Slavic languages verbs are marked for gender. In Romance languages, adjectives in self-reference are similarly marked for gender. In English there are some indicators to distinguish women's and men's speech. However, these differences are often questionable (Wardaugh 2002, 314-321). Secondly, one can employ Basil Bernstein's (1971) famous distinction beetweeen elaborated and restricted code. Although one can question Bernstein's findings, his basic theoretical framework can be useful in employing the complexity or simplicity of language as an indicator of the speaker's social background. However, this could be misleading if we take into account the risk of code-switching in an online environment, i.e. a university student may use colloquial language in online conversations. The same goes for age. One can attempt to judge the maturity of expressed opinions in order to deduce how old – more or less – subjects are. The problem here stems from the difference between life experience and age. One can act as mature even if one is young, and *vice versa*.

Amazon.com presents an interesting solution to the problem of anonymity: every user who decides to go under a real name, i.e. the one used to pay for ordered goods, receives a badge 'REAL NAME' displayed next to reviewer's 'nick'. Although it can serve as a hint for other customers by increasing the author's credibility, it does not provide extra information for the researcher. Knowing that a subject's real name is "John Smith" does not throw much light on his background. However, commercial systems, such as Amazon.com, provide the researcher with a set of information about the items purchased by a certain user. Detailed analysis of a consumer's profile could provide some data on both the user's economic status and her general taste.

Another complication in internet research is caused by the narrow population that can be examined. Together with the aforementioned complications this disadvantage contributes to the general sampling problem. A researcher cannot choose the population s/he wants to study – the population is already there. Moreover, subjects already have a specific need for online affiliation, which makes them different from people in the general population. This is a problem that may gradually disappear, however, as more and more users register on such forums and websites. Perhaps in a few years' time, the interest in internet communities will grow to such extent that everybody will participate in at least one of them. Until that happens, however, one should be cautious. Yet, studying such communities may still be worthwhile, as they consist of real people discussing real literature from a real perspective in a real manner.

At the same time one must not overlook the impact such communities have on their members. The difference between real-life conversations and online ones is that every member of the community can join the discussion and read what was said before. This situation triggers group conformism – members want to show their close ties with the group. Let me illustrate this phenomenon with a short example from BiblioNETka.pl. The following statements are taken from the autobiographical notes of six users:

> 'My name's Linda, I'm 21 and reading is my passion' / 'Reading is my passion' / 'books are my passion' / 'I've always loved books' / 'Since I was a child, I've always wanted to had a job connected to books' / 'I don't want to write too much...I just LOVE TO READ'

This particular book-lover syndrome shows the importance of indicating that a user belongs to this particular group. It seems that this confession of love serves as a sort of password to the community of other book lovers. Conformism may also affect other forms of expression, since there is no speaking *in vacuo*: speaking always means speaking TO somebody. Therefore the researcher has to be aware of the risk of group conformism in order to avoid stereotypical data.

The next disadvantage I would like to point out is the heterogeneity of the internet material. In the study of biblioNETka.pl I came across a wide range of texts of different length and purpose. The longest form of expression was an elaborated subjective review. This form allows users to express their general attitude towards a book. Some of them copy the editor's text from the cover. Sometimes, however, readers need only a short quote to describe the book. Another form is a reader's diary – an account of the individual reading processes outlining a reader's expectations, reading experience and conclusions. Sometimes users express their opinions in a more discursive way, posting short comments to statements made by others. The shortest form of evaluation is a mark (from 1 to 6) given to a particular book. If one wants to obtain reliable material, the problem of variety of expressions must not be overlooked. Among the two aforementioned variables – length and purpose – the former is not so important. One can express oneself accurately in just a few words and the researcher can compare it to the content of other longer statements. However, the latter category, namely the purpose of writing the text, may present the researcher with some difficulties in judgment. For instance, the form of a review outlines a more general and 'objective' mode of description, whereas a reader's diary is a purely subjective genre, concentrated on the reader's private experience. Hence, different forms of internet expressions may be incomparable.

At Amazon.com users can rate a book or provide a comment called "a Customer Review". Quite similarly, comments are either highly personal and subjective ("I really wanted to like this novel. I paid about $20 for it"; "Eeek! I love this book soooo much! It's splendidly artistic...")[2], or based on professional literary criticism (*"House of Leaves* is probably this century's - or the past one's - *Moby Dick*."; "*House of Leaves* is the very definition of post-modern."). Yet, we can also obtain such information as "Customers Who Bought This Item Also Bought...", or "What Do Customers Ultimately Buy After Viewing Items Like This?" Although the material found in both commercial and non-profit recommendation systems may be similar in content, one should be aware of the differences in functions of this material. Whereas material from BiblioNETka.pl could be conceived expressive (readers want to share their observations), utterances at Amazon.com serve the function of impressing (the company concentrates not on the users who submit the comments but rather on those who browse them). Hence, all that we see at Amazon.com depends highly on an algorithm, which aims at presenting the user with a highly personalised content, one s/he is likely to appreciate.

Finally, data collected from the internet can be totally irrelevant to the research topic, especially when the research question is narrowly

---

[2] Comments presented here are taken from various Customer Reviews of: Mark Danielewski's *House of Leaves*, at Amazon.com.

formulated. For instance, if we want to find out how readers react to suspense in crime fiction, it may turn out that they do not write about it or simply that they do not read such fiction. The problem with relevance is also caused by something one could call the I-have-an-exam-tomorrow syndrome: users often share their personal experience, their life problems, anxieties, or wishes instead of writing about books. The readers' community is often treated as a group of supportive friends. Therefore, researchers have to design methods that enable them to ensure the relevance of their data. That means that the method ought to be highly qualitative and the research questions carefully formulated in order to meet the specific criteria of the medium.

Some researchers tend to emphasise the ephemeral character of internet material, claiming that webmasters are free to delete users' entries at any time (see Mącik 2005, 93). Although the risk of losing data is always real, one should not overplay its significance, since all data can be retrieved from the web in the preliminary phase of the study and safely stored on the researcher's PC.

The list of disadvantages of the internet material is long and it is not always possible to avoid these problems. I would nevertheless claim that the internet is a promising medium to study people's reactions to literature. It is an unobtrusive way to observe literary reception *in actu*. So let us look in somewhat more detail at the benefits of an online research.

Advantages of internet material

The main advantage of online research is the availability of material. One does not need to organise large groups of surveyors, nor does one have to look for subjects. Data are already there, on the web, waiting for the researcher to download and analyse them. What is more, the online material is produced without the researcher's influence. Hence, the material can be considered spontaneous. Finally, the heterogeneity of this material allows researchers to find out more than they expected.

Easy access to data allows researchers to run the study at any convenient moment. What is more, materials obtained in that way are ready for analysis. For instance, a researcher does not have to transcribe any recordings or decode his survey. If one applies content analysis software (e.g. PROTAN, TextSTAT), the first results can be obtained within minutes after the material is collected. Online research can be also repeated at certain intervals to trace trends. Finally, online research is extremely cheap, which enables researchers to carry on their studies with limited funding.

An obvious advantage of materials collected this way is that a researcher does not influence them in any way. Readers respond to texts in their own way, having as much time as they need. Moreover, readers share their opinions with others only when they really want to say something about the text they have read. For the researcher that is a guarantee that their responses are genuine and not provoked by a request, as it may be the case in a reading experiment. Furthermore, any bias introduced by an experimental situation is eliminated, since subjects read texts in their favourite environment (on a couch, on the train, in a café…). Online research thus enables us to eavesdrop on readers' real experience, expressed in their own terms.

The list of disadvantages seems to be rather longer. However, in my opinion, it is an indication of the method's limits, but does not prove that it is useless.

It is important to explain in detail the approach taken in the research presented here. Shaun Moores claims that ethnography of audiences "attends to the media's multiple significances in varied contexts of reception as opposed to focusing on quantification through measurement" (Moores 1993, 3). He defines it as a "method for investigating a social world of actual audiences" (ibid., 5). The aim of this kind of research is to measure "the extent to which media messages influence the thoughts and actions of their receivers" (ibid., 5). Therefore, a media ethnographer explores the context in which the meaning-making process takes place.

That is because online research does not allow us to measure a complete individual response to certain texts: however, we can say something about different styles of reading, different strategies of dealing with literature, and about the connection between life and literature. In order to show the kind of information that can thus be gathered, I will now present a pilot research project, which I ran on the users of biblioNETka.pl.

Study of biblioNETka.pl

What follows is a list of topics that emerged in the course of the project. Through these observations we can learn more about users of an internet portal and recognise the possibilities for further internet research on literary responses.

My initial goal was to test the role that literature plays in readers' lives and to give an account of their literary experience. Therefore I chose to work on readers' diaries. In order to obtain more information about the subjects, I also examined their autobiographical statements and their responses to other users' comments.

I developed a sampling frame of 222 users who (1) submitted at least one reader's diary and (2) presented an autobiographical statement. I analysed every tenth user starting from number 1 (1, 11, 21…), then a second sample beginning from number 5 (15, 25, 35…). If a user did not meet the criteria (for instance, if the autobiographical statement was removed) I substituted him or her with the next user on the list. After the second run I considered the sample sufficiently large, since the same content started to repeat itself.

The sample consisted of 45 readers. For obvious reasons it is hard to give a detailed description of this group. Their age ranged from teenagers (attending secondary school) to adults (40-50). The gender distribution was unequal and it reflected the general structure of biblioNETka.pl users: 36 females (80%) and 9 males (20%). It is a rather common proportion, given the findings of Elizabeth Long's study on Houston book-clubs, 64% of which are female-only, 33% are mixed, and only 3% are exclusively male (Long 2003: xiii).

It should be noted that males tend to concentrate on non-fiction books, e.g. on philosophy or history. Women usually wrote shorter diaries but were very open to interaction (long discussions, invitations, comments). The average number of readers' diary entries per user varied from one to a dozen or so. The average was 3-4 entries per user. Although the material varied in length, even a single entry could be significant and contribute to the analysis.

In order to examine the material collected, I designed a double-phased procedure. In the first phase, I traced all statements that could fit into general categories, namely:

(1) what is literature?
(2) what role does it play in a reader's life?
(3) reading as an everyday activity;
(4) fiction's effect on reality.

In the second phase I applied an inductive technique of creating patterns out of data collected in the first phase. I applied content analysis to both phases.

The strategy was aimed at describing the role of literature among common readers in their own terms. I am referring here to Clifford Geertz's concept of the 'local knowledge', through which people organise the world (Geertz 1984). Analysis of categories subjects use themselves describing their experience, leads us to an understanding of reader behaviour. Therefore, what I wanted to know was a secondary goal. The primary aim was to test what readers really want to say about their experience. I put the results into four larger categories, concerning:

(1) pre-reading strategies,
(2) reading strategies,
(3) attitudes towards literature,
(4) literature and reality.

I will discuss each of these consecutively.

(1) **Pre-reading strategies** are employed in the process of choosing a particular book at a particular moment. This choice is affected by several factors. First of all, it depends largely on the temporal context. There is a special time for reading, which can be called a sort of 'internal holidays'. There are books better suited for certain periods than others. For instance, one reader observes: "Christmas is approaching, it's time to read something in Christmas mood". Readers often switch books – they start a new one having not finished the one they were reading, or they reread some books they liked before. It can depend on readers' shifting or multi-faceted practical interests, often combined with impatience, as in the case of this reader who sighs: "I would like to have all those books at last, or at least some of them, and read them, preferably all at once. I've already started the sixth book, and I'm unable to finish any of them. I hate to wait". The choice also depends on the book's availability: readers search for books in bookstores, libraries and on the internet (in that order).

Readers ascribe certain values to particular books. These categories facilitate the choice of a book, guiding readers through the decision-making process. Drawing on the study, I distinguished the following oppositions: (a) easy reading – serious reading, (b) immersive – non-immersive book, (c) required reading – reading for pleasure, (d) portable literature – stationary literature. Let me discuss those categories in brief.

(a) By serious literature readers often mean classical readings, which are conceived as must-reads in a particular culture. Serious books are described as deep, ambitious, requiring more attention and … thick. On the other hand, easy readings are more accessible, but generate a specific feeling of guilt, expressed in such terms as: "I should start to read something more ambitious". This ambivalence marks a difference between social and individual aspects of reading, between that what we *should* read and, what we *want* to read.

(b) The next opposition is closely linked to the aforementioned time management: there is time for reading and time for other activities. The best description is provided by a reader who hesitates whether she should start to read a certain book: "I know that if I start to read it, I wouldn't put it aside until I finish it. I have to find something I could put aside easily, however, not without any regret".

(c) Required readings are considered negatively with no exceptions. One reader complains: "It's no surprise that I won't be able to read a nice book during the holidays, cause my teacher decided otherwise". What is interesting, however, is that a new, non-compulsory encounter with a text previously read as required, leads to differences in response. This is the case of the reader whose attitude towards a certain author changed when she started to read his books for pleasure. Readers highly value freedom of choice which enables them to adjust reading choices to their actual needs.

(d) Reading can be either autotelic, or serve as a time-killer, e.g. on a journey or in a waiting room. One reader points out that the ideal books to read in public transportation are "divided into small chapters, so you can easily stop reading and resume it later on". He finds texts with long chapters definitely impractical.

If we take a closer look at the act of choosing a book, it becomes apparent that the act of reading is strongly connected to readers' everyday context. Books accompany readers in everyday life, corresponding to their needs and expectations drawn from the 'real' world of everyday life. It is readers' practical interest in the world that guides them in the process of book selection. This notion becomes stronger when we proceed to reading strategies.

(2) **Reading strategies.** The very act of reading is being described by readers as an activity which has physical, temporal and social dimensions. This chapter's opening quotation presented a sample of how literature is treated as a deeply physical process. There are also other physical activities undertaken in the course of reading, like for instance: underlining, marking, making notes or an index of protagonists (who has not done that while reading *One Hundred Years of Solitude*?). All these actions help the reader understand the fictional world.

Temporality is also very important in presenting the reading process as an activity. A book can be read at one sitting or in intervals, quickly or slowly. The reading time also tells readers something about the book they read: "I read a book of less than 300 pages in 2 weeks", one reader observes, "whereas usually it takes me 2 days. Isn't that weird?"

Reading also plays a role in social relations. Sharing striking or witty quotes with others (e.g. with one's family sitting in the same room) changes the highly individual process of reading into a social interaction. Some readers tend to use passages from their favourite books when they want to say something nice to somebody: "I love to share [the quotes with others], especially the 'gigglegenic' ones. Yet, I giggle a bit, and then I am walking round the house trying to convert them to literature. Unfortunately, they're really resistant ;-))".

Another aspect of the reading process is the role literature plays in readers' lives. For many readers literature serves as an escape from reality. This can be illustrated by the example of an unemployed teacher sharing her opinion about a book in which the protagonist teaches everybody how to look at the bright side of life. "I know it seems unreal," the reader writes, "but one can dream at least". Readers compare their life experience to events depicted in the book they read. They do not search for answers and ready recipes to solve everyday problems but rather concentrate on topics relevant to their situation (e.g. love, aging) and try to find something for themselves. Literature becomes a kind of impulse provoking self-reflection, enabling readers to reconsider their perception of problem-situations they are facing.

(3) **Attitudes towards literature.** The common understanding of the word "literature" seems to confirm this presumption. In general, readers consider literature as a description of life. Hence, they trace a writer's mistakes and improbable events, which make them disbelieve that the picture painted in the story is accurate. "Why almost every book has a happy ending", one of the readers asks, "Why, despite the joy, pain and suffering they describe, 98% of them has a happy end? Why do those books which describe such real life experiences have nothing to do with reality?"

What sets literature apart from non-fiction is the emotional aspect of reading. Readers not only observe the fictional world but also experience emotions. Some users express their negative feelings towards books that have not moved them. By contrast, they prefer books which provide food for thought. One reader wrote: "I love this book. I grab it very often cause it helps me a lot. It teaches life, teaches how to love, how to forgive … how to cherish hope". Concluding then, literature is commonly understood as a picture of reality, which moves readers and provokes reflections. "There are no exclamation marks in Kafka", a reader points out, "exclamation marks appear in readers". The role of fictional worlds is a very specific topic that needs to be addressed.

The very first thing to be mentioned is the way readers enter the fictional world. Subjects in my study preferred texts that were well-written; in the present context this meant texts one could read fast, being overwhelmed by them. This does not, however, necessarily imply an inclination towards simplistic writing. Well-written texts, not too complicated in style, allow readers to enter the fictional world smoothly. Let us take a look at a comment: "[this book] immerses me now and then, but there were moments when I turned pages laboriously". This laborious page-turning is an opposite of immersion – if a text is too complicated one has to pay more attention to the surface structure. Hence, if the text is difficult, readers cannot be so easily transported into the fictional realm. Gerrig and Rapp, who discuss in detail the phenomenon of transport, give empirical evidence to support their claim that "literary narratives' capacity to engage readers increases the probability that those narratives will wield an impact on life." (Gerrig and Rapp 2004, 270).

(4) **Literature and reality.** Fiction interlaces with reality in two respects. On the one hand, readers search for fictional places in the real world, on the other, they seem to trace reality in fiction. The best example of the first category is the action undertaken by a reader who went to Moscow in order to visit the places mentioned in Bulgakov's *Master and Margarita*. He even uploaded a photograph of Patriarshie Prudy, the street on which one of the protagonists was beheaded by a tram. Fiction also provokes readers to visit places where narrated events took place. Hence, reading becomes a form of tourism into semi-fictional worlds.

There are also readers who treat fictional events as if they were real. One user made a list of fictional places she encountered in books. What is more, protagonists often trigger real emotions in readers, who tend to judge fictional characters according to real-life criteria. Readers often say: "I like this character, I hate that one…" One reader claimed that the protagonist "is a kind of guy I would definitely like to impress … Probably I would like to have sex with him, cause nothing turns me on more than intelligence".

Conclusions: online reports of everyday experiences with fiction

The study reported here was aimed at discovering readers' strategies and approaches towards literature. It sketched in brief the role of literature in readers' everyday life, concentrating on the role they ascribe to fictional texts. Believing that the act of reading is a specific everyday activity, depending on the individual context, I tried to investigate what contributes to that context.

The second goal of this study was to test the possibilities of online research in studying the reception of literature. Despite some inconveniences internet material proves to be useful in certain areas of study, especially concerning emotional reactions to fiction, reading behaviour, and self-implication in literary reading, to name just a few. Hence, studies online could be treated as a complementary research technique for face-to-faces interviews and observations.

As I have shown, literature provides readers with food for thought and shows them alternative worlds; at the same time, readers use it to regulate their emotions. Experience gained in the fictional world is adopted in reality. Literature may also serve other purposes: it can provoke actions or reflections, it can help readers work out their problems and tune their emotions, or it can serve as a mirror, opening up topics relevant to readers' own worlds.

Acknowledgments

I would like to thank all participants in the discussion following this paper at the IGEL conference in Munich. Their opinions and questions were very helpful in my work on this final version. I would also like to express my gratitude to David Miall and Willie van Peer for their comments and suggestions concerning the earlier versions of this paper.

Works Cited

Bernstein, Basil. 1971. *Class, Codes and Control,* vol. 1. London: Routledge.
Geertz, Clifford. 1984. *Local Knowledge. Further Essays in Interpretive Anthropology.* New York: Basic Books.
Gerrig, Richard J. and David N. Rapp. 2004. Psychological Processes Underlying Literary Impact. *Poetics Today* 25:2: 265-281.
Long, Elizabeth. 2003. *Book Clubs: Women and the Uses of Reading in Everyday Life.* Chicago: University of Chicago Press.
Mącik, Radosław. 2005. *Wykorzystanie internetu w badaniach marketingowych. [The use of the internet in marketing research]* Lublin: Wydawnictwo UMCS.
Moores, Shaun. 1993. *Interpreting Audiences. The Ethnography of Media Consumption.* London: SAGE.
Pietrowicz, Krzysztof. 2006. Badanie internetu w ujęciu konstruktywistycznym". [*"Internet research: a constructivist approach"*] In *Re:internet-społeczne aspekty medium [Re:internet – social aspects of the medium].* Eds. Łukasz Jonak, et. al., 351-364. Warszawa: Wydawnictwa Akademickie i Profesjonalne.

Scherf, Eva Maria 1990. Motive and Goal as Determinants in the Treatment of Texts: Some Thoughts on a Functional Model of Reception. *Poetics* 19: 487-504.

Wallace, Patricia. 1999. *The Psychology of the Internet.* Cambridge: Cambridge University Press.

Wardaugh, Ronald. 2002. *An Introduction to Sociolinguistics.* Oxford: Blackwell.

CHAPTER TWENTY ONE

LITERARINESS AND THE PROCESS OF EVALUATION

MARISA BORTOLUSSI, PETER DIXON, AND BLAINE MULLINS

Abstract

In this paper, we propose a framework for the empirical study of literary evaluation. In this framework, we distinguish evaluation source from evaluation process. In turn, evaluation source can be either textual or extratextual. Textual sources can be described as pertaining to either the story or the discourse. To each of these textual sources corresponds an evaluation process: situational appreciation and language processing. Evidence for this analysis was obtained by asking readers to rate the initial pages of novels on a range of rating scales. Principal components analysis was used to identify four components underlying the responses, which we identified as Appeal, Clarity, Focus, and Style. Each component could be interpreted as pertaining to elements of the evaluation framework. We conclude that despite the controversies surrounding the notions of literariness and literary value, an empirical investigation of literary evaluation is indeed possible.

Introduction

In this paper, we are concerned with the problem of literary value. Not surprisingly, sensitivities and opinions about what constitutes literary quality have fuelled debates among critics and theorists for centuries; in fact, such debates are probably as old as literature itself. On our analysis, debates concerning literary quality, whether we call it literariness or literary value, often involve a contrast between an essentialist perspective and a relativist perspective. On the one hand, intuition suggests that some texts are inherently superior to others in terms of their language and style, the depth of their ideas, and so on. This intuition, which is embodied in formalist views regarding the intrinsic quality of certain works, has contributed to the formation of the so-called literary canon: that body of works many have identified as exemplary and influential cultural products. A central problem with the essentialist position, though, is that it is extremely difficult to obtain a strong consensus on what should be in the canon and what should not, and it is even more difficult to arrive at any agreement about the nature of the literary values that canonised works exemplify. The inescapable impossibility of achieving any universal definition of literary value has led some critics to declare the very topic of value "exiled" (Herrnstein Smith 1983).

On the other hand, there is the relativist perspective. This is the view, common in cultural-studies, that canonical works are not of interest to everyone in society and that what is valued in literature depends on socio-cultural context. Taken to its extreme, this position leads to what we refer to as the "doctrine of radical relativism": the conclusion that value is purely a function of individual, contextually determined preference, and that what an individual prefers is just as valid an index of quality as widespread critical acclaim. From this perspective, one can argue that "there are no bad books" (Long 2006), and it may even be politically incorrect in some circles to suggest that some works may have greater intrinsic value than others.

Despite the merits of the relativistic perspective, exiling the topic of intrinsic literary value may amount to throwing out the baby with the bath water. Evaluations are the pulse of literary life: They occur at every stage of the literary institution, starting with authors, through publishers, editors, marketers, book sellers, library-book purchasers, reviewers, critics, right down to the readers. Moreover, despite the prevalence of the relativistic perspective, the fields of literary and cultural studies are still permeated with assumptions about what is valued by whom and why. In particular, the assertion that value is contextually determined has merely generated different presuppositions about the nature of literary value: Instead of features of the text, the focus today tends to be on the pragmatic function that literary works perform for their readers. However, the analysis of these functions suffers from some of the same flaws as the essentialist perspective: First, in its enthusiasm for contextual influences, it is often assumed that context is the *only* factor that determines value, so that literary response is purely a function of class, race, gender, ethnicity, and so on. Second, value is typically conceived of as a unitary, global assessment, excluding the possibility that readers might recognise the distinct value of various works, independent of their own preferences, and excluding the possibility that works can be valued differentially in various ways. Finally, conclusions about literary value are generally subjective and intuitive, just as has been the case with the scholarship in the essentialist perspective. Thus, while the relativist perspective has succeeded in highlighted the importance of context, it does not provide a clear understanding of the nature of literary value.

In our view, a productive resolution to these differing perspectives can be found by investigating general properties of the *process of evaluation* rather than focusing simply on who values what in literature. A principal advantage of this approach is that evaluation can be conceived of as an empirical question, so that evidence can be garnered for one view or another, irrespective of prior ideological assumptions. Once one conceives of this sort of approach, it becomes clear that some of the scholarship on literary value is simplistic. For instance, value must be thought of as multidimensional, so that a given work can be evaluated in a variety of different respects, and the products of that evaluation could be quite disparate. For example, a reader may value the language of a work, but not its story; he or she may find the main character appealing but find the text difficult to read; and so on.

For literary scholars, there are a number of potential benefits of an empirical approach. First, such an approach allows us to identify the elements of the evaluation process that are similar across individuals, even though the results of an evaluation could vary. Chicanos living in Chicago and Alberta ranchers might value different works, but the information used to form that evaluation and the manner in which it is processed could be quite similar. Second, once the elements of the evaluation process are understood, it could be possible to study the lawful relation between value for individual readers and those readers' situation and culture. Thus, we may be able to assess the requisite context, knowledge, and skills that lead readers to value some works and not others. Finally, it might be possible to identify aspects of the text that correspond to the value placed on given works by some readers in certain contexts. It may well be that there are some aspects of all texts, popular and canonised, that readers across social groups evaluate in the same way. In this way, we may be able to come to an understanding of literariness as a textual property, without making any assumptions about the universality of that evaluation.

A Framework for Literary Evaluation

In order to engage in this type of empirical approach, we need to identify the information that contributes to evaluation and how that information is processed by readers. Therefore, we begin by describing a general framework for literary evaluation. Following this description, we proceed to discuss some empirical evidence on evaluation that hopefully demonstrates the promise of this approach. However, this evidence provides only a preliminary step towards understanding evaluation, and much more work will be needed to develop our framework into a full-fledged account of evaluation.

The main features of our proposed framework are illustrated in figure 1. We distinguish two aspects of evaluation: the source of information that forms the basis of the evaluation and how that information is used, that is, the process of evaluation. With respect to the evaluation source, we identify two broad categories: textual and extra-textual sources. We will not elaborate on extra-textual sources in the current paper but simply point out that such sources might include critical commentaries, advertising, recommendations from friends or book representatives, and so on. Such sources could contribute to the evaluation of a given text even though they provide indirect information about the text that is potentially biased or selective. Extratextual sources are potentially important to consider since it is quite possible that attributions of value have less to do with independent, individual reading experience than with consensual norms and expectations.

With respect to the textual sources, we make use of the narratological distinction between story (or the "told") and discourse (or the "telling"): "Story" pertains to information about events and characters in the story world, while "discourse" pertains to the manner of presenting that information This distinction is useful because it provides a broad delineation of the information readers encounter in reading a literary text. As noted by reception theorists, reading is an interactive process in which elements of the story and discourse contribute to the reader's evaluation of the work.

To each of these textual evaluation sources corresponds an evaluation process. On the one hand, there is situational appreciation – that is, how readers react to events, settings, characters of the story world. Clearly, situational appreciation depends on whether readers have the relevant background knowledge pertaining to the story world and the characters; a story that is embedded in a particular culture may present modes of behavior that render the text obscure to readers from outside that culture.

On the other hand, there is the appreciation of the discourse – that is, how readers process the language of the text. This includes how they react to the narrative style, whether or not they have difficulties with the vocabulary or sentence structure, and whether they have the skills to appreciate literary devices in the text. Thus, in general, we assume that the nature of the evaluation processes will depend to a large degree on characteristics of the reader. However, this does not imply that reading is a purely subjective experience; indeed, some of the results reported in this paper corroborate the reception theorists' insight that although reading is an interactive process, the text guides and constrains the reading experience.

Figure 1. A framework for literary evaluation.

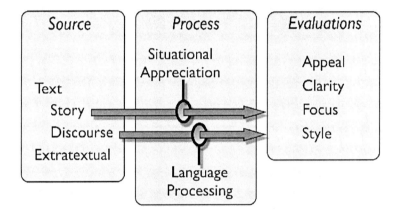

As mentioned earlier, a central ingredient in our approach is the assumption that evaluation is not a single, global assessment, but rather includes a range of different kinds of evaluations. For example, a reader can ascribe a positive value to the style of a piece of literature, but may not find the plot to be very engaging; or, a reader may understand that a work has social relevance, but consider it boring; or a reader may understand its stylistic and social importance but find it lacking in personal-relevance, and thus have no interest in reading it. Thus, regardless of one's theoretical orientation, literary value has to be thought of as multidimensional. This perspective leads to an important insight about the nature of the literary canon: The fact that a work is part of the canon should not necessarily be interpreted as a claim about an overall value assessment; instead, it may reflect an evaluation with respect to a much more limited set of criteria, and other works, not normally regarded as part of the canon, may be evaluated highly by some individuals in other respects. Thinking of value in terms of the process by which it is ascribed provides a more sophisticated analysis of the relative and partial merits of different works.

An Empirical Investigation

In what follows, we describe an initial empirical foray into understanding the process of evaluation. Our ultimate goal is to develop a process model of evaluation, and the results we describe hopefully provide a foundation on which to build. For this study, we selected the first two pages of eight novels and asked subjects to provide a variety of assessments of each selection. In this respect, the evaluation process we asked subjects to perform bears some relation to the real-life book selection that occurs in bookstores and libraries in which readers examine some initial portion of a novel to decide whether or not to purchase or borrow it. To obtain a range of different materials, our informal judgment was used to select texts varying on two dimensions: accessibility (i.e., whether the language and style of the excerpt was relatively easy or relatively difficult to understand) and orientation. For the latter dimension, we assessed whether the excerpt was "plot-oriented," consisting primarily of a description of a sequence of events, or "character-oriented," with large segments devoted to the depiction of characters and mental states. (These assessments applied only to the two-page excerpts that subjects read and would not necessarily apply to the novels as a whole.) The novels selected and their classifications on these dimensions are shown in table 1. Seven hundred and two students participated in the experiment as part of a course requirement in introductory psychology. Subjects responded to the nine evaluation rating scales shown in table 2 on a seven-point scale.

Table 1. Novel selections

Character-Oriented, Accessible
Joyce Cary, *The Horse's Mouth*
John Williams, *Cardiff Dead*
Action-Oriented, Accessible
David Elias, *Sunday Afternoon*
Timothy Findley, *The Butterfly Plague*
Character-Oriented, Inaccessible
John Hawkes, *The Lime Twig*
Shawn McBride, *Green Grass Grace*
Action-Oriented, Inaccessible
William Faulkner, *As I Lay Dying*
Langston Hughes, *Not Without Laughter*

Table 2. Evaluation rating scales

1. I would like to continue reading this novel.
2. I have friends who would enjoy this novel.
3. I found the excerpt easy to understand.
4. I can relate to the main character in the story.
5. Literary critics would enjoy this novel.
6. I found the main character in the story to be engaging.
7. I thought the excerpt was well written.
8. I was curious to find out what would happen next in the story.
9. I can relate to the situation described in the story.

Among our subjects, we identified those with high or low reading experience by administering a version of the Author Recognition Test (Stanovich and West 1989). In this test, subjects were shown a list of 75 names and were asked to select those that were well-known authors. The 75 names were divided equally among canonised authors, popular authors, and foils. Our reading-experience measure was the difference between the hit rate for popular authors and foils. (Similar results were obtained using the hit rate for canonised authors instead of popular authors, but the range of scores was somewhat smaller.) High and low reading-experience groups were created with a median split.

The rating results were analysed using principal components analysis. Principal components analysis is a statistical technique for identifying the underlying determinants of a collection of responses. For example, if all of the questionnaire responses in the present study were determined simply by whether the reader liked the text or not, the analysis would identify this single "preference" component and would specify the relationship between that preference score and the response to each question (as in linear regression). More generally, though, responses will be determined by a range of different kinds of reactions to the text, and the response to each question will depend on some combination of those reactions. Principal components analysis provides an estimate of each of those distinct reactions and the linear combination that best predicts the set of questionnaire responses. Our expectation was that those reactions, or components, would be related to different aspects of our evaluative framework, and, in particular, might correspond to the various evaluation source and process components shown in figure 1.

Components of Evaluation

The results of the principal components analysis are summarised in table 3. Although the components can be identified statistically, the technique does not provide an interpretation of what they embody. For that, we use a combination of further analysis, argument, and example, as described below. We have labeled the first component as an overall *Appeal* factor. According to the principal components analysis, Appeal is a powerful predictor of the questionnaire responses. In particular, knowing the Appeal score for each reader allows one to predict nearly half the variation in how that reader responds to all the questions. Our interpretation is that when readers like a text, they tend to rate it positively on all of the scales. However, there are also three additional components (together accounting for an additional 30% of the variation) that have more interesting relationships with the rating scales. We suggest that these components correspond, respectively, to *Clarity* (i.e., whether the story situation and context are clear or opaque from the selection); *Focus* (i.e., whether the narrative consists primarily of external events or internal thoughts and reactions); and *Style* (i.e., whether the narrative technique is distinctive or interesting for the reader). Below we provide a justification for these interpretations.

Table 3. Principal components summary

	Component			
	Appeal	Clarity	Focus	Style
Variance Proportion	.481	.110	.100	.098
Loadings				
1. Continue reading	.447	.373	-.075	-.162
2. Friends enjoy	.346	.009	.022	-.086
3. Easy to understand	.197	.427	.455	.720
4. Relate to character	.291	-.381	.497	-.064
5. Critics enjoy	.170	-.440	-.384	.356
6. Character engaging	.395	.013	-.263	.084
7. Well written	.273	-.339	-.267	.448
8. Curious about next	.478	.256	-.184	-.224
9. Relate to situation	.260	-.398	.467	-.242
Experience Group r	.349	.953	.910.	.309
Evaluation Source / Process	Situational Appreciation	Discourse Source	Story Source	Language Processing

A first step in our analysis of the components was to note that Clarity and Focus components were closely related to properties of the text, whereas the Appeal and Style components related to aspects of evaluation that were more idiosyncratic and variable across individuals. For this analysis, we considered the four component scores for each reader isolated by the principal components analysis. Because each reader evaluated a single text, we could then ask how well each component score was predicted simply by which text was read. If the component was determined purely on the basis of the text, this prediction would be perfect, with 100% of the variance explained. On the other hand, if the score reflected purely idiosyncratic preferences, so that each reader assessed each text differently, the text would have little predictive value. This analysis is illustrated in figure 2, in which we plot the proportion of the variance in each component that can be predicted on the basis of which of the eight texts was being evaluated. As can be seen, Clarity and Focus are well predicted by the text, while Appeal and Style are not.

Figure 2. Proportion of variance of the component scores predicted by text. (Error bars represent the standard error of the estimate.)

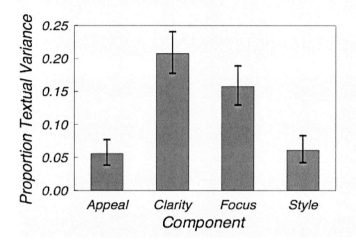

Another way to make the same point is to examine the groups of high- and low-experience readers. The average Clarity and Focus scores for these two groups show almost exactly the same pattern across the eight stories; however, there is much less correspondence between the groups for the Appeal and Style components. (The correlations of the component scores between the high and low experience groups across the eight stories are shown in table 3 under the heading "Experience Group r.") These results suggest that we should look to properties of the text in order to understand the basis of the Clarity and Focus components.

An intuitive sense of these two components can be obtained by studying the texts. For example, table 4 lists excerpts from *Sunday Afternoon*, which was high on the Clarity component and *The Lime Twig*, which was low in Clarity. It is easy understand why *Sunday Afternoon* would be considered clear: The excerpt consists of a concrete description of a recognizable situation. In contrast, *The Lime Twig* opens with a series of disorienting rhetorical questions and continues for most of the excerpt in this fashion. The contrast between these two excerpts illustrates why we think that Clarity provides a reasonable label for this component.

Table 4. Excerpts illustrating the Clarity component

High Clarity (*Sunday Afternoon*)

When a blonde in a yellow convertible pulled up to the barricade, the young private posted there could hardly believe his wild luck. He certainly hadn't expected anything so terrific looking to come driving down such a lousy little road. In fact, he hadn't counted on much in the way of traffic at all, since the road came to an abrupt end only a few hundred yards farther up. But already he'd turned back a half-dozen vehicles, all of the with the same yellow and black plates from someplace he'd never hear of called Manitoba.

Low Clarity (*The Lime Twig*)

Have you ever let lodgings in the winter? Was there a bed kept waiting, a corner room kept waiting for a gentleman? And have you eve hung a cardboard in the window and, just out of view yourself, watched to see which man would stop and read the hand-letting on your sign, glance at the premises from roof to little sign – an awkward piece of work – then step up suddenly and hold his finger on your bell? What was it you saw from the window that made you let the bell continue ringing and the bed go empty another night?

The basis of the Focus component can similarly be appreciated by examining examples high and low on Focus, as shown in table 5. The first example (from *The Butterfly Plague*) develops a clearly identified sequence of overt events. In contrast, the second example (*The Horse's Mouth*) uses a more metaphorical description of subjective internal reactions of the character. The other texts show corresponding variations in internal versus external focus. Thus, it seems reasonable to identify this component with the nature of the perspective in the narration.

Table 5. Excerpts illustrating the Focus component

External Focus (*The Butterfly Plague*)

"Mickey Balloon! Mickey Balloon, come down!"
A little boy, aged four, stood screaming on the verge of the platform.
"He got away!"
The child-owner of Mickey Balloon stamped his pretty feet, encased in patent-leather shoes, and jumped up and down.
Mickey Balloon's string hung tantalizingly close, but just as soon as the child leaped near it, up it bobbled and away it jiggled.
"Oh, Mickey Balloon – Oh – Mickey Balloon! Come back!"
But Mickey Balloon was going his merry way.
Up, up he soared, further and further into the blue, blue sky. Mickey Balloon had places to go and things to see.

Internal Focus (*The Horse's Mouth*)

I was walking by the Thames. Half-past morning on an autumn day. Sun in a mist. Like an orange in a fried fish shop. All bright below. Low tide, dusty water and a crooked bar of straw, chicken-boxes, dirt and oil from mud to mud. Like a viper swimming in skim milk. The old serpent, symbol of nature and love.
Five windows light the caverned man: through one he breathes the air;
Through one hear music of the spheres; through one can look
And see small portions of the eternal world.
Such as Thames mud turned into a bank of nine carat gold rough from the fire.

As mentioned earlier, the Appeal and Style components were not related purely to the text, and instead were related to the more idiosyncratic reactions of the reader. Consequently, an examination of the texts themselves is unlikely to help us understand what they comprise. However, the Appeal component is easy to understand: All evaluations were predicted by this component, so we infer that it is related to an overall preference for the text. Moreover, as shown in figure 3, the interaction of this component with reading experience is readily understandable. As shown in figure 3, the more experienced readers had higher Appeal scores for inaccessible texts generally, and among the accessible materials, they preferred the character-oriented texts. Presumably, the greater the reading experience, the greater the preference for the more complex texts that we labeled as inaccessible, and the greater the tolerance for the more introspective writing that we categorised as character oriented.

Figure 3. Mean Appeal score as a function of reader experience, plot/character orientation, and textual accessibility. (Error bars represent the standard error of the mean.)

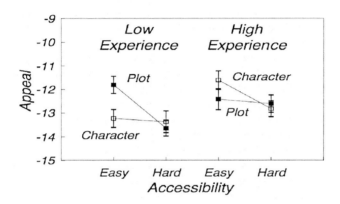

The fourth component was the hardest to label. However, a critical clue was that the items that were positively related to this component all pertained to the language of the excerpt, such as "I found the excerpt easy to understand" and "I thought the excerpt was well-written." In contrast, items that pertained to the elements of the story world (such as "I can relate to the situation described in the story" and "I was curious to find out what would happen next in the story") had a negative relationship to this component. In other words, positive score on the component were associated with positive evaluation of the discourse, while negative scores were associated with a positive evaluation of the story. Further, there was a large overall difference between experience groups in this component, irrespective of the story that was actually read: High experience readers had a value of 1.19 (SE = 0.08) and low-experience readers had a value of 0.84 (SE = 0.10). We hypothesise that readers with low experience had trouble with the style of some texts, while those with more experience might have found those styles interesting. For example, the biggest difference between the groups occurred with *Green Grass Grace*, which uses a stream of consciousness style with a significant amount of profanity; it is possible that readers with low experience might have found this disconcerting or objectionable. Thus, we argue that the fourth component is most appropriately viewed as corresponding to the interest value for the reader of the language and narrative technique.

Components in the Evaluation Framework

Although these results are far from definitive, it is possible to interpret them within the evaluation framework shown in figure 1 and to relate each component to aspects of the evaluation source and process. For example, *Clarity* was ranked consistently across individuals, so it makes sense to suppose that it is related to the textual source rather than the evaluation process. In particular, it seems to be aligned with textual discourse rather than story features since it corresponds to how clearly the text describes the story world. *Focus* is also clearly related to the text, but in this case it has to do with whether the excerpt provides internal or external information. This might be regarded as story information rather than discourse because the component distinguishes the nature of the information supplied about the story world rather than the manner in which that information is conveyed in the text. In contrast to *Clarity* and *Focus*, *Appeal* varies across individuals. Consequently, in our framework it has to be related to the evaluation *process* in figure 1. It is plausible to relate it at least in part to the subjects' reaction to the situation. We suspect, for example, that overall appeal is substantially determined by readers' evaluation of the characters and the situation. Finally, the perception and appreciation of *Style* is also fairly idiosyncratic, and we suspect that it might have something to do with language processing. In other words, high-experience readers might have distinct reading and comprehension skills, which leads them to process characteristics of style differently. Based on this analysis, we might tentatively associate the Style component with language processing in figure 1. A summary of our tentative analysis of these components is listed at the bottom of table 3.

There are a number of limitations of this analysis. To begin with, there is no doubt that the components isolated by the principal components analysis are just a few of the many factors that intervene in the process of evaluation. Moreover, the different sources and processes outlined in figure 1 will likely interact in any number of ways, and the evaluation sources and processes are unlikely to be completely independent as depicted in the figure. In contrast, because of the nature of principal components analysis, the components are of necessity orthogonal. Thus, our intuitive mapping of the derived components to source and process is simplistic at best. Nevertheless, we believe that our approach and analysis provides at least some hints concerning the nature of the major pieces of evaluation. Further, the fact that there are sensible (albeit preliminary) interpretations of the components in terms of evaluation source and process suggests that our initial analysis of the nature of evaluation has some merit and that an empirical approach to evaluation is indeed possible.

Conclusions

As argued by many critics, literary value is not a tractable research problem for investigation. However, value is a product of evaluation, and we believe that there can be an empirical science of literary evaluation. This initial study is just the beginning of such an empirical approach, but it provides at least some support for the framework we have developed. In particular, in our analysis we were able to isolate aspects of evaluation that were related to the evaluation source and the evaluation process. That is, some components were related to the texts and applied consistently across individuals; other components were clearly related not to the texts but rather to reader characteristics, of which reading experience appears to be one aspect.

This type of empirical approach goes beyond simply identifying problematic aspects of traditional assumptions about value. For example, an empirical approach may allow us to identify which specific aspects of the evaluation process are similar across different reading publics and which differ. Similarly, empirical evidence may allow us to disentangle taste or preference from an independent attribution of value. For example, it is possible that members of minority reading publics appreciate the value of canonised literature, even if they prefer works that are more closely related to their cultural perspective. Another hypothesis, suggested by the present results, is that the evaluation of literature is mediated by knowledge and reading experience: Individuals with high experience or knowledge may prefer different kinds of texts than those with less experience or knowledge. Although these ideas may be plausible, simply speculating on them does not provide definitive answers. Instead, we believe that this initial study will inspire an empirical analysis of these kinds of questions.

Works Cited

Herrnstein Smith, Barbara. 1983. Contingencies of Value. *Critical Inquiry* September:1-35.
Long, E. 2006. Beginning with Readers. Keynote address at the 10th International Conference of the IGEL Society, Aug. 5-9, at Chiemsee, Germany.
Stanovich, K. E., West, R. F. 1989. Exposure to Print and Orthographic Processing. *Reading Research Quarterly* 24: 402-433.

CHAPTER TWENTY TWO

WHAT IS, EMPIRICALLY, A GREAT BOOK? OR: LITERARY DIALOGUES AND CANON FORMATION[1]

DAVID FISHELOV

Abstract

The purpose of this chapter is to explore the relationship between literary dialogues and the process of canon formation and to suggest an empirically oriented answer to the question "What is a great book?" First, I examine different types of dialogues in real-life, communicative situations, introducing the distinction between *genuine* and *pseudo dialogues*. Then I illustrate how these categories can be applied to the literary field. Within theories of canon formation, I distinguish between two major directions: the "beauty party," emphasising aesthetic qualities as the source of a book's "greatness" and the "power party," underlining social power structures as the source of a book's reputation. After exposing some built-in shortcomings of these two prevailing "parties," I propose the *dialogical approach* to great books. At the core of that approach stands the hypothesis that *a great book is one that evokes many and diverse types of literary, artistic and critical dialogues*. To corroborate the hypothesis, I present the results of research comparing lists of works enjoying a high reputation with the number and diversity of references to these works on four data bases, representing different layers of culture and literature. Finally, I discuss possible counter-arguments, concluding that the dialogic

---

[1] Ideas elaborated in this chapter were first presented at the following conferences: IAEA (Lisbon, September 2004); Intertextuality in Literature and Culture (Tel Aviv, May 2006) and IGEL (Munich, August 2006). I would like to thank participants for their critical and constructive comments.

approach to great books enables us to establish research of canon formation on empirical grounds.

Introduction

The purpose of this chapter is to present an empirically oriented approach to the question "What Is a Great Book?" The key to the answer lies, as will be explained later, in *dialogues* that certain works evoke or generate. I prefer the term "dialogues" to the term "intertextuality", because this latter term is notoriously vague, embracing every conceivable relation between semiotic objects (still, one can decide to use it in specified meanings: Genette 1982; Ben-Porat 1985; Allen 2000). Further, "intertextuality" is usually employed in theoretical frameworks that reject certain pre-suppositions associated with the notion of "a great book" or a "masterpiece" (a term originally used in art history: Cahn 1979).[2]

The advantage of using the term "dialogue" lies not only in bypassing the undesired vagueness associated with "intertextuality" but also because it calls attention to the close affinities between dialogues in ordinary, social interactions ("real-life" dialogues) and literary and artistic "dialogues."

I. Real-life Dialogues

The seemingly simple, ordinary day-to-day dialogue is, on a closer look, a complex and multilayered phenomenon. For a social contact to be called a dialogue we need two participants and some kind of verbal exchange taking place among them (a "conversation between two or more persons" – *Random House College Dictionary*).[3] But this general requirement still leaves great room when it comes to the actual nature of verbal exchanges occurring between these two people. Actual dialogues have a variety of goals, they involve different relationships between participants and they are conducted through all sorts of channels (Jakobson 1960). A brief, information-oriented dialogue conducted among strangers ("do you know by any chance how we get to Highway 101?") does not sound like a dialogue between two intimate friends ("What's up man?"). A dialogue between a boss and an employee differs from one conducted among peers; and a chat on the Internet greatly differs from a conversation

---

[2] For some of these pre-suppositions, see Clayton and Rothstein (1991), 3-36.
[3] The principles discussed here may be applied also to multi-participants conversation.

in a café: not only in its form (written vs. spoken) and register (e.g., chat shortcuts), but also because the former provides a whole range of opportunities for playful invention of identities ("sexy Angela" is in fact middle-aged John). By adopting an empirical, open-minded approach, we should acknowledge this great variety and see how it helps us to better understand the heterogeneous field of literary dialogues, and the role these literary dialogues play in forming the "great books club".

To describe the structure of real-life dialogues it is necessary to discern two levels evident in every dialogue: the *outer* (or "formal") dimension and the *inner* (or "content") one. The outer dimension includes the actual, observable exchange of words between the two participants. This level involves questions such as "How long does the dialogue go on?" "Who is more talkative among the two?" and "In what intonation do they utter the words?" When we focus on the inner dimension, we address questions like "Do the two participants share a 'common language'?" "To what degree do they differ in their points of view?" "Do they truly listen to one another?" "Do they actually respond to each other?"

Types of Dialogue (and Monologue)

Using the distinction between the inner and the outer dimensions of the ongoing verbal interaction a scheme with some basic *types of dialogue* emerges (**Table 1**). The emerging scheme provides basic coordinates for describing the structure of actual dialogues and also brings into the picture a dialogue's (lonely) counterpart – the monologue. The parameters for such a scheme can be formulated in terms of *voices* – referring to the outer, audible (or readable), concrete level, as well as metaphorically (indicated by inverted commas) to one's points of view, ideology, sentiments etc. ("in what you're saying I can hear your wife's voice").

Table 1: Real-Life Dialogues

		Inner Level		
		One "Voice"	Two "Voices"	
Outer Level	One Voice	Genuine Monologue	Pseudo-Monologue: Dialogical Monologue	
	Two Voices	Pseudo-Dialogue: "Echo-dialogue"	Pseudo-Dialogue: Dialogue of the Deaf	Genuine-Dialogue: Dialectic Dialogue

Let us provide a brief explanation for the emerging categories:

Genuine Monologue: represents a situation where only one person is heard, and his/her voice gives expression to one point of view or sentiment or ideology. Note that, whereas it is relatively easy to determine whether we hear the (outer) voice of just one person, it is more complicated to decide whether this person expresses only one point of view, and this decision depends to a certain extent on contextual factors (e.g., acquaintance with the speaker).

Pseudo-Monologue or **Dialogical Monologue**: represents a situation where only one person is heard, but his/her voice gives expression to different points of view or sentiments or ideologies. Hamlet's famous "To be or not to be" could be invoked here as a prototypical example for such "dialogic monologue".

Pseudo-Dialogue of the type of **Echo-Dialogue**: represents cases where two persons are engaged in an exchange of words, but when we listen to what they are saying, we realise that actually only one point of view is being expressed. Whereas a typical case here would be a simple reiterating verbatim the words just heard; this category may cover also cases where an interlocutor repeats what s/he has just heard, albeit in different words. It may also refer to cases where the interlocutor simply nods in consent. A literary example of a represented echo-dialogue can be found in *Hamlet*'s Rosencrantz and Guildenstern: two (outer) voices of two characters are heard, but only one "voice" is being expressed.

Pseudo-Dialogue, Dialogue of the Deaf: represents cases where the two interlocutors utter different points of view, but because they lack the ability or the will to engage in a genuine dialogue, the (outer) conversation may go on, but no dialectical give-and-take takes place. This category can be described as simply two parallel (genuine) monologues.

Genuine Dialogue or **Dialectic Dialogue**[4]: represents cases that we usually associate with serious, true dialogues, where the two interlocutors give expression to different points of view, are attentive to each other and engage in meaningful exchange of ideas, sentiments etc. Sometimes, such dialogues reach a happy conclusion, sometimes not.

Note that the distinction between the two types of *pseudo*-dialogue may also be described as a function of the question to what extent the interlocutors share a common "language" (ideology, point of view): the higher the degree of overlap, the closer we get to the realm of echo-dialogues; the more they come from two radically different worlds, the closer we come to a dialogue of the deaf. These types are not meant to be understood as exclusive classificatory categories: a concrete, real-life dialogue may illustrate characteristics of more than one type and certainly can move from one type to the other ("Sorry, I wasn't listening; could you please repeat your question?").

II. Literary Dialogues

The dynamics of literary dialogues seem to parallel those of real-life dialogues. These parallels should not hide the obvious differences: oral vs. written, continuous conversation vs. one-time "réplique."

Genuine Literary Dialogues

It is not difficult to apply the concept of real-life genuine, dialectic dialogues to the literary arena, namely to cases where an author, after reading attentively a literary work, responds to it in a dialectical way, taking issue with some aesthetic and/or ideological dimensions of the inspiring work. An author may write a parody of the "triggering" text or develop it or subvert it. To call, for example, a literary (or artistic) work a *parody* means: (a) that the writer of the text is familiar with the "triggering", parodied work (or style or school or genre), (b) that s/he does

---

[4] My distinction between genuine and pseudo dialogue is inspired by Buber's discussion of "I and Thou" (Buber 1970) and Bakhtin's dialogic approach to language (Bakhtin 1981).

not like certain aspects of that work and (c) that s/he has decided to express this discontent by using the mechanism of parody, namely partial imitation and distortion (or deviation or substitution). Shakespeare's Sonnet 130 may (Shakespeare 1986: 141) illustrate this mechanism:

> My mistress' eyes are nothing like the Sun;
> Coral is far more red than her lips' red;
> If snow be white, why then her breasts are dun;
> If hairs be wires, black wires grow on her head.
> I have seen roses damasked, red and white,
> But no such roses see I in her cheeks,
> And in some perfumes is there more delight
> Than in the breath that from my mistress reeks.
> I love to hear her speak, yet well I know
> That music hath a far more pleasing sound;
> I grant I never saw a goddess go -
> My mistress when she walks treads on the ground.
>   And yet, by heaven, I think my love as rare
>   As any she belied with false compare.

Shakespeare's parodic treatment of Elizabethan love poetry is based on the juxtaposition of prevalent Petrarchan metaphors describing the beloved together with a series of her "naturalistic" descriptions. The effect of the "naturalistic" observations demeans the image of the beloved woman, dragging her from a conventional high pedestal to the image of an almost repelling figure. This rhetorical move is reversed in the concluding couplet: suddenly we learn that one can both look with open eyes at women of flesh and blood, including their inevitable imperfections, and at the same time be truthfully in love.

But parody is not the only way to express an author's discontent with a work or a sentiment expressed in a work. The title of Wilfred Owen's "Dulce Et Decorum Est," alludes to a maxim originally taken from a famous line from Horace's *Odes*, Book III Ode 2:

> dulce et decorum est pro patria mori:
> mors et fugacem persequitur virum,
> nec parcit imbellis iuventae
> poplitibus timidove tergo

> (It is sweet and fitting to die for one's country. Death hunts down also the man who runs away, and has no mercy on the hamstrings of the unwarlike youth and his cowardly back) (Horace 2004: 144-145).

Owen, who experienced the horrors of World War I (in which he was eventually killed on 4 November, 1918), loathes the patriotic sentiment embedded in Horace's lines and, as a rebut responds by portraying in gruesome details of the actual face of "sweat" dying. Here is the poem's last stanza (Owen 1973: 79):

> If in some smothering dreams you too could pace
> Behind the wagon that we fling him in,
> And watch the white eyes writhing in his face,
> His hanging face, like a devil's sick of sin;
> If you could hear, at every jolt, the blood
> Come gargling from the froth-corrupted lungs,
> Obscene as cancer, bitter as the cud
> Of vile, incurable sores on innocent tongues, –
> My friend, you would not tell with such high zest
> To children ardent for some desperate glory,
> The old Lie: Dulce et decorum est
> Pro patria mori.

Genuine literary dialogues form perhaps the most significant dimension of the dynamics of literary history; through the dialectics of partial acceptance and partial rejection – using either parodic humor or serious rhetoric.[5] But in addition to various forms of genuine literary dialogues, one can also find various manifestations of "pseudo" literary dialogues, similar in structure to real-life echo-dialogue and dialogue of the deaf.

Echo-dialogues in Literature

The main characteristic of a real-life echo-dialogue lies in the fact that the words of one participant are "re-heard." A literary parallel of this can be seen in the ubiquitous phenomenon of literary life – *translation*. The basic meaning of the term "translation" – "A version in a different language" (*Random House Dictionary*) – reminds of the situation of a real-life echo-dialogue: a reader of a literary work "repeats" or "echoes" a source text in a different language. As the theory of translation has demonstrated, the term "translation" in fact covers many different phenomena and can be seen as an umbrella concept.[6] Every translation

---

[5] For the important role played by parody in the "mechanism" of literary history, see Tynianov (1975).
[6] I would like to point out three important discussions of literary translation: Robinson (1991), who introduces the concept of dialogue into translation studies,

can be seen as a "compromise" between two poles: an attempt to faithfully replicate *the* original source-text but at the same time to create *an* original text in the target language. In translating or "imitating" Juvenal's Satire X, Samuel Johnson, for example, tried to "tailor" Juvenal's opening lines – "Search every land, from Cadiz to the dawn-streaked shores / Of Ganges" (Juvenal 1970: 205; for the original Latin, see Duff 1970: 58) – to contemporary English readers by changing the geographical pointers: "Let Observation, with extensive view, / Survey mankind, from China to Peru" (Johnson 1958: 51). Johnson's "The Vanity of Human Wishes" is one possible "compromise" between two poles. The specific nature of the achieved "compromise" depends on the norms of the literary period, constraints of the target system and, of course, on the talent of the individual translator. Still, despite the extremely heterogeneous and complex nature of literary translation, it resembles the structure of real-life echo-dialogues.

Despite this structural similarity, literary translations differ from real-life echo-dialogue in two important aspects. First, linguistic variations that are usually considered insignificant in real-life dialogues – e.g., the specific choice of words, register, formal patterns – may acquire greater significance in literary translations, designed to produce aesthetic effects ("the translator chose a higher register to elevate the poem's tone"). Secondly, and most importantly, whereas an *echo-dialogue* in a real-life situation is usually regarded as dull and unsatisfactory ("it is only an echo"), literary translations can fulfil an important innovative role in the target literature and culture. The very decision to translate into a given language certain works can have far-reaching consequences for the target culture by introducing new modes of expression, literary forms, ideas and sensibilities.[7] Furthermore, there are cases where the translator takes many liberties, bringing the translation close to the realm of *genuine* literary dialogue.

Literary abridgments and adaptations can also serve as examples of literary echo-dialogues: their raison d'être is to "replicate" the source text, changing only the length or the wording or the medium. And, like in literary translations, in addition to simple manipulation of the source text according to certain known principles, producing predictable texts (e.g.,

---

Lefevere (1992), and Toury (1995). Levefere's study (especially pp. 1-10) makes the important connection between translation (and other forms of rewriting) and the forming of the canon.

[7] Lefevere (1992), while putting a strong emphasis on the coercing power of the target system, does not sufficiently acknowledge the role of translations and other forms of rewriting to re-shape, in their turn, the literary target system.

moving "sensitive" issues from adaptations for children), there are cases where abridgments and adaptations take certain liberties that bring them closer to the realm of genuine dialogue (e.g., the hilarious show by the *Reduced Shakespeare Company*: http://www.reducedshakes-peare.com/).

Dialogues of the Deaf in Literature

Are there cases that can be described as literary dialogue of the deaf, i.e., where an author evokes a source-text, but without truly creating a dialogue with what the original text is saying? Dryden's *Absalom and Achitophel* (1681) may be an interesting case in point. In this long satirical poem, Dryden evokes the biblical story of how King David (II Samuel xiii-xviii) was rebelled against by his son Absalom and by Achitophel, a former counselor of King David. Dryden, however, was using the biblical story to address contemporary issues, supporting King Charles II (= King David) and denouncing his rivals, who tried to exclude the Charles' legal successor, James, Duke of York (hated for his known Catholicism) and to promote the Duke of Monmouth (= Absalom) in his stead. A central figure in trying to promote this move was Lord Shaftesbury (= Achitophel). Based on the initial resemblance between the two situations – an attempt to substitute a legal heir to a ruling king – Dryden re-tells the biblical story, conjuring up many more real and alleged similarities that serve his motivation: to support and glorify Charles II and to denounce those who were trying to challenge the legal successor.

Dryden's poem may serve his moral and political convictions and demonstrate his great artistic talent. Still, we can argue that this literary tour de force does not create a *genuine* literary dialogue with the Bible. Dryden is only using the Bible's canonical status to enhance his satirical goals. From here ensues the "bending" of historical facts and many anachronisms: (e.g., confusing the ancient Hebrews with post-biblical Jews; referring to the Sanhedrin, line 390, established long after the times of King David). These anachronisms are symptomatic of Dryden's disinterest in the original biblical story for its own sake, but his "misreading" (to borrow Bloom's term: 1973, 1975) produced a valuable literary text.

To conclude this section, we can now draw a wide spectrum of literary dialogues, illustrating different forms. One way to present this spectrum is to move according to the degree of dialectics between the responding and the source text. At one end of the spectrum we can find minimal dialectical relations in the form of *echo-dialogue*, starting with the most *passive* way of responding to a text, namely the *act of its reading*.[8] This can be paralleled to real-life listening and nodding; the next point on the spectrum will be more active forms of echo-dialogue in the forms of re-telling, abridgment, translation, adaptation, etc.; then we will be moving into the realm of genuine dialogues in the form of allusions, parody and other ways of creating dialectical relations; finally, we find at the other end of the spectrum works illustrating also minimal dialectical relations, but this time of the kind of dialogue of the deaf: works that use or "misuse" the source text without paying real attention to its form and content.

III. What Is a Great Book? The Two Parties

After demonstrating the multifaceted nature of dialogues, we should turn now to explain the term "great book" of the chapter's title. The many concrete explanations given to that term might be grouped into two major "parties".[9]

The Beauty Party

The first party may be named *the beauty party*, arguing that the status of a great book is a function of certain aesthetic qualities inherent in a literary work. There may be significant disagreements among members of the beauty party. First, they differ as to the specific nature of these aesthetic qualities. Aristotle was not speaking in modern terms of aesthetic qualities, but still one can extract from his discussion of literary and artistic works in the seventh chapter of *Poetics* that he considers highly a work that fulfils a double criterion: unity in variety (Aristotle 1951: 1451a10-11).

If we move to modern discussions of aesthetics and literary theory, there are still some important disagreements. The New Critics offered different formulations that put an emphasis on the literary work's semantic complexities: Cleanth Brooks (1949) suggested that the language of poetry (and, by implication, of literature) is the language of *paradox*; William Empson (1947) offered, in an influential book first published as early as 1930, *ambiguity* to be the true sign of good poetic work; Allen Tate (1949)

---

[8] I would like to mention in this context an important attempt of Franco Moretti (see, for example in his 1998, especially 141-197), to use empirical, quantitative methods in order to connect questions related to the history of reading with literary history and literary forms.

[9] The following description of the two "parties" is partly based on Adams (1988).

suggested that the existence of *tension* between the abstract meanings conveyed by a poem and the concrete images used in it is the hallmark of excellent poetry, distinguishing it from what he calls mass, propaganda poetry on the one hand, and "analytic" poetry, on the other. Another influential aesthetic principle was introduced by Monroe Beardsley. According to him, a good artistic work has to fulfill a dual principle, reminding us of Aristotle's dual principle of unity in variety, of *congruence and plenitude* (Beardsley 1958: 144-147).

Leaving the Anglo-Saxon tradition and moving to another influential twentieth-century school of criticism, we can cite also Shklovsky's notion of "making strange" (Shklovsky 1965). According to this Russian Formalist, every successful work of art deviates from and distorts habitual ways of perception in order to provide a fresh look on things, mores or values. An interesting development of the Russian Formalists can be found in the works of the Check structuralist Jan Mukarovsky (1976). In his work on the aesthetic function he stresses the deviation from established linguistic and literary norms as the constitutive factor for producing an aesthetic effect.

Another interesting issue that separates thinkers of the beauty party is related to the ontological or epistemic status of the relevant aesthetic qualities: are they on the same level as other qualities of a text (e.g., its length) and hence can be discussed and even measured in objective terms (see, for example, Zemach 1997)? Or are they perhaps subjective, according to the popular saying that beauty is in the eye of the beholder?

Thus, the beauty party offers a wide gallery of specific aesthetic qualities to choose from and it contains many factions with regard to the question whether the aesthetic qualities have objective, subjective or intersubjective status. But despite these differences, all partisans of the beauty party share the belief that the status of a great book (or artistic work) is a function of its (relevant) aesthetic qualities, discerned by its readers (or spectators): the more one can find them in a specific work, the better are its chances to be included in the great books club.

The Power Party

During the past few decades, followers of the beauty party are in decline and on the defensive. The contemporary dominant tone belongs to what can be labelled "the power party", claiming that a book's reputation is determined by social hegemonies.

Like with partisans of the beauty party, here too there are some interesting variations. Orthodox Marxism, at least in its simplified version, emphasises the role of social and economic infra-structure in determining cultural value: the decision as to whether a literary work is included in the great books club reflects the interests of the prevailing ideology, reflecting the interests of the ruling class, reflecting, in its turn, the economic and manufacturing structure in a society. A similar logic directs also Neo-Marxist thinkers, who suggest more sophisticated versions for the relations between infra- and super-structures in society. While accepting the idea that economic factors ultimately determine culture, they acknowledge that culture has a relatively autonomous status.[10]

Another influential faction of the power party can be found in Foucault and his followers. In fact the idea to title this party "the power party" comes directly from Foucault's emphasis on the power system underlying cultural values (Rabinow 1984). A central theme in his intellectual project was to unmask accepted cultural values and distinctions as in fact an expression of social structures of power. Another interesting contribution to the power party can be found in the thinking of Bourdieu (1992) and his concept of the cultural field and in Fish's discussion of institutionalised modes of interpretation (Fish 1980).

While these two parties shed light on the complex question of "How and why does a literary work become 'a great book'?" they also have their limitations. The beauty party fails to explain the *dynamic* nature of the literary canon. If the aesthetic qualities of literary works are inherent, universal and objective (or inter-subjective), it is reasonable to assume that the list of great books would remain unchanged throughout the ages. But literary history teaches us that this is not the case and that there are shifts, especially in the relative status of certain works within the canon. The power party, on the other hand, fails to explain the *stable* elements of the canon. If the status of a great book is a function of changing social and ideological hegemonies, we would expect the list to change dramatically with the alterations of economic, social and ideological hegemonies. But despite such influences, many literary works (e.g., Homer, Shakespeare and many others) have kept their reputation as great books throughout the ages.

IV. Dialogic Approach to Great Books

At this point, I would like to propose a new approach, based on the concept of literary dialogues and on empirically oriented principles. The

---

[10] For different versions of Marxist and Neo-Marxist approaches, see Eagelton and Milne (1996).

core of this approach can be formulated in the following hypothesis: *A great book is one that evokes many and diverse types of literary, artistic and critical dialogues* (in the form of local allusions, epigraphs, parodies, translations, adaptations, pictorial representations, scholarly interpretations, etc.). A similar investigation, namely to define the canon of artistic, musical, literary and scientific canons through traces left in print was recently undertaken by Charles Murray, resulting in his monumental *Human Accomplishment* (2003).

The term "many" in the definition should be understood as a relative term: first, to the size of the relevant cultural community and to similar, "neighbouring" literary works (e.g., of the same genre). But a sheer quantitative criterion seems to me unsatisfactory, hence the introduction of the criterion of *diversity*: not only many typical literary "echoes" and "dialogues" (e.g., literary allusions, translations) but also other kinds of dialogues in the form of paintings, movie adaptations, stage productions, critical discussions etc. It seems that the chances of a specific work to keep inspiring readers (and authors) throughout time lie in the fact that its "echoes" are heterogeneously distributed. If a literary work evokes many reactions but only of one kind (e.g., it is embraced by critics of only one school or period), its chances to join the "great books club" seem smaller than those of a work that inspires diverse reactions (e.g., it evokes responses from different schools of criticism). In that respect, cultural phenomena may resemble a principle that can be found in biology: the chances of a species to survive depend, ceteris paribus, on the *diversity* of its gene pool.[11]

The Dialogic Approach: Some Facts, for a Change

To examine the above hypothesis, I conducted a series of Internet searches. Some of these searches focused on "conservative" data bases (e.g., university libraries) while others address less traditional fields (e.g., images related to a work).

My point of departure was three existing, independent lists of "great books" from three "traditional" sources: the *Norton Anthology of World Masterpieces* (Mack 1997), Denby's *Great Books* (Denby 1996), tracing the curriculum of a Great Books course taught at Columbia University

---

[11] I have elaborated on that issue in my book (Fishelov 1993), especially pp. 37-39, 46-47. One should, however, be aware of significant differences between culture and biology. For some instructive warning against a mechanical application of biological principles to the literary and cultural field, see Todorov (1970) and Schaeffer (1989).

during the nineties, and the entries in *Masterpieces of World Literature* (Magill 1952) This existing point of departure has at least one obvious methodological advantage: it safeguards the searches from becoming circular. If I focused in my searches on works that I thought to be great books, chances are that these searches will only corroborate my initial knowledge about their fame. The lists from the three works mentioned above, by contrast, provided a valuable *independent* reference point for the searches.

Since my hypothesis stated that great books evoke "echoes" and "dialogues" on different levels of culture, I checked the "echoes" and "dialogues" found on four different data bases:

(1) *Google*; I deliberately chose this popular, all-inclusive search engine to provide a rough approximation of the work's general distribution in culture. The greatest problem with using Google for this research was to avoid as much as possible getting "junk" results. To this end, I used both the work's and the author's name in the searches.

(2) *Google-Image*; this search engine traces images related to a work: paintings of its major characters, book jackets, etc. Using that search engine may teach us something valuable not only because literary works do serve as a source of inspiration for many visual artists, but also because sometimes images related to a work become an important association or even "focal point" related to that work (e.g., Hamlet holding a skull).

(3) The *Clio*, the library's data base of Columbia University; as opposed to the first two searches, represents a more "elitist" domain. There is a serious and meticulous process of selection, done by experts, librarians and scholars, before an item is purchased and shelved in a university library.

(4) Finally, the *International Movie Data Base* (IMDB). This search engine traces all movie adaptations and productions based on specified literary works.

These four data bases can provide a heuristic picture of "traces" left by literary works on different layers of culture: different media, genres (literary as well as scholarly) and social strata (popular and elitist). [12] As

---

[12] The following results represent searches done during the period of August 25- September 1, 2005. Needless to say, since then some of the numbers have dramatically increased in the search engines of Google, indicating the extremely

expected, the results obtained in the Google searches yielded the largest numbers and those of IMDB the smallest. This comes as no surprise, because to produce a movie, even a filmed version of a play, is a relatively costly business. We should note, however, that movie production involves a variety of artists (screenwriters, camera men, director, actors, etc.) and reaches a wide audience.

First, I conducted the four searches for works listed in my three source books. Then, I put in a separate table the search results of works that appear in *all three* sources. This group, representing a relatively high consensus on their merit and status, may be labeled "the hard core" of the canon. The following table (**Table 2**) presents the results obtained for the seventeen works mentioned in all three sources.

---

rapid growth of the Internet. Still, these changes do not undermine the basic approach advocated here.

Table 2: Results of Searches of the Canon's "Hard Core"

Work	Google	Google, Image	Clio, Columbia	IMDB
Aeneid – Virgil	149,000	744	316	2
Antigone – Sophocles	119,000	542	306	14
Candide – Voltaire	186,000	820	140	6
Divine Comedy – Dante	135,000	582	190	1
Don Quixote – Cervantes	206,000	3,380	698	50[13]
Faust – Goethe	904,000	4,350	861	7
Gargantua and Pantagruel – Rabelais	16,500	107	23	0
Gulliver's Travels – Swift	120,000	737	170	15
Hamlet – Shakespeare	899,000	9,450	969	58
Iliad – Homer	340,000	2,610	852	5
Medea – Euripides	93,900	476	204	8
Odyssey – Homer	736,000	4,260	679	15
Oedipus Tyrannus – Sophocles	132,000	695	413	11
Paradise Lost – Milton	221,000	981	758	3
Prometheus Bound – Aeschylus	41,900	202	169	0
Tartuffe – Molière	77,900	802	136	13

---

[13] This number is a rough approximation, because there are a few films that are an adaptation of works that are inspired themselves by Cervantes's classical work (e.g., a filmed opera).

The search results of the "hard core" showed a relatively high degree of consistency, characterised by both high numbers of occurrences in the specific searches and a wide range of distribution among different genres and media. Further, these results formed a distinct pattern: when the search results of Google were an X digits number; the results of the Google-Image and the Clio searches were X minus two or three digits number and the results of the IMBD search were X minus four or five digits number (e.g., in searches for *Tartuffe*, Google results is a five digits number, Google-Image and Clio are a three digits number and IMBD – a two digits number).[14]

Needless to say, this pattern is based on a partial and to a certain degree arbitrary choice of the specific search engines and data bases, but still I think it is symptomatic and not insignificant. To illustrate why I believe it to be significant, let us look at some results of other works that were not part of the "hard core." The following table contains the search results obtained for four works mentioned only in Magill (1952):

Table 3

Work	Google	Google, Image	Clio, Columbia	IMDB
"Abe Lincoln in Illinois" – Rohert E. Sherwood	32,500	3[15]	11	4
Dear Brutus – J. M. Barrie	898	23	6	0
Nocturne – F. A. Swinnerton	1,400	0	4	0
Wreck of the Grosvenor – W.C. Russell	403	6	0	0

Note that these results are characterised not only by relatively small overall numbers but they also show uneven distribution in different genres and media. Among other things, they corroborated my initial impression

---

[14] This pattern is a rough approximation, representing most of the results.
[15] These were the results of a search for '"Abe Lincoln in Illinois"' AND Sherwood." Results for just "Abe Lincoln in Illinois" were 90. The reason is simple: most references of the all-inclusive Google belong to a film based on Sherwood's play, not to the play itself.

that Magill's list was based on biased selection criteria, favoring English and American works of the first half of the twentieth century. They may also tell us something deeper about the fate of works that enjoy ephemeral critical acclaim.

Objections to the Dialogue Approach

Despite my satisfaction with this outcome, the proposal to see a great book as a function of textual dialogues may be charged with circularity. We can – thus goes the argument – define works evoking many and diverse textual dialogues as "great books" and then find the books that answer that description, but then we can define a great book any way we like (e.g., a work that won the Booker prize) and then find the books answering that description. The circularity charge can be answered by the fact that *my point of departure* was the lists of "great books" made by three independent source-books.

The dialogic approach can also be challenged from a different angle by what can be named: "the *Harry Potter* case." If the large number of echoes left by a book is indeed an important criterion for introducing it into the "the great books club", then the *Harry Potter* series should automatically be considered "a great book", because of its enormous popularity. Further, its "echoes" are not restricted, as might be expected, to large readerships, movie productions and popular culture (games etc.); it also attracts, surely but not slowly, critical attention: the number of scholarly books and articles devoted to *Harry Potter* is constantly growing.[16] Thus, at least superficially, this series of books also seems to fulfill the requirement of variety of dialogues and echoes.

Despite these books' overwhelming popularity in today's culture, our intuitions tell us that Homer's *Odyssey* or Shakespeare's *Hamlet* are in a different "league" than the *Harry Potter* series. But how can we corroborate these intuitions without renouncing the dialogic approach altogether? The answer is simple: we should stipulate that the principle of variety applies also to different *periods* – a test that the *Harry Potter* series has not yet passed. This postulate can be seen as a reformulation of the good old principle that a great book has to pass the "test of time."

---

[16] As can be found in the MLA bibliography data base.

Conclusion

The purpose of the dialogic approach to the question of great books is not to deny the valuable insights of the beauty and power "parties": certain books surely contain aesthetic qualities more than others and cultural elites do play an important role in promoting certain works. But by focusing only on aesthetic qualities or cultural power structures, we might lose sight of the actual processes of literary life. Perhaps the prevailing two "parties" could explain the data presented in the above tables, but to that end they will have to add many complicated assumptions: the beauty party will face difficulties in dealing with books which do not possess conspicuous accepted aesthetic qualities and the power party will find it difficult to explain how some books became "great" despite the fact that they were not promoted by their contemporary cultural elite (e.g., a book like *Gargantua and Pantagruel* can be a challenge to both parties). The dialogic approach on the contrary is attuned, first and foremost, to the actual dynamics of literary life manifested in various forms of literary, artistic and critical dialogues.[17]

It is clear that the search tools offered so far are in some respects not sophisticated and fine-tuned enough. More adequate search tools should provide not only gross numbers, but also some kind of an algorithm for weighing them: genuine literary dialogues (e.g., re-writings, allusions), for example, should have far greater weight than the mention of a book in a commercial advertisement. We should also be aware that not every genre generates the same kinds of dialogue: while great dramatic works, for example, keep inspiring new stage productions,[18] a lyrical poem may gain its reputation when it is anthologised, re-anthologised and gets new critical interpretations. There are also important differences with regard to relevant periods: in the pre-Gutenberg era one major factor in the survival and distribution of a literary piece depended, at least in some parts of Western Europe, on its being manually copied and consequently the

---

[17] In a recently published essay, Damrosch (2006) calls attention to some changes in the canon as reflected in MLA bibliography entries devoted to certain authors and consequently suggests some interesting distinctions. His illuminating discussion, however, gives too much weight to scholarly works as a factor in canon formation without giving due attention to other, equally important forms of literary dialogue.

[18] Stage productions may be labeled "interpretations" in a sense close to playing a musical piece in a certain way. Such "interpretations" are distinguished from verbal statements that purport to convey the "meaning" of a work of art (Beardsley 1958: 9-10).

number of manuscripts would be considered an important factor. In print culture the base-line numbers change dramatically and in addition to counting individual copies we should count also the number of editions. And there are also pertinent differences between cultures: some cultures (e.g., Russian) have an established tradition of reciting poetry in public, which can be regarded as a significant way for creating a "dialogue" with a text, but in other traditions the reading of poetry is done mainly privately and individually. Thus, ensuing research, hypotheses and searches should factor in, among other things, the questions of genre, period and culture. Awareness of such factors would make the search for textual dialogues more complex and nuanced and would yield more accurate results.

But even before these needed improvements and refinements are introduced, the dialogic approach with its empirical methods can contribute to our understanding of the way literary works gain and maintain their status of "great books." First and foremost because it helps us to perceive "great books" not as static entities, revered objects "sitting there" on the shelf, but to see their active role as "focal points" in culture, inspiring the minds of individuals and groups of writers, artists and critics.[19] Consequently, the question "Is this work a great book or not?" should be substituted for the understanding that a literary work is in a continual, ongoing *process of becoming a great book.*

---

[19] I have elsewhere advocated a similar perspective in discussion of literary genres; not as static forms, but as *generating* principles, "giving birth" to new works (Fishelov 1993: 19-52, and 1999).

Works Cited

Adams, Hazard. 1988. Canons: Literary Criteria/Power Criteria. *Critical Inquiry* 14: 748-64.
Allen, Graham. 2000. *Intertextuality*. London and New York: Routledge.
Aristotle. 1951. *Poetics*. Trans. Samuel H. Butcher. New York: Dover.
Bakhtin, Michail M. 1981. *The Dialogic Imagination*. Trans. Caryl Emerson and Michael Holquist. Austin: University of Texas Press.
Beardsley, Monroe C. 1958. *Aesthetics: Problems in the Philosophy of Criticism*. New York: Harcourt and Brace.
Ben-Porat, Ziva. 1985. Intertextuality. *Hasifrut/Literature* 34: 170-178. (In Hebrew)
Bloom, Harold. 1975. *A Map of Misreading*. New York: Oxford University Press.
—. 1973. *The Anxiety of Influence*. New York: Oxford University Press.
Bourdieu, Pierre. 1992. *Les règles de l'art: genèse et structure du champ littéraire* Paris: Seuil.
Brooks, Cleanth. 1949. *The Well Wrought Urn*. London: D. Dobson.
Buber, Martin. 1970. *I and Thou*. Trans. Walter Kaufmann. Edinburgh: T & T Clark.
Cahn, Walter. 1979. *Masterpiece, Chapters on the History of an Idea*. Princeton, NJ: Princeton University Press.
Clayton, Jay and Eric Rothstein, eds. 1991. *Influence and Intertextuality in Literary History*. Madison, Wis.: University of Wisconsin Press.
Damrosch, David. 2006. World Literature in a Postcanonical, Hypercanonical Age. In *Comparative Literature in an Age of Globalization*, ed. Haun Saussy, 43-53. Baltimore: The Johns Hopkins University Press.
Denby, David. 1996. *Great Books*. New York: Simon & Schuster.
Duff, James. D., ed. 1970. *Juvenal, Satires*. Cambridge: Cambridge University Press.
Eagelton, Terry and Drew Milne, eds. 1996. *Marxist Literary Theory*. Oxford: Blackwell.
Empson, William. 1947, *Seven Types of Ambiguity*. New York: New Directions.
Fish, Stanley. 1980. *Is There a Text in this Class?* Cambridge, Mass.: Harvard University Press.
Fishelov, David. 1993. *Metaphors of Genres*. University Park: Penn State University Press.

—. 1999. The Birth of a Genre. *European Journal of English Studies* 3:1: 51-63.
Genette, Gerard. 1982. *Palimpsestes, la littérature au second degree.* Paris: Seuil.
Horace. 2004. *The Odes of Horace.* Ed. and trans. Niall Rudd. Cambridge, MA: Harvard University Press.
Jakobson, Roman. 1960. Closing Statement: Linguistics and Poetics. In *Style in Language*, ed. Thomas A. Sebeok, 350-377. Cambridge, Massachusetts: MIT Press.
Johnson, Samuel. 1958. *Rasselas, Poems, and Selected Prose*, ed. Bertrand H. Bronson. New York: Hold, Rinehold and Winston.
Juvenal. 1970. *The Sixteen Satires.* Trans. Peter Green. Harmondsworth: Penguin.
Lefevere, André. 1992. *Translation, Rewriting, and the Manipulation of Literary Fame.* London: Routledge.
Mack, Maynard, ed. 1997. *The Norton Anthology of World Literature.* New York: Norton.
Magill, Frank N. 1952. *Masterpieces of World Literature.* New York: Harper Collins.
Moretti, Franco. 1998. *Atlas of the European Novel, 1800-1900.* London: Verso.
Mukarovsky, Jan. 1976. *On Poetic Language*, Trans. John Burbank and Peter Steiner. Lisse: Peter de Ridder Press.
Murray, Charles. 2003. *Human Accomplishment: The Pursuit of Excellence in the Arts and Sciences, 800 BC to 1950.* New York: Harper Collins.
Owen, Wilfred. 1973. *War Poems and Others*, ed. Dominic Hibberd. London: Chatto and Windus.
Rabinow, Paul, ed. 1984. *The Foucault Reader.* New York: Pantheon.
Robinson, Douglas. 1991. *The Translator's Turn.* Baltimore: Johns Hopkins University Press.
Schaeffer, Jean-Marie. 1989. *Qu'est-ce qu'un genre littéraire?* Paris: Seuil.
Shakespeare, William. 1986. *The Sonnets and A Lover's Complaint*, ed. John Kerrigan. Harmondsworth: Penguin.
Shklovsky, Victor. 1965. Art as Technique. In *Russian Formalist Criticism.* Trans. Lee T. Lemon and Marion J. Reis. Lincoln: University of Nebraska Press.
Tate, Allen. 1949. Tension in Poetry. In *Critiques and Essays in Criticism, 1920-1948*, ed. Robert W. Stallman. New York: Ronald Press.
Todorov, Tzvetan. 1970. *Introduction á la littérature fantastique.* Paris: Seuil.

Toury, Gideon. 1995. *Descriptive Translation Studies and beyond.* Amsterdam: John Benjamins.
Tynianov, Jurij. 1975. Dostoevsky and Gogol: Theory of Parody. In *Twentieth-Century Russian Literary Criticism*, ed. Victor Erlich, 102-116. New Haven: Yale University Press.
Zemach, Eddy M. 1997. *Real Beauty.* University Park: Penn State University Press.

CONTRIBUTORS

Jan Auracher is junior lecturer at the University of Munich, Germany, where he teaches empirical methodology and statistical analysis in intercultural studies. His Ph.D. was on psychophysiological measurements of reader reactions to narrative perspective in suspense stories. j.auracher@lmu.de

Marisa Bortolussi is at the University of Alberta in Edmonton, Alberta, Canada. She is a professor in the Department of Modern Languages and Cultural Studies. Dr. Bortolussi and Dr. Dixon have collaborated on projects on the empirical study of literary processing for over 15 years. marisa.bortolussi@ualberta.ca

Zhiqiang Cai is a software developer at the University of Memphis. He is the chief developer of QUAID and Coh-Metrix. zcai@memphis.edu

Peter Dixon is at the University of Alberta in Edmonton, Alberta, Canada. He is a professor in the Department of Psychology. Dr. Dixon and Dr. Bortolussi have collaborated on projects on the empirical study of literary processing for over 15 years. peter.dixon@ualberta.ca

David Fishelov teaches Comparative Literature at the Hebrew University of Jerusalem. His publications include - *Metaphor of Genre: The Role of Analogies in Genre Theories* (1993), *Like a Rainfall: Studies in Poetic Simile* (1996) [In Hebrew] and *Samson's Locks: The Transformations of Biblical Samson* (2000) [In Hebrew]. fishelov@mscc.huji.ac.il

Gao Wei is currently professor of Foreign Languages at Tianjin University of Science and Technology. Her previous publications in empirical studies have appeared in *Empirical Studies of the Arts*, *Journal of Bohai University*, and *Tianjin Foreign Studies University Journal*.

Jennifer Garst received her Ph.D. from Michigan State University, and was a faculty member at the University of Maryland-College Park. She is currently the Gift Planning Manager at Planned Parenthood of Greater Iowa.

David Gil is a scientific staff member in the Department of Linguistics of the Max Planck Institute for Evolutionary Anthropology, Leipzig. His main areas of research are linguistic theory, linguistic typology, and the languages of Southeast Asia.

Art Graesser is a professor in the Department of Psychology at the University of Memphis and co-Director of the Institute for Intelligent Systems. He is editor of Journal of Educational Psychology and former editor of Discourse Processes. He has developed psychological and computational models of learning, language, and discourse processes. a.graesser@mail.psyc.memphis.edu

Melanie Green received her Ph.D. from the Ohio State University. She is currently an Assistant Professor in the Department of Psychology at the University of North Carolina at Chapel Hill. Her research explores the persuasive power of narratives.

Jèmeljan Hakemulder has a background in literary theory and comparative literature. He specialized in the psychology of literature, media, and the arts. In his research he focuses on the effects of reading literary texts on beliefs. hakemulder@let.uu.nl

Akiko Hirose is currently Ph.D. student at the department of Language and Literature, University of Munich, Germany. Her research interest is on comparative studies of German and Japanese information processing, regarding reading as well as writing. akikoausmu@aol.com

Robert Hogenraad is Honorary Senior Research Associate of the National Foundation for Scientific Research (Belgium). He is also Emeritus of the Psychology Department, Université catholique de Louvain. His distinctive concern for computer-aided content analysis steered him recently towards predicting geopolitical conflicts from the analysis of political documents. robert.hogenraad@uclouvain.be

Molly E. Ireland is currently a third-year graduate student at the University of Texas at Austin. She studies language style matching and its role in social problems and processes. meireland@mail.utexas.edu.

Moongee Jeon is a doctoral student in the department of Psychology at the University of Memphis. He has developed interactive simulation and dialogue facilities for AutoTutor, and designed and tested SEEK Web Tutor and Coh-Metrix. mjeon1@memphis.edu

Colin Key is a graduate of the doctoral program in applied social psychology at Brigham Young University. His research interests include investigating accounts for unwelcome behaviours and the causes underlying aggression.

Michael Kimmel is full-time researcher at the University of Vienna (Dept. of English; Dept. of Cultural Anthropology), where he currently is involved in empirical projects on literary metaphor and imagery used in Tango apprenticeship.

Don Kuiken is Professor of Psychology at the University of Alberta. He is editor of *Mood and Memory* (1991), and has published a number of articles on the psychology of sleep and dreams, phenomenological psychology, and aesthetics.

M. Chiara Levorato (Univ. of Padova, Italy) is a psychologist and developmental psycholinguist who published on narrative fruition and readers' responses to short stories. chiara.levorato@unipd.it

Gwyneth Lewis is an undergraduate student in Psychology and the Intitute for Intelligent Systems at the University of Memphis.

Max Louwerse is Associate Professor in Psychology at the Institute for Intelligent Systems at the University of Memphis. He has published widely in psycholinguistics and computationl linguistics, including work on symbolic and embodied cognition and multimodal communication. mlouwers@memphis.edu

Maciej Maryl is assistant lecturer at the Institute for Literary Research of the Polish Academy of Sciences (Warsaw) and a Ph.D. student at the Graduate School for Social Research (Warsaw). He graduated with distinction from Warsaw University in sociology (2007) and literature (2006). His PhD project is aimed at describing the role of literature in the context of new media.

Danielle S. McNamara is a Professor at the University of Memphis. She develops intelligent technologies (e.g., Coh-Metrix, iSTART) and conducts research to better understand comprehension and learning. dsmcnamr@memphis.edu

David Miall is professor in the Department of English and Film Studies at the University of Alberta, where he has collaborated with Don Kuiken since 1990. Their research in empirical studies of reading has appeared in numerous journals, and Miall recently published *Literary Reading: Empirical and Theoretical Studies* (2006).

Véronique Montémont is a Lecturer at University Henri Poincaré (Nancy, France) and a member of Institut Universitaire de France. She belongs to ATILF-CNRS (Nancy). veronique.montemont@uhp-nancy.fr

Blaine Mullins is a graduate student in the Department of Psychology at the University of Alberta interested in literature and language processing.

Aldo Nemesio (Univ. of Torino, Italy) published books on narrative beginning, scientific communication and empirical research in textual studies. aldo.nemesio@unito.it

Özen Odağ has recently completed her Ph.D. in psychology at Jacobs University Bremen where she has worked as both a research associate in several media-related projects funded by the German Research Association and an instructor of empirical methods.

Bradford Owen, Ph.D., is an assistant professor of Communication Studies at California State University, San Bernardino, where he teaches media studies, digital production, and screenwriting.

James W. Pennebaker is professor and chair in the Psychology Department at the University of Texas at Austin. He studies the nature of language and emotion. Pennebaker@mail.utexas.edu.

Janina Petzold is a Ph.D. candidate from the Department of Educational Studies at the Free University of Berlin. She is an assistant in the research project "Media Reception and Narration" conducted by Prof. Dr. Wieler. Her research interests include children's literature and their didactic(s), reading and media socialisation. janina.petzold@web.de

Robert D. Ridge, PhD, is an Associate Professor of Psychology at Brigham Young University. His research interests include the effects of violent media on aggression and factors influencing the initiation and perception of sexual harassment. bob_ridge@byu.edu.

Lucia Ronconi (Univ. of Padova, Italy) is an expert on statistical analyses of behavioural data collected in psychological investigation. l.ronconi@unipd.it.

Yeshayahu Shen is an associate Professor in the Program of Cognitive studies of language and its uses, and in the department of Literature at Tel Aviv University. His main areas of research are story grammars, discourse comprehension, figurative language comprehension, cognitive poetics, metaphor and conceptual structure, and literary theory.

Paul Sopčák holds an M.A. in English Literature from the Ludwig-Maximilans-University Munich, Germany and is currently pursuing a doctoral degree (ABD) in Comparative Literature at the University of Alberta, Canada. He is a Killam scholar whose academic interests include the empirical study of literature, Early Modernist English Literature, and Latin American Literature.

Cecilia Therman is a Ph.D. student at the University of Helsinki. In her work she examines theoretical assumptions related to literary interpretation by looking at how readers actually interpret literary texts. cecilia.therman@helsinki.fi.

Willie van Peer is Professor of Literary Studies and Interculturural Hermeneutics at the University of Munich. He is a former President of IGEL and of the Poetics and Linguistics Association (PALA). vanpeer@daf.uni-muenchen.de

Petra Wieler (Ph.D.) is a University Professor for Primary School Education in German Language and Literature at the Free University of Berlin. Her research includes reading and media socialisation, language acquisition, cultural learning and reconstruction of classroom-interaction. pwieler@zedat.fu-berlin.de

Jie Wu is a gradate student in Computer Science at the Institute for Intelligent Systems at the University of Memphis.

Yehong Zhang is currently Ph.D. student at the Department of German Philology, University of Göttingen, Germany. yehong.zhang@gmail.com.